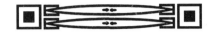

NATIVE AMERICAN

MYTH & LEGEND

AN A–Z OF PEOPLE AND PLACES

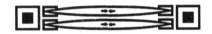

Mike Dixon-Kennedy

BLANDFORD

In loving memory of Charles
One in a million

A BLANDFORD BOOK

First published in the UK 1996 by Blandford
A Cassell Imprint
Cassell Plc, Wellington House,
125 Strand, London WC2R 0BB

Distributed in the United States by Sterling Publishing Co., Inc.,
387 Park Avenue South, New York, NY 10016-8810

Distributed in Australia by Capricorn Link (Australia) Pty Ltd
2/13 Carrington Road, Castle Hill, NSW 2154

A Cataloguing-in-Publication Data entry for this title is available from the British Library

ISBN 0-7137-2623-7

Typeset by York House Typographic Ltd., London
Printed and bound in Great Britain by
Hartnolls Ltd, Bodmin, Cornwall

Companion volumes by Mike Dixon-Kennedy:

ARTHURIAN MYTH & LEGEND
An A–Z of People and Places

CELTIC MYTH & LEGEND
An A–Z of People and Places

CONTENTS

PREFACE

This book, the third I have written along the same lines, is the result of many, many years' research, research that has involved every world race and religion, culture and cult, from the Aztecs to the Zulus, from Christianity to Zoroastrianism. This book covers the native beliefs of a large number of people from a huge geographical division – the Americas. For the first time in a single volume, the myths and legends of the native American peoples, from the Ona of Tierra del Fuego to the Inuit of the Arctic Circle are included in a single volume.

Of course this has meant, due to the physical limitations of such a book, that I have had to be selective about what has found its way into the text, a problem posed to me on many occasions when I was in two minds. I have tried to cover as many peoples as I possibly could, but some of them regrettably get a very small mention. There are two reasons for this, the first of which leads to the second. First, many of the native American peoples have over the centuries either been totally or very nearly wiped out, or have been assimilated into other tribes and peoples which has all but eradicated the evidence needed to research their ancient beliefs and rites. This is particularly true in South and Central (Meso) America, but also, due to the Indian Wars, relevant in North America. This in turn leads to the second reason for omission. Many of the legends that now exist have been Christianized to such an extent that they no longer reflect the true beliefs of the native peoples. The Spanish conquistadors, to give a well-known example, systematically destroyed the pagan texts they encountered during their various conquests, and those that now exist date from a post-conquest period.

Sorting through the mire that has been left has been a passion of mine for almost longer than I now care to reveal. What started as a hobby became an obsession, an obsession that has left me with a list of over 15,000 texts I have researched and condensed into a huge database. This book covers just a small part of that database, but a truly remarkable one. The native Americans were unique in many of their beliefs, but some of these exhibit well-known characteristics from around the world. In almost all the American cultures there is reference to at least one flood (some cultures record successive catastrophic floods) that wiped out mankind, a theme well-known in every corner of the earth.

Yet, until Christopher Columbus 'discovered' the New World, these peoples appear to have remained isolated and to have had no contact with other cultures.

Thor Heyerdahl found, however, that the South American Indian peoples could have had contact with the South Pacific peoples, and I believe they did. Equally, I believe that the New World was visited many years prior to Columbus, or indeed any other explorer, possibly even by the Celts who would most likely have travelled from Ireland to the Atlantic seaboard of North America. Pure supposition I know, but supposition which scholars have been arguing about for countless years, and will continue to do so for many years to come.

Within the pages of this book I hope you will all find something to interest you. The native American people were extremely diversified, and left behind them a similarly diversified mythology. Some of the myths are pure religious fantasy, but others make you think very deeply about the historicity of the events they describe. I know that while I have been preparing the text, I have been amazed by the beauty of the legends, a beauty I hope I have been able to convey accurately in words. I sincerely hope that you will derive as much pleasure from the myths and legends I have recorded in this book as I have gained from researching them. I know that there are omissions from the text, in part due to the reasons I have already given, and in part due to constraints imposed by the length of the book. I also know that I will probably have made some error of assumption somewhere. Should you wish to bring anything to my attention, I should only be too pleased to hear from you. Please address your letters to me via the publishers who will see that they reach me.

No book such as this could ever be completed without the help of a great many individuals, some of whom are sadly no longer with us. To list them all here would take far too much space. Suffice it to say that they know who they are, and that they have my thanks and gratitude for all the help they have given. There are, however, some people I simply cannot go without saying thank you to publicly. They are Stuart Booth (of Blandford) at Cassell for commissioning this book, and Alison Leach for her copy-editing of a complex subject. The other five people are very close to my heart – my wife Gill and our four children, Christopher, Charlotte, Thomas and Rebecca. I thank them for their amazing tolerance and patience. Never once (well, not too often) have they complained while I have been involved in my research, or in self-imposed solitary confinement preparing the text.

Mike Dixon-Kennedy
Lincolnshire

HOW TO USE THIS BOOK

Even though this book is arranged as a straightforward dictionary, several conventions have been adopted to make cross-referencing much easier, and the text therefore more decipherable.

Where headwords have alternative spellings that simply consist of the omission or addition of letters, then the relevant letters within the headword are enclosed in brackets. Where variants are created by different spellings, the entry is made under the most correct form of the word, the variant endings being given as, e.g., **Arna(r)ku(su)agsa~k, ~q** which gives six legitimate variants: *Arnakuagsak, Arnakuagsaq, Arnarkuagsak, Arnarkuagsaq, Arnarkusuagsak* and *Arnarkusuagsaq*. This system is also sometimes used for complete words that might vary; e.g., **Azaka ~Baing Baing, ~Mede**. Where names normally have a part of their full form omitted, that part is enclosed in brackets, e.g., **Coniraya (Viracocha)**.

The use of SMALL CAPITALS indicates that there is a separate entry for the word or words in question. The use of *italics* indicates that the reference is to a text (*italicized* SMALL CAPITALS indicate a text for which there is a separate entry), or to words in a foreign language.

Where more than one entry appears under a headword, each entry is preceded by a number. Further references to these words within the text of the book are followed by the appropriate number in superscript, e.g., MILKY WAY[2].

Where countries or geographical divisions are indicated under a headword, these do not imply that the relevant myth or legend was solely restricted to that place, but rather indicate the place of origin, and it may well be that the myth or legend was known further afield. For example, those myths given as Aztec are identified within this book as having originated in Mexico, which indeed they did, but Aztec myth spread throughout Central America, and even ventured into both the north and the south of the continent.

SPELLING AND PRONUNCIATION GUIDE

With so many languages spread among so many different peoples it has been no mean feat to sort out the plethora of variations that exist for the characters and legends I have recorded in this book. To the best of my ability I have tried to ensure that I have used the most correct form of each headword, but where multiple variants exist in much the same usage, it is difficult to decide which is the correct one.

While many of the names that appear in this book may look peculiar to the Western reader, they are not that difficult to pronounce. The following brief instructions should enable you to pronounce the words correctly.

North America
The spelling and therefore pronunciation of all North American Indian names, including those of the Inuit (Eskimo), are phonetic. Accents, where indicated, emphasize the particular letter.

Central and South America
The pronunciation of names from Central and South America do require a certain amount of care. As a general rule the guidelines below should be followed.

Consonants:
- g: as in English except where followed by an i or an e when it becomes as in *hot*
- h: as *hw* (there is no true English comparison for this, instead it should be pronounced as the phonetic *h* rolled into the phonetic *w*)
- j: as in *hot*
- qua: as in *quick*
- que: as in *kick*
- qui: as in *kick*
- quo: as in *quick*
- tl: as in a*tl*as
- x: as in *sh*ed
- z: as in *s*at

Vowels:

- a: as in c*a*rt
- e: as in s*ay*
- i: as in ch*ie*f
- o: as in gn*o*me
- u: as in m*oo*n

Accents:

These usually fall on the penultimate syllable in Aztec, Chichimec and Toltec names. In other languages the accent only falls on the penultimate syllable of words that end in vowels, or in the letters *n* or *s*, and falls on the final syllable for words ending in other consonants.

Diphthongs:

Each vowel is pronounced individually and given its full value.

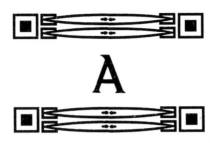

A

A CENTRAL AMERICA (*Maya*)
A deity who is usually identified with the god of death, and named by the classical MAYA people as AH KINCHEL, AH PUCH or HUNHAU and YUM CIMIL by the modern Yuacatec Maya. He is depicted in the various CODEX with naked vertebrae and skull, where, because his identity is not 100 per cent certain, he is simply referred to as the god A. Some sources have identified the god A with the AZTEC god of death MICT-LÁNTECUHTLI, though that deity presided over the north (or south), and the god A presided over the west. His Mayan hieroglyph is a corpse's head and a skull together with a flint or obsidian sacrificial knife, and his symbol is, quite appropriately, that for the day of CIMI which is associated with death.

Ab Kin Xoc CENTRAL AMERICA (*Maya*)
The god of poetry who is also known as PPIZ HIU TEC.

Aba NORTH AMERICA – WOODLANDS
(*Choctaw*)
The supreme spirit of the CHOCTAW people.

Abirá SOUTH AMERICA – COLOMBIA
(*Antioquia*)
The creator who, according to sixteenth-century reports, was associated with the mother-goddess DABIECIBA, and opposed by the evil CHANICUBÁ.

Abnaki NORTH AMERICA – WOODLANDS
Indigenous IROQUOIS people living in the WOODLANDS culture zone.

Acacitli CENTRAL AMERICA – MEXICO
(*Aztec*)
One of the AZTEC leaders who left their original homeland of AZTLAN to seek out and find a new kingdom, the other leaders being named AHATL, AUEXOTL, HUICTON, OCELOPAN, TEÇACATETL, TENOCH and XOMIMITL. They were accompanied on their journey by the four guardians of HUITZILOPOCHTLI, who are named CHIPACTONAL, OXOMOCO, TLALTECUIN and XOCHICAHUACA.

Acamama SOUTH AMERICA (*Inca*)
The city to which the CHILDREN OF THE SUN proceeded after HUANA CAURI had died *en route*, occupying the city without encountering any resistance. CUSCO HUANCA became the first INCA king of Acamama, and duly changed its name to CUZCO. He was later succeeded as king by his brother, the great MANCO CAPAC.

Acatl CENTRAL AMERICA – MEXICO
(*Aztec*)
The thirteenth day of the AZTEC twenty-day MONTH[1]. Depicted by the symbol of the arrow shaft, the day represented the east and had as its patron deity the great TEZCATLIPOCA.

achachila SOUTH AMERICA – BOLIVIA
AND PERU (*Aymará*)
Sacred or revered object (cf. HUACA). To
the AYMARÁ the achachilas included the
mountain peaks of the Bolivian cordillera:
CHURUQUILLA, HUAYANU POTOSÍ, ILANYAU,
ILLAMPU and ILLIMANI.

Achiyala ~ bopa, ~ topa NORTH
AMERICA – PUEBLO, SOUTHWEST (*Zuñi*)
The knife-feathered monster, a gigantic
mythical celestial being covered in feathers of flint.

Acolnaucatl CENTRAL AMERICA –
MEXICO (*Aztec*)
A variant name sometimes applied to
MICTLÁNTECUHTLI.

Adaheli SOUTH AMERICA – ORINOCO
REGION (*Carib*)
The personification of the Sun who, troubled that there were no people on the Earth,
descended from his heaven, and soon afterwards people were born of the Cayman
(a sort of alligator). All the women were
extremely beautiful, but some of the men
were so ugly that their fellows found them
intolerable to their gaze. So they separated, the ugly ones going to the east, the
others to the west, each with their respective wives.

Adawulcanak NORTH AMERICA –
NORTHWEST COAST (*Tlingit*)
'Old-Man-Who-Foresees-All-the-
Troubles-of-the-World'. One of the man-
servants who lived with NASCAKIYETL, and
attended his daughter. The other man-
servant was TLIEWATUWADJIGICAN – 'He-
Who-Knows-Everything'.

Adekagagwaa NORTH AMERICA –
WOODLANDS (*Iroquois*)
The spirit of personification of summer.
During the winter Adekagagwaa rests in
the south, leaving his 'sleep spirit', winter,

to watch over the Earth. He always promises the EARTH MOTHER on the evening
before his departure for the south that he
will return, and when he does HINO will
lower his voice, GA-OH lock away his fierce
winds, and GOHONE depart.

Adja (Bosu) HAITI (*Voodoo*)
An alternative name sometimes given to
ADJASSOU-LINGUETOR.

Adjassou-Li(n)guetor HAITI (*Voodoo*)
A powerful LOA who is sometimes known
as ADJA or ADJA BOSU. Adjassou-Linguetor
is easily recognized by his foul temper and
his protuberant eyes. He lives under a tree
near a spring whose water he governs, and
in which he drowns those who have offended him.

Adjassou-Miro HAITI (*Voodoo*)
A LOA who is, according to some author-
ities, simply a variant of the powerful
ADJASSOU-LINGUETOR.

Agaone HAITI (*Voodoo*)
One of the many LOA of the VOODOO cult,
though some sources have sought to say
that Agaone is simply a variant of
AGAOU.

Agaou (~ Tonné, ~ Wedó) HAITI
(*Voodoo*)
One of the RADA LOA whose variant of
Agaou Wedó is sometimes replaced by its
own variant of DAMBALLA.

Agarou HAITI (*Voodoo*)
A LOA whose name is said, by some, to be
a variant of AGAOU, but this is unsub-
stantiated.

Agasu HAITI (*Voodoo*)
A variant of ADJASSOU-LINGUETOR.

Age HAITI (*Voodoo*)
An alternative name for LOMI AGO.

Age of Beginnings NORTH AMERICA – SOUTHWEST (*Navajo*)
The appropriate way by which the NAVAJO people refer to the very start of time. In this period, which started far beneath the surface of the Earth in the RED WORLD, four streams flowed from the centre of the Earth to the four cardinal points (north, south, east and west), and thence into the sea. In this world the very first people came to life, mostly in the form of insects, though they also included bat people and, according to some versions, ATSE HASTIN, ATSE ESTSAN and the trickster COYOTE. See ASCENT OF THE NAVAJO.

Ages of Man CENTRAL AMERICA (*Maya*)
The MAYA spiritual pilgrimage with which a direct parallel may be drawn in the complex CREATION[4] myth. On the first day, IMIX, from *Im* (womb), the child begins his journey through life. On the second, IK, the spirit is bestowed on him even though he has yet to be born. On the third, AKBAL, the child is born. On the fourth, KAN, he begins to realize that there is evil in the world. On the fifth, CHICCHAN, he gathers together all the experiences of his life. On the sixth, CIMI, he dies. On the seventh, MAN-IK, from *Manzal-Ik* (pass through the spirit), he overcomes his own death and enters the realms of eternal afterlife. On the eighth, LAMAT, the sign of VENUS[2], he plunges into the lowest, infernal regions whose depravations he must now overcome. On the ninth, MULUC, he is rewarded for his efforts. On the tenth, OC, he enters into the lowest form of matter so that on the eleventh, CHEUN, he may burn without flame, and thus suffers the utmost agony. On the twelfth, EB, he starts to ascend the ladder. On the thirteenth, BEN which symbolizes growing maize, he continues his ascent until on the fourteenth, IX the day of the jaguar god, he emerges washed clean of all earthly sin. On the fifteenth, MEN, he becomes perfect, but still has a way to go until he achieves full consciousness on the sixteenth day, CIB. On the seventeenth, C'HABAN, he throws off the last traces of ash, a word that is specifically used and thus suggests ritual cleansing by fire. On the eighteenth, EDZNAB, he is finally made perfect. On the nineteenth, CAUAC, his divine nature begins to manifest itself. Finally, on the twentieth and last day, AHAU (god), he reaches heaven and becomes at one with the divinities living there who welcome him into their fold.

Through this complex process the Maya believe that they each have their own creation that is quite separate to the creation of the Earth, and that they will all reach heaven, whether they have led blameless lives or not, for to the Maya there is no permanent hell, but rather it is a place they must all pass through in order to achieve full consciousness and enter heaven.

Agomme Tonnère HAITI (*Voodoo*)
A variant of OGOUN TONNÈRE which is, in turn, a variant of OGOUN.

Agoué Oyo HAITI (*Voodoo*)
Possibly originated from the Yorunda (a Nigerian people), Agoué Oyo is a LOA of the sea who is variously also named AGUÉ, AGUÉ WOYO, AGWÉ and AGWÉ WOYO.

Agriskoue NORTH AMERICA – WOODLANDS (*Huron*)
A variant of AIRSEKUI.

Aguasu HAITI (*Voodoo*)
A variant of ADJASSOU-LINGUETOR.

Agué (Woyo) HAITI (*Voodoo*)
Variant name(s) for AGOUÉ OYO.

Agwé (Woyo) HAITI (*Voodoo*)
The god of the sea whose name is a variant of AGOUÉ OYO. Elaborate ceremonies take

11

place to feed this proud LOA. VOODOO cultists send down ships loaded with gifts to his magnificent submarine palaces.

Ah Chuy Kak CENTRAL AMERICA (*Maya*)
The fire destroyer, a symbolic war-god (cf. AH CUN CUN).

Ah Cun Cun CENTRAL AMERICA (*Maya*)
The serpent charmer, a symbolic war-god (cf. AH CHUY KAK).

Ah holpopoh CENTRAL AMERICA (*Maya*)
'Those at the head of the mat', a lay caste on the same social level as the NACOM who acted as intermediaries between the HALACH UINIC and the general populace. Its name suggests that the Ah holpopoh possibly presided at gatherings of the three lowest social castes: the TUPILES, the common people and the slaves.

Ah Hoya CENTRAL AMERICA (*Maya*)
'He who urinates', an alternative name for CHAAC, the MAYA god of rain.

Ah Kinchel CENTRAL AMERICA (*Maya*)
One of the many names given to the god of death, and identified in the various CODEX as the god A. Other names applied to this deity are AH PUCH and HUNHAU. To the modern Yuacatec MAYA he is YUM CIMIL.

Ah Kinchil CENTRAL AMERICA (*Maya*)
The sun-god who is possibly regarded as an aspect of ITZAMNÁ. At night he travelled beneath the Earth, most sources saying that during this journey he assumed jaguar form. There is some confusion about this

deity, and the one named AH KINCHEL. At one stage it was thought that they were simply aspects of, or even variant spellings for the same deity, but this now seems unlikely.

Ah Kukum Xiu CENTRAL AMERICA (*Maya*)
Historical member of the XIU clan whose sacred language had to be known, and understood, by those aspiring to become ALMENHENOB. Ah Kukum Xiu apparently rebelled against the MAYA hierarchy as he helped Francisco MONTEJO the Younger in his conquest of the Yucatán, though this might have simply been an attempt to ingratiate himself with the invaders, and thus not only save his own neck, but also secure himself a position of some importance under the new regime.

Ah Puch CENTRAL AMERICA (*Maya*)
One of the various names given to the god of death who is identified in the various CODEX as the god A. He was portrayed as a skeleton, or as a bloated corpse. Other names applied to this deity by the MAYA peoples are AH KINCHEL and HUNHAU. He was the chief of the demons who presided over the ninth and lowest of the UNDERWORLDS, the horrible MITNAL. Ah Puch may also have been called CUMHAU and CIZIN, and was associated with NACON and EKAHAU. The modern Yuacatec Mayans call him YUM CIMIL, 'lord of death', who prowls the houses of the sick in his endless search for victims.

The Maya peoples have always had a great fear of death and dying, unlike their more warlike neighbours. The Spanish conquistadors were amazed at the overwhelming grief displayed by the bereaved. It was the Mayan custom, during the day, to weep in silence, but at night, when the Earth was thought to duplicate the ghastly darkness of Hunhau's realm, to raise loud and awful cries that were unbearable to all who came within hearing range.

The bodies of the humble people were buried under the floors of their houses, or behind them, their mouths invariably being filled with maize, and jade beads placed in their hands for use as money in the Underworld. The bodies of the noble dead were cremated, their ashes being placed in great urns which then had shrines built over them. In northern Yucatán the ashes of the dead were even placed in hollow wooden or pottery statues made in the image of the dead person.

Ah Tzenul CENTRAL AMERICA (*Maya*)
'He who gives food to others', an alternative name, or title, of CHAAC.

Ahalcana CENTRAL AMERICA (*Maya*)
One of the ghastly lords of XIBALBA. His name was learned by the twins HUNAHPU and XBALANQUÉ who sent out an unidentified animal named XAN, possibly a dog, ahead of them with the order to prick the leg of everyone it met. When Xan did so, the lord cried out, and the others, enquiring of the problem, gave away his name which was duly reported to the twins.

Ahalpuh CENTRAL AMERICA (*Maya*)
One of the lords of XIBALBA whose name was learned by HUNAHPU and XBALANQUÉ in the same manner as they learned the names of all the lords of Xibalba. See AHALCANA.

Ahatl CENTRAL AMERICA – MEXICO (*Aztec*)
One of the AZTEC leaders who left AZTLAN to seek out a new homeland on the mainland. The other Aztec leaders were ACACITLI, AUEXOTL, HUICTON, OCELOPAN, TEÇACATETL, TENOCH and XOMIMITL. They were accompanied on their journey by the four guardians of HUITZILOPOCHTLI: CHIPACTONAL, OXOMOCO, TLALTECUIN and XOCHICAHUACA.

Ahau CENTRAL AMERICA (*Maya*)
In the creation story of the MAYA, Ahau is referred to as the beginning of time, a period known long ago as the eleven Ahau when AHMUCENCAB, who is possibly cognate with the night, covered the Earth. Through this association Ahau became known as the day on which evil men are condemned to eternal purgatory in hell, for that is how the Maya saw the time before the creation of the Sun and the Moon. In this respect, the day Ahau has been associated with the mysterious god known simply as D from the ambiguous CODEX, the god of the Moon and night. The Maya CREATION[4] myth of the AGES OF MAN, the spiritual pilgrimage that all undertake, says that Ahau is the twentieth and last day of this pilgrimage, and that on which man at last becomes as one with the gods living in heaven who welcome him to their number.

Ahau Chamahez CENTRAL AMERICA (*Maya*)
One of the two 'medicine gods', the other being CIT BOLON TUM. Ahau Chamahez's name has been interpreted, albeit tentatively, as 'Lord of the Magic Tooth', thus suggesting that he was, in effect, an early Mayan dentist.

Ahayuta NORTH AMERICA – PUEBLO, SOUTHWEST (*Zuñi*)
Generic name for gods of war who were ruled over by the Sun.

Ahitescatoneh NORTH AMERICA – WOODLANDS (*Montagnais*)
Reciprocal rite when NIPINOUKHE and PIPOUNOUKHE, the spirits of spring and winter respectively, change places at the

end of their designated time in any part of the world.

Ahkinshok CENTRAL AMERICA –
YUCATÁN, MEXICO (*Modern Maya*)
The guardian spirit of the day to the modern Yuacatec MAYA people.

Ahkushtal CENTRAL AMERICA –
YUCATÁN, MEXICO (*Modern Maya*)
The goddess of childbirth to the present-day Yuacatec MAYA people.

Ahmakiq CENTRAL AMERICA –
YUCATÁN, MEXICO (*Modern Maya*)
To the modern Yuacatec MAYA, a beneficent god who, when the winds threaten to spoil the crops, locks them up out of harm's way.

Ahmucencab CENTRAL AMERICA
(*Maya*)
During the eleven AHAU, a period long ago, Ahmucencab (possibly cognate with the night) covered the faces of OXLAHUN-TIKU who had been captured and held by BOLONTIKU. Fire, salt, stones and trees were brought down to Earth and Oxlahuntiku was knocked about and carried away. His serpent (his symbol of authority) was taken from him as was his TIZNÉ. The first BOLON DZACAB then covered the Earth with a thick layer of seed and went away, satisfied that his work was done, to the thirteenth and highest heaven. As the serpent of Oxlahuntiku had been taken, a great flood now came which made heaven collapse on to the Earth which was destroyed by CANTULTIKU, the four BACAB.

When the chaos subsided, Cantultiku set KANZIBYÚI on to the Earth to reorganize it. Many different coloured trees were planted at each of the world's cardinal points and the heavens were propped up. Thus the new world was created.

This creation story comes from the *Book of* CHILAM BALAM OF CHUMAYEL. Though

the exact purpose of Ahmucencab is not revealed, it seems likely that it is the representation of the all-pervading darkness that covered the face of the Earth in a time before the creation of the Sun and the Moon.

Ahsonnutli NORTH AMERICA –
SOUTHWEST (*Navajo*)
A variant of ESTANATLEHI.

Ahu-uc-cheknale CENTRAL AMERICA
(*Maya*)
'He-Who-Makes-Fruitful-Seven-Times'.
Ahu-uc-cheknale features in a creation story of the MAYA people in which he was alleged to have said that the world had come from the Earth's seven bosoms. Then he descended from the centre of the Earth to fructify ITZAMKABAIN, the alligator-footed whale. As he came, the four lights and four regions of the stars began to revolve, the Sun and the Moon awoke, and the world as it is known today came into being.

Ahuacan CENTRAL AMERICA (*Maya*)
'Lord Serpent', the priestly caste which was on a par with the HALACH UINIC in the MAYA social structure, and just one place down from the nobility, the highest caste within this structure.

Ahuizotle NORTH AMERICA – PUEBLO,
SOUTHWEST (*Zuñi and Hopi*)
A mythical beast that roamed the banks of rivers. About the size of a dog, it had the cry of a human baby but, should anyone approach to investigate, it would seize them by a monkey-like hand at the end of its long, prehensile tail. Three days later the corpse would be found minus eyes, teeth and nails, the favourite titbits of the Ahuizotle.

Ahulane CENTRAL AMERICA (*Maya*)
The archer who is usually portrayed holding an arrow. A symbolic war-god, he had a shrine on the island of COZUMEL (cf. AH CHUY KAK, AH CUN CUN).

Ai Apaec SOUTH AMERICA (*Mochica*)
A late name for an active god of the MOCHICA who ranged beneath the throne of the almost totally indifferent supreme being and creator deity, a sky-god whose throne was usually situated on the top of a high mountain. Ai Apaec was possibly the son of the mountain god, and shared the feline mouth of the nameless creator deity. He was usually portrayed wearing a jaguar head dress and snake-head earrings.

Aida-Wédo HAITI (*Voodoo*)
The rainbow-snake, an important LOA.

Airsekui NORTH AMERICA –
WOODLANDS (*Huron*)
Also called ARESKOUI and AGRISKOUE, Airsekui was the GREAT SPIRIT of the HURON AMERINDIANS. During times of great danger he is called AIRSEKUI SUTANDITENR. The first fruits of hunting and battle are always offered to him. He resembles, though is not the exact equivalent of, KITSHI MANITOU, the ALGONQUIAN supreme spirit.

Airsekui Sutanditenr NORTH AMERICA – WOODLANDS (*Huron*)
'Airsekui Saviour' – the aspect in which AIRSEKUI was invoked during times of great danger.

Akbal CENTRAL AMERICA (*Maya*)
The third day of the MAYA spiritual pilgrimage – the AGES OF MAN. On this day the child is born, his soul having been bestowed on him during IK, the preceding day. This day is not to be confused with that known as THIRTEEN AKBAL, the day

during the twenty days of the Maya CREATION[4] when the first true men were modelled out of clay.

Aktunowihio NORTH AMERICA – GREAT PLAINS (*Cheyenne*)
The soul of the Earth, a subterranean spirit whose name means 'Wise-One-Below'.

Akycha NORTH AMERICA – ALASKA (*Inuit*)
The spirit of the Sun, and thus of great importance to this ESKIMO people who spend a greater amount of the year in darkness.

Alacita SOUTH AMERICA – BOLIVIA AND PERU (*Quechua*)
Annual fairs that are held at COCHAMBAMBA, ORURO and LA PAZ, each of which has become associated with the cult of EKKEKKO, the god of good fortune.

alautun CENTRAL AMERICA (*Maya*)
An extremely long period of time over which the MAYA used to calculate their calendar. One alautun was formed from twenty KINCHILTUN and totalled 23,040,000,000 days, or over 63,000,000 years.

Alawe HAITI (*Voodoo*)
A LOA whom some authorities believe has been combined with DIJI to make the loa LALOUÉ-DIJI.

alec pong SOUTH AMERICA – PERU (*Chimu*)
Name given to ancestral TOTEM stones that were worshipped in CHIMOR.

Algonqui(a)n NORTH AMERICA – WOODLANDS
Indigenous AMERINDIAN people inhabiting the eastern WOODLANDS culture region to the south and east of Hudson Bay. They formerly lived along the banks of the River

Ottawa, and the northern tributaries of the mighty St Lawrence. Today they inhabit reserves in East Ontario and West Quebec. The Algonquian group of languages, which consists of more than twenty languages, is spoken by many native peoples on the Atlantic coast, and elsewhere, including ARAPAHO, BLACKFOOT, CHEYENNE and CREE.

Alkuntam NORTH AMERICA –
NORTHWEST COAST (*Bella Coola*)
Possibly identifiable with SISIUTL, Alkuntam was the assistant of SENX in the Creation of mankind and the animals. She was alleged to be the daughter of the cannibal goddess who sucks the brains of men out through their ears. Her mother was regarded as a personification of the mosquito which, in many myths from this region of North America, was said to have sprung from the ashes of the cannibal goddess.

Almenhenob CENTRAL AMERICA (*Maya*)
'Those who had mothers and fathers', a social caste whose membership was decided by the HALACH UINIC who sat as judges on those rising through the caste system to determine who had the right to be called Almenhenob. It appears that this classification does not owe its origins to whether or not the individual's parents were married, but rather to the Halach uinic being the 'parents' who looked to the individual to prove themselves worthy of being called their 'child'. The key to this was knowledge and understanding of a sacred language called ZUYUA, the language of the XIU clan.

Aluberi SOUTH AMERICA – GUYANA
(*Arawak*)
The GREAT SPIRIT who, in contrast to the creator KURURUMANY, was a remote and aloof being.

Amaiaua CARIBBEAN (*Taíno*)
One of the two caves from which the first people are said to have emerged, the other being called CACIBAGIAGUA. Originally the mouths of these caves were guarded by a night-watchman called MAROCAEL, but one morning he was caught by the Sun's rays which petrified him, thus allowing mankind to escape.

Amalivaca SOUTH AMERICA – GUYANA
(*Arawak*)
A trickster-hero of the ARAWAK people whose true purpose and attributes have sadly been lost to us.

Amarok NORTH AMERICA – GREENLAND
(*Inuit*)
A great wolf-like monster alleged to live in the interior wastelands of Greenland.

Amayicoyondi NORTH AMERICA (*Perico*)
The wife of NIPARAYA, the creator of the universe.

Amazon SOUTH AMERICA – BRAZIL
1 Vast river of the South American continent, the world's second longest, 4,080 miles long, containing the largest in volume of water. The river drains almost half of the South American land mass, and discharges such an immense volume of water that forty miles out to sea, fresh water remains at the surface.
2 Early Spanish visitors to Brazil identified the women of the Brazilian Indians who fought alongside their menfolk with the Amazons of classical Greek mythology.

Amelia, Maîtresse HAITI (*Voodoo*)
One of the many LOA of the VOODOO religion.

A'men CENTRAL AMERICA (*Maya*)
The name given to SHAMAN diviners who have god-given powers that enable them to control cosmic forces.

Amerindian
The term Amerindian, an amalgamation and shortening of American Indian, is freely applied to many different indigenous peoples of North, Central and South America. They were first called Indians by Christopher COLUMBUS who thought that he had found a new route to India, and had not in fact discovered the 'New World'. The ancestors of the diverse tribes are thought to have entered North America from Asia between 60,000 and 35,000 BC, crossing the former land bridge of Beringia that then joined Siberia to Alaska.

The tribes are usually identified as inhabiting specific areas of the Americas as follows:

North America:
Arctic: INUIT (ESKIMO)
Sub-Arctic: ALGONQUIAN, CREE, Ottawa
Northeast WOODLANDS: HURON, IROQUOIS, Mohican, Shawnee (Tecumseh)
GREAT PLAINS: BLACKFOOT, CHEYENNE, COMANCHE, PAWNEE, SIOUX
NORTHWEST COAST: CHINOOK, TLINGIT, TSHIMSHIAN
Southwest (PUEBLO): APACHE, HOPI, MOJAVE, NAVAJO, SHOSHONE, ZUÑI
Southeast WOODLANDS: CHEROKEE, CHOCTAW, CREEK, Hopewell, NATCHEZ, SELISH

Central America: AZTEC, MAYA, MEXICA, NAHUA, TOLTEC

South America:
Eastern: CARIB, XINGÚ
Central: GUARANÍ, Miskito
Western: ARAUCA, AYMARÁ, CHIMOR, INCA, JIVARO, QUECHUA

It should be noted that these are by no means all the indigenous peoples of the Americas. The above obviously excludes island cultures, such as the Taíno of the Caribbean, and the VOODOO cult of Haiti, though the latter is a relatively modern religious development.

Amitolane NORTH AMERICA – PUEBLO, SOUTHWEST (*Zuñi*)
The spirit of the rainbow.

Amminan HAITI (*Voodoo*)
A LOA whose characteristics and attributes remain a secret of VOODOO cultists.

Amotken NORTH AMERICA – WOODLANDS (*Selish*)
To the SELISH, one of the oldest of the North American AMERINDIAN peoples, Amotken was the creator, dwelling in heaven, solitary and alone, an old man, wise and kind, never changing in the concern he had for his creation. His messenger was the familiar COYOTE who exhibited none of the trickery associated with him among the southern tribes. According to the Selish cosmology, Amotken dwells in the highest level of the universe – the other two levels being Earth and the UNDERWORLD – each level being capable of habitation and supported by a gigantic pillar or post.

One Selish myth relates that Amotken made five young women from five hairs plucked from his head, and then asked them what they wanted to be. The first replied that she wanted to become the mother of wickedness; the second the mother of goodness; the third mother-earth; the fourth the mother of fire; and the fifth the mother of water. Amotken duly fulfilled their wishes, saying that at first the wicked would be in the majority, but later the good would overcome them and rule the world.

amoxaoque CENTRAL AMERICA –
MEXICO (*Aztec*)
The name used to refer to a wise man.
Several such wise men were said to have
left the travellers from AZTLAN at
TAMOANCHAN. Four, however, remained,
being the guardians of HUITZILOPOCHTLI:
CHIPACTONAL, OXOMOCO, TLALTECUIN and
XOCHICAHUACA.

Anago HAITI (*Voodoo*)
A LOA whose name is derived from that of
the West African Nago tribe of the Yorunda people of Nigeria.

Anáhuac CENTRAL AMERICA – MEXICO
(*Aztec and Toltec*)
The 'place at the centre, in the midst of
the circle', the holiest place of the TOLTEC
people, the source of their very existence.
Though the exact location of Anáhuac
remains unclear, the place features as the
destination to which QUETZALCÓATL set
off after he had been defeated by TEZCATLI-
POCA and left the city of TOLLAN to return
to TLILLAN-TLAPALLAN.

anamaqkiu NORTH AMERICA –
WOODLANDS (*Algonquian*)
Malignant spirits of the UNDERWORLD who
were said, in the HARE cycles of the ALGO-
NQUIAN people, to have dragged MOQWAOI
under the ice he was walking on. For four
days his brother MÄNÄBUSCH mourned his
loss, but on the fifth he met his brother's
shade whom he told to go to the furthest
point to the west, and to build a large fire
there which he was to tend, this fire to
serve as a beacon to guide the dead towards their new home, and to keep them
warm on their journey.
Mänäbusch was determined to avenge
the death of his brother, and tricked the
two great bear chiefs of the anamaqkiu to
their death. In revenge the anamaqkiu
raised a great FLOOD[3], the waters of which
chased Mänäbusch up a mountain, then

up a large pine tree that grew on the
summit. Still the waters chased him, so
Mänäbusch made the tree grow to four
times its original height. It was only when
the waters had reached Mänäbusch's armpits that the GREAT SPIRIT intervened and
arrested the waters which immediately
subsided.

anaye NORTH AMERICA – SOUTHWEST
(*Navajo*)
The name used by the NAVAJO people to
refer to unnatural or alien gods, a grouping
of giants and monsters who were born to
virgins who had engaged in unnatural
practices. These included the hairy headless THEELGETH; the feathered TSHANA-
HALE; the BINAYE AHANI, a terrible pair of
limbless twins who killed men with a single
glance; YEITSO a fearsome giant; and the
flesh-eating antelope DELGETH.
Many of the anaye were killed by NAYA-
NEZGANI and THOBADZISTSHINI when they
returned to Earth, but they were unable to
overcome them all, so they sought the help
of TSHOHANOAI, the Sun-Bearer, who gave
them four magical hoops. Using these, the
goddess ESTANATLEHI sent a terrible storm
which not only destroyed all but four of
the remaining anaye, but also reshaped the
very Earth itself.
The four anaye who remained were OLD
AGE, COLD, POVERTY and HUNGER, these
only being allowed to survive after they
had convinced Estanatlehi that, if they
died, mankind would no longer prize the
good things of life, or even life itself.

Ancient-bodied One NORTH AMERICA –
WOODLANDS (*Iroquois*)
The CHIEF-SKY-RULER and grandfather of
ATAENTSIC.

angako ~ k, ~ q (pl. angakut) NORTH
AMERICA – ARCTIC (*Inuit*)
The name given to SHAMAN(s), men or
women, though women are said to lack the

courage to do evil. Since the religious ideas of the Arctic inhabitants have never been formalized, angakut are repositories of ancestral lore, judges in matters of tradition, and the means of communication with the spirit world. An angakok who can propitiate evil, and call down misfortune on his fellows is known as an ILISITSOK, in which case the victim would be attacked by a TUPILAK, a magical animal under the power of the angakok, and usually taking the form of a seal.

To become an angakok the individual must secure the help and protection of a single, very powerful TORNAK, or guardian spirit, of which there are three specific kinds: those in human form, those in the form of stones, or those who inhabit bears, the last being believed to be the most powerful. With the assistance of the tornak, an angakok cures the sick, controls the weather, and secures good hunting through the propitiation of the hungry sea-goddess SEDNA-NERRIVIK. When INUIT hunters are unable to find any prey, their angakok sends his spirit to plead with this sea deity.

To reach the home of the goddess, the angakok must pass through the land of the dead over which Sedna-Nerrivik rules, and then pass over an icy whirlpool which threatens to engulf the angakok. Next come three mighty tasks. The first is to pass by an enormous cauldron of boiling seals; the second is to evade the great goddess's fearsome guarddog; and the last is to cross an abyss on a path so thin that it formed a knife's edge. Having passed all these obstacles the angakok finally arrives at Sedna-Nerrivik's fabulously appointed palace.

Once in front of the goddess, the angakok dances and chants to induce the great goddess to help the angakok's people. Finally she tells the shaman spirit that the Inuit must either move and build a new settlement – otherwise they will surely starve to death – or she agrees to help them by sending seals and other prey. Now the angakok spirit retraces its steps and relays the message from Sedna-Nerrivik to the waiting people.

angakut NORTH AMERICA – ARCTIC (*Inuit*)
The plural of ANGAKOK.

Angpetu Wi NORTH AMERICA – GREAT PLAINS (*Dakota*)
The spirit of the Sun.

Anguta NORTH AMERICA – ALASKA (*Inuit*)
A shadowy being, the father of the great sea-goddess SEDNA-NERRIVIK with whom he lives in her undersea realm, and to which he drags down the dead with his maimed hand. According to some accounts it was Anguta who, having firstly rescued his daughter from her abductor, then threw her overboard in order to save himself.

Aningan NORTH AMERICA (*Inuit*)
The spirit of the Moon.

anishinabeg NORTH AMERICA – WOODLANDS (*Chippewa*)
The name given to the helpless primordial people, the ancestors of mankind, upon whom the good MINABOZHO took pity.

anitsutsa NORTH AMERICA – WOODLANDS (*Cherokee*)
The spirits of the stars within the PLEIADES[2] star cluster.

Annals of Cakquichel CENTRAL AMERICA (*Maya*)
An important source of MAYA culture though the text was not written until after the Spanish conquest. However, it was written by the southern Quiche Maya peoples of Guatemala, and may possibly reflect

rather more of TOLTEC than Maya culture and tradition. This assumption is made as it is historically recorded that by the time of the Spanish conquest, the Maya of Guatemala knew very little about the builders of their great cities. It is also based on the fact that they told the Spanish their legend about their exile from TOLLAN, a story that resembles one found among the central Mexican Toltec who certainly penetrated as far south as Guatemala, if not further.

Anpao NORTH AMERICA – GREAT
   PLAINS (*Dakota*)
The spirit of the dawn.

Antoine, Sainte HAITI (*Voodoo*)
Saint Anthony, the Roman Catholic saint who features as a LOA in some VOODOO cults.

Apache NORTH AMERICA
One of the indigenous North American AMERINDIAN peoples who are related to the NAVAJO and lived as hunters. Today there are about 10,000 Apache who live in reservations in Arizona (the Apache state), southwest Oklahoma and New Mexico. During the eighteenth and nineteenth centuries the Apache were known as fierce raiders and horse warriors. Their name also applies to any of several ATHAPASCAN languages and dialects spoken by these people.

apachita SOUTH AMERICA (*Inca*)
The name given to the piles of stones that are placed at danger spots on roads, and at the summits of passes. They are a category of HUACA – sacred objects that are perceived as permeated by a spirit.

Apitay SOUTH AMERICA (*Inca*)
The place where HUANA CAURI, one of the CHILDREN OF THE SUN, chose to remain. He died there and the mountain nearby was renamed HUANACAURI in his honour.

Apoyan Tachu NORTH AMERICA –
   SOUTHWEST (*Zuñi*)
The Sky-Father who was, according to some, created from the sea-foam by AWONAWILONA.

Apu-Punchau SOUTH AMERICA (*Inca*)
Alternative name for INTI.

Arada HAITI (*Voodoo*)
A LOA whose name is derived from that of the West African Allada tribe.

Arapaho NORTH AMERICA – GREAT
   PLAINS
Indigenous North American AMERINDIAN people who inhabited the GREAT PLAINS culture region. Their language was one of the ALGONQUIAN family that connected them linguistically with the BLACKFOOT, CHEYENNE and CREE peoples. Traditionally the Arapaho people lived to the east of the Rocky Mountains, to the south of the Cheyenne people, and to the north of the COMANCHE nation.

Arauca SOUTH AMERICA – CHILE
Though the name Arauca is normally used to refer to a single tribe of AMERINDIAN people living in Chile, the term is more correctly used to refer to any of the original indigenous inhabitants of that country as well as the Argentine pampas. These people gradually assimilated into a contiguous group that was composed not only of both farmers and hunters, but also renowned warriors who defeated the INCAS and resisted the incursion of the Spanish for 200 years. Originally living in small village communities, almost 200,000 Araucanian Indians today live on reservations. Authorities are divided over whether their language belongs to the Penutian or the Andean-Equatorial family.

Arawak SOUTH AMERICA
Indigenous AMERINDIAN people of the Caribbean and northeast AMAZON[1] basin. They lived mainly by shifting cultivation of the tropical forests, and were driven out of the Lesser Antilles by another Amerindian people, the CARIBS, shortly before the arrival of the Spanish in the sixteenth century. Subsequently their numbers on Hispaniola declined from some four million in 1492 to just a few thousand following their exploitation by the Spanish in their search for gold. Additionally, smallpox was introduced in 1518 which, along with other diseases, eradicated the remainder. Arawakan languages belong to the Andean-Equatorial family.

Areskoui NORTH AMERICA –
    WOODLANDS (*Huron*)
A variant of AIRSEKUI.

Arica SOUTH AMERICA (*Collao*)
Coastal city and port at the northern end of Chile, just south of the border with Peru. COLLAO myth states that the body of THUNAPA was carried to the coast at Arica along the River DESAGUADERO from Lake TITICACA, some 200 miles to the northeast, after the rush boat that was carrying Thunapa's body struck the lake shore at COCHAMARCA with such force that it formed the river. The legend is an anachronism as the river does not flow into the Pacific Ocean, but is land-locked and empties into Lake POOPÓ.

Arika NORTH AMERICA – GREAT PLAINS
Indigenous North American AMERINDIAN people, one of the CADDO-speaking peoples, who inhabited the GREAT PLAINS culture region. Linguistically they are linked with the Caddo and PAWNEE peoples, and dwelt in the region that lay between the ATHAPASCAN-speaking peoples to the west, and the ALGONQUIAN speakers to their east.

Arkaonyó SOUTH AMERICA – BRAZIL
    (*Tupari*)
A sorcerer who used liquid beeswax to stick VALEDJÁD's fingers together – so that he could perform no magic – and to seal his eyes and nostrils. Finally, after many attempts, Arkaonyó found a bird that was strong enough to carry Valedjád away to the north.

Arna(r)ku(su)agsa ~ k, ~ q NORTH
    AMERICA – ALASKA (*Inuit*)
'Old Woman', the GREAT GODDESS, a water-spirit and goddess of the sea, the ruler of the dead and the source of all life. To the Alaskan Inuit she is known as Arnakuagsak or Arnarkusuagsak and SEDNA-NERRIVIK, while the Inuit of eastern Greenland simply call her NERRIVIK ('food-dish').

Arna(r)quagssaq NORTH AMERICA –
    ALASKA (*Inuit*)
A variant of ARNA(R)KU(SU)AGSAK.

Aroteh SOUTH AMERICA – BRAZIL
    (*Tupari*)
One of the primitive VAMOA-POD who lived in a tent with his companion TOVA-POD. The first men, who lived underground, came and stole the vamoa-pod's food. Aroteh and Tovapod tracked the thieves to a hole in which they dug. Streams of the underground people poured out of the hole until the two vamoa-pod stopped it up again. These first people had tusks which Tovapod removed, and webbing between the fingers and toes, which he also removed, thus giving the people their present beautiful teeth, hands and feet.

Arunaua SOUTH AMERICA (*Inca*)
A variant of TUAPACA.

Ascent of the Navajo, The NORTH AMERICA – SOUTHWEST (*Navajo*)

The following myth is not peculiar to the NAVAJO people. Neighbouring peoples, such as the PUEBLO-dwelling SIA and HOPI Indians of New Mexico and Arizona, have similar myths detailing their ascent through several lower worlds to emerge upon the Earth. The Navajo story however, is, possibly the most complete of all these myths.

In the RED WORLD during the AGE OF BEGINNINGS four streams flowed from the centre of the Earth to the four cardinal points (north, south, east and west), and thence into the sea. In this world the very first people came to life, mostly in the form of insects, though they also included bat people and, according to some versions, ATSE HASTIN ('First Man'), ATSE ESTSAN ('First Woman') and the trickster COYOTE.

These first people, the inhabitants of the Red World, angered their gods because they freely committed adultery, and were punished when the gods sent a great flood. As they fled upwards seeking a way to escape the inevitable drowning in the ever-advancing waters, a blue head appeared through the sky and invited the Red World people up into the BLUE WORLD of the SWALLOW PEOPLE.

Their time in the Blue World was cut short when, on the twenty-fourth night after their arrival, one of their number committed adultery with the Swallow chief's wife, and they were expelled, once more being forced to flee upwards. Their flight was guided by the voice of the wind NILTSHI who led them to an opening in the sky through which they passed into the YELLOW WORLD of the GRASSHOPPER PEOPLE. Again they made free with their hosts' wives, and were once more expelled. Helped again by Niltshi they came into the next world, a multicoloured one.

This world was totally different from the three lower ones. Its four cardinal points were marked by snow-capped mountains, and it was already inhabited by the KISANI and the MIRAGE people. They had four gods: WHITE BODY, BLUE BODY, YELLOW BODY and BLACK BODY. The Kisani, who were farmers, fed the new arrivals on pumpkins and maize, and from ears of white and yellow maize the four gods of this world created Atse Estsan and Atse Hastin – 'First Woman' and 'First Man'.

This couple bore five pairs of twins, the oldest pairing being androgynous and inventing pottery and wicker water-bottles. The four younger pairs intermarried with the Mirage and Kisani people, and so the tribe of Atse Hastin multiplied.

One day they saw the sky bending down towards the earth, which in its turn rose up to meet it. As they touched, Coyote and BADGER came down from the world above. While Coyote stayed among the people of Atse Hastin, Badger continued his descent through to the Yellow World. It was at this time that men and women were living apart, having quarrelled over something that remains uncertain. Finding themselves short of food, the women decided that the time had come to rejoin their menfolk, but as they crossed the stream that divided their two territories, the last two women were seized by the water-monster TIEHOLTSODI and dragged down into his watery realm.

Alarmed by the loss, the people sought the advice of the four gods, and upon receiving this, a man and a woman were sent down to undertake the rescue. Unknown to them, Coyote secretly followed their passage and abducted two of Tieholtsodi's offspring.

Enraged, the water-monster caused a flood to cover the world, and in desperation the people of Atse Hastin fled upwards, the animals making the trees sprout higher and higher in a vain attempt to outrun the ever-rising waters. Finally, two men appeared with a little soil in which they grew a mighty hollow reed inside which all the people took refuge, but only just in time, for hardly was the bunghole sealed than they heard the waters surging over it.

Although they were now safe from the waters, they were also trapped for, even though the reed reached right up to and touched the sky, there was no way through into the world above. GREAT HAWK flew up and clawed at the sky until he glimpsed light filtering through from the world above, then LOCUST made a tiny hole and crawled through.

Here he was met by four grebes, the guardians of the four cardinal points of the New World, and they engaged him in a contest of power (as would happen between rival SHAMANS). Locust managed, at length, to win half the world for his people who remained trapped in the world below. Badger, who had apparently come back up from the Yellow World by then, enlarged the hole through which Locust had crawled, and all the people climbed through to their New World. Thus they came to our world, arriving on an island in the middle of a lake.

The gods accompanied them to the shore of the lake where they assembled to discover their fate by throwing a hide scraper into the water, watching it intently to see whether it would float or sink. It floated, meaning that they would have immortality, but Coyote threw a large stone into the water, the waves from which made the scraper sink. Furiously the people turned on him, but Coyote hurriedly explained that it was better that their lives should be limited by time, otherwise the world would become overpopulated.

Death, it seemed, would come very swiftly for them when the flood waters from the world they had just left came surging through the hole by which they had escaped. Luckily, Coyote's abduction of Tieholtsodi's children was discovered in time and, throwing them back into the lower world, the waters receded with a roar.

Atse Hastin, Atse Estsan, Blue Body and Black Body now fashioned the Navajo land starting with seven mountains. These they firmly anchored to the Earth with such things as a sunbeam, a rainbow, a huge stone knife and a thunderbolt. Then they decorated each mountain with various kinds of weather, light, crops, shells and semi-precious stones, and at the summit of each they placed a nest of eggs so that the mountains might have feathers to wear.

In the southern mountain, Mount TAYLOR, they set TURQUOISE BOY and CORN GIRL. In the northern, Mount SAN JUAN, they set POLLEN BOY and GRASSHOPPER GIRL. In the eastern, PELADO PEAK, they set ROCK-CRYSTAL BOY and ROCK-CRYSTAL GIRL, and in the western, Mount SAN FRANCISCO, they set WHITE-CORN BOY and YELLOW-CORN GIRL. Next, Atse Hastin and Atse Estsan made the Sun, Moon and stars, appointing as Sun-Bearer and Moon-Bearer the two men who had found the soil and grown the reed in the world below, their names being TSHOHANOAI and KLEHONOAI.

During their time in the lower, multi-coloured world, when the men and the women had lived apart, some of the women (usually described as virgins) had engaged in evil, unnatural practices. Now they gave birth to all manner of man-eating monsters, the ANAYE ('alien gods'), who included the feathered TSHANAHALE; the hairy, headless THEELGETH; a terrible pair of limbless twins who killed with a single glance, the BINAYE AHANI; YEITSO, a fearsome giant; and DELGETH, the flesh-eating antelope.

The people also fell victim to a celestial gambler who tricked them into staking and losing their freedom, and who was simply known as HE-WHO-WINS-MEN. However, two powerful beings, the great YEI – HASTSHEYALTI and HASTSHEHOGAN – came to their rescue and, with the help of the spirits of wind and darkness, as well as animal deities, they enabled a young brave to overcome the celestial gambler. With a magic bow this young brave shot He-Who-Wins-Men back into the sky, from which he later descended to rule over the Mexican people.

Now the yei created two goddesses, ESTANATLEHI ('Woman-who-changes'), and YOLKAI ESTSAN ('White-Shell-Woman'), forming the first out of turquoise and the second from white shell. Next the twin heroes NAYANEZGANI and THOBADZISTSHINI were born. Some versions of the myth make these heroes the sons of Estanatlehi and Tshohanoai, while others make Nayanezgani the son of those deities, and Thobadzistshini the son of Yolkai Estsan and WATER.

These twins made a perilous journey to the HOGAN of the Sun-Bearer, Tshohanoai, helped by Niltshi, the spirit of the wind, and SPIDER-WOMAN. There, by surviving many trials, they won the confidence of the Sun-Bearer who gave them magical weapons by way of recognition. These were arrows of lightning, sunbeams and rainbow; a huge stone knife (possibly a representation of a thunderbolt); and armour from every joint of which lightning flashed.

Now the twins returned to Earth and made war on the anaye, killing a great number of them, but, unable to overcome them all, they once again sought the help of Tshohanoai. This time he gave them four magic hoops with which the goddess Estanatlehi raised a terrible storm which not only killed almost all the remaining anaye, but also reshaped the very Earth

itself. When the storm abated, only four of the anaye remained: COLD, HUNGER, OLD AGE, POVERTY, and they were only allowed to live having convinced Estanatlehi that, if she killed them too, men would no longer prize the good things of life, or even prize life itself. Their task completed, Nayanezgani and Thobadzistshini went to their allotted mountain home, and there, even today, Navajo braves go to ask for success in battle.

Freed from the terrible anaye, Tshohanoai now peopled the reshaped Earth with animals, then he went away to the far west where he built himself a lodge way beyond the waters, taking with him Estanatlehi, the goddess of fertility and rain.

Estanatlehi's sister Yolkai Estsan was now left alone on the Earth until the good yei Hastsheyalti came to her. Together they decided to create new people, making a man from an ear of white corn, and a woman from an ear of yellow corn. The spirit of the wind, Niltshi, breathed life into them. Rock-Crystal Boy gave them their minds. Grasshopper Girl gave them the ability to speak. Yolkai Estsan gave them the gifts of maize and fire. Then she married the man to GROUND-HEAT GIRL, and the woman to MIRAGE BOY, their children becoming the first true Navajo. Her work done, Yolkai Estsan went away to become the wife of Klehonoai, the Moon-Bearer.

Asgaya Gigagei NORTH AMERICA – WOODLANDS (*Cherokee*)
Literally meaning 'red-man', Asgaya Gigagei is the thunder-god of the CHEROKEES, an AMERINDIAN tribe that was long under the domination of the IROQUOIS. They also have a group of lesser gods who are known as the 'thunder-boys', these gods possibly originating as the offspring of Asgaya Gigagei.

Ashiwanni NORTH AMERICA – PUEBLO, SOUTHWEST (*Zuñi*)

The most important religious grouping of the ZUÑI AMERINDIANS, the rain priesthood. It comprises fourteen rain-priests (the ASHIWI), two priests of the bow and a fertility priestess. Together with the priest of the Sun and the two leaders of the KOTIKILI, the Ashiwanni are the earthly counterparts of the COUNCIL OF GODS that meets in KOTHLUWALAWA.

ashiwi NORTH AMERICA – PUEBLO, SOUTHWEST (*Zuñi*)

The fourteen rain-priests within the religious grouping of the ASHIWANNI. The name is also that of the first people to emerge from the UNDERWORLD, who were originally ugly, smelly creatures with webbed feet and hands, moss-covered bodies, long ears and short, hairless tails. They were guided to the Earth's surface by a group of gods who rectified their defects *en route*. As the ashiwi emerged on to the Earth, they were accompanied by ten invisible CORN MAIDENS who travelled with them for four years until, at SHIPOLOLO, the 'Place of Mist and Cloud', they were discovered by two witches who had been the last to emerge from the Underworld. These witches presented the Corn Maidens with the seeds of maize and squash. As the ashiwi continued their journey, the Corn Maidens remained at Shipololo where they lived in a cedar bower roofed with clouds. There they danced while each held a beautiful THLAWE.

One day the Corn Maidens were discovered by the twin gods KOWWITUMA and WATSUSII, sons of the Sun-god. The Sun priest told the divine twins to bring the Corn Maidens to the people, which they did, the Corn Maidens dancing before the people in a courtyard decorated with cornmeal paintings of clouds.

Gradually, as night fell, everyone fell asleep; but still the Corn Maidens danced; then the flower and butterfly god PAYATAMI came and saw them. He was immediately smitten by their loveliness, especially that of their leader, the YELLOW-CORN MAIDEN. However, the Corn Maidens became frightened as they could read his thoughts, and as soon as he too had fallen asleep, when dawn began to break in the east, they hurried away and hid under the wings of ducks in Shipololo spring.

A great famine then spread across the land, so the people begged Kowwituma and Watsusii to find the Corn Maidens for them again. To help, the ashiwi sat in their KIVA (temple) and thought only of the Corn Maidens and the life-giving rain. The twin gods enlisted the assistance of BITSITSI, their father's musician who descended to earth and telepathically conveyed the prayers of the ashiwi to the Corn Maidens, assuring them that if they returned, he would ensure their safety, and that they would be treated with the respect and reverence due to them.

Led by Bitsitsi, the Corn Maidens returned to the people and, each holding her thlawe, danced from dawn to dusk to the music of Payatami's flute and the singing of a choir. Yellow-Corn Maiden and BLUE-CORN MAIDEN, the eldest of the Corn Maidens, led the dance. First the Corn Maidens on the north of the courtyard passed west to join their sisters on the south, and then returned to their places. Then those on the south passed west to join their sisters on the north, and then returned likewise to their places. At the end of the dance the Corn Maidens left and the ashiwi never saw them again.

Assez Media HAITI (*Voodoo*)

One of the countless LOA of the VOODOO religion.

Assinaboin(e) NORTH AMERICA –
GREAT PLAINS
Indigenous North American AMERINDIAN
people inhabiting that part of the GREAT
PLAINS culture region that lay between the
ALGONQUIAN-speaking peoples of the east,
and the ATHAPASCANs to the west. Speak-
ing one of the SIOUX languages, they
shared occupancy with the CROW, DA-
KOTA, MANDAN, OMAHA, OSAGE and WIN-
NEBAGO, all Sioux tribes, and the CADDO-
speaking peoples of the ARIKA, Caddo and
PAWNEE.

Atacrou HAITI (*Voodoo*)
One of the many LOA of the VOODOO
religion.

Ataen(t)sic NORTH AMERICA –
WOODLANDS (*Iroquois*)
The Earth-goddess, granddaughter of the
ANCIENT-BODIED ONE (the CHIEF-SKY-
RULER) and wife of the celestial CHIEF-
WHO-HOLDS-THE-EARTH. She came to Earth
with her daughter, GUSTS-OF-WIND, when
her husband unjustly accused her of being
unfaithful to him. Gusts-of-Wind married
the WIND-RULER and bore the twins
YOSKEHA or HAHGWEHDIYU ('sapling'),
and TASWISCANA or HAHGWEGDAETGAH
('flint') who were enemies while still in
their mother's womb, to the extent that
their ante-natal fighting killed Gusts-of-
Wind.

Taswiscana persuaded Ataentsic that
Yoskeha was wholly responsible for the
death of Gusts-of-Wind, so Ataentsic expelled Yoskeha from the Earth, and from
the body of Gusts-of-Wind she made the
Sun and the Moon which she then hid
under the Earth's surface with the help of
Taswiscana, though some variants of the
myth of Ataentsic say that Yoskeha created the Earth from the corpse of
Ataentsic.

Yoskeha sought out his father who gave
his son a bow and arrows, and some maize,
signifying his lordship over animals and
plants. However, when Yoskeha first prepared maize for mankind who were about
to be born, Ataentsic spoiled it by scattering ashes over it.

Atahocan NORTH AMERICA –
WOODLANDS (*Montagnais*)
The GREAT SPIRIT who was seen as the
creator of all things.

Atahualpa SOUTH AMERICA (*Inca*)
The last INCA ruler (c. 1502–1533). On
the death of his father, HUAYNA-CAPAC, in
1525, he received the northern half of the
Inca empire with its capital at QUITO, and
in 1532 overthrew his brother, HUÁSCAR,
who ruled the southern half from its capital at CUZCO. However, a year later he was
captured by a force of invading Spaniards
under the command of Francisco PIZARRO
who proceeded to conquer Peru. Although
his subjects paid a vast ransom, described
by some as enough gold to fill a room, and
enough silver and precious stones to fill
two more rooms, Atahualpa was condemned to death for treason and sen-
tenced to be burned. Following his conver-
sion to Christianity, into which faith he
was baptized, the sentence was commuted
to strangulation.

Athapascan NORTH AMERICA – GREAT
PLAINS
Indigenous North American AMERINDIAN
people from the GREAT PLAINS culture region who occupied a vast area covering,
roughly, from Alberta to Alaska. Their
nearest neighbours were the BLACKFOOT,
BELLA COOLA, KWAKIUTL and TSHIMSHIAN
peoples, though linguistically the Athapascan were quite independent of these
races.

Ati Dangné HAITI (*Voodoo*)
One more of the numerous LOA of the
VOODOO cult.

Atira NORTH AMERICA – GREAT PLAINS (*Skidi Pawnee*)
'Sky-Vault', the wife of TIRAWA who was the chief of TIRAWAHUT, the heaven's circle.

Atius Tirawa NORTH AMERICA – GREAT PLAINS (*Pawnee*)
The creator who is better known simply as TIRAWA, and is said to have ordered the courses of the Sun, the Moon and the stars. The conception of this creator deity may owe something to European settlers whom the PAWNEE encountered on the GREAT PLAINS, but astral worship had always been a feature of their beliefs, and it may be that Atius Tirawa simply had his character better defined following this contact.

Atl CENTRAL AMERICA – MEXICO (*Aztec*)
The ninth day of the twenty-day MONTH[1] employed by the AZTECs. The day symbolized the element water, represented the east, and was presided over by XIUHTE-CUHTLI, a fire god.

Atlatonan CENTRAL AMERICA – MEXICO (*Aztec*)
A goddess about whom very little is known other than she was one of the wives of TEZCATLIPOCA.

Atlaua CENTRAL AMERICA – MEXICO (*Aztec*)
An obscure deity known as the 'master of the waters', but also associated with arrows as shown in the parallel roots of the words *atlatl* (arrow), and *atl* (water). Armed with arrows which, by derivation, are as soft as water and thus unbreakable, this god needs no helmet or other armour. When armed with reed arrows he is able to emerge as the QUETZAL bird, the holy AZTEC symbol of regeneration, and in such

a conception duality is eventually conquered.

Atonatiuh CENTRAL AMERICA – MEXICO (*Aztec*)
The name of the first era preceding the coming of the AZTEC people, and which ended with the FLOOD[2] and the transformation of the people into fish. The second era that followed was that of OCE-LOTANATIUH.

Atota(r)ho NORTH AMERICA – WOODLANDS (*Iroquois*)
The great warrior and SHAMAN who was bitterly opposed to the plans of HAIOWA-THA. His head was covered with a tangle of serpents and his anger so great that anyone who crossed his gaze died – a remarkable similarity to the Gorgon of classical Greek mythology. During one tribal council it is said that Atotarho called down a huge white bird that fell on Haiowatha's only daughter, killing her. Later Atotarho was persuaded to join the Iroquoian confederacy proposed by Haiowatha, and to which he had previously been so violently opposed.

Atraiomen CARIBBEAN (*Carib*)
A terrible fish-like monster which the soul of KALINAGO inhabited after he had been murdered by his jealous sons. In this fish form he pursued his sons who fled in all directions, and thus dispersed the CARIB people across a great many islands.

Atse Estsan NORTH AMERICA – SOUTHWEST (*Navajo*)
The first woman who was created from an ear of yellow maize by the four gods, WHITE BODY, BLUE BODY, YELLOW BODY and BLACK BODY, who at the same time created the first man, ATSE HASTIN from an ear of white maize. The couple had five pairs of twins, the eldest of which were androgynous and the inventors of pottery and

wicker water-bottles. Their younger children intermarried with the MIRAGE and KISANI people, thus multiplying the tribe of Atse Estsan.

. Atse Estsan, Atse Hastin, Black Body and Blue Body fashioned the NAVAJO land, beginning with the seven sacred mountains, after which they made the Sun, the Moon and the stars. The full story of Atse Estsan may be found in the ASCENT OF THE NAVAJO.

Atse Hastin NORTH AMERICA – SOUTHWEST (*Navajo*)

The first man who was created from an ear of white maize by the four gods, WHITE BODY, BLUE BODY, YELLOW BODY and BLACK BODY, who at the same time created the first woman, ATSE ESTSAN from an ear of yellow maize. The couple had five pairs of twins, the eldest of which were androgynous and the inventors of pottery and wicker water-bottles. Their younger children intermarried with the MIRAGE and KISANI people, thus multiplying the tribe of Atse Estsan.

Atse Estsan, Atse Hastin, Black Body and Blue Body fashioned the NAVAJO land, beginning with the seven sacred mountains, after which they made the Sun, the Moon and the stars. The full story of Atse Hastin may be found in the ASCENT OF THE NAVAJO.

At(s)eats ~ an, ~ ine NORTH AMERICA – SOUTHWEST (*Navajo*)

Variant(s) of ATSE ESTSAN.

Auexoti CENTRAL AMERICA – MEXICO (*Aztec*)

One of the AZTEC leaders who left AZTLAN, their original homeland, to seek out a new domain on the mainland. The other leaders are named as ACACITLI, AHATL, HUICTON, OCELOPAN, TEÇACATETL, TENOCH and XOMIMITL. They were accompanied on their journey by the four guardians of HUITZILOPOCHTLI: CHIPACTONAL, OXOMOCO, TLALTECUIN and XOCHICAHUACA.

Aunyainá SOUTH AMERICA – BRAZIL (*Tupari*)

An evil sorcerer, tusked like a boar, who fed on children. One day when he was out hunting the VAMOA-POD, they escaped to the skies by climbing up a long creeper. He attempted to chase after them, but a parrot gnawed through the creeper. Aunyainá fell to the ground and was killed. From his arms and legs grew Caymans (a type of alligator) and iguanas, and from his fingers and toes came all sorts of small lizards.

Aurora Borealis

Famous celestial phenomena that occurs in both the northern and the southern hemispheres, though the Aurora Borealis is the name given to the eerie glow that can be seen in northern skies. It is familiar to many peoples, and not just the North American AMERINDIANS, all of whom tend to apply a spiritual characterization to the spectacle. The following is by no means a complete list of these characterizations.

1 NORTH AMERICA – NORTHWEST COAST (*Kwakiutl*)
Symbolical representation, according to some sources, of the cannibal spirit BAXBAKUALANUCHSIWAE as a war-god. It may possibly be regarded as his origin.

2 NORTH AMERICA – NORTHWEST COAST (*Klamath*)
According to the KLAMATH, KEMUSH was called upon by MORNING STAR[5] to create the Earth from the ashes of the Aurora Borealis.

3 NORTH AMERICA – WOODLANDS (*Iroquois*)
Unidentified spirit that the celestial chief who lived under the ONODJA TREE became jealous of, along with FIRE DRAGON WITH A BODY OF PURE WHITE COLOUR, with both of whom he suspected

AWENHAI of having had an affair. As a result he threw Awenhai and her two alleged lovers from heaven, though the spirits of the supposed lovers remained with him.

Avilix CENTRAL AMERICA (Maya)

The deity that was given to BALAM AGAB to preside over his clan at TULAI ZUIVA, the PLACE OF SEVEN CAVES AND SEVEN RAVINES. Avilix turned into stone following the creation of the Sun when he came into contact with its strengthening rays.

Awenhai NORTH AMERICA –
WOODLANDS (Iroquois)

A beautiful girl who offered her hand in marriage to the celestial chief who lived beneath the ONODJA TREE whose blossom lit up the world. The chief accepted her offer and made her pregnant by a single exhalation of his breath. However, he apparently did not know this for, when the baby began to show, he became jealous of AURORA BOREALIS[3], and of FIRE DRAGON WITH A BODY OF PURE WHITE COLOUR, both of whom he suspected of having seduced her. He uprooted the Onodja Tree and pushed both Awenhai and the two he suspected through the resulting hole in the sky, though their ghosts remained with him in heaven.

As Awenhai fell towards the vast sea, GREAT TURTLE surfaced and caught her, and MUSKRAT raised sufficient mud from the sea-bed to make land for her to live on. Here she gave birth to a daughter who was herself made pregnant by an arrow left at her bedside by an anonymous suitor. Twins were conceived, but they began to quarrel even before they left the womb; one, OTERONGTONGNIA emerged through her armpit, killing her. His brother, TAWISKARON, was born in the normal manner.

Greatly displeased at the death of her daughter, Awenhai threw Oterongtongnia out, and placed the dead body of her daughter on a tree, where it became the Sun. The head she placed in the branches of another tree where it became the Moon. Oterongtongnia made the Earth and all the good and beautiful things, while Tawiskaron jealously did his utmost to obstruct the good deeds of his brother, and did manage to spoil several perfectly good projects before Oterongtongnia built an immense fire and frightened him off. Then he pursued him with such fury that he shattered to pieces and formed the Rocky Mountains.

The latter part of this story should be compared with the story of ATAENTSIC, YOSKEHA and TASWISCANA, as it is simply a variant of that legend.

Awitelin Tsita NORTH AMERICA –
PUEBLO, SOUTHWEST (Zuñi)

'Fourfold-containing-Earth-Mother'. According to some myths, Awitelin Tsita was created by SHIWANOKIA from spittle. According to others she was created from seafoam along with APOYAN TACHU (the sky) by AWONAWILONA.

Within the four wombs of Awitelin Tsita stirred the seeds of all life. Inside each womb, unfinished creatures crawled over each other in the darkness, writhing as they tried to gain the warmth of the Sun's rays. Among them was POSHAIYANG-KYO, the wisest of all men who contrived a plan to escape. He found a passage and followed it upwards and outwards until he came into the light. Then, standing silently in the lapping waters of the primeval ocean, he besought the Sun to release all the other creatures. So Awonawilona sent the divine twins to the 'place of generation', and there cleft open the Earth with thunderbolts before descending into the Earth on spider's web threads. They then led those for whom Poshaiyangkyo had been praying into the light. However, there were numerous casualties since some fell back, and these only escaped later as monsters, cripples and idiots.

Awonawilona NORTH AMERICA – PUEBLO, SOUTHWEST (*Zuñi*)
The androgynous supreme power, 'all-container', the dual creator deity, first expressed in the Sun-Father, but pervading all things (cf. WAKONDA). As the Sun-Father and the Moon-Mother travelled across the sky, their faces are hidden by shields. Awonawilona gradually withdraws the veil which hides the Moon-Mother's shield, and then replaces it, which is why she is not always visible, and explains the phases of the Moon.

Awonawilona existed before all else, and it was by his/her volition that life came into being. From his/her being came the Sun that fecundated the primeval ocean across which a green scum spread. This scum became firm and divided into AWITE-LIN TSITA, the Earth Mother, and APOYAN TACHU, the Sky Father. From this divine pair sprang all living things.

Within the four wombs of Awitelin Tsita stirred the seeds of all life, life that Awonawilona released in response to the prayers of POSHAIYANGKYO, the first being to escape, though some of those led to safety fell back and were only later to emerge as monsters, cripples, or idiots. The first men to stand on the earth were strange beings as they had, during their gestation, adapted for life within the womb, and thus possessed scales, short tails, huge owl-like eyes, enormous ears and webbed hands and feet. They greeted the first sunrise with howls of terror, and only adjusted to life on Earth very slowly, their adjustment being greatly assisted by the medicine-man YANAULUHA.

axólotl CENTRAL AMERICA – MEXICO (*Aztec*)
The larvae into which XÓLOTL transformed himself before he was finally caught and sacrificed. The axólotl is, in truth, the tadpole-like larvae of any of several species of salamander, the name actually being the AZTEC for 'water monster'.

Ayar Cachi SOUTH AMERICA (*Inca*)
One of the CHILDREN OF THE SUN who is called AYAR CACHI ASAUCA in the accounts of the INCA people given by Pedro DE CIEZA DE LÉON, and TOPA AYAR CACHI in those of Fray Martin DE MONIA. *Ayar* appears to mean 'male' or 'man'.

Ayar Cachi climbed Mount HUANA-CAURI and, by slinging stones from the summit, split the surrounding hills, thus arousing the jealousy of his brother who lured him into a cave and entombed him there. When the remaining Children of the Sun camped at TAMBU QUIRU, they were visited by Ayar Cachi's spirit who told them to found a city at CUZCO. Then he turned himself into a stone on the summit of Mount Huanacauri where he was thenceforth honoured as a god.

Another version of this myth says that AYAR UCHO as well as Ayar Cachi became the cult stone after having first taught AYAR MANCO the right of passage for adolescent youths.

Ayar Cachi Asauca SOUTH AMERICA (*Inca*)
The name by which AYAR CACHI, one of the CHILDREN OF THE SUN, is referred to in the writings of Pedro DE CIEZA DE LÉON. He is given the name TOPA AYAR CACHI by Fray Martin DE MONIA. Due to this confusion he is usually referred to by that part of his name that is common to both variants – Ayar Cachi.

Ayar Manco SOUTH AMERICA (*Inca*)
One of the CHILDREN OF THE SUN who is called Ayar Manco (*Ayar* seemingly meaning 'male' or 'man') in the accounts of the INCA people of Pedro DE CIEZA DE LÉON,

and MANCO CAPAC in those of Fray Martin DE MONIA.

Having been told to found a city at CUZCO by the spirit of his dead brother AYAR CACHI, he was taught the right of passage for adolescent youths by AYAR UCHO. The city of Cuzco was duly founded and where Ayar Manco, according to Martin de Monia, took the name Manco Capac when he succeeded his brother CUSCO HUANCA as king of the city.

Ayar Ucho SOUTH AMERICA (*Inca*)
Seemingly one of the CHILDREN OF THE SUN, he is mentioned in the accounts of the INCA people written by Pedro DE CIEZA DE LÉON, but does not feature in the accounts of Fray Martin DE MONIA. He is said to have taught AYAR CACHI the right of passage for adolescent youths before joining Ayar Cachi in the form of a cult stone at the summit of Mount HUANACAURI where he and his brother were worshipped as gods.

Aymará SOUTH AMERICA – BOLIVIA AND PERU
Indigenous South American AMERINDIAN people, the builders of a great culture, they were conquered by the INCAS, and subsequently by the Spanish. Their language survives and elements of their ancient beliefs have been incorporated into their Roman Catholicism. The myths, legends, folklore and history of the Aymará were orally preserved, a special class of learned man being employed to preserve and transmit these traditions. Today about 1,400,000 Aymará farm and herd llamas and alpacas in the highlands, speaking their native tongue, which belongs to the Andean-Equatorial family of languages.

Azaca Si HAITI (*Voodoo*)
A variant name for MAMBO ZACCA.

Azaka ~ Baing Baing, ~ Mede HAITI (*Voodoo*)
Variant name(s) for MAMBO ZACCA.

Aztec CENTRAL AMERICA
From approximately the end of the eighth, or the beginning of the ninth, century until the beginning of the twelfth century, successive bands of warlike NAHUAtlan tribes migrated into Mexico from the north. The first of these tribes were the TOLTECS. They were followed by the CHICHIMECS, and the MEXICA or Aztecs. The god of the Toltecs was the Sky Father MIXCÓATL ('Cloud Serpent') with whom they seem to have identified the great war leader under whom they conquered central Mexico. More important was his son, the god, culture hero, SHAMAN, and priest-king, QUETZALCÓATL – the Green Feathered Serpent.

It is virtually impossible to disentangle history from myth in the accounts of these people's arrival in Mexico. It has, however, been noted that their pantheon seems to resemble that of the North American AMERINDIANS closely in so far as prime importance was given to the son of the Sky Father and the Earth Mother, who, like the heroes of the northern myths, were credited with the re-establishment of culture.

According to one Aztec myth, Quetzalcóatl recreated the earth after the FLOOD[2]. He was also credited with the restoration of the Toltec civilization by establishing the legendary city of TOLLAN (possibly modern TULA) and introducing all the arts of living. Tollan fell to the Chichimecs who established themselves in the lakeside city of TEZCOCO, their fortunes being made by their dominance of the lake's salt pans.

Finally there came the Aztecs who may originally have been poor vassals of the Toltecs. After they had been expelled from various cities they began, in 1325, reclaiming the marshy island of TENOCH-TITLAN (in what is the centre of modern Mexico City), on which they built their capital. From there they gradually came to dominate the whole region. Under MON-TEZUMA I (reigned from 1440) they created an empire in central and southern Mexico. The Aztec language is called Nahuatl which belongs to the Uto-Aztecan family.

The Aztec people were renowned for their architecture, their gold, jade and turquoise jewellery and their textiles. Their form of writing combined the pictograph and the hieroglyph, and they used a complex form of calendar which contained a sacred period of 260 days within the solar year of 365 days. Once in every fifty-two years the beginning of both the sacred period and the solar year coincided. During this 'dangerous' period, propitiatory rites were performed, and all temples rebuilt, a fact that has provided archaeologists with a useful dating tool.

Their own god was HUITZILOPOCHTLI ('Humming-bird Wizard'), but they also worshipped the feathered-serpent Quetzalcóatl whom they had inherited from the conquered Toltecs. They practised human sacrifice on a grand scale, tearing the heart from the living body, or flaying people alive, as in the worship of XIPE TOTEC.

The study of the myths and legends of this empire is complicated by the fact that Aztec myths expressed highly syncretistic religious and cultural beliefs in which gods of the subject were assimilated to those of the dominant group and city. Indeed the Aztec capital of Tenochtitlan contained a special temple housing the statues of the deities of all their subject people, this perhaps symbolizing their inferiority to the great Aztec Sun-god Huitzilopochtli. This subjugation was gruesomely expressed by the ritual sacrifice of prisoners of war to this deity. Human sacrifice was also made to the Aztec fertility deities, but here the purpose was, so it seems, not so much to do them honour, but to enact their annual death and resurrection. Pictographs show that the Aztecs played a type of football (TLACHTLI) in which legs rather than the feet were used to propel a hard rubber ball. Custom dictated that one team was sacrificed after the game, though it remains uncertain whether those sacrificed were the losers, or the winners who would thus have been promoted to the next world in honour of their victory.

However, as the importance of the cult of the great Toltec deity Quetzalcóatl indicates, the Aztecs saw themselves as the heirs, and in some ways, the upholders of the Toltec culture. This makes it very difficult, and often virtually impossible, to disentangle the various religious and mythical traditions.

Aztlan CENTRAL AMERICA – MEXICO
(*Aztec*)
The legendary first home of the AZTEC people, an island, which they left to found their empirical capital of TENOCHTITLAN. Very little is known about Aztlan, other than it is described as being near a sea-girt mountain called CULHUACAN, and that it might have been the eponym of the Aztec people, or vice versa.

One of the many legends preserved by the Aztecs concerning their arrival in Mexico is known as the Journey from Aztlan (as given below). This story not only tells of the southerly migration of the Aztec people, but also of other NAHUAtlan peoples who periodically went their separate ways from the Aztecs *en route*. Aztlan is also the subject of a legend which tells of when MONTEZUMA II sent messengers to the ancestral homeland of the Aztecs.

One of the legends that was preserved by the AZTEC people themselves says that they left their ancestral island home, Aztlan, and travelled across the water to PAN-OTLAN ('Place-of-Arrival-by-Sea') from where they travelled to TAMOANCHAN. There all but four of their AMOXAOQUE left them, those remaining being CHIPACTO-NAL, OXOMOCO, TLALTECUIN and XOCHI-CAHUACA. Those who left were the other leaders who had left Aztlan with them: ACACITLI, AHATL, AUEXOTL, HUICTON, OCELOPAN, TEÇACATETL, TENOCH and XO-MIMITL. The four who remained invented the calendar so that the people might have a means of organizing their lives.

From Tamoanchan the people travelled to TEOTIHUACÁN where they built pyram-ids to the Sun and the Moon, sacrificed and elected their first kings. These kings were thought of as gods and were later buried at Teotihuacán. Leaving that place they travelled to the PLACE OF SEVEN CAVES where they paid due honour to their gods. Those other people with whom the Aztecs had left Aztlan now went their own sepa-rate ways; the TOLTECS to TOLLAN, the OTOMÍ to COATEPEC, and the other NA-HUAtlan peoples to other places, leaving only the Aztec people to travel on.

Their god HUITZILOPOCHTLI led them to the COLHUACAn city of CHAPUTEPEC, but they were driven out and their lord, HUIT-ZILIHUITL, captured and killed. Now, ac-cording to one version, the Aztec people travelled to TIZAPAN, another Colhuacan city where they fought as allies of the Colhuacan against XOCHIMILO, whom they defeated, but were soon afterwards driven out, several explanations existing as to why this should have happened.

One says that their Colhuacan overlord required the Aztec people to bring him evidence of the number of the enemy that they had killed. They did this by cutting off all the ears of their victims and presented them to the ruler. He was so horrified by this barbarity that he immediately had them expelled from the city. Another ver-sion says that they captured, sacrificed and then flayed the daughter of the Colhuacan ruler, presumably in a ritual dedicated to

XIPE TOTEC, and then invited the ruler to a banquet at which the attendant priest was dressed in the dead girl's skin (a common practice in the rites of Xipe Totec).

Finally, after many further wanderings, the Aztec people came to the TEZCOCO and, receiving a divine omen in the form of an eagle with a snake in its talons flying up from a nearby rock, they settled and foun-ded the city of Tenochtitlan.

Following their southerly migration the Aztec people founded an empire that cov-ered most of central and southern Mexico, but apparently they never forgot the land of their ancestors as the following myth illustrates. Although this is represented as a journey back to Aztlan, it appears possi-bly to have gone, in fact, to Tezcoco, the city built around the 'floating gardens' – artificial islands – on Lake Tezcoco.

The fifth ruler of the Aztec empire, Montezuma II, decided to send ambassa-dors to the ancestral homeland of the Aztecs for there, so he had heard, Huitzilo-pochtli's mother COATLICUE still lived. A sage named TLACAELEL described Aztlan as being an island near a sea-girt mountain named Culhuacan. Led by the spirits, the embassy eventually reached the mountain where they found floating gardens and fisherfolk. The fact that the strangers could speak the native language aroused great surprise, but when the ambassadors said that they had come with gifts for Coatlicue, they were led to her steward to whom they delivered the messages from Montezuma and Tlacaelel.

The steward, somewhat confused, asked who Montezuma and Tlacaelel were, for those who had left Aztlan had been the leaders Acacitli, Ahatl, Auexotl, Huicton, Ocelopan, Teçacatetl, Tenoch and Xomi-mitl, along with the four guardians of Huitzilopochtli whose names were Chi-pactonal, Oxomoco, Tlaltecuin and Xo-chicahuaca. The ambassadors explained that they were all dead, a statement that only served to confuse the steward further, for those who had chosen to remain in Aztlan at that time were still alive. At length the steward was persuaded to lead the ambassadors to Coatlicue.

However, as they attempted to climb the mountain on which she lived, their feet sank into the soft ground. The steward, who moved easily over it, as if he were gliding, was once more puzzled by these events, and asked them why they were so heavy. They replied that they lived on meat and coca, and the steward then realized that it was this diet that had caused the deaths of all those who had left Aztlan where, with a simple lifestyle, people survived eternally.

The steward took the messengers to Coatlicue who, being in mourning for her son Huitzilopochtli, was ugly and terrible to look at. Having received the gifts and the messages of Montezuma, she gave a message to the ambassadors, reminding Huitzilopochtli that before he had left, he had prophesied that, after leading the seven tribes to their chosen new lands, and establishing them there, he would be conquered, and when this happened, he would return to Aztlan and his mother. Coatlicue then gave the ambassadors gifts for her son and commanded them to remind her son of his promise.

Descending the mountain again, the steward explained to the ambassadors that the people of Aztlan retained their youth because, when they grew old, they simply climbed the mountain to Coatlicue and by so doing, they were rejuvenated. At the foot of the mountain the ambassadors took their leave and duly returned to Montezuma to whom they related all they had seen and learned.

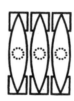

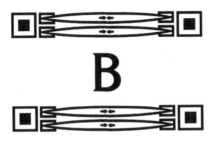

B

B CENTRAL AMERICA (*Maya*)
Usually identified as the god CHAC, the god B is so described in the various CODEX as the identity of this deity is not known for certain. He is normally depicted with a long nose, protruding teeth and tongue, and is usually accompanied by a number of serpents, weather symbols and the symbols for the four cardinal points. It seems quite feasible that the god B is indeed to be identified with Chac, for that deity is one of the four BACAB, a group of deities who represent the four main compass points.

Babe NORTH AMERICA (MODERN)
The huge blue ox that was the constant companion of Paul BUNYAN, and therefore present when his master, and friend, created the Black Hills of Dakota and the Grand Canyon.

Bacab, Four CENTRAL AMERICA (*Maya*)
Generic name given to the four deities that represented the four cardinal points, each being placed in their respective position to give the world a firm support, and to keep the sky in place after it had once fallen on to the Earth following a great flood. Also linked with the four winds, in which guise they were called the Four BALAM, and the guardians of the divisions of the sacred 260-day calendar, the four are named as KAN who was associated with the colour yellow and the south; CHAC – red and east; ZAC – white and north; and ED – black and west. The Four Bacab appear to be the MAYA equivalents of the

four TEZCATLIPOCAS, or QUETZALCÓATL and the three Tezcatlipocas.

Bacam CENTRAL AMERICA (*Maya*)
One of the two magicians, the other being XULU, with whom the twins HUNAHPU and XBALANQUÉ conferred when they became aware that they would be condemned to death, and by this consultation arranged for their resurrection.

Bachué SOUTH AMERICA – COLOMBIA
(*Chibcha*)
Soon after the Sun, ZUHÉ or XUHÉ, and the Moon, CHIÁ, had been created, a woman, sometimes called FURACHOGÚE, emerged from Lake IGUAGUÉ near TUNJA carrying a young boy whom she later married when he had grown to maturity. Thus they populated the world as Bachué always bore quadruplets or sextuplets. The children of this divine couple were taught all the laws and arts of civilization by their parents who, having adjured them to live in peace, returned to the lake near Tunja beneath whose waters they disappeared in the form of serpents.

Badé(-Si) HAITI (*Voodoo*)
Also called GBADÉ, this LOA is of West African origin, possibly Yoruba.

Badger NORTH AMERICA – SOUTHWEST
(*Navajo*)
Originally an inhabitant of the Earth before the NAVAJO people arrived, Badger

and COYOTE travelled down into the multi-coloured world during the ASCENT OF THE NAVAJO, Coyote remaining with the Navajo people of ATSE HASTIN, but Badger continued downwards into the YELLOW WORLD. However, when the Navajo were being threatened by a flood caused by TIEHOLTSODI after Coyote had abducted two of that monster's children, Badger enlarged the hole LOCUST had made in the sky, and thus enabled the Navajo people to escape from the reed in which they were trapped and make their way to the Earth, arriving on an island in the middle of a lake.

badjican HAITI (*Voodoo*)
The name given to an assistant of a HOUNGAN.

baka HAITI (*Voodoo*)
Name given to a ZOMBIE that has been transformed into an animal by its wicked HOUNGAN master.

Baker, Mount NORTH AMERICA – WEST COAST (*Skagit*)
Sacred mountain, known as KOBATH to the SKAGIT people, and one of the two peaks that were not submerged during the great FLOOD[6], the other being TAKOBAH (Mount RAINIER).

Bakoos NORTH AMERICA – NORTHWEST COAST (*Kwakiutl*)
The summer names of the clans and tribal ranks that are changed at the onset of the supernatural season of TSETSEKA (winter) so that they directly relate to the winter spirits.

baktun CENTRAL AMERICA (*Maya*)
A division of the CALENDAR that was calculated as twenty KATUNs, a katun being a period of 7,200 days. Thus a baktun was equal to 144,000 days, or roughly 400 years.

Balam, Four CENTRAL AMERICA (*Maya*)
Generic name given to the four guardians of the world's cardinal points. The four are named as KAN who was associated with the colour yellow and represented the south; CHAC – red in the east; ZAC – white in the north; and ED – black in the west. Represented as jaguars, and as such considered as priests, the four are still believed by the modern Yuacatec MAYA to stand invisibly on guard where they hold creation together, for without them the world might fall apart.

Balam Agab CENTRAL AMERICA (*Maya*)
One of the four brothers who were created by the gods after they had decided to create mankind. They were formed from ground yellow and white maize which the gods discovered grew at the PLACE OF THE DIVISION OF WATERS. The flour was mixed with nine broths brewed by XMUCANÉ. From the resulting mixture were born the brothers Balam Agab ('Night Jaguar'), BALAM QUITZÉ ('Smiling Jaguar'), IQI BALAM ('Moon Jaguar') and MAHUCUTAH ('Renowned Name'). The gods soon found, much to their horror, that they had done their work a little too perfectly, for the newly created men were so intelligent that they seemed likely to challenge the very gods who had given them life.

Therefore HURAKAN breathed on the men which clouded their vision of distant things, and reduced their understanding to a more appropriate level for mortal beings. The four brothers were then cast into a deep sleep during which time the gods created four women to be their wives. All was well with mankind at first, for they all lived peaceably together, all spoke the same language, and all revered the gods who had created them, praying to them to bless mankind with children and with light, for as of yet the Sun had not been created.

Time passed, and while the brothers were all blessed with children, their prayers for light went unanswered. Growing anxious, the four brothers travelled from TOLLAN, their home, to TULAI ZUIVA, the PLACE OF SEVEN CAVES AND SEVEN RAVINES. There the gods gave each brother a tutelary deity to preside over their clan, Balam Agab being given the god AVILIX.

TOHIL, the tutelary deity of Balam Quitzé, gave mankind fire, and when the rain extinguished it, he rekindled the life giving flame by striking his shoes together. Seeing that the MAYA had fire, men from other tribes came asking for some of the divine gift, but they were turned away. Tohil interceded, but demanded of the people, to whom he gave fire, that they *embrace him under the armpit and under the girdle*, an expression taken to mean that they should offer him human sacrifices.

Though the people were now warm, they still lived in darkness. Every day they sacrificed and prayed to their creators, and watched diligently for the MORNING STAR, the herald of the Sun. Still the Sun did not appear, so the brothers decided to resume their travels – otherwise they thought they would never witness the birth of the Sun.

After travelling through many lands, the brothers came to HACAVITZ's mountain, Hacavitz being the tutelary deity awarded to Mahucutah. There they burned incense, sacrificed and prayed to the gods. At long last their prayers were answered for they witnessed the arrival of the Morning Star and a short time later the birth of the Sun. All the people and the animals welcomed the Sun with joy. As the Sun grew in strength its heat dried the damp earth, and its rays, touching the old animal gods – lion, tiger and viper – and the gods Tohil, Avilix and Hacavitz, turned them all to stone.

Seeing that their quest had been completed, and instinctively knowing that their time on Earth was close to an end, the four brothers took leave of their wives and children saying that they would return to Tollan to take the Sun there with them. They left behind them a sacred bundle called MAJESTY ENVELOPED which they instructed the Maya people never to open.

Balam Quitzé CENTRAL AMERICA (Maya)

With a name meaning 'Smiling Jaguar', Balam Quitzé was one of the four brothers created by the gods from the flour of white and yellow maize that was mixed with the nine broths brewed by XMUCANÉ. His brothers were BALAM AGAB ('Night Jaguar'), IQI BALAM ('Moon Jaguar') and MAHUCUTAH ('Renowned Name'). He and his brothers were at first almost the equals of their creators until HURAKAN breathed on them and reduced their intellect to a level more befitting mortal men. With wives created by the gods, the four brothers became the ancestors of the MAYA people and originally lived at TOLLAN from where they set out to discover the Sun.

At TULAI ZUIVA, the PLACE OF SEVEN CAVES AND SEVEN RAVINES, the four brothers were given tutelary deities to preside over their clans, Balam Quitzé receiving the god TOHIL who presented the Maya people with fire which he once rekindled after it had been extinguished by the rain by striking his shoes together. From Tulai Zuiva the brothers travelled to the mountain of HACAVITZ, the tutelary deity of Mahucutah, and there witnessed the arrival of the MORNING STAR, the herald of the Sun, and a short time later the birth of the Sun itself. A little later, knowing that they had accomplished their mortal tasks, the four brothers took leave of their families to return to TOLLAN, and left behind a sacred bundle known as MAJESTY ENVEL-OPED which they instructed should never be opened.

Balongahoya NORTH AMERICA – PUEBLO, SOUTHWEST (*Hopi*)
The brother of POOKONGHOYA and thus one of the twin sons of the solar deity. The brothers are the HOPI equivalents of the divine twins MAASEWE and UYUUYEWE, and of NAYANEZGANI and THOBADZISTSHINI.

balsa SOUTH AMERICA – BOLIVIA AND PERU
Generic name given to a boat or raft that is made from the wood of the balsa tree.

Baquicie HAITI (*Voodoo*)
Simply referred to as a LOA.

'Batala HAITI (*Voodoo*)
Also known as OBTALA or GRAND BATALA, 'Batala is a LOA derived from the Yoruba god Orishnala, the chief of the lesser gods of this people who was seen as an inter-mediary between god and man.

Bats, House of CENTRAL AMERICA (*Maya*)
One of the trial houses used by the gods of XIBALBA, the MAYA UNDERWORLD, and in which HUNAHPU and XBALANQUÉ were forced to spend the night. Having already survived the House of COLD and the House of FIRE, Hunahpu was not so lucky in this trial house as he injudiciously raised his head from the ground on which he was lying and was immediately decapitated by the terrible bat-lord CAMAZOTZ[2].

Baxbak ~ ualanuchsiwae, ~ walanuxsiwae NORTH AMERICA – NORTHWEST COAST (*Kwakiutl*)
The cannibal spirit whose name appears to mean 'The Cannibal at the North End of the World'. Baxbakualanuchsiwae was perceived as a male deity by the KWAKIUTL,

though most other North American AMER-INDIAN peoples saw the cannibal spirit as female. He is one of the two main tutelary deities of the Kwakiutl, the other being WIXALAGILLIS. Baxbakualanuchsiwae was thought to live in the Arctic, at the exact north of the world, in a house whose cen-tral pole was either the MILKY WAY[1], or sometimes, the RAINBOW[1]. Red smoke, symbolizing the blood of those he has gorged on, was said to rise from the smoke hole of his home. When the autumn storms whipped into a frenzy, the Kwakiutl saw this as signifying the approach of Bax-bakualanuchsiwae as he travelled south-wards to visit mortals before whom he would dance chanting his cry of *Hap! Hap!* ('Eat! Eat!'). Some authorities have sought to define the origins of Baxbakualanuchsi-wae as a war-god who was symbolized by the AURORA BOREALIS[1].

Bazo HAITI (*Voodoo*)
Also known as BOSU, BOSU-CESSÉ or KADIA-BOSU, this LOA is thought to have a West African provenance.

Bazon-Mainnain HAITI (*Voodoo*)
Although the attributes and function of the LOA remain a secret, some think this is simply another variant of the loa BAZO.

Bear

1 NORTH AMERICA – NORTHWEST COAST (*Tlingit*)
One of the companions of YETL by whom he was killed on a fishing trip when Yetl the RAVEN cut off some of his flesh. Yetl then tore out CORMORANT's tongue to prevent him from telling of the murder. Bear's wife was then killed by Yetl who lured her into eating halibut bladders that had been stuffed with red-hot stones. Yetl finally trapped DEER in a pitfall and ate him.

2 NORTH AMERICA – SOUTHWEST
    (*Navajo*)
One of the four animal spirits (the others were SNAKE, FROG and TURTLE) that appear in the NAVAJO myth of the HOZONI chant when they went to an undersea village to capture two of its young women. Frog and Turtle were elected to do the kidnapping, but were disturbed while escaping with their hostages. In their haste they killed the women, whom they quickly scalped. The older woman's hair was decorated with white shell, and the younger one's with turquoise.

The villagers fell on Frog and Turtle and tried to roast them alive, but they escaped and rejoined Bear and Snake, and all four set off for home. *En route* they encountered eight men from their own village who saw the women's scalps and wanted them for themselves. Two of the men, thinking they would outsmart mere animals, suggested a shooting match, and even put up their own daughters as the prize, thinking that by so doing, they could discover who was the strongest, and thus who could wrest the scalps away from the animals. Both Bear and Snake protested that they were far too old to participate in any such contest, but much to the other's chagrin they not only won the shooting contest, but also every other contest that was suggested. However, as no one was prepared to give Bear and Snake their fairly won prizes, they all set off back to their village to hold a scalp dance.

Instead of joining the others, Bear and Snake built themselves a shelter outside the village and sat down to smoke. Soon the perfume from their tobacco reached the two girls who were their rightful prizes and who, entranced by the delicious aroma, left the dance to seek out the source of the smoke.

As the girls approached Bear and Snake's shelter, the two animal spirits made themselves appear to the two young women as handsome braves. Snake was richly adorned in rainbow colours, while Bear was dressed all in black. Both were heavily bejewelled. Both agreed to let the girls share their tobacco, Snake giving his turquoise pipe to the younger, and Bear his white shell pipe to the older of the two. The smoke quickly rendered the girls senseless and when they awoke the next morning, they found that the men they had so eagerly united with the night before were now old men, but they were bound by the smoking of their pipe to remain with them.

Beaver NORTH AMERICA – WOODLANDS
    (*Algonquian*)
The second of the four animals that, during the FLOOD[3] which covered the entire world, attempted to bring back a single grain of soil so that MÄNÄBUSCH could recreate the Earth. Beaver died in the attempt, as did OTTER – the first to try, and MINK – the third. Finally MUSKRAT succeeded in bringing back a single grain of sand with which Mänäbusch recreated the world.

Beetle NORTH AMERICA – PUEBLO,
    SOUTHWEST (*Sia*)
The animal to whom UTSET entrusted a sack containing all the stars of the heavens. Beetle could not resist the temptation of having a quick look, but as he opened the sack, the stars escaped, thus explaining why there is no order to their distribution in the night sky.

Bella Coola NORTH AMERICA –
    NORTHWEST COAST
Indigenous North American AMERINDIAN people who inhabit a part of the NORTHWEST COAST culture region along with the

CHINOOK, HAIDA, KWAKIUTL, NOOTKA, SALISH and TSHIMSHIAN peoples, though none of these tribes are linked linguistically. The Bella Coola people lived in an area that today lies in British Columbia, Canada, at the northern end of the Rocky Mountains, their southern neighbours being the Kwakiutl, and their northern the Tshimshian. They also bordered on the Haida though these people lived offshore on the Queen Charlotte Islands.

Ben CENTRAL AMERICA (Maya)

The thirteenth day of the MAYA spiritual pilgrimage known as the AGES OF MAN. On this day, which symbolizes the growing maize, the spirit continues the ascent he started on EB, the twelfth day, and which he completes on IX, the fourteenth day.

Binaye Ahani NORTH AMERICA – SOUTHWEST (Navajo)

The collective name for a pair of terrible limbless twins who had the ability to kill men with their gaze. They were one of the fearsome ANAYE who were born to women, usually virgins, who had engaged in unnatural practices during the ASCENT OF THE NAVAJO.

Bitsitsi NORTH AMERICA – PUEBLO, SOUTHWEST (Zuñi)

The musician of the father of the twin deities WATSUSII and KOWWITUMA. When his help was sought by the twins to locate the CORN MAIDENS, Bitsitsi descended to Earth on a gossamer thread and then telepathically conveyed the prayers of the ASHIWI to the Corn Maidens, assuring them that, if they returned, they would have his protection, and that they would be treated with the honour and respect they deserved. The Corn Maidens agreed and were led back to the ashiwi by Bitsitsi himself.

Black Body NORTH AMERICA – SOUTHWEST (Navajo)

One of the four gods of the MIRAGE and KISANI peoples who inhabited the fourth world which the NAVAJO people encountered during their ascent to the Earth. See ASCENT OF THE NAVAJO.

Black Body helped ATSE ESTSAN, ATSE HASTIN and BLUE BODY to fashion the Navajo land, beginning with the seven sacred mountains which the gods anchored firmly to the ground with such magical implements as lightning, sunbeams, rainbows and huge flint or obsidian knives. They then decorated each mountain with all sorts of weather, crops, shells, semi-precious stones and light, and finally placed a nest of eggs on the summit of each to ensure that each mountain would have feathers to wear. The gods then set various tutelary deities on the four cardinal mountains. They placed ROCK-CRYSTAL BOY and ROCK-CRYSTAL GIRL on the eastern mountain – PELADO PEAK. On the western Mount SAN FRANCISCO they placed WHITE-CORN BOY and YELLOW-CORN GIRL. On the northern Mount SAN JUAN they placed POLLEN BOY and GRASSHOPPER GIRL, and on the southern Mount TAYLOR they placed TURQUOISE BOY and CORN GIRL.

Blackfoot NORTH AMERICA – GREAT PLAINS

Indigenous North American AMERINDIAN people who lived predominantly in Saskatchewan, Canada, as well as in Montana, USA, and were one of the many GREAT PLAINS Indian peoples. Originally divided into three sub-tribes – the Blackfoot proper, the Blood and the Piegan – they take their name, not from the colour of their feet, but rather from their black moccasins. Their language is one branch of the ALGONQUIAN family.

Blanco, Ruiz SOUTH AMERICA –
GUYANA
Seventeenth-century Spanish missionary
who reported that IBOROQUIAMIO was the
personification of evil among the people of
Guyana, though he omitted to say among
which native people.

Blue Body NORTH AMERICA –
SOUTHWEST (*Navajo*)
One of the four gods of the KISANI and
MIRAGE peoples who the NAVAJO encountered in the fourth world they came to
during their ascent to the Earth (see AS-
CENT OF THE NAVAJO). Together with
BLACK BODY, ATSE HASTIN and ATSE EST-
SAN, Blue Body helped to form the land of
the Navajo people and, with the aid of the
other gods, placed tutelary deities on the
four cardinal mountains that he had
helped to create. See BLACK BODY.

Blue-Corn Maiden NORTH AMERICA –
PUEBLO, SOUTHWEST (*Zuñi*)
One of the two oldest of the CORN MAID-
ENS, her sibling of comparable age being
YELLOW-CORN MAIDEN. After the Corn
Maidens had been persuaded to return to
the ZUÑI, and convinced that they had
nothing to fear from the attentions of
PAYATAMI, these two sisters led the dance
to the music of Payatami's flute and the
singing of a choir before the Corn Maidens
departed, never to be seen again.

Blue World NORTH AMERICA –
SOUTHWEST (*Navajo*)
One of the coloured worlds that the NAV-
AJO people passed through during their
ascent to the Earth. See ASCENT OF THE
NAVAJO. Prior to the Blue World, the Navajo had been living in the RED WORLD but,
because they made free and committed
adultery, they were punished by the gods
who sent a great flood from which they
were forced to flee upwards towards the

sky. As they were seeking a way to escape
the inevitable drowning they all feared, a
blue head poked through the sky and invited the people up into the Blue World,
the home of the SWALLOW PEOPLE. However, on the twenty-fourth night after their
arrival, one of the Navajo refugees committed adultery with the wife of the chief
of the Swallow People, and once again the
Navajo people were forced to flee upwards.

Bochica SOUTH AMERICA – BOLIVIA AND
COLOMBIA (*Chibcha*)
The supreme being of the CHIBCHA people,
a solar deity, the Father of the Gods and
inventor of all the arts of civilization who
was sometimes identified with the culture
hero CHIMIZAPAGNA or NEMTEREQUETEBA.
An invisible entity, perceived by some as
pure energy, Bochica was said to have had
his material self in ZUHÉ, the Sun. Bochica
saved mankind from the FLOOD[4] sent by
the evil CHIBCHACUM who had grown
angry with the petty bickering of mankind.
Bochica made himself known to mankind
during this troubled time as a rainbow that
struck the rocks which opened and swallowed the waters, creating the great waterfall TEQUENDAMA. Bochica then materialized as Zuhé, dried out the land, and
defeated Chibchacum who was forced to
retreat beneath the Earth from where he
has never returned. Since then the world,
firmly supported on pillars in Lake GUAYA-
CÁN, has rested on Chibchacum's great
shoulders. When he tires of his burden, or
simply shifts his position – which is quite
often – the ground shakes as earthquakes
split the earth open.

Bois l'en Dingué HAITI (*Voodoo*)
Simply described as one of the many LOA
of the VOODOO religion.

Bokwus NORTH AMERICA – NORTHWEST
COAST (*Kwakiutl*)
A wild spirit who dwells in thick forests
and woodlands and draws to his home the
spirits of those who have drowned.

Bolodjoré HAITI (*Voodoo*)
Simply described as a LOA, one of the many
within the VOODOO religion whose attributes and purpose remain the secret of cult
members.

Bolon ~ Dzacab, ~ Zacab CENTRAL
AMERICA (*Maya*)
The guardian of the world whose name
may mean 'Many Matrilineages', possibly
because he is one of the MAYA deities
associated with ancestral genealogies.
During the KAN years his statue was erected in city centres. At some time during
the creation he was said to have covered
the Earth in a thick layer of seeds before
travelling to the thirteenth and highest
heaven.

Bolontiku CENTRAL AMERICA (*Maya*)
The collective name for nine unnamed
deities who, during the creation, captured
OXLAHUNTIKU, a group of thirteen other
unnamed gods, while AHMUCENCAB covered the face of Oxlahuntiku. This was
said to have happened long ago in a period
known as the eleven AHAU.

Bonampak CENTRAL AMERICA (*Maya*)
Ancient MAYA city in what is today the
Chiapa district of Mexico. It lies midway
between the ruins of Tikal and PALENQUE
near the course of the River USUMACINTA.
Paintings discovered at Bonampak illustrate the elongated, flattened forehead
with which YUM CAAX is usually depicted,
and which was cultivated by the Maya
aristocracy who tied boards to the heads of
their children while the bones of their
skulls were still soft. The paintings at Bonampak, rediscovered in 1948, have led to

a rational rethinking of Maya life, which
was originally seen as peaceable. The
paintings, however, proved otherwise for
they depicted scenes of battles, torture and
human sacrifice, aspects of life that had
not previously been attributed to the Maya
civilization.

bope SOUTH AMERICA (*Bororo*)
Generic name for evil spirits who attack
the dead and who are impersonated by the
tribal members during the eight-day funeral ceremony in an attempt to keep
them at bay. At the end of the ritual the
body is secretly taken to the river where
the flesh is scraped away to leave clean
bones. The spirit of the dead person then
escapes and becomes embodied in a frog, a
bird, or a deer.

Borrommée HAITI (*Voodoo*)
Roman Catholic saint who is regarded as a
LOA by some VOODOO cultists.

Bosu(-Cessé) HAITI (*Voodoo*)
Variant(s) of BAZO.

Bow Priests NORTH AMERICA – PUEBLO,
SOUTHWEST (*Zuñi*)
Honorific title given to members of the
warrior caste who are the guardians of the
twin war-gods. When they die, they are
believed to ascend to the skies where their
arrows might still be seen as bolts of
lightning.

Brave HAITI (*Voodoo*)
One of the many LOA of the VOODOO
cult.

Bright Star NORTH AMERICA – GREAT
PLAINS (*Skidi Pawnee*)
The 'Mother-of-all-Things' who was the
personification of the planet VENUS[1] when
that planet was seen as the EVENING STAR.
Bright Star was placed in the west of the

heavens by TIRAWA, the chief of TIRAWA-HUT. Tirawa told Bright Star that he was going to send her wind, lightning and thunder spirits whom she was to position between herself and her garden. They would then be transformed into people, each person wearing a downy feather in his or her hair to symbolize the breath of life, a buffalo robe and moccasins. Each would also hold in his or her right hand a rattle that symbolized Bright Star's garden, and to these spirits Bright Star would allocate the task of creating the Earth.

As the wind, lightning and thunder spirits formed a great storm that filled the void, Tirawa dropped a pebble into the storm which was tossed about until the storm abated. As the clouds cleared, a vast tract of water was revealed. Acting on Tirawa's instructions, Bright Star now commanded the UPHOLDERS-OF-THE-HEAVENS to strike the surface of the water with their clubs. As they did so, the waters divided and land appeared. Bright Star now instructed the Upholders-of-the-Heavens to sing of the Earth's shaping, which they did. As the song progressed, the wind, lightning and thunder spirits returned and shaped the Earth into hills and valleys. As these spirits left, the song changed and the Earth was clothed with trees and grass, its waters purified, and seeds germinated.

Tirawa now called on SAKURU, the Sun, and PAH, the Moon, to unite. From their union was born the first man. Bright Star was then told to unite with GREAT STAR (the planet Venus as the MORNING STAR[4]), and from their union was born the first woman. Both were set upon the newly created Earth. However, both as yet lacked life, so Bright Star, again acting on the orders of Tirawa, ordered the wind, lightning and thunder spirits to sing about bestowing life on the couple. As they sang, a great storm raged around the inert couple. Lightning flashed, the rain poured and

the wind blew, and as the storm once more abated, the couple came to life.

The new couple quickly had a child of their own, and all three of them were cared for by Tirawa and Bright Star who came to the man, whose name was CLOSED MAN, in visions, and taught him how to make sacrifices to the gods, and how to prepare a sacred bundle which he was to place in his lodge. During this time the Upholders-of-the-Heavens had been creating more people, and soon the earth was populated with four tribes who lived in the southwest, the southeast, the northwest and the northeast. Each tribe prepared their own sacred bundles, but as of yet no one knew the purpose of the bundles, so Bright Star explained to Closed Man that each bundle contained a species of corn: white for the southwest people; yellow for the northwest; red for the southeast; and black for the northeast. She also told Closed Man that all the people should be called together, for they would shortly be taught the purpose of the bundles.

Closed Man called together all four tribes. When they were gathered, a man came forward who had been taught the purpose of the bundles in a series of visions, and he instructed the SKIDI PAWNEE people the songs and ceremonies appropriate to their particular bundle. When at length Closed Man's time on Earth came to an end, his skull was placed on top of his sacred bundle, and thus his spirit was said to have remained with the Skidi Pawnee people.

Brigitte, Maman HAITI (*Voodoo*)
An important LOA, Maman Brigitte was the patron of death and cemeteries.

Buckeye Bush NORTH AMERICA –
SOUTHWEST COAST (*Wintun*)
One of the three beings who, along with SHOOTING STAR and FIRE DRILL, set the

world on fire to avenge the theft of FLINT after which it was recreated by OLELBIS.

Buffalo Dance NORTH AMERICA –
GREAT PLAINS (*Blackfoot*)

The Plains Indians employed a unique method in their hunting of buffalo for they herded them towards a cliff, at the foot of which they had built a corral. The buffalo were driven over the cliff to their deaths, the corral ensuring that those who survived the fall should not escape.

However, once long ago the hunters were unable to entice a herd of buffalo towards the cliff's edge. Every time they tried, the animals turned away at the last moment. This had been going on for some time and the people were slowly starving to death. One day a young woman was out on the plains when she noticed a herd of buffalo grazing close to the edge of the cliff. In desperation she promised that she would become the wife of one of the buffalo if the herd would leap over the cliff.

Immediately the herd flung itself over the precipice into the corral at its foot. There a great bull leapt over the wall and claimed the young woman as his bride. A short while later the young woman was missed by her people who were feasting on the buffalo they had slaughtered, so her father went out to look for her. The bull sensed the man's presence and lead the other bulls in an attack and trampled the woman's father to death.

She was beside herself with grief, but her bull husband told her that all she was experiencing was what they had felt for many years every time one of their number had been killed by her people. However, the bull took pity on her and promised that both she and her father might return home if she could restore her father to life.

The young woman enlisted the help of a magpie who, after much searching, found a scrap of the dead man's corpse which it

brought to the girl who then chanted over the fragment and restored her father to life. The buffalo were amazed by what she had managed to do. Her bull husband kept his word and allowed the woman and her father to return to their home, but before they went they taught them their dance and chant, so that in future all the buffalo that were killed for food could also be restored to life, the dancers in this Buffalo Dance to wear bull's skin robes and wear bull's horns.

The purpose of the Buffalo Dance was, in one aspect, to avoid slaying a relative, but was more importantly to ensure the survival of the herds of buffalo on whose meat the Indians were totally dependant.

Bumba loa HAITI (*Voodoo*)

A group of LOA which is derived from the gods of the Congolese Bumba tribes.

Bunyan, Paul NORTH AMERICA
(*Modern*)

A gigantic lumberjack about whom tales appeared in the early twentieth-century lumber camps in the mid-west of America. He was always in the company of his huge blue ox BABE, and is credited with the creation of the Black Hills of Dakota as well as the Grand Canyon.

Busk Festival NORTH AMERICA –
WOODLANDS (*Creek*)

The Anglicized name for the great New Year festival of the CREEK people of PUSKITA which is held in the late summer when the first ears of maize have ripened. During the festival all old fires are extinguished and new ones kindled, all used dishes and household goods destroyed and replaced by new ones, and a general amnesty declared for all criminals except murderers.

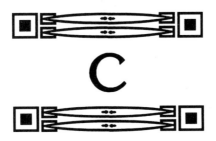

C

C CENTRAL AMERICA (*Maya*)

One of the many MAYA deities about whom very little is known. He is referred to as the god C as that is how he appears in the various CODEX. He is depicted with an ornamental face and hangs from the sky on a thread, this latter characteristic perhaps symbolizing that the god C was a sky-god, possibly XANAN EK, the spirit of the pole star, or even the spirit of URSA MAJOR[2]. Some have sought to connect him with the planet VENUS[2] which would therefore make the god C an aspect of KUKULCÁN. One thing that is definitely known about this deity is that he is associated with the Mayan day of ONE CHEUN, the first created day of the Mayan series, that day on which the god-above-all, MONTH[2], brought forth the heavens and the earth. See CREATION[4].

Cabra ~ ca(n), ~ ka(n) CENTRAL AMERICA (*Maya*)

The demolisher of mountains, god of the earthquake, the younger son of the giant VUKUB-CAKIX and CHIMALAMAT, and brother of ZIPACNÁ. After HUNAHPU and XBALANQUÉ had killed both Zipacná and Vukub-Cakix, they went in search of Cabraca, an arrogant giant who claimed that he could overturn the Earth and shake the sky. They discovered him as he was levelling a great mountain. They engaged the giant in polite conversation, telling him that they were simple hunters, and offered to lead him to a splendid mountain that he could level. On their journey Cabraca was amazed to find that the hunters needed no ammunition in their blowpipes, and simply brought down the birds they shot at with no more than their own breath. Hunahpu and Xbalanqué roasted the birds and offered them to Cabraca who could not resist the tempting meal that was placed before him. However, Cabraca did not know that the brothers had poisoned the birds, and so Cabraca met his death.

Cachimana SOUTH AMERICA – VENEZUELA, ORINOCO REGION

The Great Spirit who is opposed by the highly motivated IOLOKIAMO, the TRICKSTER of this region.

Cacibagiagua CARIBBEAN (*Taïno*)

One of the two caves from which the first men escaped, the other cave being called AMAIAUA. Originally people were kept captive underground as the entrances to these caves were watched over by the night-watchman MAROCAEL, but one morning he lingered just a while too long at dawn and was caught by the Sun's rays which petrified him and allowed mankind to emerge under the leadership of GUAGUGIANA.

Caddo NORTH AMERICA – GREAT PLAINS

Indigenous North American AMERINDIAN people who entered the GREAT PLAINS culture region from AD c. 800, and brought with them knowledge of agricultural techniques that far surpassed those being used at that time. The Caddo-speaking peoples, which included the ARIKA and PAWNEE, inhabited an area, along with seven SIOUX tribes, that lay between the ALGONQUIAN-speaking peoples to the east, and the ATHAPASCANS to the west.

Caesars SOUTH AMERICA – CHILE
A mythical city of gold that is alleged to exist on the shores of a lake. The city is surrounded by an inexhaustible tobacco plantation and no one who lives there ever has to work. It will only become generally visible at the very end of the world, which is why it still remains undiscovered. The concept of this city appears to combine elements of the EL DORADO legend and the Christian concept of the New Jerusalem – 'the Golden'. The naming of the city seems to owe its origins from a memory of an expedition to discover the fabled golden city of El Dorado that was led by the sixteenth-century explorer César.

calabtun CENTRAL AMERICA (*Maya*)
An ancient period of time that was equal to 20 PICTUNs, or 57,600,000 days, which is roughly 158,000 years. See CALENDAR.

Calendar CENTRAL AMERICA (*Aztec and Maya*)
Both the AZTEC and MAYA peoples based their calendars on cycles of eighteen-day periods arranged in multiples of twenty – 20 x 18 = 360 days. To these were added five days that were considered to be 'outside the calendar' to make the 365 days of the solar year which was in Maya terminology called a HAAB. The fact that the Aztecs and Mayans used the same system of calendar proves, with almost unerring certainty, that these two civilizations have a common origin. In both NAHUA and Maya lands the people were excessively careful not to fall asleep during the daylight hours of the extra days of the calendar, for to do so would mean almost certain death. Nor did they quarrel or fall as they walked, for

they feared that what they did during those 'unholy' days, they would do for all eternity. The people therefore tended to confine themselves to their houses where they were extremely careful not to do anything unpleasant, or to do household chores lest they were condemned to these forever.

The 365-day length of the year was corrected in such a way that the Maya people fixed the true length of the solar year (the time it takes for the Earth to complete one orbit of the Sun) as 365.242 days, a remarkable degree of accuracy when it is considered that today, with all the technology we have at our disposal, the current measurement of the solar year is 365.2422 days, just two ten-thousandths of a day short (17.28 seconds). The Gregorian calendar that is in almost universal use fixes the solar year at 365.2425 days – three ten-thousandths of a day too long (26 seconds).

Each period of 360 days was called a TUN. A KATUN was 7,200 days, calculated as twenty cycles of the sacred division of 260 days. The 7,200 days are roughly equal to twenty years (19.71 to be exact), but is exactly the time it takes the planet VENUS to complete twelve and a half cycles. A BAKTUN was twenty katuns, or 144,000 days, about 400 years. A PICTUN was twenty baktuns, or 2,880,000 days – about 8,000 years. A CALABTUN was twenty pictuns – 57,600,000 days – about 158,000 years. A KINCHILTUN was twenty calabtuns – 1,250,000,000 days – about 3,000,000 years. Twenty kinchiltun formed one ALAUTUN – 23,040,000,000 days – over 63,000,000 years. All this shows that the Maya and Nahua peoples certainly had long-term plans about their ultimate survival when their calendar was devised.

Through this arrangement it just so happened that a katun could only ever end on the day known as AHAU, and every 260 tuns the same Ahau, numbered in sequence, would turn up. Ultimately, through the passage of time, so the Nahua and Maya believed, history would begin to repeat itself significantly enough to come under the influence of the greater forces of the cosmos. For instance, katun 8 Ahau was believed to herald disturbances, war and political upheavals. This theory would seem to have proved itself when a usurping family called ITZÁ that had ruled over the Maya lands for centuries was not defeated until AD 1697, their final defeat coming just before the start of the katun that heralded disaster.

Within the larger cycle of the calendar which was seen to herald good or bad fortune, and also within the natural cycle of the Earth around the Sun, a smaller period was defined as 260 consecutive days that were sub-divided into twenty periods of thirteen days each. This was called the TZOLKIN by the Maya, and the TONALPOHUALLI by the Aztecs.

Both Maya and Aztec further subdivided time into periods of fifty-two days. The Tonalpohualli of the Aztecs was divided into five parts that were seen as corresponding to the four cardinal points and the centre, and has an exact parallel in the fifty-two-year cycle at which the Sun had to be revived, or the world would come to an end. The number five was specifically associated with the god QUETZALCÓATL and his quincunx symbol, and also with Venus, that planet itself forming one aspect of Quetzalcóatl. The synodic period (the time it takes for a planet to go through all its phases) of Venus is 584 days. This sacred period was grouped into five's by the Nahua, so that 5 x 584 = 2,920 days, or exactly eight years. At the conjunction of the solar year and the Venusian cycle feasts and rites were performed to XIUHTECUHTLI or HUEHUETÉOTL, god of the year and god of the centre who stood at the very middle of the four cardinal points. He is represented in the TLECUIL, or brazier, that was the hearth to be found at the centre of every Aztec or Maya home or temple. Thus, the god was often associated with the cross with emphasis on the connections between each point and the hub.

The Maya and Aztec day, it appears, consisted of just twenty-two hours that would have each been slightly longer than the sixty minutes of today (approximately 65 minutes 27 seconds), though some sources suggest that the Aztec day had just twenty hours (see MONTH[1]). The day was clearly divided into day and night, the former having thirteen divisions, and the latter with just nine. Each division had its own guardian deity. Those of the day were Xiuhtecuhtli; TLALTECUHTLI, an earth-god; CHALCHIUHTLICUE, the water-goddess; TONATIUH the Sun god; TLACOLTÉUTL, an earth-goddess and goddess of love; MICTLÁNTECUHTLI, god of death; XOCHIPILLICINTÉOTL; TLÁLOC, the rain god; Quetzalcóatl; TEZCATLIPOCA; CHALMECATECUHTLI, god of sacrifice; TLAHUIXCALPANTECUHTLI, god of dawn; and ILAMATECUHTLI, or possibly CITLALINICUE, goddess of the MILKY WAY[2]. Those of the night (some of them duplicated from the day) were Xiuhtecuhtli; ITZLI, god of the sacrificial knife; PILTZINTECUHTLITONATIUH, a Sun god; CINTÉOTL, the god of maize; Mictlántecuhtli; Chalchiuhtlicue; Tlacoltéutl; TEPEYOLLOTL, the heart of the mountain; and Tláloc.

Current thinking places the order of the Aztec hours as follows:

Day:

1 Xiuhtecuhtli
2 Tlaltecuhtli
3 Chalchiuhtlicue
4 Tonatiuh
5 Tlacoltéutl
6 TEOYAOMQUI, or preferably Mictlántecuhtli

7 Xochipilli-Cintéotl $> > > >$ **midday**
8 Tláloc
9 Quetzalcóatl
10 Tezcatlipoca
11 Mictlántecuhtli or Chalmecatecuhtli
12 Tlahuixcalpantecuhtli
13 Ilamatecuhtli, or possibly Citlalinicue
Night:
1 Xiuhtecuhtli
2 Itzli
3 Piltzintecuhtli-Tonatiuh
4 Cintéotl
5 Mictlántecuhtli $> > > >$ **midnight**
6 Chalchiuhtlicue
7 Tlacoltéutl
8 Tepeyollotl
9 Tláloc

Calli CENTRAL AMERICA – MEXICO
(*Aztec*)
The third day of the twenty-day MONTH[1] employed by the AZTEC people. It symbolized the temple, represented the west, and was presided over by TEPEYOLLOTL. In artistic representations of the calendar, Calli is represented as being carried by a falling eagle.

calumet NORTH AMERICA (*Delaware*)
A ritual smoking of the HOBOWAKAN (peacepipe) that came about when the other tribes of the north decided that they would exterminate the DELAWARE people. However, as they held their council of war, a great white bird appeared and hovered over the head of the chief's only daughter. The bird commanded the girl to tell the assembled council that the GREAT SPIRIT was both sad and angry with them for planning to drink the blood of his firstborn, the LENNI-LENNAPI. The bird added that in order to appease the Great Spirit they were to wash their hands in the blood of a fawn and then go to the Lenni-Lennapi taking gifts and their Hobowakan with them. Having presented them with

the gifts, they were then to smoke the Hobowakan together, thereby pledging eternal brotherhood. This ceremony was called the calumet. In it the Hobowakan is lifted first to the sky, then to the Earth, and then to each of the four quarters, each time the guardian deity of that direction was asked to look kindly upon those taking part and confirm their promises.

Camalotz CENTRAL AMERICA (*Maya*)
Alternative name for CAMAZOTZ[1].

Camaxtli CENTRAL AMERICA – MEXICO
(*Aztec*)
The tutelary god of TLACALE, coloured red, the chief god of the TLAXCALA, Camaxtli was an aspect of the flayed god XIPE TOTEC, who appears to have originally been a nature deity and the god of the four quarters. One of the four sons of TONACATECUHTLI and TONACACÍHUATL, his brothers were QUETZALCÓATL, TEZCATLIPOCA and HUITZILOPOCHTLI.

Camazotz CENTRAL AMERICA (*Maya*)
1 Also called CAMALOTZ, Camazotz was one of the four great birds sent by TEPEU and GUCUMATZ to attack the wooden bodies of the humans they had carved, the other three birds being named XECOTCOVACH, COTZBALAM and TECUMBALAM. Each bird attacked a different part of the body, and by doing so destroyed the first attempts of the gods to create mankind.
2 The lord of the House of BATS, a bloodthirsty bat with large teeth and claws and a nose that was the shape of a flint knife which he used to decapitate his victims. He did just that to HUNAHPU when he and his twin brother XBALANQUÉ were placed in his domain as one of the many tests they had set for them by the lords of XIBALBA if they were to defeat the powers of evil. Hunahpu made the mistake of lifting his head

from the floor on which he and his brother had prostrated themselves, and by so doing presented Camazotz with an easy target in the dark.

Canicubá SOUTH AMERICA – COLOMBIA (*Antioquia*)
The personification of evil who was opposed by the creator ABIRÁ and the mother-goddess DABIECIBA.

Cannibal Mother NORTH AMERICA
1 WOODLANDS – (*Kwakiutl*)
Called TSONOQUA, the Cannibal Mother was an important figure in clan rituals. She lived in the woods where she feasted on corpses and on children she stole from their homes, or those who got lost in the woods. She was killed by the SKY-YOUTH with whose reflection she had fallen in love. See also 3 below.

2 WOODLANDS – (*Creek*)
The Cannibal Mother is simply referred to as a man-eating monster by the CREEK who lived in constant fear of her, for she could strike at any time, and no one knew how to defeat her, or how to protect themselves against her voracious appetite.

3 NORTHWEST COAST – (*Kwakiutl*)
The KWAKIUTL who lived in the NORTHWEST COAST culture region of North America called the Cannibal Mother BAXBAKUALANUCHSIWAE, though to these people the Cannibal Mother was in fact the Cannibal Father for, unlike just about every other AMERINDIAN tribe, they perceived this man-eating monster as male. The Kwakiutl who lived in the WOODLANDS culture region of North America referred to the Cannibal Mother as TSONOQUA. See 1 above.

Baxbakualanuchsiwae was thought of as living in the Arctic at the exact north of the world. There his home has, as its central 'cannibal' pole, the MILKY WAY[1] or, sometimes, the RAINBOW[1]. Red smoke rises from the roof of his home, this smoke symbolizing the blood of those he had gorged himself on. One of the two main tutelary deities of the Northwest coastal Kwakiutl along with WIXALAGILLIS, some commentators have sought to define Baxbakualanuchsiwae's origins as a war-god who was symbolized by the AURORA BOREALIS[1].

Cantultiku CENTRAL AMERICA (*Maya*)
During the creation of the world, when the Earth was covered with a flood, Cantultiku caused the heavens to collapse. When the chaos had ended, Cantultiku sent KANZIBYÚI down to Earth to reorganize it. At each of the four cardinal points different coloured trees were planted, and the heavens propped up so that they could never again fall on to the Earth.

Capac SOUTH AMERICA – PERU (*Chimu and Mochica*)
A Chimu leader who led an invasion into the valley ruled over by NAYMLAP and FEMPELLEC and, having routed them, made PONY MASSA the new ruler.

Cari SOUTH AMERICA – BOLIVIA (*Collao*)
One of two legendary chieftains, the other being ZAPANA, who were said to have engaged in an internecine war, as a result of which the INCA people were easily able to conquer their kingdom.

Carib SOUTH AMERICA AND CARIBBEAN
Indigenous AMERINDIAN people of the north coastal regions of South America and the islands of the southern West Indies in the Caribbean Sea. The Caribs who moved north to take the islands from the ARAWAK people were alleged, by the Spanish, to be fierce cannibals. In 1796 most of them were deported from the West Indies by the English who placed them on Roatan

Island off Honduras. Since that time they have spread extensively throughout Honduras and Nicaragua. Their languages belong to the Ge-Pano-Carib family. The Carib gave their name to the Caribbean Sea which was named after them by the Spanish.

Carrefour, Maît(re) HAITI (*Voodoo*)
One of the many LOA of the VOODOO cult.

Cassé Brisé HAITI (*Voodoo*)
Simply described as a LOA whose characteristics and attributes remain a closely guarded secret of VOODOO cultists.

Catherine, Sainte Haiti (*Voodoo*)
The Roman Catholic saint who is regarded as a LOA by some VOODOO cultists.

Cauac CENTRAL AMERICA (*Maya*)
The nineteenth day of the MAYA spiritual pilgrimage known as the AGES OF MAN. On this day man's divine nature begins to manifest itself. Cauac is not to be confused with NINE CAUAC, the ninth day of the CREATION[4]. For some reason the Maya considered Cauac to be a harbinger of disaster, as they did IX, and considered those years that started on the day of Cauac to be malign. During these years, governed by the western of the Four BACAB, the western gates of the city were guarded by EK-U-UAYEYAB, while the centre of the city was guarded by ZAC-MITUN-AHAU.

Cavillaca SOUTH AMERICA (*Quechua*)
The beautiful goddess with whom CON-IRAYA fell in love. He secretly impregnated her by transforming some of his sperm into fruit which she ate. When her mysteriously conceived child was one year old, Cavillaca called together all the gods to discover the identity of her child's father.

Since none of the assembled company admitted paternity, Cavillaca said that the child should crawl to its father, which it did. As soon as she realized that the father was Coniraya, Cavillaca, humiliated by that discovery, took her child and fled to the coast where, at PACHACAMAC[2], she transformed herself and her child into rocks.

Cayuga NORTH AMERICA – WOODLANDS
Indigenous North American AMERINDIAN people who were one of the six member tribes of the IROQUOIS confederation which consisted of the Cayuga, MOHAWK, ONEIDA, ONONDAGA and SENECA peoples, with the TUSCARORA joining in 1715. The confederation was traditionally founded by HAIOWATHA in 1570.

Ce Actl Topiltzin CENTRAL AMERICA –
  MEXICO (*Toltec and Aztec*)
'Our-Lord-Reed-One', the son of MIXCÓATL and CHIMALMAN. After the murder of his father, Ce Actl Topiltzin fled into exile, but later returned and avenged his father's death. Ce Actl Topiltzin then became high priest of the god QUETZALCÓATL whose name he took.

Celia, Sainte HAITI (*Voodoo*)
The Roman Catholic saint who is regarded as a LOA by some VOODOO cultists.

Cemanahuac CENTRAL AMERICA –
  MEXICO (*Aztec*)
The name given to the Earth after it had been formed from the sea-monster CIPACTLI. The name would appear to bear witness to the origins of the AZTEC as a NAHUA people as it seems to mean 'Land of the Nahua' coming from *Cema* and *Nahua*.

cemis CARIBBEAN (*Taïno*)
A fairly simple variant of ZEMIS.

Centéotl CENTRAL AMERICA (*Aztec*)
Simple variant of CINTÉOTL.

Central American Mythology

The main mythology of the high Mexican tableland was not, as might be thought, created by the AZTEC people, but rather by their NAHUA-speaking predecessors who include the TOLTECS, and others who lived in the region many aeons earlier. The pre-Hispanic population of Mexico was composed of a large variety of peoples. The Nahua were confined almost exclusively to the high central plain. The Gulf coastline was populated by the OLMEC and TOTONAC peoples, while further south lived the HUASTEC, MIXTEC and ZAPOTEC civilizations. Central Mexico, as it is known today, was home to the TARASCAN and ZACATEC peoples, while the CORA and HUICHOL Indians occupied the most westerly portion of the country. All these peoples were further supplemented by various nomadic tribes who lived in the north and who were gradually assimilated into the peoples they came into contact with. All of these inhabitants gradually assimilated, or were annihilated, to leave the Aztec people in almost sole control of the Mexican tableland. Today, when people refer to Central American Mythology they usually think of the Aztec and MAYA peoples, but the area is rich in myth and legend that predates both of these mighty civilizations by some considerable period.

Centzonhuitznáua CENTRAL AMERICA –
　MEXICO (*Aztec*)
The generic name of the 400 sons of COAT-LICUE, the stellar deities of the southern sky who are sometimes referred to as the 'Four Hundred Southerners' (cf. CENTZON-MIXIXCOA). At the instigation of COYOL-XAUHQUI, the daughter of Coatlicue, the Centzonhuitznáua planned to kill their mother. However, as they approached her, she gave birth to HUITZILOPOCHTLI who

emerged from her womb fully armed with a blue shield and spear, and his serpent torch XIUHOCÓATL with a single blow of which Huitzilopochtli killed Coyolxauhqui. He then set off after the Centzonhuitznáua and succeeded in killing almost all of them as well. The few that managed to escape his fury escaped south to HUITZLAMPA the 'Place of Thorns'.

Centzonmixixcoa CENTRAL AMERICA –
　MEXICO (*Aztec*)
The 400 stellar gods of the northern sky whom some suggest are the sons of COATLICUE, and thus the brothers of COYOLXAUHQUI and the 400 CENTZONHUITZNÁUA.

Centzontotochtin CENTRAL AMERICA –
　MEXICO (*Aztec*)
The collective name for the 400 PULQUE gods who are commonly known as the 'Four Hundred Rabbits'. Among their number is PATÉCATL, lord of OCPATLI, the PEYOTE from which a sacred intoxicating drink is made.

Ceterni SOUTH AMERICA – PERU
　(*Mochica*)
The wife of NAYMLAP whom she accompanied to LAMBEYEQYE, along with the remainder of his retinue: FONGASIDE, LLAPCHILULLI, NINACOLLA, NINGENTUE, OCHOCALO, PITAZOFI and XAN.

C'Haban CENTRAL AMERICA (*Maya*)
The seventeenth day of the MAYA spiritual pilgrimage known as the AGES OF MAN on which, having completed his mortal life, the soul throws off the last remnants of ash, a phrase specifically used to suggest ritual cleansing by fire (cremation). C'Haban in this context is not to be confused with SEVEN C'HABAN, the seventh day of the Maya CREATION[4].

Cha(a)c CENTRAL AMERICA (*Maya*)

1 The rain-god, also called AH HOYA ('he who urinates'), AH TZENUL ('he who gives food to others'), and HOPOP CAAN ('he who lights up the sky'), Chaac is the MAYA equivalent of the AZTEC deity TLÁLOC. A gruesome festival was held in his honour. During this festival babies and young children were sacrificed, cooked and eaten by the rain-god's priests. If the children cried, it was taken as a sign that rain would soon fall. Chaac was portrayed with two wide eyes, a long turned-up nose, two curved fangs and hair made up from a tangle of knots. His four aspects depended on which direction the life-giving rain he sent came from. In the east he was red; in the west, black; in the north, white; and in the south, yellow. He made thunder with great stone axes, the lightning being created by their sparking, and threw down the rain from gourds full of water.

Though his festival was particularly gruesome, Chaac was a beneficent deity and the friend of man. He taught them how to grow food and was patron of their cornfields. However, Chaac could also summarily deal with those who transgressed, either against him or against his fellow man. In these cases he would simply strike them dead with a thunderbolt.

2 One of the Four BACAB, Chac was coloured red and represented the east. His companions were KAN who was associated with yellow and south, ZAC – white and north, and ED – black and west.

Cha(a)c Mool CENTRAL AMERICA (*Maya*)

The name given to reclining figures at CHICHEN ITZÁ that represent the attendants of the rain-god CHAAC. These figures, adorned with shallow dishes in which to catch the rain, were carved in a lumpy fashion so that they emulated rain clouds. Similar figures, possibly of TOLTEC origin, have been found at the great Toltec centre of TULA. However, here the figures are simply thought to represent seated figures of the gods themselves, rather than attendants.

Chacs CENTRAL AMERICA (*Maya*)

Collective name given to four fertility and rain-gods who obviously take their name from the great MAYA rain-god CHAAC. They lived at the four corners of the world, manifested themselves in thunder and lightning, and were honoured every spring along with the Four BACAB, and again at the March festival of ITZAMNÁ, another Maya rain-god. The early chronicler LANDA recorded that the title Chacs was also given to four old men who were chosen each year to assist the priests at the various ceremonials. It is possible that the Chacs have their origin with CHAC[2], one of the Four BACAB whose role may have been expanded until it surpassed that of his companions whose names were then dropped.

Chac-u-Uayeyab CENTRAL AMERICA (*Maya*)

The guardian of the eastern gates of a city during the MULUC years which were governed by the eastern of the Four BACAB. During this time the god KINICH AHAU presided over the centre of the town. See also EK-U-UAYEYAB, KAN-U-UAYEYAB, ZAC-U-UAYEYAB.

Chahuru NORTH AMERICA – GREAT PLAINS (*Pawnee*)

The water-spirit.

Chakekenapok NORTH AMERICA – WOODLANDS (*Potawatomi*)

'Flint', the fourth brother of NANABOOJOO, the Great HARE, and the killer of their mother. Nanaboojoo avenged her death by killing Chakekenapok. The fragments of his corpse, for Nanaboojoo had torn his brother to shreds, were transformed into rocks. His intestines became vines, and patches of flint stone marked the places where he and his brother did battle, the flint stone seemingly being formed from Chakekenapok's blood as it was spilled.

Chalchiuhtlicue CENTRAL AMERICA –
MEXICO (*Aztec*)
'Lady-of-the-Turquoise-Skirt' or 'Lady of the Jade Petticoat'. The goddess of marriage, babies and chastity who, nonetheless, married her brother TLÁLOC. She presided over the baptism of infants, a ceremony that was recorded as having impressed the Spanish conquistadors as Christian in its style and implications. Her symbols were maize and snakes. An ambivalent deity who was also the goddess of running water, this role stemming from the fact that she was also said to have been married to the water-god TLACOTECUHTLI, Chalchiuhtlicue governed shipwrecks and death by drowning. She was also credited with the invention of the RAINBOW[2] as a spiritual bridge between Earth and heaven without which mankind could not have survived.

Chalchiuhtlicue ruled the era of the FOURTH SUN during which time maize was first introduced to mankind. This era ended after 312 years when she caused it to rain so hard, and for so long, that the Earth was entirely covered with water and all the people were transformed into fish, so that mankind might survive. She then had a son by QUETZALCÓATL whom that god threw into a fire from which he emerged as the FIFTH SUN. The gods then determined that the heavens should be firmly propped up. To do this four giants called FALLING EAGLE, SERPENT OF OBSIDIAN KNIVES, RESURRECTION and THORNY FLOWERS were placed at the four corners of the Earth to hold the heavens up. Quetzalcóatl and TEZCATLIPOCA also lent a hand, the former becoming the PRECIOUS TREE, and the latter the TREE OF MIRRORS.

Although Chalchiuhtlicue is of great ritual importance, she plays little part in the known AZTEC narratives. She was depicted in blue and yellow and wearing a green stone necklace and turquoise earplugs and a blue cap with a spray of quetzal feathers, a depiction that definitely has watery connotations. Her skirt and shift were decorated like water and adorned with water lilies, and she carried a clapper, the traditional symbol of a water deity.

Chalchiutotolin CENTRAL AMERICA –
MEXICO (*Aztec*)
An aspect of TEZCATLIPOCA.

Chalmecatecuhtli CENTRAL AMERICA –
MEXICO (*Aztec*)
God of sacrifice, and thus of great importance to a culture that placed immense importance on sacrifice, both human and otherwise. Chalmecatecuhtli presided over the eleventh hour of the twenty-two-hour AZTEC day, though sometimes MICTLÁNTECUHTLI is also quoted as having this role. See CALENDAR.

Chamacoco SOUTH AMERICA – BOLIVIA
An indigenous South American Indian people who say that they originally lived underground and were incredibly small which is why they referred to themselves as the INSECT MEN. They tried to climb into the sky up a hugh tree, but they all fell back to the Earth which killed a large proportion of the climbers. That is why, according to the Chamacoco, there are so few of them.

Chamiabak CENTRAL AMERICA (*Maya*)
One of the terrible lords of XIBALBA, his co-rulers being AHALCANA, AHALPUH, CHAMIAHOLOM, CUCHUMAQIQ, HUN CAME,

PATAN, QUIQRE, QUIQRIXGAG, QUIQXIL, VUKUB CAME and XIQIRIPAT, though some sources say that Xibalba was ruled by Hun Came and Vukub Came, and that all the other lords were subordinate to that pair.

Chamiahol(o)m CENTRAL AMERICA (*Maya*)
One of the eleven terrible lords of XIBALBA (see CHAMIABAK).

Chan Chan SOUTH AMERICA – PERU (*Chimu*)
The huge maze-like capital of the pre-INCA kingdom of CHIMOR that was located in MOCHE valley and covered fourteen square miles.

Chanca SOUTH AMERICA (*Inca*)
Confederation of neighbouring peoples who all but vanquished the INCAS in the middle of the fifteenth century. This defeat came shortly before PACHACUTI came to power and led the Inca nation in an expansionist policy that ended up with the Inca empire covering most of Ecuador, Bolivia and Peru, together with large areas of Argentina and Chile.

Chanicubá SOUTH AMERICA – COLUMBIA (*Antioquia*)
The personification of evil who was, according to sixteenth-century reports, opposed to the creator ABIRÁ and the mother-goddess DABIECIBA.

Chantico CENTRAL AMERICA – MEXICO (*Aztec*)
The goddess of the hearth, both in the home and in the temple, who was also associated with volcanoes and volcanic fire, her moods being said to be represented by the activity of volcanoes. When they were quiet she was happy, but when they erupted she was thought to have been offended in some way, and sacrifices were hurriedly made to appease her (cf. TLECUIL).

Chaputepec CENTRAL AMERICA – MEXICO (*Aztec*)
The COLHUACAn city to which HUITZILOPOCHTLI led the travellers from AZTLAN. They were not welcomed and were quickly and forcibly driven out, their lord HUITZILIHUITL being taken captive and killed.

Chavin SOUTH AMERICA – PERU
A highly developed civilization of great temple builders that, after the gradual development of fishing and agricultural villages along the Peruvian coast from *c.* 4000 BC, quite suddenly arose *c.* 1000 BC. The civilization appears, from archaeological evidence anyway, to have been peaceable rather than warlike, and quickly spread over much of the Andean region of Peru. The name Chavin comes from one of the greatest temples these people built – CHAVIN DE HUÁNTOR. They appear to have worshipped a jaguar deity as jaguar motifs dominate their temple carvings. However, two representations of an anthropomorphic deity have also been found – the EL LANZÓN and the RAIMONDI steles, both of which depict a man with serpent hair and cat-like features.

The origins of this great civilization remain a mystery. Some authorities state that it has definite associations with the OLMEC civilization of Central America, while others have even, quite fantastically, suggested a Chinese provenance. While their rise to predominance remains an unsolved mystery, so does their equally puzzling disappearance *c.* 300 BC.

Chavin de Huántor SOUTH AMERICA (*Chavin*)
Archaeological site in the Peruvian Andes 10,000 feet above sea level which is the

location of the greatest temple of the mysterious CHAVIN civilization, and the one which has given them their name.

Chebel Yax CENTRAL AMERICA (*Maya*)
A goddess who is credited with the invention of woven textile designs, designs that have become an unmistakable trademark of the MAYA people.

chenoo NORTH AMERICA – WOODLANDS
(*Abnaki and Micmac*)
The generic name given to stone giants that are common to all IROQUOIS peoples, and not solely the ABNAKI and MICMAC tribes. Ignorant of the use of bows and arrows, these mythical monsters used rocks as their weapons, and in fights among themselves used to uproot trees to use as clubs. The chenoo could sometimes be tamed by a human, in which case they became very useful tools to their SHAMAN masters.

Chenuke SOUTH AMERICA – TIERRA DEL FUEGO (*Ona*)
The personification of evil who was fought, and conquered, by KWANYIP.

Cherokee NORTH AMERICA –
WOODLANDS
Indigenous North American AMERINDIAN people who were under the domination of the ferocious and frequently internecine IROQUOIS. They originally lived in the mountain country of what is now Alabama, the Carolinas, Georgia and Tennessee. Their great leader, Sequoyah (*c.* 1770–1843) devised the syllabary used for writing their language which was one branch of the Macro-Siouan family. In 1829, the Cherokee nation was transported to a reservation in Oklahoma by a forced march known as the 'Trail of Tears' by order of President Andrew Jackson as a punishment for aiding the British during the American Revolution. Today the

Cherokee live mainly in North Carolina, where they were allowed to re-establish a tribal centre in 1984, and in Oklahoma where they established their capital at Tahlequah. The Cherokee people claim their descent from KANATI and SELU.

Cheun CENTRAL AMERICA (*Maya*)
The eleventh day of the MAYA spiritual pilgrimage known as the AGES OF MAN on which, having been transformed into the lowest form of matter on the tenth day, OC, he may burn without flame and thus suffers the utmost agony. This point is the lowest spot in the twenty-day spiritual pilgrimage, as from here forwards the spirit starts a long ascent to heaven until on the twentieth day, AHAU, the spirit manifests its divine nature and is welcomed to the home of the gods. Cheun in this context is not to be confused with ONE CHEUN, the first day of the Maya CREATION[4].

Cheyenne NORTH AMERICA – GREAT
PLAINS AND WOODLANDS
Indigenous North American AMERINDIAN people who originally inhabited the WOODLANDS culture region, but migrated under pressure from the first settlers to the GREAT PLAINS. Their language is one of the ALGONQUIAN group whose other speakers include the ARAPAHO, BLACKFOOT and CREE.

Chiá SOUTH AMERICA – COLOMBIA
(*Chibcha*)
The name that CHIMINIGAGUÉ, the creator, gave to the Moon which he created at the same time as ZUHÉ, the Sun.

Chibcha SOUTH AMERICA – COLOMBIA
Indigenous South American INCA people who lived in Colombia. Their civilization was overthrown and totally annihilated by the Spaniards in 1538. Their practice of completely covering their leader with gold dust on an underlying layer of gum is

thought to have given rise to the legends of the fabled city of gold – EL DORADO.

Chibchacum SOUTH AMERICA – COLUMBIA (*Chibcha*)

Also called CHICCHECHUM, Chibchacum was the Earth-god and patron of farmers and merchants, though he is usually portrayed as an evil deity, the god of earthquakes. Chibchacum once grew very angry with mankind and sent a FLOOD[4] to punish them. In response to the frantic prayers of man, BOCHICA showed himself to mankind as a RAINBOW[3] which struck the rocks and caused them to split open. As they did so the waters flowed away, thus creating the great waterfall TEQUENDAMA. Bochica then sent ZUHÉ, the Sun, to dry out the land, and then forced Chibchacum to retreat underground where he has remained ever since bearing the weight of the Earth on his shoulders. Chibchacum often grows tired of his load and when he shifts the burden, which is quite often, earthquakes split the Earth open.

Chibiabos NORTH AMERICA – WOODLANDS (*Potawatomi*)

Also called CHIPIABOS or CHIPIAPOOS. The second brother of NANABOOJOO, the Great HARE. He was drowned by evil UNDERWORLD spirits, after which he became the lord of the dead.

Chicama SOUTH AMERICA – PERU (*Mochica*)

One of the two valleys, the other being MOCHE, around which the MOCHICA civilization, the civilization that followed the mysterious CHAVIN civilization, was centred.

Chicchan CENTRAL AMERICA (*Maya*)

The fifth day of the MAYA spiritual pilgrimage known as the AGES OF MAN on which man gathers together all the experiences of his life before he dies on the sixth day,

CIMI. Chicchan is associated with the serpent and is the day of KUKULCÁN in his serpent aspect. Chicchan in these contexts is not to be confused with TWO CHICCHAN, the fifteenth day of the Maya CREATION[4].

Chicchechum SOUTH AMERICA – COLOMBIA (*Chibcha*)

Alternative name for CHIBCHACUM.

chicha SOUTH AMERICA – BRAZIL (*Tupari*)

Unfermented beer that is given to a PABID when it first comes to the village of the dead by PATOBKIA, the chief SHAMAN.

Chichen ltzá CENTRAL AMERICA – YUCATÁN, MEXICO (*Maya*)

Ancient MAYA city in Yucatán, Mexico that flourished between the tenth and thirteenth centuries. The city was excavated between 1924 and 1940 by Sylvanus Griswold Morley (see Bibliography). The magnificent remains include temples with sculptures and colour reliefs, an observatory, and a sacred well into which votive offerings, as well as human sacrifices, were thrown. The city, it is thought, was probably founded c. AD 500 by the ITZÁ and displays both Classic and post-Classic architecture which has a strong TOLTEC influence.

Chichimec CENTRAL AMERICA – MEXICO

The 'Race of Dogs', an indigenous NAHUA tribe that numbered among the emigrants from North America who settled in Mexico. They established themselves in the lakeside city of TEZCOCO after the great TOLTEC city of TOLLAN had fallen to the Chichimec invaders. Their fortunes, and power, were based on their dominance of the salt pans of Lake Tezcoco. Their great god and war-leader was XÓLOTL who, in many ways, resembles the TRICKSTER of North American AMERINDIAN myth. He appears to be an extremely old deity and probably originated as the totemic ancestor of the Chichimec people who, according to one myth, were descended from a man and a bitch (hence their name) who were the sole survivors of the FLOOD[5].

Chicksaw NORTH AMERICA – WOODLANDS
Indigenous North American AMERINDIAN people who inhabited the southern parts of the WOODLANDS culture region. Their language was a branch of the MUSKHOGEE that was also spoken by the CREEK people.

Chicomecóatl CENTRAL AMERICA – MEXICO (*Aztec*)
'Seven Snakes', an early fertility deity who is also called XILONEN. The goddess of maize, and thus an extremely important deity to a people whose diet was based around this particular cereal. Depicted as a savage snake-like woman, Chicomecóatl had absolute power over man's nourishment, though she was also a benign goddess adorned with water lilies and carrying a Sun shield, both elements, Sun and water, being essential to the growth of the maize she oversaw. She is cognate with COATLICUE, the great Earth Mother.

Chicomexochtli CENTRAL AMERICA – MEXICO (*Aztec*)
'Seven Flowers', an alternative name for TONACATECUHTLI in which guise he is associated with the MILKY WAY[2].

Chicuna SOUTH AMERICA – PANAMA
The supreme being of the AMERINDIANS of Panama during the nineteenth century.

Chicunauhapan CENTRAL AMERICA – MEXICO (*Aztec*)
One of the nine rivers of MICTLÁN, the UNDERWORLD, across which the soul of the dead was carried by the dog that was ritually sacrificed and buried alongside its newly deceased master. Having crossed all nine rivers, the soul finally came to its eternal resting place in CHICUNAUHMICTLÁN.

C(h)icunauhmictlán CENTRAL AMERICA – MEXICO (*Aztec*)
The ninth and final region of MICTLÁN, the UNDERWORLD of AZTEC belief, and the final resting place of the souls of the dead who were carried there by a dog which had to cross nine rivers on its long and hazardous journey. According to some accounts, this region is the final destination of all those who die after their soul has spent four probationary years in outer regions of the Underworld.

Chief-Sky-Ruler NORTH AMERICA – WOODLANDS (*Iroquois*)
Title given to the grandfather of ATAENTSIC, he was also known as the ANCIENT-BODIED ONE.

Chief-Who-Holds-The-Earth NORTH AMERICA – WOODLANDS (*Iroquois*)
Husband of ATAENTSIC and father of GUSTS-OF-WIND. He falsely accused his wife of being unfaithful to him, whereupon she left the heavens and descended to the Earth.

Chilam Balam of Chumayel, The Book of CENTRAL AMERICA – YUCATÁN, MEXICO (*Maya*)
A collection of chronicles and other miscellaneous information about the MAYA peoples that dates from the sixteenth century. It is one of the most important sources of Maya beliefs, and the myths they associated with such events as the Creation.

Chilane CENTRAL AMERICA (*Maya*)
Name given to diviners who were on a parallel in the priestly hierarchy of the

MAYA with the ALMENHENOB. Those attaining the rank of Chilane could either be elected, or would attain their status through hereditary inheritance.

Chilchi NORTH AMERICA – PEUBLO, SOUTHWEST (*Zuñi*)
An extremely important KATCHINA.

Children of the Sun CENTRAL AMERICA (*Maya*)
The collective name given to the ancestors of the INCA people. Originally mankind had lived beneath the Earth but eventually, from a cave with three mouths at PACCARITAMBO – 'Inn of Origin', also called TAMBOTOCCO – 'Place of the Hole', four brothers and four sisters emerged, though some sources say that there were only three of each gender. They left the dark confines of the UNDERWORLD through the central mouth of the cave as, according to some versions of the story, the ancestors of the lesser Inca tribes emerged from the other two entrances.

The names of the Children of the Sun are variously given. Pedro DE CIEZA DE LÉON says that the Inca nobility told him that the brothers' names were AYAR CACHI ASAUCA, AYAR MANCO and AYAR UCHO, and their sisters MAMA COYA, MAMA HUACO and MAMA RAHUA. Fray Martin DE MONIA, who had obviously heard a great number of variations of the story, says that the most 'plausible' names for the children, in this case four brothers and four sisters, were the brothers CUSCO HUANCA, HUANA CAURI, MANCO CAPAC and TOPA AYAR CACHI, and the sisters CORI OCLLO, IPA HUACO, MAMA COYA and TOPA HUACO.

Both commentators agree that the children were dressed in beautiful woollen tabards and cloaks, TAPACU – the royal vesture of the Inca – and each of the brothers carried a golden sling. By their

natural superiority the Children of the Sun won immediate ascendancy over all the other Inca peoples who had emerged from the cave at the same time.

Seeing that the cave was not a suitable area to settle, they set off north. *En route*, one of the brothers, Ayar Cachi (that is Ayar Cachi Asauca or Topa Ayar Cachi) climbed Mount HUANACAURI where, by firing stones from its summit with his golden slingshot, he caused the surrounding hills to split open. This aroused such jealousy in his brothers that they lured him into a cave which they sealed, so imprisoning him there.

Leaving Mount Huanacauri, the remaining brothers and sisters camped at TAMBU QUIRU where they were visited by their dead brother's spirit who told them to found a city at CUZCO. Ayar Cachi then transformed himself into a stone on the summit of the mountain in which he had been entombed, and was thenceforth revered as a god. A variant of this says that both Ayar Cachi and Ayar Ucho (otherwise called Huana Cauri – see below) became the cult stone; Ayar Ucho, in this instance, being said to have first taught Ayar Manco (Manco Capac) the right of passage for adolescent youths. Ayar Manco and his sisters then went on to found the city of Cuzco where Ayar Manco became the first Inca king and changed his name to Manco Capac.

Fray Martin de Monia says, however, that the oldest brother, Huana Cauri, chose to remain in APITAY, their first stopping place, where he died; the mountain he died on being named Mount Huanacauri in his honour. The others then proceeded to the city of ACAMAMA which they occupied without meeting any resistance. Cusco Huanca became the first Inca king and changed the name of the city to Cuzco. He was later succeeded by his brother, the great Manco Capac.

Chimalamat CENTRAL AMERICA (*Maya*)
The wife of VUKUB CAKIX and the mother
of his monstrous offspring ZIPACNÁ and
CABRACA. When HUNAHPU and XBALAN-
QUÉ fought and killed her husband and
children, Hunahpu lost an arm which she
proceeded to roast on a spit.

Chimalman CENTRAL AMERICA –
MEXICO (*Toltec*)
'Prostrate-Shield', the wife of MIXCÓATL
and mother of CE ACTL TOPILTZIN.

Chiminigagué SOUTH AMERICA
(*Chibcha*)
The creator. At first everything was in
darkness as light was contained within the
body of Chiminigagué. He then created
four large birds to whom he gave the light
and told them to carry it across the world.
He then created the Sun ZUHÉ and the
Moon CHIA so that the light might have a
home and the birds could rest.

Chimizapag ~ na, ~ ua SOUTH
AMERICA – BOLIVIA AND COLOMBIA
(*Chibcha*)
'Messenger of CHIMINIGAGUÉ, an alterna-
tive name for NEMTEREQUETEBA.

Chimor SOUTH AMERICA – PERU
(*pre-Inca*)
Great South American civilization that
flourished for a little over 200 years
between *c.* 1240 and *c.* 1470, and succeeded the dissolution of TIAHUANACO.
The great kingdom of Chimor, whose inhabitants are known as Chimu, was centred on the coastal valleys of northern and
central Peru and had as its capital the
hugh maze-like city of CHAN CHAN, in
MOCHE valley near Trujillo. According to
legend, Chimor was founded by a prince
who came 'over the sea', and was named
either TACANAYMO or NAYMLAP who, it is
now thought, possibly originated from the
region of Ecuador. Chimor was a highly

centralized civilization, the ruler of which
was worshipped as a god. Other deities
included, as would be expected the Sun,
the Moon and sea gods, but also included
ancestral TOTEM stones known as ALEC
PONG. They produced fine articles in gold,
made realistic portrait pottery as well as
savage fanged images in clay, and possibly,
though by no means certainly, a system of
writing that involved the painting of beans
in a particular series of patterns. It is,
however, the building prowess of the
Chimu people that really stands out. They
built aqueducts that carried water for
many miles, and enormous adobe brick
mounds, or *huacas*, as the base of temples
and palaces. Chan Chan itself consists of
nine complexes, possibly built by successive kings, that were to form their tombs
eventually. The aqueduct system was very
important to the Chimu as being able to
transport water easily was the very foundation of their agricultural system. Within
this system, which appears feudal in nature, it has been discovered that any peasant who defaulted – say, in the payment of
his tithe – would be ritually mutilated. An
extremely effective method, so it would
appear, of keeping the peasants in line!

The northern highlands, in contrast to
the united might of lowland Chimor, consisted of a loosely knit confederation of
villages, each divided into two moieties
and centred around the hardly any larger
village of CHUCUITO which was ruled by
two omnipotent leaders. To the south the
confederation appears not to have held,
for here the small villages were always at
war with each other.

Not much remains of the Chimor society, as they were to be assimilated with the
INCA people who were assured of victory in
their invasion when they cut the Chimu
aqueducts, and therefore starved the people of water. With the Chimu subjugated,
the Inca all but erased any memory of the
earlier Chimu beliefs and doctrines.

Chin CENTRAL AMERICA – YUCATÁN, MEXICO (*Maya*)
The god of lust.

Chinook NORTH AMERICA – NORTHWEST COAST
Indigenous North American AMERINDIAN people inhabiting the NORTHWEST COAST culture region, and whose name means 'snow-eater'. Their neighbours included the BELLA COOLA, HAIDA, KWAKIUTL, NOOTKA, SALISH and TSHIMSHIAN people, though linguistically all these peoples speak different languages. The Chinook have given their name to a warm dry wind that blows downhill on the eastern side of the Rocky Mountains, most often occurring in the spring and winter when it produces a rapid thaw – hence its name.

Chipactonal CENTRAL AMERICA – MEXICO (*Aztec*)
The name of one of the four AMOXAOQUE (wise men) who remained with the travellers from AZTLAN after the others had left them at TAMOANCHAN. The others who remained were OXOMOCO TLALTECUIN and XOCHICAHUACA. These four, who were also known as the guardians of HUITZILOPOCHTLI, are credited with the invention of the calendar so that the AZTEC people might have a proper means by which to organize their lives.

Chipia ~ bos, ~ poos NORTH AMERICA – WOODLANDS (*Potawatomi*)
Variant(s) of CHIBIABOS, the lord of the dead.

Chipiripa SOUTH AMERICA – COSTA RICA (*Curra or Cueva*)
The rain-god.

Chipmunk NORTH AMERICA – NORTHWEST COAST
Indigenous North American AMERINDIAN people who inhabited a portion of the NORTHWEST COAST culture region. According to the KLAMATH, the Chipmunk people, along with the Klamath, MAIDU and MAKLAK tribes were created by KEMUSH.

Chippewa NORTH AMERICA – WOODLANDS
Indigenous North American AMERINDIAN people inhabiting the far north of the WOODLANDS culture region. Their language was one branch of the ALGONQUIAN family which linguistically links the Chippewa with the CREE, DELAWARE, MENOMINEE, MONTAGNAIS and POTAWATOMI.

chixu NORTH AMERICA – GREAT PLAINS (*Pawnee*)
The name given to the spirit of the dead, i.e. a ghost.

Choctaw NORTH AMERICA – WOODLANDS
Indigenous North American AMERINDIAN people who inhabited the southeastern WOODLANDS culture region. Like many other Amerindian peoples, the Choctaw claim to have originated in an UNDERWORLD domain from which they were led to the surface, the point of emergence for the Choctaw being NANIH WAYA.

Cholula CENTRAL AMERICA – MEXICO (*Maya and Aztec*)
City that stands close to Puebla on the road from Mexico City where the POCHTECA had their main centre, and from where they travelled into the Gulf lands, carrying not only the goods they had to sell, but also their ideas, far into MAYA territory. It has been suggested that the pochteca were largely responsible for the spread of the cult of QUETZALCÓATL, as the city of Cholula was one of the chief centres of the Quetzalcóatl cult. The city is also mentioned in a story when TEZCATLIPOCA,

in the form of an ocelot, chased Quetzalcóatl from city to city until they came to Cholula, a story that is clearly a remembrance of a terrible storm in which the wind-god Quetzalcóatl swept over the land, but abated as it reached the city, an event that would have undoubtedly strengthened the cult of Quetzalcóatl.

Chot SOUTH AMERICA – PERU (*Chimu*)
The name of a temple that was built by NAYMLAP and his people after they had landed at LAMBEYEQYE (south of Cape Santa Elena). They placed a great stone-carving of a king in the temple that was thenceforth known as LLAMPALLEC – 'figure of Naymlap'.

Chu(i)cuito SOUTH AMERICA – PERU (*Chimu*)
Village in the northern highlands of the ancient pre-INCA empire of CHIMOR that led the loosely knit confederation of villages, each village being divided into two moieties. The choice of Chuicuito was somewhat curious as it was hardly any larger than the villages that surrounded it.

Chulavete CENTRAL AMERICA – MEXICO (*Cora*)
The MORNING STAR and one of the CORA peoples' most important deities.

Churuquilla, Mount SOUTH AMERICA – BOLIVIA (*Aymará*)
One of the two ACHACHILAS of SUCRÉ, the other being Mount SICASICA. These two mountains were said to embody a pair of spirits, one male and one female, the female spirit of Mount Sicasica sometimes manifesting itself as a seductive, yet unapproachable young woman.

Cib CENTRAL AMERICA (*Maya*)
The sixteenth day of the MAYA spiritual pilgrimage known as the AGES OF MAN, on which day the spirit reaches full consciousness during the long ascent to heaven. Cib is not to be confused with SIX CIB, the sixth day of the Maya CREATION[4].

cibas CARIBBEAN (*Taïno*)
White shells with which, along with yellow shells (GUIANOS), GUAGUGIANA was taught the lore and art of making sacred necklaces by the sea-goddess GUABONITO.

Cibi HAITI (*Voodoo*)
One of the many LOA of the VOODOO religion.

Cicunauhmictlán CENTRAL AMERICA – MEXICO (*Aztec*)
Simple variant of CHICUNAUHMICTLÁN.

Cihuacóatl CENTRAL AMERICA – MEXICO (*Aztec*)
'Snake Woman', the greatest and most powerful of all the AZTEC goddesses whose roaring signalled the start of a war. She was also called TONANTZIN ('Our Mother'); ILAMATECUHTLI ('the Goddess'), in which aspect she was sometimes depicted as the toad TLALTECUHTLI swallowing a knife; ITZPAPÁLOTL ('Obsidian Butterfly'); TEMAZCALTECI ('Grandmother of the Sweatbath'); and TETEOINNAN ('Mother of the Gods'). With a cult that may have originated among the peoples of the East Mexican coastal area, Cihuacóatl was also a lunar fertility goddess in whose honour phallic symbols were carried during the annual harvest festival.

cihuapipiltin CENTRAL AMERICA – MEXICO (*Aztec*)
Name sometimes used as an alternative to CIHUATETEO.

cihuateteo CENTRAL AMERICA – MEXICO (*Aztec*)
Generic name given to women who had either died in war, or during childbirth.

They are said to live in TAMOANCHAN, the western paradise (see XOCHIQUETZAL), from where they escort the Sun's palanquin into their realm where they are relieved of their charge by the lords of the UNDERWORLD. Sometimes called CIHUAPIPILTIN, these spectral souls are from time to time identified with the TZIZIMIME, the stars that follow the descent of the Sun. Usually benign, they also have a malevolent aspect in which they are said to attack mankind in the shape of an eagle. These attacks afflict children with a disease akin to epilepsy, while men are afflicted with an incurable lust.

Cimi CENTRAL AMERICA (Maya)

The sixth day of the MAYA spiritual pilgrimage that is known as the AGES OF MAN on which man ends his mortal life. As such the day of Cimi has become associated with death, and with the mysterious god known simply as A. Cimi is not to be confused with THREE CIMI, the sixteenth day of the twenty-day CREATION[4] on which death was created, though the general meaning of the word Cimi remains constant.

Cintéotl CENTRAL AMERICA – MEXICO (Aztec)

The corn god, the son of TLAZOLTÉOTL and husband of XOCHIQUETZAL.

Cipactli CENTRAL AMERICA – MEXICO (Aztec)

A sea-monster from whom CEMANAHUAC, the Earth, was said to have been formed during the creation.

Cipactonal CENTRAL AMERICA – MEXICO (Aztec)

The first woman who was created at the same time as OXOMOCO, the first man, some 600 years after the Earth had been created by the gods CAMAXTLI, TEZCATLIPOCA, QUETZALCÓATL and HUITZILOPOCHTLI. The time lapse was said to have been caused by the gods having to rest after the great effort involved in the creation of the Earth.

Cirape NORTH AMERICA – GREAT PLAINS (Crow)

'Little Coyote', the brother of COYOTE, the TRICKSTER of the CROW people.

Cit Bolon Tum CENTRAL AMERICA (Maya)

The god of medicine and herbs. His name has been tentatively translated as 'Boar with Nine Tusks'. He was one of the two medicine gods of the MAYA people, the other being AHAU CHAMAHEZ.

Citalicue CENTRAL AMERICA – MEXICO (Aztec)

The Earth Mother who gave birth to all the earthly demi-gods who sprang from a stone knife she gave birth to. Her children asked her to let them create mankind to act as her servants. She agreed and told them to ask MICTLÁNTECUHTLI for a bone or some ashes of the dead to work with, though this must have referred to a bone or the ashes of a dead god if mankind had yet to be created.

XÓLOTL made the journey down to MICTLÁN and was given a bone, though some accounts say that he stole it and then fled. No matter how he came into possession of the bone, he dropped it on his way back to the Earth and it broke. Gathering up the pieces, making sure that he collected even the smallest fragment, Xólotl brought the remains up to the Earth where he placed them in a bowl and mixed them with gods' blood donated by his brothers. On the fourth day a man emerged from the bowl, and was followed four days later by a woman, the first people to walk on the Earth.

Citlalinicue CENTRAL AMERICA –
 MEXICO (*Aztec*)
The goddess of the MILKY WAY[2], an alternative name for OMECÍHUATL in which
case her husband is named as CITLALTO-
NAC rather than OMETECUHTLI. Under this
variant she is the patroness of the thirteenth hour of the twenty-two-hour long
AZTEC day, though ILAMATECUHTLI is
sometimes named in this role.

Citlatépetl CENTRAL AMERICA – MEXICO
 (*Aztec*)
The AZTEC name for the snow-capped
mountain of ORIZABA that is to be found a
short distance north of the city of Orizaba
to the southeast of Mexico City.

Citlaltonac CENTRAL AMERICA –
 MEXICO (*Aztec*)
Alternative name for OMETECUHTLI under
which his wife, normally called OMECÍ-
HUATL, is named as CITLALINICUE. Under
either variant, Citlaltonac or Ometecuhtli, this deity is one half of the omnipotent dual creator OMETÉOTL.

Citli CENTRAL AMERICA – MEXICO
 (*Aztec*)
'Hare'. Once Citli bet on which quarter of
the sky the Sun would appear in, but he
lost. So angry was he with the Sun that he
shot an arrow at it, but the Sun caught the
arrow and threw it back with such accuracy that it struck Citli on the forehead.

Ciuacóatl CENTRAL AMERICA – MEXICO
 (*Aztec*)
The chief of the sinister goddesses, those
deities who foretold of doom and despair,
or brought it about. Ciuacóatl had a benevolent aspect in which she was depicted
as dressed in white and the inventor of the
hoe and the tump line, the means of labour
for mankind. However, her face was painted half black and half red, and at night
she would run weeping and lamenting,

forecasting forthcoming wars or periods of
misery, such as famine. Her horrible appearance, enough to bring despair to mankind upon just a fleeting glimpse, was
somewhat alleviated by her feather head
dress, her golden earplugs and a turquoise
weaving stick she carried. It seems that she
may have been a female, darker aspect of
QUETZALCÓATL, a maleficent rather than a
benevolent serpent deity.

Cizin CENTRAL AMERICA (*Maya*)
Though the identity, attributes and characteristics of this deity remain a mystery, it
has been theorized that Cizin may be a
variant name for AH PUCH.

Clérmeil, Président HAITI (*Voodoo*)
A powerful LOA who is, unusually, a white
man. Like a true president, he is omnipotent. Also known as Monsieur DIFFICILE
CLÉRMEIL, he is said to make the rivers
break their banks when he is annoyed,
which he can become extremely easily.

Clérmézine HAITI (*Voodoo*)
One of the numerous LOA of the VOODOO
religion.

Closed Man NORTH AMERICA – GREAT
 PLAINS (*Skidi Pawnee*)
The first man who was instructed in the
use of the sacred bundles of the SKIDI
PAWNEE people by BRIGHT STAR who told
him that each bundle contained a particular species of corn depending on the geographical location of the relevant tribe.
The bundles of the southwestern-living
Skidi Pawnee contained white corn, the
northwestern yellow corn, the southeastern red corn and the northwestern black
corn. After Closed Man had died, his skull
was according to the instructions of TIR-
AWA that had been passed on by Bright
Star, placed on top of his sacred bundle. By
so doing, the Skidi Pawnee believe that his

spirit remained with them to act as a guide between mankind and the gods.

Coatepec CENTRAL AMERICA – MEXICO (*Aztec*)

'Serpent Mount', the home of the earth-goddess COATLICUE, her daughter, the Moon-goddess COYOLXAUHQUI, and her 400 star-god sons, the CENTZONHUITZ-NÁUA. The travellers out of AZTLAN stopped at the mountain during their journeying.

Coatl CENTRAL AMERICA – MEXICO (*Aztec*)

The fifth day of the twenty-day MONTH[1] employed by the AZTECS. The day symbolizes the snake, represents the east, and is presided over by the goddess CHAL-CHIUHTLICUE.

Coatlicue CENTRAL AMERICA – MEXICO (*Aztec*)

'Goddess of the Serpent Petticoat' or 'She of the Serpent Woven Skirt', Coatlicue was the mother of the Sun as well as being his wife and sister simultaneously. The suffix to her name, *cue*, means petticoat, and is an apt title to apply to such an omnipotent lady. The mother of the gods who is portrayed in some carvings and statues as the description of the cosmic process rather than as a female deity, Coatlicue is said by some to be one of the five Moon-goddesses of the AZTEC people, though others argue that she is rather a single deity with a five-fold aspect, symbolized as a quincunx, representing the four cardinal points with the goddess at the centre. However, Coatlicue is normally seen as the earth-goddess in whom the spirit and matter are fused, for her purpose is to solidify the spirit into the tangible Earth. Interestingly, her son QUETZAL-CÓATLs function was exactly the converse, and allowed matter to be redeemed in spirit.

Coatlicue is therefore considered not just as the mother of the gods, but also as the mother of mankind, for she made life possible, though she could not accomplish this task single-handedly, and needed the help of the Sun and some mysterious, un-named magicians. Until these magicians correctly guessed the mystery of her existence, she remained hidden in a cloud, alone and sterile. However, the magicians called upon the Sun who came to take Coatlicue as his bride, and so life began.

Coatlicue thus represents a merging of myth and reality, for Coatlicue is at once both mother and myth, and represents the rhythm of life merging into death. She is the guardian of the thirteen mythical heavens ruled over by HUITZILOPOCHTLI, the Sun; she demands the sacrifice necessary to maintain the gods and to uphold the cosmic order (she is connected with the horrific ceremonies associated with XIPE TOTEC); she is the mother of the heavenly twins Quetzalcóatl and XÓLOTL; she is the queen of OMEYOCAN, the palace in which the divine god-above-all resides; she is the Moon, the consort of the Sun; and she is the Earth. Coatlicue is the dynamic force behind the cosmos who gives life and maintains death in the desperate struggle to maintain true balance, a balance that is sometimes only achieved through war, and thus she ultimately has both benevolent and malevolent aspects, for she can give life, and she can take it away again. Thus she reigns supreme, for no other Aztec deity wielded such awesome power who, in simplistic terms, represents stability and endurance.

Coatlicue lived on COATEPEC (Mount Serpent or Snake Hill – a name that occurs as far south as Guatemala) with her daughter, the Moon-goddess COYOLXAUHQUI ('She Whose Face is Painted with Bells'), and her 400 star-god sons, the CENTZON-HUITZNÁUA. One day Coatlicue and her four sisters, who remain unnamed, thus fuelling the theory that Coatlicue has a five-fold aspect, were doing penance for some unrecorded reason on the slopes of Coatepec. There, Coatlicue, a virgin, gathered some white feathers and placed them in her bosom. One alternative version says that she swallowed the feathers, and others that she swallowed an emerald. Whatever the truth, Coatlicue found that she was pregnant.

At Coyolxauhqui's instigation, the Centzonhuitznáua planned to kill their disgraced mother. However, as they drew near to do the ghastly deed, Coatlicue gave birth to either Quetzalcóatl, if one is telling the early NAHUA version of the story, or Huitzilopochtli if one is dealing in later Aztec terms. The child was born fully armed with a blue shield and spear, his left leg being adorned with hummingbird feathers and his head with a plume of feathers. With a single blow of his serpent-torch XIUHOCÓATL, which he was also born with, Huitzilopochtli killed the treacherous Coyolxauhqui, and then set off in pursuit of the 400 Centzonhuitznáua, the majority of whom he also killed except for a few who managed to escape south to HUITZLAMPA, the 'Place of Thorns'.

Despite her omnipotent status, there are actually very few narratives built around the character of Coatlicue. Perhaps the Aztec people were too much in awe of her powers to risk offending her. However, one dramatized version of the magical conception and birth by Coatlicue does exist, in which the goddess is referred to as LA, perhaps in an attempt to hide the identity of the central player of the story from the wrath of the goddess herself. In this version she is a widow, and her 400 sons have long since left and are no more than a memory. One day a multicoloured feather appears, falling slowly from the sky. La places the feather in her bosom and then continues to sweep the heavens, which she did every day at twilight so that she might at least see her sons in the sky at night.

Having completed her chores, La sits down and remembers the feather but when she looks for it, she finds that it has disappeared. Saddened by her loss, she suddenly feels a slight movement within her, and, remembering how she felt when her 400 sons had been gestating, she realized that she was pregnant and all signs of her melancholy immediately lifted.

Her happiness is not to last for long, for her 400 sons learn of their mother's condition, and demand to know who the father is, adding that whoever he is, they want him dead. However, La cannot answer the demands and so the sons begin to plot her death. However, before they can come to kill their mother, the child is born – a boy who immediately declares himself to be Huitzilopochtli. He then sets out to kill the 400 who have plotted to kill their own mother. The actual number of sons need not be taken literally; indeed they are sometimes said to number 4,000, for this number is actually meant to represent the number of stars that the Sun extinguishes each morning.

In another version of the story the child in nine years old before he sets out to kill the murderous 400 who, at that time, inhabited the MILKY WAY[1] where they seethed with their hatred for the boys' father – the Sun itself, though Huitzilopochtli is also the Sun. This anomaly, however, exactly fits the cosmology. Stars and Sun kill each other alternatively as day follows night follows day, the Sun being said to be reborn as the son every morning and to die as the father every evening.

Huitzilopochtli, having defeated the murderous Centzonhuitznáua, later left his mother when the Aztec people journeyed away from their ancestral homeland of AZTLAN, taking with him four guardians. Many years later the Aztec ruler MONTEZUMA sent a number of ambassadors

back to Aztlan with a message for Coatlicue whom they encountered on Mount
Coatepec as a hideous hag whose appearance was caused by her mourning the loss
of her son.

coca SOUTH AMERICA – ANDES REGION
The dried leaves of a plant that has been
cultivated in the Andean valleys for an
extremely long time, and which is today
better known as cocaine. Chewed by the
Andean Indians, they found that it produced an euphoric state of indifference to
such things as hunger, fatigue and cold,
and has thus long been regarded as sacred
by these AMERINDIAN peoples. As well as
being used as a narcotic, the leaves were
burned as fumigants to exorcize demons,
and as ritual sacrifices to the spirits of the
dead, as well as to the earth-goddess PA-
CHAMAMA. The first coca bush is alleged to
have either grown from the body of a
murdered prostitute, or was alternatively a
gift from the gods to the people who had
been attacked by KHUNO. During the INCA
domination the use of coca was reserved
for the use of the nobility, but attempts to
curtail its more widespread dissemination
appear to have been fruitless.

Cocoa SOUTH AMERICA – PERU
  (*Quechua*)
One of the very few cat deities of South
America. This mythical creature was just
two feet long, extremely small to be a
deification, with a tail half as long again.
Entirely covered in stripes, an excellent
camouflage that meant it was not often
seen, the cocoa had a large head and
mournful eyes from which hail continuously rained to the ground.

Cochamarca SOUTH AMERICA (*Collao*)
The place where the rush boat carrying the
body of THUNAPA across Lake TITICACA
struck the shore with such force that it

formed the River DESAGUADERO. The legend would seem to indicate that the raft
struck the shore at present day Guaqui
which lies just south of the Chilean border,
though the river that enters Lake Titicaca
at that point is not the Desaguadero. The
legend further states that the river carried
the raft to the shore at ARICA. This is a
further anachronism as the River Desaguadero does not empty into the Pacific
Ocean, but rather flows into Lake POOPÓ.

Cochambamba SOUTH AMERICA – PERU
  AND BOLIVIA (*Quechua*)
City in Bolivia, midway between Santa
Cruz and LA PAZ, where an ALACITA, an
annual fair associated with the cult of
EKKEKKO, is held. Other such fairs are held
at La Paz and ORURO.

Cocijo CENTRAL AMERICA – MEXICO
  (*Zapotec*)
The ZAPOTEC name for TEZCATLIPOCA.

Codex (pl. Codices) CENTRAL AND
  SOUTH AMERICA
The generic name given to the fragmentary and extremely vague illustrated texts
relating to the ancient South and Central
American cultures, though these texts
were not compiled until after these em-
pires had fallen to the Spanish. They must
therefore be treated with a little scepti-
cism, as it was not unusual for the Spanish
to use legends that in some way tallied
with Spanish and Roman Catholic doctrines. They are, however, essential sources
of reference to the student of ancient
South and Central American culture, as
contemporary records were systematically
destroyed by the conquistadors.

Coeviacá SOUTH AMERICA – BRAZIL
  (*Xingú*)
A very tall man with extremely long hair
who was given the task of making fires

wherever he went by the gods, thus bringing that life-giving force among the people.

Cold NORTH AMERICA – SOUTHWEST (*Navajo*)

One of the four ANAYE to survive after some of the others had been destroyed by NAYANEZGANI and THOBADZISTSHINI, and the remainder by ESTANATLEHI who sent a terrible storm that not only wiped out all but four of the anaye, but also reshaped the Earth. The other three anaye who were allowed to survive only after they had convinced Estanatlehi that, if they died, mankind would no longer prize life, were OLD AGE, HUNGER and POVERTY.

Cold, House of CENTRAL AMERICA – MEXICO (*Aztec*)

One of the trials which the heavenly twins HUNAHPU and XBALANQUÉ were put through by the lords of XIBALBA. They survived the deathly cold of this test by lighting pine cones to keep them warm.

Colhuaca CENTRAL AMERICA

An ancient indigenous AMERINDIAN race mentioned in the AZTEC myths surrounding the journey undertaken by the Aztec people from their ancestral homeland of AZTLAN. Very little is known of these people, who may be mythical, but the Aztecs were said to have visited the cities of CHAPUTEPEC and TIZAPAN during their travels.

Colhuatzincátl CENTRAL AMERICA – MEXICO (*Aztec*)

'Winged-One', an important PULQUE-god, and thus one of the CENTZONTOTOCHTIN.

Collao SOUTH AMERICA

An ancient realm or province of the INCA empire that included the city of TIAHUA-NACO, though some authorities identify the Collao as a civilization that developed quite independently of the Incas, and only later became identified with that great culture through assimilation. Various stories collected by the Spaniards from these people in the sixteenth century show that, perhaps, Collao was a penal colony to which vanquished peoples were banished. Therefore, the stories collected by the Spaniards cannot be said, for certain, to be indicative of or accurately reflect the earlier beliefs of the region. When the Spaniards came to Collao and met the inhabitants of Tiahuanaco, they recorded that the people had no knowledge of that city's founders whom they simply regarded as mysterious giants. This lends further weight to the theory that Collao was an area in which the Inca deposited undesirables, or displaced conquered people.

One Collao story collected by the Spaniards says that the Earth was made by TUAPACA – the Collao name for the character more usually known as CON TICCI VIRACOCHA. Having made the Earth, Tuapaca returned to the island in the middle of Lake TITICACA from whence he had appeared, and disappeared leaving the Earth in darkness. Some time later Con Ticci Viracocha returned, this time coming from the south in the guise of a tall, bearded white man who changed hills into valleys, valleys into hills, and summoned water from the rocks as he passed. As he came, the Sun rose from the island in Lake Titicaca to which the man also came, and there created the Moon and the stars, the Sun also being credited as his invention. He then made stone effigies of people of all ages and from every walk of life to whom he gave names, and placed in Collao.

Then Tuapaca summoned his followers, the VIRACOCHA, and told them to study the stone figures carefully and remember all their names, for these were the exact likeness of the first people who would soon emerge from caves, fountains, rivers and

rocks. When he was satisfied that the viracocha had memorized the names and
faces of the effigies, he sent all but two of
them out to summon the people, and to
give them their names and positions in
life.

The Spaniards were greatly impressed
by the imagery conjured up by the stories
of Tuapaca, the white, bearded creator
and teacher whom they identified with
Saint Thomas the Apostle.

Columbus, Christopher

Anglicized variant of Cristóbal Colón
(1451–1506), the Italian navigator and
explorer who made four voyages to the
New World: 1492 to San Salvador Island,
Cuba and Haiti; 1493–96 to Guadeloupe,
Monserrat, Antigua, Puerto Rico and Jamaica; 1498 to Trinidad and the mainland
of South America; and 1502–04 to Honduras and Nicaragua.

Born in Genoa, Columbus went to sea
at an early age and settled in Portugal in
1478. There he sought patronage to prove
that Asia could be reached by sailing west-
ward, and eventually gained the support of
King Ferdinand and Queen Isabella of
Spain. On 3 August 1492 he sailed from
Palos with three small ships: the *Niña*, the
Pinta, and his flagship the *Santa María*. He
sighted land on 12 October 1492 (San
Salvador island), and had, within weeks,
reached Cuba and Haiti before returning
to Spain in March 1493. After his third
voyage in 1498 he became involved in a
quarrel with the colonists sent to Haiti and
was sent back to Spain in chains by the
governor in 1500. He was released and
compensated by the king, and made his
last voyage between 1502 and 1504 during
which he hoped to find a strait leading to
India. He died in abject poverty in Valla-
dolid and is buried in Seville cathedral.
The wreck of the *Santa María*, sunk off
Hispaniola on 25 December 1492, was
located in 1968.

Comanche NORTH AMERICA – GREAT PLAINS

Indigenous North American AMERINDIAN
people from the southern portion of the
GREAT PLAINS culture region, an area that
today would roughly correspond with the
state of Texas. They speak the SHOSHO-
NEan language.

Commentarios réales de los Incas SOUTH AMERICA

One of the most important of all the records of INCA culture, myth and history. It
was written by Garsilasco DE LA VEGA who
claimed to have been of royal Inca descent, though he was in truth born and
raised in Spain.

Con SOUTH AMERICA (*Quechua*)

A creator deity who was pure energy, for
the early myths say that the boneless Con
came from the north and declared that he
was a child of the Sun. His power appears
to have been immense, for he is recorded
as having been able to move mountains
purely by will.

Con, having shaped the landscape,
turned his attention to the creation of
people whom he gave all the necessities of
life. However, his creation soon aggra-
vated Con to such an extent that he transformed their fertile land into a wasteland
where no rain ever fell. Yet he did not
want to destroy mankind totally, so he left
them the rivers with which they could,
with great effort, irrigate the land and
return it to its former fertile state.

A short time later the true creator PA-
CHACAMAC[1], the son of the Sun and Moon,
came and expelled Con, transforming all
his people into monkeys which lived in the
canopy of the great forests Pachacamac
then created. Satisfied that the Earth was
once again a lush and fertile place, Pachacamac created a new race of people, the

people of today, and gave them all they needed to flourish. In return, the people worshipped Pachacamac as their god and built a temple to him near what is present-day Lima.

Con Ticci Viracocha SOUTH AMERICA (*Inca*)

The creator who was known as TUAPACA by the inhabitants of the INCA province of COLLAO. Two versions exist of the manner in which he created the Earth and people. In the first, Con Ticci Viracocha made the Earth which he took over by emerging from an island in the middle of Lake TITI-CACA. However, he departed leaving everything in darkness. A while later he returned and created the Sun, the Moon, and the stars, and brought with him his attendants who were known as the VIR-ACOCHA.

Con Ticci Viracocha then made a large number of stone effigies of people of all ages, and from all walks of life. He gave each a name, and then instructed his attendants to memorize the faces and names of these images, for he told them that the people would soon emerge on to the Earth, and they were to give them their names and their positions in life. Satisfied that the viracocha had learned all the names of the effigies, Con Ticci Viracocha sent them to summon the people from beneath the ground, and to give them their names, and set them in their rightful positions within the new society.

The second story of Con Ticci Viracocha says that mankind was already living on the Earth when he came in answer to their prayers for light, for the world remained in permanent darkness. As he approached from the south, transforming the landscape as he passed, the Sun rose from an island in Lake Titicaca. He then came to the people and gave them their laws and told them to live peaceably together.

Condorcoto, Mount SOUTH AMERICA (*Quechua*)

Mountain whose summit was not submerged during the FLOOD[9] that destroyed the world, and on whose slopes lay the golden eggs from which five men were born after the waters had receded, one of those men being PARIACACA.

Confrit HAITI (*Voodoo*)

A LOA whose name is possibly derived from the French *confrère* (brother).

Congo HAITI (*Voodoo*)

A handsome, but lethargic and slow-witted LOA who is said to have little power. He seems to be derived from a West African deity having the same name and attributes.

Coniraya (Viracocha) SOUTH AMERICA (*Quechua*)

The creator of all things and the inventor of agriculture. Coniraya came to the Earth in the guise of a beggar and fell in love with the immensely beautiful goddess CAVIL-LACA, whom he secretly impregnated by transforming his sperm into some fruit which the goddess unwittingly ate. A year after the child had been born, the goddess called together all the other gods and demanded to know who the father of her child was. Since no one admitted paternity, Cavillaca instructed the child to crawl to its father, which it did. When Cavillaca saw the dishevelled Coniraya, she snatched up the child and, totally humiliated by the thought that the father of her child was a beggar, fled to the coast where at PACHACAMAC[2] she transformed herself and her child into rocks.

Coniraya set out to search for them, and *en route* received help from a wide variety of creatures, though not all the help or news was good or useful. Those who gave him good news and useful advice, including the condor, the lion and the falcon, he blessed. Those who gave him bad news or useless advice, including the fox and parrot, he cursed. As he reached the coast, he met the daughters of the goddess URPI-HUACHAC, but his advances towards one of them were spurned. In retaliation, Coniraya emptied Urpi-huachac's fishpond into the sea which has thenceforth been copiously inhabited by sea fish.

Another story says that he gave HUAYNA-CAPAC a shining woman in a box. When the box was opened to release the woman, the world was filled with light.

It is entirely possible that CON was either another version of Coniraya, or an aspect of the god, though it is equally feasible that they were separate deities or culture heroes that have become assimilated with the god Pachacamac.

Cora CENTRAL AMERICA – MEXICO

Ancient NAHUA people who, along with the HUICHOL, inhabited the most westerly portion of Mexico. Regrettably, very little is today known about these people, or their ancient culture and beliefs. One of their most important deities was CHULAVETE, the personification of the MORNING STAR[1].

Cori Ocllo SOUTH AMERICA (Inca)

One of the four female CHILDREN OF THE SUN whose name only appears among the list proposed as the most 'plausible' for these ancestral deities by Fray Martin DE MONIA. In some of the legends this character is called MAMA OCLLO but in these stories there are just two Children of the Sun, Mama Ocllo and her brother MANCO CAPAC.

Cormorant NORTH AMERICA – NORTHWEST COAST (Tlingit)

Cormorant once went on a fishing trip with YETL, the RAVEN and BEAR. However, Yetl cut off some of Bear's flesh, thus killing him, and then tore out Cormorant's tongue so that he could not reveal the murder.

Corn Girl NORTH AMERICA – SOUTHWEST (Navajo)

Tutelary deity who was, along with TURQUOISE BOY, set on the southern sacred mountain of the NAVAJO, Mount TAYLOR, by ATSE ESTSAN and ATSE HASTIN towards the end of their creation of the Navajo land. See ASCENT OF THE NAVAJO.

Corn Maidens NORTH AMERICA – PUEBLO, SOUTHWEST (Hopi and Zuñi)

The most important deities of the PUEBLO-dwelling AMERINDIAN peoples who appear in most of their ritual ceremonies. They were said to have accompanied the first people on to the surface of the Earth; the ZUÑI and HOPI peoples telling much the same story of their arrival. That told here is the Zuñi version.

When the first people, the ASHIWI, came from the UNDERWORLD to live on the surface of the Earth they were followed by ten invisible Corn Maidens who accompanied them for four years, until at SHIPOLOLO, the 'Place of Mist and Cloud', they were discovered by the two witches who had been the very last people to emerge on to the Earth. These two witches recognized the importance of the Corn Maidens and gave them the seeds of maize and squash, the staple diet of the Pueblo Indians.

As the ashiwi continued on their way, the Corn Maidens remained at Shipololo where they lived in a cedar bower that was roofed with clouds. There they danced, each of the Corn Maidens holding the beautiful plumed Underworld plant, the THLAWE.

One day the twin gods KOWWITUMA and WATSUSII, sons of the Sun deity, came across the Corn Maidens, and were told to bring them to the people, which they did. There the Corn Maidens danced for the people in a courtyard decorated with corn-meal paintings of clouds. As they danced and night fell, the people gradually fell asleep, but the Corn Maidens danced on. Then the butterfly and flower god PAYATAMI came and saw them and was immediately smitten by their loveliness, especially that of their leader, YELLOW-CORN MAIDEN. However, as the Corn Maidens could read Payatami's thoughts, they became scared of him, and as dawn broke, when Payatami also fell asleep, they fled back to Shipololo where they hid themselves under the wings of a flock of ducks.

After the Corn Maidens had departed a great famine descended on the people who begged Kowwituma and Watsusii to search out the Corn Maidens. The ashiwi sat in their KIVA (temple) where they fasted and thought only of the Corn Maidens, and of the life-giving rain. Answering the prayers of the people, Kowwituma and Watsusii went to BITSITSI, their father's musician, who descended to Earth on a gossamer thread and telepathically conveyed the prayers of the ashiwi to the Corn Maidens, adding that if they returned, they would be under his protection, and he would ensure that they were treated honourably.

The Corn Maidens consented and were led back to the ashiwi by Bitsitsi. There they once more danced for the people, each Corn Maiden holding her thlawe, from dawn to dusk to the music of Payatami's flute and the singing of a choir. Yellow-Corn Maiden and BLUE-CORN MAIDEN, the older sisters, led the dance. When the dance was over, the Corn Maidens departed once more and the ashiwi

have never seen them again from that day to this.

Cortés, Hernándo
Spanish fortune hunter and conquistador (1485–1547) who travelled to the West Indies as a young man, and in 1518 secured command of an expedition to Mexico where he landed with just 600 men. He was at first welcomed as the returning incarnation of QUETZALCÓATL by the AZTEC emperor MONTEZUMA II. He was later to be expelled from TENOCHTITLAN following a revolt, but with the aid of Indian allies he recaptured the city in 1521 and then went on to overthrow the entire Aztec empire. His conquests finally included most of Mexico and northern Central America.

Cotzbalam CENTRAL AMERICA (*Maya*)
The name of one of the four massive birds, the others being XECOTCOVACH, CAMAZOTZ[1] and TECUMBALAM, that were sent by TEPEU and GUCUMATZ to attack the wooden bodies of the men they had carved. Each bird attacked a different part of the body and so destroyed the first attempt of the gods at creating mankind.

Council of Gods NORTH AMERICA –
PUEBLO, SOUTHWEST (*Zuñi*)
The assembly of deities that meets in KOTHLUWALAWA and has its earthly counterpart in the ASHIWANNI.

Coxcox CENTRAL AMERICA – MEXICO
(*Aztec*)
Mysterious deity who appears in some versions of the story of XOCHIQUETZAL as the god who survived the FLOOD[2] along with the goddess, though this god is sometimes named as TEOCIPACTLI. Coxcox and Xochiquetzal had many children, but they had no voices until a dove landed in a high tree and gave them each a voice, and a different language.

Coyolxauhqui CENTRAL AMERICA –
MEXICO (*Aztec*)
The Moon-goddess daughter of COATLI-
CUE and thus sister to the 400 CENTZON-
HUITZNÁUA. She lived with both her
mother and brothers on Mount COATEPEC.
When her mother became mysteriously
pregnant, Coyolxauhqui goaded her
brothers into attempting to murder their
disgraced parent. However, as the Centzonuitznáua came to do the ghastly deed,
Coatlicue gave birth to HUITZILOPOCHTLI
who killed Coyolxauhqui with a single
blow from his serpent torch, XIUHOCÓATL,
after which he set out after the treacherous brothers and killed most of them
too.

Coyote NORTH AMERICA – SOUTHWEST
(*Navajo*)
The TRICKSTER of the NAVAJO people. He
first came to the Navajo, in the company
of BADGER, during their long ascent from
the various worlds beneath ground that
they passed through before finally emerging on to the Earth (see ASCENT OF THE
NAVAJO). Coyote followed a man and a
woman down into the realm of the monster TIEHOLTSODI whose task was to rescue
two women whom the monster had dragged down into his realm. Coyote abducted
two of Tieholtsodi's children and made off
with them. When the monster discovered
that his offspring had been kidnapped, he
sent a great flood which forced the Navajo
to flee upwards to the next world, their
escape only coming after Badger had extended a small hole in the sky made by
LOCUST. However, the flood waters began
to surge out of the hole until the two
children of Tieholtsodi were thrown back
down through it, whereupon the waters
receded. The new people had arrived on
Earth on an island in the midst of a lake.
They threw a hide scraper on to the water
to determine their fate. It floated, which
meant they would have immortality, until

Coyote threw a rock into the water and
made it sink. This infuriated the people as
it now meant that their lives would be
finite, and they turned on Coyote who
hurriedly explained that it was better for
people's lives to come to an end, otherwise
they would no longer prize the good things
of life, or even life itself.

The characterization of the Coyote as
the Trickster is not solely confined to the
Navajo people, but their story is perhaps
the clearest illustration of the behaviour of
this character and his continual attempts
to thwart the good things of life, though, as
in the case of SEDIT, things do not always
work out exactly as planned.

Cozcaquauhtli CENTRAL AMERICA –
MEXICO (*Aztec*)
The name given to the sixteenth day of the
twenty-day MONTH[1] employed by the
AZTEC people. The day symbolized the
eagle, represented the west, and was presided over by ITZPAPÁLOTL, the obsidian
butterfly.

Cozumel CENTRAL AMERICA –
YUCATÁN, MEXICO
Island off the east coast of the Yucatán
peninsula that was the site of a shrine to
AHULANE, a symbolic war-god of the MAYA
people.

Creation
1 NORTH AMERICA – CALIFORNIA
  (*Achowami*)
  This Californian AMERINDIAN tribe say
  that the creator, who remains nameless,
  originally came from a cloud and was
  accompanied by his assistant, usually
  personified as a COYOTE, who came from
  a land of eternal mist.
2 NORTH AMERICA (*Omaha*)
  In the beginning all things existed solely
  in the mind of WAKONDA, the GREAT
  SPIRIT. From his thoughts, Wakonda

brought forward man and all other creatures as disembodied spirits who wandered through space in their search for somewhere they might be able to take bodily form. Having visited both the Moon and the Sun, both of which they considered wholly unsuitable, they next came to the Earth but, as of yet, there was no land, as the Earth was entirely covered in water.

Wakonda saw their distress and caused a great rock to erupt to the surface of the water, whereupon it burst into flames. The waters around it steamed and dried up and exposed the land on which grass and trees quickly sprouted. The spirits, giving thanks to Wakonda, descended on to the newly formed landscape and took their present human and animal forms.

3 NORTH AMERICA (*Inuit*)
Long, long ago the Earth fell out of the skies. Babies were then born from the Earth and remained among the willow trees until they were found by a man and a woman. She made clothes for them and he stamped on the ground which brought forth the dogs upon which humans rely.

These first people were immortal, but they lived in perpetual darkness, for there was neither Sun nor Moon. Two women sat and discussed this situation, one deciding darkness was a small price to pay for immortality. The other, however, decided that mortality would likewise be a small price to pay for light.

The Sun and Moon had already been created as brother and sister, but in the darkness neither knew the other, so they lay together. However, they then lit torches so that they could see each other. When the girl realized that she had been sleeping with her brother, she tore off her breasts which she threw at her brother. She then ran away, taking her torch with her, and was pursued by her brother right up into the sky. As the girl ran, her torch flared brighter and brighter, but her brother's died down until it was no more than a mere spark. Thus she became the INU of the Sun, and he the inu of the Moon.

The people rejoiced as the world could at last be seen. One day a group of hunters and their dogs chased a bear far out on to the ice floes. The bear rose into the sky to escape certain death, but the hunters pursued unfalteringly, and can yet been in the night sky as the PLEIADES[1] chasing the GREAT BEAR. A similar story accounts for the formation of the constellation Orion. The planet VENUS[3], seen low in the Western sky as spring approaches, is said to be the spirit of an old man who was chased into the air by the parents of some children he had imprisoned after they had disturbed him when he was hunting seals.

4 CENTRAL AMERICA (*Maya*)
The first thing to be created was the MONTH[2] who then created the day, and then the heavens and the Earth in the form of a ladder – water first, then earth, then rocks and then trees – after which he created all things on Earth and in the sea. In ONE CHEUN he created infinity and the heavens and the Earth. In TWO EB he formed the first ladder so that god could descend into the midst of the sky and the sea, and return to heaven once more. In THREE BEN he made the whole diversity of creation – things in the heavens, in the sea, and on the Earth. In FOUR IX heaven and Earth were complete and embraced each other. In FIVE MEN things were given life. In SIX CIB the first candle was made, as at this time there was neither Sun nor Moon, and so light was brought to the creation. In SEVEN C'HABAN the Earth itself was born. In EIGHT EDZNAB the first people

were created. In NINE CAUAC the first attempt was made to create a hell. In TEN AHAU the first sinners were sent to hell as God the Word had yet to appear, and men did not know the difference between right and wrong. In ELEVEN IMIX stones and trees were made. In TWELVE IK wind blew for the first time, the wind thenceforth being known as IK (spirit), for he alone on earth is immortal. In THIRTEEN AKBAL the first true men as they are still known were modelled out of clay.

In ONE KAN his spirit was sickened by the evil things he had created. In TWO CHICCHAN evil made its presence known to man. In THREE CIMI death was created. In FOUR MAN-IK the spirit of man for the first time passed over from Earth to heaven. In FIVE LAMAT the great sea lake was created. In SIX MULUC all the valleys were brought to life, and the creation was completed. On the last day Month rested and surveyed all he had done. Thus the world was created in the twenty days of the MAYA month.

A direct parallel to this complex Creation myth may be drawn with the Maya spiritual pilgrimage – the AGES OF MAN.

5 CENTRAL AMERICA – GUATEMALA (Maya)

The famous Guatemalan POPUL VUH gives a very clear interpretation of the Guatemalan MAYA concept of the Creation. In the beginning – a phrase used almost universally in Creation stories – the sky and the sea lay in the silent dark. The creator TEPEU and the maker GUCU-MATZ consulted with HURAKAN, and they decided that the time had come for the sea to withdraw and the Earth to appear so that they might create mankind, with the sole purpose that they should glorify and honour the gods. The waters withdrew on the command of the gods and the Earth formed like a cloud, and the mountains rose up covered with pine and cypress trees. Gucumatz was understandably happy.

Next Gucumatz and Tepeu created the animals and gave them their homes, but Tepeu was not wholly satisfied for these animals had no language and could not worship the gods. Thus they made men from damp soil, but these proved just as unsatisfactory for, although they had speech, they were blind and lame. Gucumatz and Tepeu washed them away. Now they sought the advice of Twice Grandmother, XPIYACOC, Twice Grandfather, XMU-CANÉ, Hurakan and the Sun. They divined with maize kernels and the red berries of the TZITÉ plant, the result of which was that they decided to carve their next men from wood. However, these both lacked intelligence and, more importantly, failed to honour their creators, of whom they apparently remembered nothing. So the gods sent four great birds – XECOTCOVACH, CAMA-ZOTZ[1], COTZBALAM and TECUMBALAM – to attack them, each targeting a different part of the wooden men. These men had more than just the huge birds to contend with, for they had been cruel and heartless masters, and all their animals and even their utensils turned against them. When they tried to shelter under the trees, the trees drew away from them, and when they tried to hide in the caves, the caves closed their entrances. So the wooden men and all their descendants were destroyed except for the monkeys.

There is a gap in the text at this point, but it appears that during the next stage of the Creation the Earth was inhabited by the giant VUKUB CAKIX and his equally monstrous sons, all of whom were defeated by the twin deities, HUNAHPU and XBALANQUÉ.

Now the gods came together again, frustrated by their many failures, and discussed how they might people the Earth. It was decided that they should use the yellow and white maize that grew in the PLACE OF THE DIVISION OF WATERS. They gathered the maize which they ground into a flour. This flour was mixed with nine broths brewed by Xmucané. Thus were formed the four brothers, BALAM AGAB ('Night Jaguar'), BALAM QUITZÉ ('Smiling Jaguar'), IQI BALAM ('Moon Jaguar') and MAHUCUTAH ('Renowned Name').

This time the gods found that they had done their work too perfectly, for these four men were so highly intellectual that they threatened to rival their creators. Hurakan, to rectify this regrettable situation, breathed over the men which clouded their vision and reduced their levels of reasoning to more mortal levels. Then the brothers were placed in an enchanted sleep while the gods created four women to be their wives, though the names of the women are not recorded.

For a while everything was fine, the people lived happily and peaceably together, and prayed to their creators, asking them to bless them with children and to provide them with light, for the Sun had yet to be created. Although their prayers for children were answered, their pleas for light seemed to go unanswered and the people began to grow anxious. The four brothers therefore decided to set out to find the Sun and left their home in TOLLAN to travel to TULAI ZUIVA, the PLACE OF SEVEN CAVES AND SEVEN RAVINES. There the gods gave each brother a tutelary deity to preside over their respective clans. Balam Quitzé was given TOHIL; Balam Agab received AVILIX; Iqi Balam – NICAHTAGAH; and Mahucutah – HACAVITZ.

Tohil gave the brothers the gift of fire which he rekindled after it had been extinguished by the rain by striking his shoes together. Now the brothers were warm and had light to see by, this light soon attracted other peoples who asked to be given some of the life-giving fire. The brothers repulsed them, but Tohil told them that they could have some of the fire provided they honoured him 'under the armpit and under the girdle', a phrase that has been taken to mean that he demanded human sacrifices in return for the fire.

Even though the people were now warmer, and had light to see by, they still lived in perpetual darkness, even though they fasted and kept a constant vigil for the herald of the Sun, the MORNING STAR[3]. As the Sun still did not appear, the four brothers decided that they must resume their travels otherwise they might never witness the birth of the Sun.

Having journeyed through many lands they finally came to Hacavitz's home mountain. There they sacrificed and burned incense. Having completed their rituals, they saw the Morning Star rise, followed a short while later by the birth of the Sun itself. Prostrating themselves on the ground the four brothers gave thanks to the gods for their ultimate gift. As the Sun grew in strength, it dried out the damp Earth and turned the old animal gods – lion, tiger and viper, as well as the gods Avilix, Tohil and Hacavitz – to stone with its rays.

With the creation complete, the four brothers realized that their time on Earth was nearing an end. Thus, taking leave of their wives, the four brothers set off to return to Tollan to take the gift of the Sun with them. When they departed, never to be seen again, they left behind them the sacred bundle MAJESTY CREE

ENVELOPED which they instructed must never be opened.

This wonderfully recorded story of the Creation clearly shows that the gods were not entirely infallible, and that the ultimate completion of their work depended on men themselves, and the respect these men, their creations, gave to their makers.

Cree NORTH AMERICA
An indigenous AMERINDIAN people whose language belongs to the ALGONQUIAN family. The Cree people are distributed over a vast area in Canada from Québec to Alberta, but the majority of those in the USA today live in the Rocky Boys reservation in Montana.

Creek NORTH AMERICA – WOODLANDS
Indigenous North American AMERINDIAN people from the southern WOODLANDS culture region who are, perhaps, more correctly known as the MUSKHOGEE, for that is the language they spoke. As they are, however, more widely known as the Creek people than the Muskhogee, the former term is used throughout this book.

Crocodile People, The SOUTH AMERICA – ORINOCO REGION (*Carib*)
The name by which the CARIB refer to themselves, for they believe that, during the Creation, ADAHELI, the Sun, concerned that the Earth had no human beings on its surface, descended from the sky. Soon afterwards the first people were born of the Cayman (a type of alligator). All the women were beautiful, but some of the men were so ugly that their fellow humans found them intolerable and forced them to leave. So they separated, the ugly folk and their wives, going to the east, while the rest went to the west.

Crow
1 NORTH AMERICA – NORTHEAST COAST
An alternative to the more usual RAVEN as the TRICKSTER.
2 NORTH AMERICA – GREAT PLAINS
Indigenous North American AMERINDIAN people, one of the SIOUX tribes, who inhabited the mid-GREAT PLAINS culture region, their closest neighbours, also Sioux-speaking tribes, being the ASSINABOIN, DAKOTA, MANDAN, OMAHA, OSAGE and WINNEBAGO, along with the CADDO-speaking ARIKA, Caddo and PAWNEE.

Cuchumaqiq CENTRAL AMERICA – MEXICO (*Aztec*)
One of the thirteen lords of XIBALBA. His co-rulers are named as AHALCANA, AHAL-PUH, CHAMIABAK, CHAMIAHOLOM, HUN CAME, PATAN, QUIQRE, QUIQRIXGAG, QUIQ-XIL, VUKUB CAME and XIQIRIPAT. Some sources, however, say that Xibalba was ruled by Hun Came and Vukub Came, and that all the other lords were subordinate to them.

Cuero SOUTH AMERICA
An unpleasant mythical sea-monster, a giant octopus having claws at the end of its tentacles and huge ears that are covered with eyes that can be made either large or small at will (cf. HIDE, IMAP IMASSOUR-SUA).

Culhuacan CENTRAL AMERICA – MEXICO (*Aztec*)
The name of the sea-girt mountain near which TLACAELEL described the ancestral homeland of the AZTEC people, AZTLAN, as lying. It is possible that the name is a derivation of COLHUACA, an ancient race mentioned in the Aztec myths concerning the return of the Aztec people to their ancestral homeland.

76

Cumhau CENTRAL AMERICA (*Maya*)
A name that is sometimes used to refer to
the god of death AH PUCH.

Cuni-Cuni, Lake SOUTH AMERICA –
PARAGUAY (*Guaraní*)
Lake that was said to be the location of the
island of PAITITI, the land of gold that was
ruled over by EL GRAN MOXO and was
guarded by TEYÚ-YAGUÁ, the jaguar-
lizard.

Cusco Huanca SOUTH AMERICA (*Inca*)
One of the male CHILDREN OF THE SUN
according to the texts of Fray Martin DE
MONIA. Cusco Huanca became the first
INCA king of the city of ACAMAMA which
he renamed CUZCO. He was succeeded by
his brother MANCO CAPAC.

Cuzco SOUTH AMERICA – PERU
City in southern Peru, the capital of Cuzco
department, in the Andes that lies over
11,000 feet above sea-level, and some 350
miles southeast of Lima. The city was
founded in the eleventh century as the
ancient capital of the INCA empire, the
Incas now being thought to have settled in
Cuzco valley *c.* 1250, though at first they
encountered considerable resistance from
the neighbouring peoples. In the middle of
the fifteenth century they were all but
vanquished by the CHANCA confederation
of these peoples. The city was captured by
PIZZARO in 1533. According to the legends
of the CHILDREN OF THE SUN, as recorded by
both Fray Martin DE MONIA and Pedro DE
CIEZA DE LÉON, the city was founded by the
Children of the Sun who were told by the
spirit of AYAR CACHI to build in this place.
It is mentioned as being just north of the
penultimate resting place of MANCO CAPAC
and MAMA OCLLO, a village called PACCAR-
ITAMBO, the 'Inn of Dawn'. It is also just to
the north of the hill or mountain of HUA-
NACAURI. De Monia says that the city was
originally called ACAMAMA, which they occupied with no opposition, its name being
changed by CUSCO HUANCA, the first Inca
king who was later succeeded by his
brother Manco Capac. The city became
known as the City of the SUN and so many
came to live there that the city had to be
divided into two distinct regions, the
upper part being named HANAN CUZCO and
the lower HURIN CUZCO. There are many
Inca remains to be seen on the site, and
during the 1970s and 1980s the Inca irrigation canals and terracing near to the city
were restored to increase the fertility of the
surrounding area.

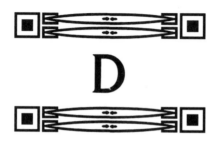

D

D CENTRAL AMERICA (*Maya*)
Yet another of the deities whose true identity, thanks to the ambiguous nature of the various CODEX, is simply referred to as the god D. The god of the Moon and of night, he is depicted as a Roman-nosed ancient man who has no teeth except for one in the lower jaw. His day is AHAU, the day on which evil men are condemned to eternal purgatory in hell, though, contradictorily, he is never shown with any of the traditional symbols of death. Instead he sometimes wears the conch shell on his head, this shell being the symbol of birth and one of the signs for life itself. Some authorities identify him with KUKULCÁN, while others with ITZAMNÁ. It has been suggested that he is the representation of the perpetual cycle of life, death and rebirth.

Dabiaba SOUTH AND CENTRAL AMERICA – PANAMA–COLOMBIA BORDER
A river or water-goddess who was the mother of the creator, according to the sixteenth-century writer Peter MARTYR ANGLERIUS.

Dabieciba SOUTH AMERICA – COLOMBIA (*Antioquia*)
The mother-goddess who was recorded in sixteenth-century texts as being associated with the creator ABIRÁ, and opposed by the evil CHANICUBÁ.

Daganoweda NORTH AMERICA– WOODLANDS (*Iroquois*)
A variant name for HAIOWATHA.

Dagué (~ -Amminan, ~ Cala Michaud) HAITI (*Voodoo*)
Variant(s) of AGOUÉ OYO.

Dagué-Lissa HAITI (*Voodoo*)
A LOA derived from the West African god Lisa of the Fon people, Lisa being the male primeval twin who married his sister and then taught mankind all the arts of civilization.

Dahomain HAITI (*Voodoo*)
A LOA whose name is derived from the West African country and people of Dahomey.

Dakota NORTH AMERICA – GREAT PLAINS
Indigenous North American AMERINDIAN people inhabiting the central portion of the GREAT PLAINS culture region. A SIOUX-speaking people, the Dakota were neighbours to the ASSINABOIN, CROW, MANDAN, OMAHA, OSAGE and WINNEBAGO tribes, all of which spoke the Sioux language, along with the CADDO-speaking ARIKA, Caddo and PAWNEE.

Damballa(h) (Wedó) HAITI (*Voodoo*)
Sometimes called AGAOU WEDÓ, this LOA has his origins in the West African divine python or Rainbow Snake Dan Ayido Hwedo. The VOODOO cultists identify him with Saint Patrick, in whose likeness he is usually portrayed. One of the most powerful of all the loa, Damballa governs snakes and floods, and can either afflict people

with the most serious diseases, or cure them.

Dan Houéza HAITI (*Voodoo*)
A variant of DAMBALLA.

Dan Yi HAITI (*Voodoo*)
Simply named as a LOA, one of the many to be found in VOODOO cults.

Dangbe HAITI (*Voodoo*)
One of the numerous LOA of the VOODOO religion.

Danger HAITI (*Voodoo*)
Thought by some to be cognate with DANGBE, possibly solely due to the similarity of their names. This LOA lives up to his name for if annoyed he can be the most dangerous adversary.

Danger Mina HAITI (*Voodoo*)
One of the LOA of the VOODOO religion. He is said to have his origins in the West African Mina tribe.

Dawn NORTH AMERICA – WOODLANDS (*Iroquois*)
Goddess of daybreak who caught the hunter SOSONDOWAH after he had chased the spirit SKY-ELK up into the highest heaven which lay way beyond the Sun itself. Dawn made Sosondowah her watchman, from which position he looked down on Earth and fell in love with the beautiful GLENDENWITHA whom he abducted in the form of a hawk. Dawn, however, found out about Sosondowah's trips to the Earth and angrily tied him to her door-posts and transformed Glendenwitha into a star which she then placed in Sosondowah's forehead, forever beyond his reach.

de Cieza de Léon, Pedro
Spanish historian and writer who recorded one version of the story of the CHILDREN OF THE SUN which he said was told to him by the INCA nobility.

De Hi No NORTH AMERICA – WOODLANDS (*Huron*)
An alternative name for the thunder-god HENG.

de la Vega, Garsilasco (Inca)
An important Spanish writer and historian (*c.*1540–1616) who was born in CUZCO, the son of one of the conquerors of Peru and an INCA princess. At the age of twenty he travelled to Spain where he spent the rest of his life. His account of the conquest of Florida by Fernando de Soto (1605) was followed in 1609 by his great COMMENTARIOS RÉALES DE LOS INCAS, a text that remains one of the single most important sources of Inca tradition, ritual and religion, and in which he movingly describes the legends and beliefs of his mother's people.

de Landa, Diego CENTRAL AMERICA – YUCATÁN, MEXICO
The first Spanish bishop of Yucatán, Mexico, and one of the most enthusiastic destroyers of the heathen texts of the MAYA peoples whose actions have, almost single-handedly made the study of early Maya tradition, religion and ritual very difficult, to say the least. He was, however, extremely interested in the Maya system of hieroglyphics and asked their scholars to explain them to him. It is the information that he collected directly from the Maya that today forms the basis of almost all the keys to unravelling the mysteries of the Maya culture.

de Monia, Fray Martin
Important Spanish monk who recorded and reported on the INCA religion, rites, and customs. He is one of the main sources for the legends of the CHILDREN OF THE SUN, about whom he had heard various

79

stories. As a result he puts forward eight members of this divine family; these members, which he felt were the most 'plausible', being named in his writings as the brothers CUSCO HUANCA, HUANA CAURI, MANCO CAPAC and TOPA AYAR CACHI, and the sisters CORI OCLLO, IPA HUACO, MAMA COYA and TOPA HUACO.

Deer NORTH AMERICA – NORTHWEST
COAST (*Tlingit*)
The first animal to be trapped and eaten, Deer was caught in a pitfall by YETL who, by so doing, introduced the hunting and eating of meat to mankind.

Dekanawida NORTH AMERICA –
WOODLANDS (*Oneida*)
Chief who became a staunch ally of HAIO-WATHA and with him converted the MO-HAWK and CAYUGA peoples to Haiowatha's confederacy plan. When the confederacy, known as the LEAGUE OF THE LONG HOUSE was finally established, after ATOTARHO had altered his stance and joined, Dekana-wida became the confederacy's law-giver.

Delaware NORTH AMERICA –
WOODLANDS
Indigenous and largely peaceable North American AMERINDIAN people who inhabited a portion of the WOODLANDS culture region to the east of the Appalachian Mountains. They spoke one branch of the ALGONQUIAN family of languages, which linguistically links them with the likes of the CHIPPEWA, CREE, MENOMINEE, MON-TAGNAIS and POTAWATOMI peoples.

Delge(e)th NORTH AMERICA –
SOUTHWEST (*Navajo*)
The flesh-eating antelope, one of the ANAYE born to women, usually virgins, who had engaged in evil practices during the ASCENT OF THE NAVAJO when the men and the women lived apart for a short while.

Dent Friand HAITI (*Voodoo*)
One of the many LOA of the VOODOO religion.

deohako NORTH AMERICA –
WOODLANDS (*Iroquois*)
Generic name given to the spirits of plants, especially those that were essential to the survival of the IROQUOIS people, namely beans, maize and squash.

Desaguadero, River SOUTH AMERICA
(*Collao*)
The river created when the rush boat carrying the body of THUNAPA across the waters of Lake TITICACA struck the shore at COCHAMARCA. The river carried the body to the coast at ARICA where it joined the sea. The legend is an anachronism as the river does not empty into the Pacific Ocean, but is land-locked and empties into Lake POOPÓ.

Desportes, Monsieur HAITI (*Voodoo*)
Simply named as one of the LOA of the VOODOO religion.

Dévis Pas Pressé HAITI (*Voodoo*)
One of the untold LOA of the VOODOO religion.

Diable Tonnère HAITI (*Voodoo*)
'Thunder Devil', a powerful LOA.

diablesse HAITI (*Voodoo*)
Name given to the fiendish spirit of a woman who has died as a virgin. Dia-blesses are compelled to purge this 'sin' by inhabiting the woods for many years until God feels that he is able to admit them to heaven.

Diegueño CENTRAL AMERICA – MEXICO
Indigenous Central-American AMERIN-DIAN people who are linguistically and culturally similar to their neighbours, the MOJAVE.

Diejuste, Monsieur HAITI (*Voodoo*)
A benevolent LOA.

Difficile Clérmeil HAITI (*Voodoo*)
A variant of Président CLÉRMEIL.

Diji HAITI (*Voodoo*)
This being, who no longer survives as a separate LOA within the VOODOO religion, is thought to have been combined with ALAWE to form Maîtresse LALOUÉ-DIJI.

Dismiraye HAITI (*Voodoo*)
One of the LOA of the VOODOO religion.

Djeneta NORTH AMERICA –
  WOODLANDS (*Chippewa*)
A mythical giant about whom nothing is now known.

Dohkwibuhch NORTH AMERICA –
  NORTHWEST COAST (*Shohomish*)
The creator TRICKSTER of these people.

Dokibatl NORTH AMERICA –
  SOUTHWEST COAST (*Chinook*)
The TRICKSTER who was responsible for causing the flood.

Don Pedro HAITI (*Voodoo*)
Unidentified and possibly historical person who was said to have introduced the easily annoyed PETRA LOA – named after him – to the VOODOO religion from San Domingo.

Doquebuth NORTH AMERICA – WEST
  COAST (*Skagit*)
The second creator of the world, the son of the only two survivors of the FLOOD[6] who rode out the deluge in a dugout canoe into which they had loaded two of everything on Earth, an aspect that was probably added after the SKAGIT came into contact with Christians. Doquebuth was a SHAMAN who was told, in a trance, how to recreate the Earth and repopulate it.

Dosu-Dosua HAITI (*Voodoo*)
A LOA.

Dreamers, The NORTH AMERICA –
  OREGON
An historical cult that was led by SMOHALA (born c.1820) and which was based on a mixture of Roman Catholicism and AMERINDIAN beliefs. In c.1860 he was challenged by a rival SHAMAN called MOSES who left him for dead beside a river. Smohala was carried downstream on the flood waters and was rescued by a white farmer. He then wandered extensively through the Southeast and into Mexico before he returned to Oregon. There he claimed to have actually drowned in the river, his spirit conversing with the GREAT SPIRIT who had rebuked him for abandoning the 'old ways' in favour of the white man's religion. His 'miraculous' return convinced many people that Smohala had been chosen by the Great Spirit to be his spokesman, and since the Indians had owned the Earth long before white men appeared, and had a responsibility to take it back again, that Smohala was speaking the words of the Great Spirit. The cult, which at one stage had a very large following, proved a major obstacle to government policy, and took its name from the trance-like state the shamans entered when they conversed with and sought the advice of the gods.

Dresden Codex CENTRAL AMERICA
  (*Maya*)
One of the three remaining contemporary CODEX that regrettably reveal little about the MAYA culture as they are incredibly ambiguous in nature. This *Codex* is so called as it is today housed in Dresden, Germany.

Dsilnaotil NORTH AMERICA –
SOUTHWEST (*Navajo*)
Unidentified location near where the
twins NAYANEZGANI and THOBADZISTSHINI
saw smoke rising from the ground, smoke
that led them to the underground home of
SPIDER-WOMAN.

Ducá SOUTH AMERICA – BRAZIL (*Xingú*)
A mythical animal, a sort of jaguar or
puma, that was said to have been the
father of the hero SINAA.

Dumballah HAITI (*Voodoo*)
A variant of DAMBALLA.

Dzarilaw NORTH AMERICA –
NORTHWEST COAST (*Haida*)
The son of the Bear Chief who married
RHPISUNT, a human girl who bore him two
sons. However, Rhpisunt's brothers were
outraged when they learned of her marriage and set out to kill Dzarilaw, and as
they approached, Dzarilaw taught his wife
his sacred bear song which he completed
moments before he was killed.

Dzerlarhons NORTH AMERICA –
NORTHWEST COAST (*Haida*)
The goddess of the volcano who is some-
times also called the goddess of frogs.

Dzhe Manito NORTH AMERICA –
WOODLANDS (*Chippewa*)
The Good Spirit, the brother of the GREAT
SPIRIT, KITSHI MANITOU, and second in im-
portance to him. His manservant is named
as MINABOZHO.

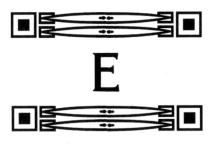

E

E CENTRAL AMERICA (*Maya*)
A maize-god who is simply identified as the
letter E in the various CODEX. He is possibly to be identified with YUM CAAX.

Earth Monster CENTRAL AMERICA –
MEXICO (*Nahua*)
The primeval female principle of Creation,
a monster with numerous mouths, who, in
a NAHUA creation myth, swam in the vast
primeval ocean devouring anything and
everything in her path. At about this time
the gods QUETZALCÓATL and TEZCATLI-
POCA decided that the time was right for
the Earth to be created. Seeing the Earth
Monster in the ocean, the gods turned
themselves into huge serpents and caught
the Earth Monster, one serpent taking
hold of her right hand and left foot, and
the other her left hand and right foot. The
three of them fought long and hard until
the Earth Monster was torn in two, her
lower half rising to form the heavens, and
her upper half becoming the Earth.

The Earth Monster thus became the
fecundity of life itself. Her hair became the
long grass, trees, flowers and crops; her
eyes became little caverns, fountains and
wells; her mouths formed great caves in
which men could shelter; and her many
noses formed the hills and valleys between
them. The Nahua acknowledged that all
matter returns to the Earth that sustains
man during his lifetime, but that the Earth
also has a voracious appetite. Sometimes
she weeps at night when she longs to taste

human hearts. She refuses to stay quiet
unless she is fed, and will not bear fruit
unless her skin is sprinkled with blood.
Thus the provider of life must have life
returned to her by sacrifice, a simple fact
later hideously distorted by the AZTEC
peoples who used this as a pretext to sacrifice their enemies and tear out their
hearts.

Earth Mother
A familiar concept among almost every
AMERINDIAN people, whether from the
north, the south, or in the centre. She is
the very essence of life itself. The Amerindians live on her body and feast from the
many varied fruits and crops she puts
forth. When they die, they are united with
her, though the soul of the buried person
does not always form unity with the Earth
Mother, but rather transcends the realms
of mortal man and becomes at one with
the gods in the heavens above.

Eb CENTRAL AMERICA (*Maya*)
The twelfth day of the MAYA spiritual pilgrimage that is known as the AGES OF MAN.
On this day, having died and suffered the
utmost agony, the spirit finally begins the
long ascent of the ladder that leads to
heaven. Eb in this context is not to be
confused with TWO EB, the day during the
Maya CREATION[4] when MONTH created the
ladder so that the gods could descend from
heaven to Earth, and vice versa.

Ecantonatiuh CENTRAL AMERICA –
MEXICO (*Aztec*)
The name given to the age of the FOURTH
SUN in the *Annals of Quahititlan*. This age
was destroyed by wind, while our own age
will be destroyed by earthquakes, and
man's own doing – famine, war and confusion.

Ed CENTRAL AMERICA – MEXICO (*Maya*)
One of the Four BACAB, or Four BALAM, Ed
was coloured black and was the representation and guardian of the west in
which guise he would take the form of a
jaguar.

Edznab CENTRAL AMERICA (*Maya*)
The eighteenth day of the MAYA spiritual
pilgrimage, the AGES OF MAN, on which the
spirit is finally made perfect. Edznab is not
to be confused with EIGHT EDZNAB, the
eighth day of the Maya CREATION[4].

Ehécatl CENTRAL AMERICA – MEXICO
(*Aztec*)
The wind-god, among other aspects, who
is a manifestation of the great QUETZAL-
CÓATL. In this form he appears in the
CODEX where he is depicted as breathing
life into the god of death, MICTLÁNTE-
CUHTLI.

Ehécatl brought the power of love to
mankind when he himself became besot-
ted with the maiden MAYAHUAL. He found
the maiden in the company of many others, all asleep, in the charge of an ancient
guardian named TZIZIMITL who was also
asleep. Ehécatl woke Mayahual who
agreed to go with him. Their love was
manifested in a beautiful tree that grew on
the spot where they confirmed and consummated their passion for each other on
the Earth. This great tree had two branches. One was known as the PRECIOUS
WILLOW and belonged to Ehécatl. The

other branch – the one that was covered in
flowers – belonged to Mayahual.

In the meantime Tzizimitl had woken
up and discovered that Mayahual was no
longer where she should have been. Furiously she gathered together an army of
young gods and set off in search of her
wayward ward. On Earth they soon came
to the tree in whose flowering branch Tzizimitl recognized the characteristics of
Mayahual. Realizing that the maiden had
been seduced, Tzizimitl broke the flowers
from the branch and gave them to the gods
accompanying her who immediately ate
them. Then she and her henchmen returned to the heavens.

After they had gone, Ehécatl resumed
his proper shape and changed the other
branch back into the now-dead Mayahual
whom he buried in a field. There her body
brought forth a magical plant that provided man with an intoxicating drink
which would induce in mankind the same
feeling that Ehécatl had felt when he held
Mayahual.

Eight Deer CENTRAL AMERICA – MEXICO
(*Mixtec*)
Lord of TILANTONGO, the spiritual brother
of NINE OLLIN who presided at the palace of
the plumed serpent where he sat on an
ocelot-skin cushion. Following the sacrifice of Nine Ollin, his ashes would be
brought to Eight Deer who would adorn
them with a feather head dress and a
turquoise mask. Finally a quail would be
sacrificed as the ashes were once more
cremated, the quail being a symbol of the
Sunrise.

Eight Edznab CENTRAL AMERICA (*Maya*)
The eighth day of the MAYA CREATION[4] on
which MONTH created the first people.
Eight Edznab should not be confused with
EDZNAB, the eighteenth day of the AGES OF
MAN.

Eithinoha NORTH AMERICA –
WOODLANDS (*Iroquois*)
The Earth Mother whose daughter was
ONATAH, a Corn Maiden.

Ekahau CENTRAL AMERICA (*Maya*)
The black-faced god of travellers and merchants who is also associated with the gods
of death and war, the association possibly
springing from the fact that trade was
often a dangerous business and could frequently lead travelling merchants into
war.

Ekchuah CENTRAL AMERICA (*Maya*)
The god of travellers who is identified in
the various CODEX as the god L.

Ekkekko SOUTH AMERICA – PERU AND
BOLIVIA (*Quechua*)
The god of good fortune who is usually
depicted as a pot-bellied, cheerful dwarf
who carried all sorts of domestic goods – a
sort of divine tinker. His cult has become
especially associated with the ALACITAS,
annual fairs that are held at COCHAM-
BAMBA, LA PAZ and ORURO.

Ek-u-Uayeyab CENTRAL AMERICA
(*Maya*)
The guardian deity of a city's western gates
during the malign CAUAC years, that were
governed over by the western of the Four
BACAB. During these years the centre of
the city was guarded by ZAC-MITUN-AHAU.
See also CHAC-U-UAYEYAB, KAN-U-UAYEYAB,
ZAC-U-UAYEYAB.

Ekutsihimmiyo NORTH AMERICA –
GREAT PLAINS (*Cheyenne*)
The MILKY WAY³, the 'Hanging Road' that
is suspended between, and links, heaven
and Earth, and along which the TASOOM

travels after death to the sky home of
HEAMMAWIHIO.

El Dorado SOUTH AMERICA
The fabled and famous city of gold that
was believed by the sixteenth-century Spaniards, as well as other Europeans, to exist
somewhere in the area of the ORINOCO and
AMAZON rivers. El Dorado means 'the
Gilded Man' or 'the Gold Man', and has
since that time become a figure of persist-
ing legend that has induced a great many
hopeful people to go in search of his fab-
ulous treasure. The story of such a man,
the great priest-king who was ritually covered in gold dust, and his golden city
undoubtedly derives from confused stories
of the INCA people which the Spanish
conquistadors were told by primitive
tribes. The city of El Dorado, – the city of
the Gold Man – has been associated with
Lake GUATAVITA and with the mythical
Lake PARIMA that, until VON HUMBOLDT
disproved it, was said to have lain beyond
the Orinoco in a fabled land called MANOA
or OMOA.
  El Dorado has not, however, always
been a city. The legends appear to have
started out telling of a single, huge golden
statue, and it is the immensity of that
statue, and the evidence of the immense
wealth of the South American peoples
that the Spanish brought out of the interior with them that has led to the inflation
of the single object into a whole city. In
this case the statue is said to be that of the
king of the city of gold where it may be
found along with a female statue that is,
quite logically, called LA DORADA.

El Gran Dios CENTRAL AMERICA –
YUCATÁN, MEXICO (*Modern Maya*)
The name given by the modern Yuacatec
MAYA to the Christian God who lives in
the seventh heaven, and gives orders to
the YUMCHABOB who live below him in the
sixth heaven.

El Gran Moxo SOUTH AMERICA –
PARAGUAY (*Guaraní*)
The ruler of the fabled PAITITI said to be
situated in Lake CUNI-CUNI and guarded by
the jaguar-lizard TEYÚ-YAGUÁ.

El Lanzón SOUTH AMERICA – PERU
(*Chavin*)
A stele that is a representation of an anthropomorphic deity, a deity with serpent
hair and feline features who is also shown
on the RAIMONDI stele. It is assumed that
as so little is known of the CHAVIN culture,
this deity is the supreme god of the Chavin
people, but this is by no means certain, and
he may simply have been a guardian spirit,
or a tutelary deity.

Eleven Imix CENTRAL AMERICA (*Maya*)
The eleventh day of the MAYA CREATION[4]
during which MONTH made the first stones
and trees. Eleven Imix is not to be confused with IMIX, the first day of the AGES OF
MAN.

Ellal SOUTH AMERICA – PATAGONIA
(*Puechlo*)
The personification of evil who opposed
everything that was good on the Earth, as
well as in heaven.

Emisiwaddo SOUTH AMERICA – GUYANA
(*Arawak*)
One of the two wives of KURURUMANY, the
creator, his other wife being WUREKADDO.
Her name has been translated as 'She
Who Bores Through the Earth', and she
has been identified with a species of South
American ant, thus suggesting that she
may have been connected with a long lost
Creation myth that the Earth was created
from either one or many ant hills.

Er ~ zilie, ~ zulia HAITI (*Voodoo*)
A very important LOA who has a West
African provenance. The goddess of sexual
love, she is depicted as a very beautiful,
seductive and amorous woman, though

she has also been identified by VOODOO
devotees as the Christian 'Mater Delor-
osa'.

Eskimo NORTH AMERICA
'Foul eaters of raw meat', the name first
given to the Arctic-dwelling peoples of
North America by the ALGONQUIAN Indians. Today the term is still in popular
usage, but is greatly disliked by the people
to whom it refers, the INUIT and the Asiatic
Aleut. There are a number of Eskimo-
speaking peoples who live in the Arctic
regions of North America, the main
grouping being the Inuit whose name is
now generally applied to all these peoples.
To be correct, the Inuit inhabit the most
northerly reaches of northern Canada,
while the Eskimo-speaking peoples of
Greenland are the KALAALLIT and those of
Alaska, the INUPIAT and the YUPIK. As the
term Eskimo is disliked by the Inuit, the
latter term is used throughout this book to
refer to these Arctic-dwelling peoples.

Estanatlehi NORTH AMERICA –
SOUTHWEST (*Navajo*)
'Woman Who Changes', one of the two
goddesses created by the YEI under the
guidance of HASTSHEYALTI, the other goddess created at the same time being YOLKAI
ESTSAN. Estanatlehi was formed from turquoise while her companion was made
from white shell, hence her name which
means 'White Shell Woman'. Estanatlehi
was responsible for killing almost all of the
ANAYE when she was given four hoops that
had been made by the Sun-Bearer, which
she used to raise a terrible storm that not
only almost wiped out the anaye, but also
altered the very shape of the Earth itself.

Estanatlehi became the goddess of rain
and fertility and left the Earth with TSHO-
HANOAI to live with her husband in a lodge
that is situated beyond the waters. See
ASCENT OF THE NAVAJO.

Etienne, Sainte HAITI (*Voodoo*)
The Roman Catholic Saint Stephen who is regarded as a LOA by some VOODOO cultists.

Eupai SOUTH AMERICA (*Inca*)
The god of the UNDERWORLD who, greedy for subjects of his dark realm, invented death and thus persuaded mankind to become his subjects eventually. The INCA lived in such fear of Eupai that they annually sacrificed 100 children to him in the hope that this would satisfy his lust.

Evening Sky NORTH AMERICA –
NORTHWEST COAST (*Klamath*)
The daughter of KEMUSH, the creator, who accompanied her father to the lodges of the spirits who inhabited the PLACE OF THE DARK. For five nights, father and daughter danced with the spirits in a circle around their fire until SHEL at last called upon the spirits of the Earth, and all those in the

Place of the Dark were turned into dry bones. Having disposed of the evil spirits, Kemush followed Shel's trail to the very summit of the sky where he built himself a lodge, and there he still lives with SUN HALO and his daughter, Evening Sky.

Evening Star NORTH AMERICA – GREAT
PLAINS (*Skidi Pawnee*)
The name given to the planet VENUS[1] when seen in the twilight. Under this name the planet was seen as the personification of BRIGHT STAR. The concept of the Evening Star is not solely confined to the SKIDI PAWNEE people. Throughout America, and indeed throughout the world, the planet Venus seen in the evening sky has been personified as any number of deities who herald the onset of night. As the concept is so widespread, it is sufficient to say that whenever a deity is referred to as the Evening Star, this is the meaning of that phrase.

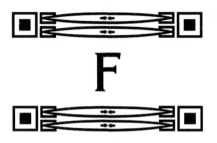

F

F CENTRAL AMERICA (*Maya*)
A war-god who is simply known by the letter F in the various CODEX, and is possibly to be identified with NACON. He is distinguished by vertical slash marks on his face, which has led some to postulate that his origins lie with the AZTEC flayed-god XIPE TOTEC, but this link seems tenuous.

Fair Weather NORTH AMERICA –
NORTHWEST COAST (*Comox*)
The mother of the two sons who conquered TLAIK.

Falling Eagle CENTRAL AMERICA –
MEXICO (*Aztec*)
One of the four giants who were turned into the pillars which support the heavens and separate the realm of the gods from the realm of mortal men. It is said to symbolize the descent of heavenly and activating principle into the Earth, a principle that maintains all life on Earth. If the pillars were to be removed, not only would the heavens crash on to the Earth, but mankind would die without the life-giving essence that the pillars conduct from heaven. The other three giants were RESURRECTION, SERPENT OF OBSIDIAN KNIVES and THORNY FLOWERS. QUETZALCÓATL and TEZCATLIPOCA also became pillars at this time, the former becoming the PRECIOUS TREE and the latter the TREE OF MIRRORS.

False-Face Society NORTH AMERICA –
WOODLANDS (*Iroquois*)
More properly called the HADIGANSO SHANO, the False-Face Society is an organized group of SHAMAN healers who supervise all religious rituals. As healers, they cure the sick with the aid of large wooden masks, of which there are twelve basic types. The members of the society always function as a group and undergo a grotesque noisy dance at the house of the afflicted, scattering ashes over him, shaking their turtle-shell rattles and chanting magical incantations.

The masks worn by the members of the society were referred to as 'faces' because they were carved portraits in which the spirits the members called upon were manifest. A 'face' was never made, but rather 'discovered' as the shaman carved his interpretation of the spirit into a living tree from which the 'face' was then cut free. Red-painted 'faces' were carved in the morning while black-painted ones were carved in the afternoon – the time of carving depending on the spirit whose image was being created.

Fat God, The CENTRAL AMERICA
A deity of apparently immense importance and popularity between approximately AD 300 and 900. His significance remains a mystery, but images of this deity, so named because of his appearance, are found throughout Central America.

Fempellec SOUTH AMERICA (*Chimu*)
The tenth king of CHIMOR, after NAYMLAP, who decided to move the sacred statue LLAMPALLEC. He was subsequently seduced by a fiend who took the form of a beautiful woman, after which an unprecedented deluge followed. The deluge was so intense that it ruined the crops and a famine ensued. To counter the effects of this famine, the priests of Chimu tied Fempellec's hands and feet together and threw him from the cliffs into the sea, thus killing the last of Naymlap's descendants.

Fifth Sun CENTRAL AMERICA – MEXICO (*Aztec*)
The name given by the AZTEC to the era of mankind – our present era. Only when this Fifth Sun NAOLLIN ('Four Movement') was born was it possible for all the separate elements of the Creation to come together and form the Earth as it is known today. The Aztecs, however, did not assume that even this Sun was immortal, and thus performed extensive rituals to maintain it.

At the end of the fourth era of the Creation, that known as FOURTH SUN, the gods met to discuss who should have the task of lighting the next era. At first there was only one volunteer, TECCIZTÉCATL, the god of the death's head day MIQUIZTLI who later became the Moon-god, who thought that he could raise his status by undertaking what at first glance was a simple task. The other gods were sceptical that Tecciztécatl would carry out the allotted task, and so asked for a second volunteer. One by one the assembled gods made their excuses until there was just one god left, NANAUTZIN, a sorry sight as he was covered in scabs and tried to hide in the shadows.

It suddenly dawned on all the other gods that here they had the perfect volunteer, for no one would miss a god who was so gross to look upon. Therefore they volunteered Nanautzin who could do

nothing other than accept. Tecciztécatl and Nanautzin then spent four days in penance preparing themselves for the task ahead. Having completed their penance, the two lit a fire on a hearth of rock. Ritual sacrifices were then offered. Tecciztécatl, a proud god, offered rich feathers in place of the customary dead branches; nuggets of gold rather than hay; precious stones shaped like thorns instead of the thorns from the maguey cactus; thorns of red coral in place of those obligatory thorns that had to be tipped with blood; and the finest quality opals.

Nanautzin, though proud, was very poor, and offered nine green reeds tied in bundles of three; hay; the thorns of the maguey cactus; thorns anointed with his own blood; but in place of opals he gave scabs that he removed from his own sores.

During this time the other gods had built a large tower, as high as a mountain beside the fire, and now the assembled company did a further four days' penance. Then they let the fire burn for a further four days before destroying the receptacles into which the offerings had been placed. The gods then lined up and ordered Tecciztécatl to throw himself into the fire. Four times Tecciztécatl made ready, but always shied away at the last moment. As it had been decreed that no one was allowed to make more than four attempts, Nanautzin was then called forward to take his place.

Summoning all his courage and closing his eyes, Nanautzin rushed blindly forwards and leapt into the flames. Ashamed by his cowardice, Tecciztécatl followed Nanautzin's example and threw himself into the fire. Thus were the Sun, (Nanautzin) and the Moon, (Tecciztécatl) born, the lowliest of all the gods showing the true way. The Sun, which was later to be made one of the central reasons for tearing the hearts out of living victims, owed its very existence to a much greater, voluntary sacrifice.

The story of Nanautzin represents the central idea and purpose of the myths of QUETZALCÓATL, for he is the lowliest of all the manifestations of the great god whose self-sacrifice not only saves the cosmos from extinction, but also represents the opening up of all the latent possibilities for both men and the gods.

Firavitoba SOUTH AMERICA – COLOMBIA (*Chibcha*)
The brother-in-law of NAMPANEM, the legendary and divine king whom he succeeded.

Fire, House of CENTRAL AMERICA – MEXICO (*Aztec*)
One of the numerous trials devised by the lords of XIBALBA that the twins HUNAHPU and XBALANQUÉ were put through, and one through which they passed unscathed.

Fire Dragon with a Body of Pure White Colour NORTH AMERICA – WOODLANDS (*Iroquois*)
One of the two spirits by whom the celestial chief thought AWENHAI had been seduced, the other spirit being the AURORA BOREALIS[3]. The celestial chief uprooted the ONODJA TREE which he lived under and pushed Awenhai and the two suspects through the resulting hole in the sky, though their ghosts remained with him in heaven.

Fire Drill NORTH AMERICA – SOUTHWEST COAST (*Wintun*)
One of the three beings who, along with SHOOTING STAR and BUCKEYE BUSH, set the world on fire to avenge the theft of FLINT.

First Sun CENTRAL AMERICA – MEXICO (*Aztec*)
The first era of the Creation that is symbolized by the ocelot. A time when animals and men lived in the dark and the animals were the more powerful of the two; a fact that was confirmed when the ocelots devoured all the humans. However, some versions of the AZTEC Creation myth say that the first era was called the Sun of Water and ended in a great flood which two humans survived when they hid in a cave. The second era of the Creation that followed is, naturally enough, referred to as the SECOND SUN.

Five Lamat CENTRAL AMERICA (*Maya*)
The eighteenth day of the MAYA CREATION[4] on which MONTH[2] created the great sea lake.

Five Men CENTRAL AMERICA (*Maya*)
The fifth day of the MAYA CREATION[4] on which MONTH[2] first gave things life, though the first people were not to be created until EIGHT EDZNAB. Five Men is not to be confused with the MEN, the fifteenth day of the Maya spiritual pilgrimage – the AGES OF MAN.

Five Suns CENTRAL AMERICA – MEXICO (*Aztec*)
An AZTEC Creation myth that seems to predate the one related elsewhere in this book under FIRST SUN, SECOND SUN, THIRD SUN, FOURTH SUN and FIFTH SUN. This myth is, perhaps, the earlier NAHUA myth on which the later one is based, for some of the central concepts remain, particularly the naming of the five eras as First, Second, Third, Fourth and Fifth Sun.

In the ninth and highest heaven lived the god TONACATECUHTLI ('Lord Nourishment') and his consort TONACACÍHUATL ('Lady Nourishment'). They had four sons, who originally seem to have been nature deities and the guardians of the four cardinal points, but were later to become identified as the gods of the Aztec empire's different peoples. They were CAMAXTLI, the chief god of the TLAXCALA whose colour was red; HUITZILOPOCHTLI, tutelary deity of the Aztecs; QUETZALCÓATL, the wind-god and chief deity of the TOLTECS; TEZCATLIPOCA, the black god of night and the war-god of the great city of TEZCOCO.

After resting for 600 years these deities started the Creation by inventing fire and the calendar, and making a half-sun, and the man OXOMOCO and the woman CIPACTONAL. At the same time they also created the UNDERWORLD of MICTLÁN and the rulers of that domain, MICTLÁNTECUHTLI and MICTLÁNTECUHTL. They then formed the twelve lower levels of heaven, the sea, the water-god TLALTECUHTLI and his wife CHALCHIUHTLICUE, and the sea-monster CIPACTLI from whom they formed the Earth which they named CEMANAHUAC.

The gods saw that the half-sun gave only a feeble light, so they made it whole and Tezcatlipoca became the SUN-BEARER and ruler of the First Sun era during which the giant inhabitants of Earth lived on acorns.

After 676 years Quetzalcóatl killed Tezcatlipoca who was transformed into a jaguar that then devoured all the giants. He is still to be seen in the night sky as the constellation URSA MAJOR[1] as it falls towards the water into which he was cast by Quetzalcóatl.

Quetzalcóatl now recreated man and became the ruler of the second era of the Creation, that of the Second Sun until, after another 676 years he was killed by TLÁLOC, the wind-god who caused a great wind and storm to rise up and blow almost all the people away, those who remained being transformed into monkeys.

Tláloc now became the ruler of the Third Sun era which lasted considerably less than the previous two, only 364 years, until it ended in a rain of fire from which only a few people managed to escape in the form of birds.

Chalchiuhtlicue now became the ruler of the Fourth Sun era during which maize was introduced to the Earth. This era lasted just 312 years and ended with a great FLOOD[2], the people who survived the deluge being transformed into fish.

The gods then created four giant men who raised the heavens to their present position, with the aid of Quetzalcóatl and Tezcatlipoca, here miraculously resurrected, but gods cannot really be killed. These two deities became the rulers of the sky.

During all this time the first true human, PILTZINTECUHTLI, the son of Oxomoco and Cipactonal, had survived, as had his wife who had been created from a hair from the goddess XOCHIQUETZAL. A son was born to this pair, and the gods set about creating other people who lived in the darkness, except for the light from their fires, for the Sun had yet to be created for the final era of the Creation.

Quetzalcóatl rectified this situation when he threw his own son by the goddess Chalchiuhtlicue into a fire from which he emerged as the Fifth Sun. Tláloc threw his son into the embers of the fire and he emerged as the Moon who casts far less light than the Sun, as the fire from which he had been created had cooled. The gods, having sacrificed their own children to provide mankind with light, said that man should feed the Sun with hearts and blood, and thus invented war to provide sacrifices for him.

It can be seen that many aspects of this story tally with the later renditions of the five Aztec stages of the Creation, though in many cases the names of the deities concerned are different. It is thought that this story is the original from which all the various derivations have come, and is also thought to have influenced the Creation

91

stories of other Central and South American peoples.

Flint

1 NORTH AMERICA – SOUTHWEST COAST (*Wintun*)
The theft of Flint was avenged by BUCK-EYE BUSH, FIRE DRILL and SHOOTING STAR who set the world on fire.

2 NORTH AMERICA – WOODLANDS (*Menominee*)
The son of NOKOMIS according to the MENOMINEE. He stole a bowl of blood from his mother from which WABUS, the Great HARE, grew. Later Wabus became a man whereupon he took the name MÄNÄBUSCH.

Flood

Stories of a great flood that all but destroyed mankind are common, not just throughout the Americas, but worldwide, their commonness perhaps indicating some historicity behind the stories. Those given below are simply a representative selection of the flood myths of the Native American peoples.

1 NORTH AMERICA (*Inuit*)
At first the INUIT were the only people on the Earth . Then there came a great Flood. When the waters receded, a girl bore some white children fathered by a dog, this aspect demonstrating that the Inuit thought of white people as unnatural. The mother put these children in the sole of a boot and cast them on to the sea, telling them to go away and find their own country. A long time after, the descendants of these children returned to the Inuit lands in ships that resembled the sole of a boot.

2 CENTRAL AMERICA – MEXICO (*Aztec*)
The deluge which ended the era of the FIRST SUN, that of ATONATIUH, when all the people were turned into fish. One AZTEC myth says that the world was recreated by QUETZALCÓATL after this flood. However, various Aztec myths give varying accounts of the flood. In some cases there was more than one flood, each era of the Creation coming to a similar end under just such an inundation.

3 NORTH AMERICA (*Algonquian*)
The deluge sent by the ANAMAQKIU in retaliation for the death of their two BEAR chiefs at the hands of MÄNÄBUSCH. Mänäbusch climbed a huge pine growing on the summit of a mountain to escape the advancing waters, but they relentlessly chased after him. Mänäbusch made the tree grow to four times its original height, but still the waters came on until they had reached Mänäbusch's armpits. Only then did the GREAT SPIRIT intervene and arrest the waters.

The entire surface of the Earth was now covered with water. Mänäbusch told the animals who had escaped with him that he could recreate the Earth if he had so much as a single grain of soil. First OTTER, then BEAVER, and then MINK plunged down into the waters to look for some, but each of them died in their attempt. Finally MUSKRAT succeeded and Mänäbusch set about the recreation of the Earth .

4 SOUTH AMERICA – BOLIVIA AND COLOMBIA (*Chibcha*)
The inundation sent by the evil CHIBCHACUM who had grown tired of mankind's petty bickering. Mankind was saved by BOCHICA who made himself visible as a rainbow that struck the rocks which opened and imbibed the waters, creating the great waterfall TEQUENDAMA in the process. Bochica then dried out the sodden land when he materialized as ZUHÉ, the Sun, and then turned on, and defeated, Chibchacum.

5 CENTRAL AMERICA (*Chichimec*)
According to the CHICHIMEC people, they descended from a man and a bitch who were the sole survivors of the deluge, hence their name which means the 'Race of Dogs'.

6 NORTH AMERICA – WEST COAST (*Skagit*)
According to the SKAGIT people, only two people survived the Flood, riding on the waters in a dugout canoe into which they had loaded two of everything, an aspect that probably did not become an integral part of the story until after the Skagit had come into contact with Christian beliefs. The son of these two survivors was DOQUEBUTH, the second Creator of the world who was told how to conduct the recreation in a SHAMANistic trance. The Flood did not completely cover the surface of the Earth, for the peaks of two sacred mountains, KOBATH and TAKOBAH, still remained visible.

7 CENTRAL AMERICA – YUCATÁN, MEXICO (*Modern Maya*)
The Flood completely destroyed the Earth and made the heavens fall into the waters. CANTULTIKU therefore sent KANZIBYÚI to reorganize the Earth ready for the recreation, which he did by propping up the heavens on different trees that he planted at the four cardinal points.

8 CENTRAL AMERICA (*Maya*)
The MAYA people, suffered not just a single deluge but several, for they said that each of the preliminary eras of the CREATION[4] came to end in a great flood.

9 SOUTH AMERICA (*Quechua*)
Inundation destroyed the world, but did not cover the summit of Mount CONDORCOTO on whose slopes lay the golden eggs from which five men, among them PARIACACA, were born after the waters had receded.

Flute Dance NORTH AMERICA – PUEBLO, SOUTHWEST (*Hopi*)
A summer ritual that is celebrated in a two-year alternating cycle with the SNAKE DANCE. The Sun-god takes an important place in this rite and is represented by a disc circled with ribbons and the feathers of an eagle.

Fongaside SOUTH AMERICA – PERU (*Mochica*)
One of the servants of NAYMLAP who walked ahead of his master and scattered shells before him.

Four Earthquake CENTRAL AMERICA – MEXICO (*Aztec*)
The name given to the era of the FIFTH SUN which is taken to be our present era, and one that will end with earthquakes and the man-made catastrophes of war, famine and general confusion.

Four Ix CENTRAL AMERICA (*Maya*)
The fourth day of the MAYA CREATION[4] on which MONTH[2] completed the creation of the heavens and the Earth. Four Ix is not to be confused with IX, the fifteenth day of the AGES OF MAN, the Maya spiritual pilgrimage.

Four Man-Ik CENTRAL AMERICA (*Maya*)
The seventeenth day of the MAYA CREATION[4] on which, for the first time, the spirit of man passed from Earth to heaven. Four Man-Ik is not to be confused with MAN-IK, the seventh day of the Maya spiritual pilgrimage, the AGES OF MAN, though the context is the same, for on that day man overcomes his own death and enters the after-life.

Four Ocelot CENTRAL AMERICA – MEXICO (*Aztec*)
The name given to the era of the FIRST SUN in the AZTEC myth of the FIVE SUNS. The era was ruled over by TEZCATLIPOCA, who

became the SUN-BEARER, the inhabitants of Earth being described as brutish giants who lived on acorns. After 676 years QUETZALCÓATL struck down Tezcatlipoca whom he transformed into a jaguar that devoured all the giants. Thus ended the era of the First Sun. Tezcatlipoca was thrown into the sea by his brother, and may still be seen as the constellation URSA MAJOR[1] in the night sky, still falling towards the water.

Four Rain CENTRAL AMERICA – MEXICO (*Aztec*)
The era of the THIRD SUN in the AZTEC myth of the FIVE SUNS. The era was ruled over by the wind-god TLÁLOC and lasted for 364 years until it ended in a rain of fire which only a few of the people managed to survive in the form of birds.

Four Water CENTRAL AMERICA – MEXICO (*Aztec*)
The era of the FOURTH SUN according to the AZTEC myth of the FIVE SUNS. This era, which lasted for 312 years, was ruled over by the goddess CHALCHIUHTLICUE who introduced maize to mankind. It ended with a great flood which some of the people managed to survive in the form of fish.

Four Wind CENTRAL AMERICA – MEXICO (*Aztec*)
The name given to the era of the SECOND SUN in the AZTEC myth of the FIVE SUNS. This era was ruled over by the great QUETZALCÓATL and lasted 676 years until TLÁLOC deposed the SUN-BEARER and caused a great wind and storm to ravage the Earth which blew away almost all the people, those who remained being transformed into monkeys.

Fourth Sun CENTRAL AMERICA – MEXICO (*Aztec*)
The fourth era of the Creation that was sometimes known as the SUN OF WATER, as during this era the fishes were created, though the Sun of Water is also sometimes used to refer to the FIRST SUN. The era ended with a great flood and was followed by our present era which is known as the FIFTH SUN. The first four stages of the Creation are taken to represent the four elements essential to the creation of mankind, and to the sustenance of the Creation itself. The Fourth Sun era is also referred to as the SUN OF EARTH in some accounts, at the end of which men rescued certain nourishing plants and flowers from the flood waters, and were thus able to sustain life in the next era.

As the era came to an end, the supreme god sent for the human couple TATA and NENA and told them to make a hole in a huge tree and hide in it. Thus they would be saved from the flood, but only if they ate no more than a single cob of maize each. Tata and Nena followed the gods' instructions and duly rode out the flood in complete safety. However, as the waters receded, they saw a fish which they caught and placed on a spit over a fire they built. The gods saw the smoke rising and were angry that their instructions had been disobeyed. As a punishment they transformed both Tata and Nena into dogs and removed from them that portion of the brain that distinguishes man from the animals.

Frog NORTH AMERICA – SOUTHWEST (*Navajo*)
One of the four animals who volunteered to travel to an underwater village to capture two of its female inhabitants. His companions were BEAR, SNAKE and TURTLE. Frog and Turtle were chosen to be the kidnappers, but they were surprised by the people of the village and had to kill the girls whom they quickly scalped. The older girl's hair was decorated with white shell jewellery, and the younger girl's hair with turquoise. Frog and Turtle were captured

but, having survived the attempts of the villagers to roast them and then to drown them, they escaped and rejoined their companions, and all four set off for home.

Furachogúe SOUTH AMERICA (*Inca*)
The first woman, sometimes called BACHUÉ, she emerged on to the Earth from Lake IGUAGUÉ near TUNJA carrying a young boy. When this boy reached maturity, they married and their children quickly became the Earth's population, as Furachogúe always bore either quadruplets or sextuplets. The divine parents taught their children their laws and all the arts of civilization. Then they returned to the waters of the lake in the form of serpents, having beseeched their children to live in peace.

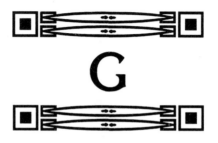

G

G Central America (*Maya*)
A solar deity who is known simply as the god G in the various CODEX. He is thought to be cognate with KINICH AHAU.

Ga-oh North America – Woodlands (*Iroquois*)
The wind-giant who lives in a house guarded by a bear whose prowling brings the north wind and whose whining the strong west wind. A moose also stands on guard whose breathing brings the wet east wind, while a fawn, also in attendance, returning to its mother, brings the gentle south wind.

Gagavitz Central America – Guatemala (*Cakchiquel*)
One of the two eldest warriors under the leadership of TIUH TIUH, the other warrior of comparable age being ZACTECAUH. The warriors would have liked to have disposed of ZAKIQOXOL, but they bowed to his supernatural nature (he was the spirit of fire) and gave him clothing and a blood-red dagger and shoes so that man could recognize him. Gagavitz once climbed a mountain, in all probability a volcano, in the company of the only man brave enough to go with him, ZAKITZUNUN, though the purpose of this ascent is not known. Later, as Tiuh Tiuh led his people across the land they came to a sea they could not cross. There the two fell asleep on the sea shore and were drowned.

Gahonga North America – Woodlands (*Iroquois*)
'Stone-throwers', one of the three tribes of JOGAH, dwarf nature-spirits, the other two being the GANDAYAH and the OHDOWS. The Gahonga inhabit rocks and rivers.

Galibi Caribbean (*Carib*)
The name given by the island-dwelling CARIB to those of their people who have left the islands to live on the mainland.

Gandayah North America – Woodlands (*Iroquois*)
One of the three tribes of JOGAH, dwarf nature-spirits, the other two being the GAHONGA and the OHDOWS. The Gandayah maintain the fertility of the Earth.

Ganga Haiti (*Voodoo*)
Possibly having a Hindu provenance, Ganga is yet another of the numerous and diverse LOA of the VOODOO religion.

gangan Haiti (*Voodoo*)
An inferior SHAMAN who is, due to a lack of prowess, unable to attain the status of HOUNGAN.

gans North America – Great Plains (*Apache*)
Generic name for mountain spirits that were sent by the GREAT SPIRIT to teach the APACHE people all the arts of civilization. Distressed by the corruption of their teaching by the Apache, the gans left and hid in caves from which they have never

emerged. Their memory is upheld in the GANS DANCE.

Gans Dance NORTH AMERICA – GREAT PLAINS (*Apache*)
A ritual dance in which four dancers and an attendant clown impersonate the GANS and thus uphold their memory.

Garsilasco (Inca) de la Vega
See DE LA VEGA, Garsilasco (Inca).

Gbadé HAITI (*Voodoo*)
Alternative name for BADÉ-SI.

Georges, Sainte HAITI (*Voodoo*)
The Christian saint who is regarded as a LOA by some VOODOO cultists.

Geyaguga NORTH AMERICA – WOODLANDS (*Cherokee*)
The spirit of the Moon.

Ghanan CENTRAL AMERICA (*Maya*)
Alternative name sometimes applied to YUM CAAX in which instance he is regarded as an aspect of KUKULCÁN.

Ghost Dance(s) NORTH AMERICA
The origin of these revivalist ritual dances bear a striking resemblance to the Melanesian Cargo Cult rituals. The first wave of the dances began c.1870 among the PAIUTE people of the California–Nevada border regions led by the prophet WODZIWOB who foresaw that all their ancestors would return on a large train (the railroad had just been completed) and would announce their arrival with a great explosion. All the white people would be swallowed up in the resulting cataclysm leaving all their possessions for the Indians whereupon the GREAT SPIRIT would return to live among his people. The dances Wodziwob had been taught in a vision would, so he asserted, hasten this new Indian beginning.

The second series of Ghost Dances began in 1890 and were inspired by WOVOKA, the son of Wodziwob's assistant. The tribes of the GREAT PLAINS now became involved in the ritual that was fast gaining popularity. The cult was taken up by the disillusioned SIOUX who, under the leadership of the great Sitting Bull, distorted Wovoka's peaceable teachings and spread a new belief that the dances would also induce a landslide that would engulf all the white people, while the costumes of the dancers, their 'ghost shirts', would be invulnerable to bullets. This movement culminated with the massacre of the Sioux at Wounded Knee on 29 December 1890.

Giadruvava CARIBBEAN (*Taíno*)
The servant of GUAGUGIANA who was caught by the Sun's rays and turned into a beautiful bird with a wonderful song, when his master sent him out to find a medicinal herb. Every year, on the anniversary of his transformation, Giadruvava fills the night air with his beautiful song, imploring Guagugiana to come and rescue him.

Gitche Manito NORTH AMERICA – WOODLANDS (*Chippewa*)
A variant of KITSHI MANITO.

Glendenwitha NORTH AMERICA – WOODLANDS (*Iroquois*)
A beautiful maiden with whom SOSONDOWAH became smitten and was subsequently wooed by him, firstly in the spring as a bluebird, then in the summer as a blackbird, and lastly in the autumn as a night-hawk in which form he carried her away. Glendenwitha was then transformed

into a star and set in Sosondowah's fore-head, forever out of his reach, by DAWN.

Glisma NORTH AMERICA – SOUTHWEST
(*Navajo*)
A culture-heroine, of which there are very few among the AMERINDIAN people in gen-eral. She was the younger of the two sisters that had been captured by BEAR and SNAKE who took her to the UNDERWORLD realm of the SNAKE PEOPLE where she was taught the words and painting rituals of the HO-ZONI CHANT. After two years she was freed and subsequently taught the rituals to her brother, the new powers he thus learned turning him into a powerful SHAMAN.

Gloom, House of CENTRAL AMERICA
(*Maya*)
One of the houses or places of trial in the UNDERWORLD kingdom of XIBALBA. It fea-tures in two series of stories, the first con-cerning HUNHUN AHPU and VUKUB AHPU, and the second the culture heroes, HU-NAHPU and XBALANQUÉ. In both cases the brothers are placed in the house and in-structed that they must not let their tor-ches go out. In the first case Hunhun Ahpu and Vukub Ahpu failed and were put to death, but in the case of Hunahpu and Xbalanqué the brothers tricked the lords of Xibalba by painting red flames on to their torches after they had gone out.

Gl ~ ooscap, ~ uscap NORTH AMERICA
– WOODLANDS (*Micmac*)
The MICMAC name for the Great HARE.

Gohone NORTH AMERICA –
WOODLANDS (*Iroquois*)
The spirit of the winter who is perceived as an old man who raps the trees with his club, which can be heard to make the trees split when there has been a particularly hard frost. Gohone departs from the land when ADEKAGAGWAA, the spirit of summer, returns.

G(o)ug(o)une HAITI (*Voodoo*)
Variant(s) of OGOUN.

Grand Batala HAITI (*Voodoo*)
Variant of 'BATALA.

Grand Bois HAITI (*Voodoo*)
'The Tree of Life', the personification of the forces of nature who is, along with ORAJI BRISÉ, one of the most powerful of all the LOA, even though he represents a far more primitive form of the loa than the classical West African derivatives such as OGOUN and DAMBALLA.

Grasshopper NORTH AMERICA –
WOODLANDS (*Choctaw*)
Unidentified nature-spirit who was said to have emerged from NANIH WAYA with the first CHOCTAW people.

Grasshopper Girl NORTH AMERICA –
SOUTHWEST (*Navajo*)
One of the tutelary deities created by ATSE ESTSAN and ATSE HASTIN. She was, along with POLLEN BOY, set on the northern sa-cred mountain, Mount SAN JUAN, and gave the first man and woman created by HAST-SHEYALTI and YOLKAI ESTSAN the power of speech.

Grasshopper Mother NORTH AMERICA
– WOODLANDS (*Choctaw*)
The mother of GRASSHOPPER who, when her daughter emerged from NANIH WAYA with the first CHOCTAW people, stayed be-hind and was killed by those Choctaw who had yet to make it to the surface. Those who had already made their home on the Earth prayed to ABA, the GREAT SPIRIT, to close the tunnel so that the murderers should remain in the UNDERWORLD where they were transformed into ants.

Grasshopper People NORTH AMERICA –
SOUTHWEST (*Navajo*)
The original inhabitants of the YELLOW
WORLD through which the NAVAJO passed
during their ascent to the Earth. They
did not remain long in the Yellow World,
as they made free with their hosts' wives
and were expelled. See ASCENT OF THE
NAVAJO.

Great Bear NORTH AMERICA (*Inuit*)
The common name for the constellation
URSA MAJOR[3] that is seen by the INUIT as a
bear who, having been chased out on to
the ice floes by some hunters and their
dogs could find no other way of escaping
than to take to the skies. The hunters were
not to be deterred and followed the bear,
and today may be seen in the night sky as
the PLEIADES[1] who still chase the Great
Bear across the sky.

Great Goddess NORTH AMERICA (*Inuit*)
Whereas for most other peoples the archetypal Great Goddess is the EARTH MOTHER,
for the INUIT, who are primarily dependant
on the sea for their food, and thus for life,
the Great Goddess is a sea deity. She has
several names. In eastern Greenland she is
NERRIVIK; in Alaska she becomes SEDNA, or
sometimes SEDNA-NERRIVIK, and is also
known as NULIAJOQ and ARNA(R)KU-
(SU)AGSAK. Like her land-based counterparts, the Great Goddess has an ambivalent nature, being the ruler of the dead
as well as the source of all life.

Great Hare
See HARE, Great.

Great Hawk NORTH AMERICA –
SOUTHWEST (*Navajo*)
During the ASCENT OF THE NAVAJO, Great
Hawk flew up to the sky and clawed at the
sky until he made a small hole which was
subsequently enlarged by LOCUST, this
opening allowing the NAVAJO people to
continue their ascent to the Earth.

Great Plains NORTH AMERICA
Semi-arid region to the east of the Rocky
Mountains that stretches as far as the
100th meridian through Oklahoma, Kan-
sas, Nebraska and the Dakotas. Covering
one-fifth of the USA, the Great Plains
extend from Texas in the south for over
2,000 miles north to Canada.

Long before the arrival of the white
man, from whom they obtained guns and
horses, the AMERINDIAN peoples of the
eastern plains supplemented hunting with
a very basic form of agriculture. From c. AD
800 SIOUX immigrants entered the region
from the northwest, while CADDO-
speaking Indians came from the south and
southeast, bringing with them knowledge
of better agricultural techniques.

The Amerindian people of the more
arid western plains were far more dependent on hunting. From the middle of the
sixteenth century, when the first white
explorers arrived, they almost totally neglected agriculture in favour of hunting as
their acquisition of both horses and guns
had made them far more mobile, and
hunting, at least in the short term, seemed
to reap greater rewards than farming.

All the plains Indians were nomadic or
semi-nomadic and were, by necessity,
highly disciplined with rituals that centre
on the hunter and warrior castes. Many
lived in skin tents or *tipis*, wore war paint,
buffalo robes, and eagle feather head dres-
ses, characteristics that were later adopted
by many other tribes.

Linguistically the Indians of the Great
Plains are divided between the ATHAPAS-
CANS who occupied a region from Alaska
to Alberta, but also include the southern
APACHE tribe; the ALGONQUIAN-speaking
peoples of the ARAPAHO, BLACKFOOT,
CHEYENNE and CREE; and the SHOSHONEan-

speaking COMANCHE of Texas. In the inter-lying region were the numerous Sioux and Caddo tribes, the former including the ASSINABOIN, CROW, DAKOTA, MANDAN, OMAHA, OSAGE and WINNEBAGO; and the latter the ARIKA, Caddo and PAWNEE.

Great Spirit NORTH AMERICA
The Supreme Being, a popular concept among the AMERINDIAN peoples, who was perceived as the creator of all things and the giver of life. The Great Spirit would, in monotheistic cultures, simply be referred to as God.

Great Star NORTH AMERICA – GREAT PLAINS (*Skidi Pawnee*)
The personification of the planet VENUS[1] as the MORNING STAR[4] who was set in the east by TIRAWA. Her opposite was BRIGHT STAR whom Tirawa set in the west as the personification of Venus as the EVENING STAR. Bright Star and Great Star united and from this union was born a daughter who, along with the son of SAKURU and PAH, was set on the newly created Earth as the first people from whom all others are descended.

Great Turtle NORTH AMERICA – WOODLANDS (*Iroquois*)
When AWENHAI was thrown from the heavens, along with AURORA BOREALIS[3] and FIRE DRAGON WITH A BODY OF PURE WHITE COLOUR, Great Turtle surfaced from the primordial ocean and caught her, thus saving her from certain death.

Grey Wolf NORTH AMERICA – NORTHWEST COAST (*Klamath*)
Tutelary deity placed on Mount SHASTA by KEMUSH during the Creation.

Ground-Heat Girl NORTH AMERICA – SOUTHWEST (*Navajo*)
The divine girl to whom the first man was married by YOLKAI ESTSAN. The first

woman was likewise married to MIRAGE BOY, their children becoming the first NAVAJO people from whom all others can claim their descent.

Guabonito CARIBBEAN (*Taïno*)
The sea-goddess who resided at the bottom of the ocean amongst the shells. She taught GUAGUGIANA the lore and arts of medicine as well as how to make sacred necklaces from CIBAS (white shells) and GUIANOS (yellow shells).

Guagugiana CARIBBEAN (*Taïno*)
Also known as VAGONIONA, Guagugiana was one of the first people who emerged from the caves of CACIBAGIAGUA and AMAIAUA after the night watchman MAROCAEL had tarried a little too long one morning and the rays of the Sun petrified him, thus allowing mankind to emerge on to the Earth. Seeing that the entrance to the caves was now unguarded, Guagugiana sent his servant GIADRUVAVA out to look for a medicinal herb, but he too was caught in the Sun's rays and transformed into a bird whose beautiful song fills the night sky on the anniversary of his transformation, imploring his master to come to his rescue.

Saddened by the loss of his servant, Guagugiana decided to venture forth from the cave. He called all the women to him and told them to abandon their husbands and follow him, promising them untold riches if they did so. The women complied. Guagugiana led them to the island of MATENINO where he abandoned them, taking their children away with him.

According to some versions of this story, which survives only in fragmentary form, Guagugiana then abandoned the children beside a stream, or on the shore line, where their pleas for milk led to their transformation into dwarf-like TONA or, according to another variant, frogs.

Guagugiana continued his travels across the Earth and on one occasion met GUA-BONITO, the sea-goddess who taught him the lore of medicine and how to make sacred necklaces from CIBAS and GUIA-NOS.

Guamán Poma de Ayala, Don
Felipe SOUTH AMERICA
Spanish historian and writer who claimed royal INCA descent through his mother. He was responsible for the illustrated CODEX NUEVA CORONICA Y BUEN GOBIERNO, one of the two most important sources of Inca culture and doctrine.

Guaraní SOUTH AMERICA
Indigenous South American AMERINDIAN people who inhabited the area that is today Paraguay, southern Brazil and Bolivia. Traditionally, the Guaraní lived by hunting, cultivation and ritual warfare, but few of those living today retain these traditions. Their language belongs to the Tupian family.

Guarap SOUTH AMERICA – BRAZIL
(Xingú)
A simple variant of KUARUP.

Guatavita, Lake SOUTH AMERICA –
COLOMBIA (Chibcha)
A lake that was said to have been in-habited by a serpentine deity who, from time to time, came to collect the votive offerings left for him at his shrine on the shore. This mysterious deity is thought to represent a chthonic fertility god and a lord of the dead to whom vast quantities of gold were thrown in offering, this leading the lake to be identified, by some, with the fabled EL DORADO.

One story still survives surrounding the deity of this lake. In this an adulterous wife leaped into the water with her young child to escape her husband who had unmasked her infidelity, impaled her lover and forced the woman to eat his genitalia. Some time later the man asked the village SHAMAN to bring his wife back to him. The shaman descended to the bottom of the lake where he found the woman and the child living in the palace of the god. He returned empty-handed, but was immediately sent back, and this time returned with the child's eyeless corpse.

Guatrigakwitl NORTH AMERICA –
SOUTHWEST COAST (Wishok)
'Old Man Above', the creator deity who made the entire universe and the living things within it, when he spread his hands out over the primordial vacuum.

Guayacán, Lake SOUTH AMERICA (Inca)
The Earth was allegedly supported on pillars located in this lake in a time before CHIBCHACUM was defeated and made to retreat underground since when the Earth has rested on his shoulders, the pillars in the lake then being considered to hold the heavens aloft and prevent them from falling on to the Earth.

Guayavacuni SOUTH AMERICA –
PATAGONIA (Tehuelcho)
According to some sources, Guayavacuni was the SUPREME SPIRIT of the TEHUELCHO people.

Gucumatz CENTRAL AMERICA (Maya)
'Plumed Serpent' who, along with the creator TEPEU, consulted HURAKAN in order to determine how they might make men who would serve and glorify the gods. First the three gods made the Earth and then Gucumatz and Tepeu created the animals, and finally mankind.

guecufü SOUTH AMERICA – CHILE
(Arauca)
The generic name given to fiends of all types and descriptions.

Guédé HAITI (*Voodoo*)
The very first man to die who was resurrected, and thus saved, by LEGBA who summoned his soul to return to his body, that soul being said to have returned from beyond the waters of death. cf. GUÉDÉS.

guédés HAITI (*Voodoo*)
Name given to the spirits of the dead that are sometimes considered to take possession of the VOODOO cultists. The name is of Nigerian Yoruba derivation. On All Souls Day (2 November), a day of prayer for those in purgatory, the guédés are personified by dancers who dress in the clothes of mourning, and powder their faces a deathly shade of white. They wield phallic batons and dance in a provocative manner that is supposed to appease the dead spirits, the phallic symbology being used to suggest a life after death.

guianos CARIBBEAN (*Taïno*)
The name given to sacred yellow shells with which GUAGUGIANA was taught to make sacred necklaces, along with CIBAS, the sacred white shells, by the sea-goddess GUABONITO.

Guinechén SOUTH AMERICA – CHILE (*Arauca*)
The supreme being of the ARAUCA who is also sometimes called GUINEMAPUN.

Guinemapun SOUTH AMERICA – CHILE (*Arauca*)
An alternative name for the ARAUCA supreme spirit who is more usually called GUINECHÉN.

Gunarh NORTH AMERICA – NORTHWEST COAST (*Tlingit*)
The mythical killer-whale, one of the many animal spirits of the TLINGIT.

Gunarhnsengyet NORTH AMERICA – NORTHWEST COAST (*Tlingit*)
An heroic mythical hunter whose name comes from the fact that he was alleged to have once hunted GUNARH, the mythical killer-whale.

Gunnodoyah NORTH AMERICA – WOODLANDS (*Iroquois*)
A small boy whom the thunder-god HINO carried away to the sky where he armed him with bow and arrows and sent him out to fight a huge serpent. Gunnodoyah proved no match for the serpent who quickly swallowed him. However, Gunnodoyah's plight was revealed to Hino who summoned all his warriors and killed the serpent, released Gunnodoyah and made him his celestial servant.

Gusts-of-Wind NORTH AMERICA – WOODLANDS (*Iroquois*)
The daughter of the sky CHIEF-WHO-HOLDS-THE-EARTH and the goddess ATAENTSIC. She was made pregnant by the WIND-RULER but died due to the ante-natal quarrelling of the twins YOSKEHA and TASWISCANA.

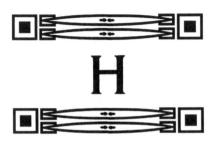

H

Ha Wen Neyu NORTH AMERICA –
WOODLANDS (*Iroquois*)
The GREAT SPIRIT.

Haab CENTRAL AMERICA (*Maya*)
The MAYA term for a solar year.

Hacavitz CENTRAL AMERICA (*Maya*)
The tutelary deity that was given to MAHU-
CUTAH at TULAI ZUIVA (the PLACE OF SEVEN
CAVES AND SEVEN RAVINES) to preside over
Mahucutah's clan. When the Sun rose for
the first time, its rays petrified Hacavitz,
along with TOHIL, AVILIX, and all the old
animal deities such as lion, tiger and viper
(cf. BALAM AGAB, BALAM QUITZÉ, IQI
BALAM, NICAHTAGAH).

Hadiganso Shano NORTH AMERICA –
WOODLANDS (*Iroquois*)
The proper name for the FALSE-FACE medicine society, an organized group of SHA-
MAN healers who were the supervisors of
religious rites and rituals. Their most important role was in the cure of the sick for
which they used carved wooden masks, or
faces, of which there are twelve basic
types. The members of the Hadiganso
Shano are somewhat unusual in that they
only ever operated as a group, performing
a noisy, grotesque dance at the house of
the sick person whom they are attempting
to cure. They scatter ashes from a sacred
fire over the ailing person, shake their
turtle-shell rattles and chant complex incantations.

The masks the members of the Hadiganso Shano wear are not called masks,
but rather 'faces', for they are perceived as
portraits in which the spirits being called
upon manifest themselves. A new 'face' is
'discovered' by the shaman as he carves
the portrait of the spirit into a living tree,
and then cuts the 'face' free. Red-painted
faces were carved in the morning, while
black-painted ones were 'discovered' in
the afternoon.

Hahai Wügti NORTH AMERICA –
PUEBLO, SOUTHWEST (*Hopi*)
The SPIDER-WOMAN.

Hahgwegdaetgah NORTH AMERICA –
WOODLANDS (*Iroquois*)
Alternative name for TASWISCANA that is
only used when HAHGWEHDIYU is used as
the alternative for YOSKEHA.

Hahgwehdiyu NORTH AMERICA –
WOODLANDS (*Iroquois*)
Alternative name for YOSKEHA that is only
used when HAHGWEGDAETGAH is used as
the alternative for TASWISCANA.

Haida NORTH AMERICA – NORTHWEST
COAST
Indigenous North American AMERINDIAN
people inhabiting a portion of the NORTH-
WEST COAST culture region. Their neigh-
bours include the likes of the BELLA COOLA,
CHINOOK, KWAKIUTL, NOOTKA, SALISH and

TSHIMSHIAN Indians with whom they share certain customs and myths.

Haidu NORTH AMERICA – WOODLANDS (*Iroquois*)

The evil ally of TASWISCANA whom YOS-KEHA had to fight. Having defeated Haidu, the source of disease and decay, Yoskeha extricated from him the secret lore of medicine and the sacred tobacco cere-mony which Yoskeha then taught to mankind.

Haietlik NORTH AMERICA – BRITISH COLUMBIA (*Nootka*)

Sometimes spelt HEITLIK. The lightning snake, the demon serpent of the NOOTKA who was related to the great THUNDERBIRD of the North American AMERINDIAN. Ver-sions of Haietlik can be found along the entire Pacific coastline of North America, as well as inland along the many mighty rivers. These variants include the NAITAKA of Lake OKANAGAN. Haietlik also appears to be akin to PAL-RAI-YÛK of the INUIT people.

Haietlik is recorded in two petroglyph sites on Vancouver Island where the demon serpent was considered very pre-cious. There fishermen offered, for a scrap of his flesh, the skins of twenty sea-otters, for they believed that if they carried a fragment of Haietlik's flesh in their canoe, they would be assured of killing a whale. Near NANAIMO, a site in British Columbia that is sacred to Haietlik, a group of three images has been found on a flat rock, while a huge horse-headed image, usually identi-fied as Haietlik, has been discovered lying on its back, split by a fault, amid other designs of fish and game. An image of the serpent is also to be found above Lake NICOLA, an image that was avoided at all costs by the fishermen who believed that if they looked at it, an evil wind would im-mediately blow up and capsize their canoes.

Haiowatha NORTH AMERICA – WOODLANDS (*Onondaga*)

Semi-legendary ONONDAGA teacher and chieftain who lived in the late sixteenth century and united the six nations of the IROQUOIS into the confederation of the LEAGUE OF THE LONG HOUSE. He is perhaps best known by the ALGONQUIAN variant of his name – HIAWATHA, though some have suggested that this name was simply the invention of LONGFELLOW. As Hiawatha is the better known of the two names, the legends associated with this character are to be found under that heading.

Hako NORTH AMERICA – GREAT PLAINS (*Pawnee*)

A great fertility ritual that symbolized the marriage of the Earth and the sky. The central emblems of the ceremony are winged staves that represent the eagle – the greatest of all the birds that travel between the Earth and the sky; white down that represents the clouds; and an ear of maize to symbolize W'ATIRA, Mother Corn. At the start of the ritual, the leading SHAMAN draws a circle on the ground with his eagle staff, an act that symbolizes both the building of it's nest by the eagle, and TIRAWA creating the world. The circle also denotes the kinship of the tribe.

Halach uinic CENTRAL AMERICA (*Maya*)

'True man', a caste that was on a par with the priestly caste of the AHUACAN in the MAYA caste system. Both were just one position down the social scale from the nobility. The Halach uinic sat as judges on those rising through the caste system to determine who had the right to be called ALMENHENOB, 'those who had mothers and fathers'. It seems that this classification does not owe its origins to whether or not the individual's parents were married, but rather to the Halach uinic being the par-ents who looked to the individual to prove themselves worthy of being called their children.

Hamatsu NORTH AMERICA –
NORTHWEST COAST (*Kwakiutl*)
The cannibal society.

Hamedicu NORTH AMERICA –
WOODLANDS (*Huron*)
The SUPREME BEING of the HURON peoples.

Hanan Cuzco SOUTH AMERICA (*Inca*)
The name given to the upper part of CUZCO, the CITY OF THE SUN, cf. HURIN CUZCO.

Hanghep Wi NORTH AMERICA – GREAT PLAINS (*Dakota*)
The spirit of the Moon when it illuminates the night sky, and is not visible during any daylight hours.

Hanhau CENTRAL AMERICA (*Maya*)
Simple variant of HUNHAU.

Haokah NORTH AMERICA – DAKOTA (*Sioux*)
The thunder-god who is personified as a drummer who used his drum-sticks to beat his thunder-drum. Heat made him shiver while the cold made him sweat. When he was happy, he would bow his horned head and weep, and conversely laugh when he was sad.

Hapikern CENTRAL AMERICA –
YUCATÁN, MEXICO (*Lacandone*)
Serpent with whom the LACANDONE believe NOHOCHAKYUM will enter into a fatal fight at the end of time, Hapikern's breath killing all mankind.

hapni-ñuñus SOUTH AMERICA – PERU (*Inca*)
A generic name for fiends that also appears to have been applied to the many peoples whom the INCAS conquered.

Hare NORTH AMERICA – WOODLANDS (*Algonquian*)
Sometimes referred to as RABBIT, but more usually as the Great Hare, this character is the chief figure in stories of the ALGONQUIAN-speaking AMERINDIAN peoples of the North American forests. He is both demi-urge and culture hero, as well as the TRICKSTER. Creator and transformer, Hero of the Dawn, the personification of Light and the provider of all things necessary to life, as well as god of water, wind and snow. Different peoples give him different names: GLOOSCAP – MICMAC; MÄNÄBUSCH – MENOMINEE; MANABOZHO or MINABOZHO – CHIPPEWA; MESSOU – MONTAGNAIS; NA-NABOOJOO or NANIBOZHO – POTAWATOMI.

Other important characters in the cycle of stories that are told about the Great Hare, a cycle that is commonly simply referred to as the Hare Cycle, are Hare's grandmother, the earth-goddess who is called NOKOMIS by the Menominee, and his younger brother who is also an animal – lynx, marten, or wolf. Stories about Hare and his brother (or brothers) sometimes also contain elements of the same myths as the IROQUOIS tell of the rival twins, TAS-WISCANA and YOSKEHA. Though Hare is sometimes called Rabbit, some variants of the cycle call Rabbit one of Hare's younger brothers. In later times the poet LONG-FELLOW incorporated many of the Hare stories into his epic poem concerning the legendary Iroquoian chief HIAWATHA.

The Hare cycle, in a much condensed form, is basically as follows. It should be noted that many of the names used in the following are Menominee, for theirs is the best recorded version of the cycle.

The daughter of Nokomis bore twins, but died during the final stages of child-birth along with one of the babies. Noko-mis took a wooden bowl (a symbol of the heavens) and placed it over the surviving baby to protect it. When she later removed the bowl, she discovered that the baby was a little white rabbit with long, trembling ears. She called the child Mänäbusch.

While still very young, Mänäbusch de-cided that he would steal fire to keep both his grandmother and himself warm. Noko-mis pleaded with him not to attempt such a feat, but Mänäbusch would not be dis-suaded and set off eastwards in his canoe until he came to the island on which the old man who owned fire lived. Arriving wet and cold outside the old man's wig-wam, Mänäbusch was found by the old man's two daughters who took pity on him and took him inside where they placed him by the roaring fire to dry and warm up. Waiting until the old man and his daugh-ters were otherwise occupied, Mänäbusch snatched a glowing brand from the fire and hurried out to his canoe. As he fled, the old man and his daughters noticed him and gave chase. Mänäbusch, however, rowed too quickly for the chasers and soon outran them. As he fled, the wind caused the brand to burst into flame, and so Män-äbusch brought fire home to his grand-mother. Nokomis entrusted the sacred flame to the THUNDERERs and their chief KENEUN, the Golden Eagle, in whose custo-dianship it has remained to this very day.

Mänäbusch had a brother, MOQWAOI, the Wolf. One day, as Moqwaoi walked across the frozen surface of a lake, the ANAMAQKIU, malignant underworld spir-its, dragged him under the ice. For four days Mänäbusch mourned the loss of his brother. On the fifth he met with his brother's shade whom he told to go to the west where he should build and tend a great fire that would guide the dead to their new home, as well as to keep them warm on their journey.

Mänäbusch now determined to avenge the death of his brother and made war on the anamaqkiu whose two BEAR chieftains he tricked to their death. The anamaqkiu retaliated by raising a great flood that cov-ered the whole Earth. Mänäbusch climbed a huge pine tree to escape the advancing waters, but still they chased after him. Mänäbusch made the tree grow to four times its original height, but still the waters came after him, only being arrested by the GREAT SPIRIT when they had reached Män-äbusch's armpits.

With the world destroyed, Mänäbusch told the other animals that he could create a new world if he had so much as a single speck of soil. First OTTER, then BEAVER, then MINK plunged down to look for some, but they all died in their attempt. At last MUSKRAT succeeded and brought back the single grain of soil that Mänäbusch then used to recreate the Earth.

Various other animals take part in this episode depending on which people are relating the cycle. For example, in the Montagnais version the first attempt was made by RAVEN. However, all versions concur that it was Muskrat that suc-ceeded.

The Potawatomi Hare cycle names Na-naboojoo as the oldest of four brothers who were born to a spirit father and an earthly mother. The second brother was CHIPIAPOOS, or CHIBIABOS, who was drowned by evil underworld spirits and duly became the lord of the dead. The third was WABASSO who took fright the first time he saw light and fled away to the north where he became a white rabbit, and is revered as the great MANITOU. The fourth brother, CHAKEKENAPOK killed their mother and was killed by Nanaboojoo in revenge, patches of flint marking the spots where the two brothers fought. Fragments of Chakekenapok's corpse were transformed into rocks and his intestines formed the vines that hang from the trees.

The Hare cycle tells how Hare introduced the sacred rites and teachings of the MIDEWEWIN, the medicine society, and of his various battles with giants and other monsters. His greatest feat, apart from the recreation of the Earth, was perhaps his victory over a terrible water-monster who had been swallowing mankind. In some versions of the cycle this episode is connected with the death of Hare's brother, while in others it remains quite independent.

In the Menominee cycle this fiend is called MASHENOMAK, or MISIKINEBIK. Hare allowed himself to be swallowed and then, along with all its other victims, held a war dance in the monster's stomach, stabbed it in the heart, and finally hacked his way out.

After his work on Earth was completed, Hare went away to live in the VILLAGE OF SOULS in the far west where he still lives with his grandmother and brother who had gone there before him. Sometimes braves have journeyed there to visit him. One story tells of how four – though some sources say seven – braves made the perilous journey and entertained Hare who promised each brave a wish. One man asked to be a successful hunter. Another wanted to be a great warrior. However, the last wished for immortality, so Hare turned him into a stone – some say a tree.

A Montagnais variant on this says that Hare partly agreed to the wish and gave the man a little packet of immortality, telling the brave that all men would be immortal while the packet remained closed. However, in due course the man's inquisitive wife could no longer resist the temptation and opened the packet, out of which the immortality flew and so men became mortal.

Hast(s)(h)eyalti NORTH AMERICA – SOUTHWEST (*Navajo*)
One of the two great YEI, the other being HASTSHEHOGAN. When mankind lost their freedom to the celestial gambler HE-WHO-WINS-MEN, Hastsheyalti and Hastshehogan came to the rescue and assisted by animal deities and the spirits of wind and darkness, enabled a young brave to overcome the gambler. With a magic bow the youth shot the celestial gambler back into the sky from where he later descended to rule over the Mexican peoples.

The yei then created two goddesses – ESTANATLEHI and YOLKAI ESTSAN – forming the first from turquoise and the second from white-shell. Yolkai Estsan and Hastsheyalti decided that they should create a new race of men. They first made a man from an ear of white corn, and then a woman from an ear of yellow corn. The wind-spirit NILTSHI then breathed life into them. ROCK-CRYSTAL BOY gave them their minds. GRASSHOPPER GIRL gave them the power of speech. Yolkai Estsan gave them the gifts of fire and maize. She then married the man to GROUND-HEAT GIRL and the woman to MIRAGE BOY. These couples became the ancestors of the NAVAJO people.

Hast(s)(h)ehogan NORTH AMERICA – SOUTHWEST (*Navajo*)
The house-god, one of the two great YEI, the other being HASTSHEYALTI.

Hastseltsi NORTH AMERICA – SOUTHWEST (*Navajo*)
The god of racing who was euphemistically called 'Red Lord'.

Hastsezini NORTH AMERICA –
SOUTHWEST (*Navajo*)
The fire-god who was given the euphemism 'Black Lord'.

Havstrambe NORTH AMERICA –
GREENLAND (*Inuit*)
A mysterious sea-creature that is simply described as a sort of merman.

Hayicanke NORTH AMERICA –
NORTHWEST COAST (*Tlingit*)
'Old-Woman-Under-the-Earth'. She was placed in charge of the foreleg of the beaver that had been killed by YETL and which was used to prop up the Earth.

He-Who-Wins-Men NORTH AMERICA –
SOUTHWEST (*Navajo*)
Celestial gambler to whom the NAVAJO fell victim and were tricked into staking and losing their freedom. However, He-Who-Wins-Men was not to enjoy his overlordship for long, as the two YEI – HASTSHEYALTI and HASTSHEHOGAN – came to the rescue of the Navajo and, with the help of the spirits of wind and darkness, along with various animal deities, enabled a young brave to overcome the gambler and then to shoot him back into the sky with a magic bow. He-Who-Wins-Men later descended, according to the Navajo, to rule over the Mexican people.

Heammawihio NORTH AMERICA –
GREAT PLAINS (*Cheyenne*)
The GREAT SPIRIT who was symbolized by the Sun. He appears to have been originally perceived as a spider for the root of his name, *wihio*, (spider). (cf. AKTUNOWIHIO)

Heitlik NORTH AMERICA – BRITISH
COLUMBIA (*Nootka*)
Variant of HAIETLIK.

Heller SOUTH AMERICA – PATAGONIA
(*Tehuelcho*)
The son of the Sun who created men and bestowed on them all the arts of civilization.

Heloha NORTH AMERICA – WOODLANDS
(*Choctaw*)
The female THUNDERBIRD.

Heng NORTH AMERICA – WOODLANDS
(*Huron*)
The thunder-god who was also known as DE HI NO. The guardian of the skies, and the eternal enemy of all things evil, Heng was extremely important to the HURON people. (cf. HINO)

Henga NORTH AMERICA – GREAT PLAINS
(*Osage*)
The eagle-spirit.

Heno NORTH AMERICA – WOODLANDS
(*Iroquois*)
A variant of HINO.

Hereshguina NORTH AMERICA –
WOODLANDS (*Winnebago*)
The great evil-spirit who is identified with WAKDJUNKAGA by the semi-Christianized followers of the PEYOTE rite.

Heron NORTH AMERICA (*Tlingit*)
A very tall and very wise man who was created by NASCAKIYETL. Some sources say that Nascakiyelt's sister had given birth to many sons, but her brother killed them all in a jealous rage. Advised by Heron, she swallowed a red-hot pebble and subsequently gave birth to YETL, the RAVEN, her child being named after the impregnable stone ITC AK, and called TAQLIKIC, 'Hammer-father', as he was so tough and

flexible. Nascakiyetl recognized his prowess and made him the world's head man.

Hex Chun Chun CENTRAL AMERICA (*Maya*)

The god of the usurping ITZÁ dynasty, a symbolic and highly dangerous war-god.

Heyerdahl, Thor

Twentieth-century Norwegian anthropologist, ethnologist, adventurer and explorer who sailed, with five colleagues, the BALSA-wood raft KON-TIKI, named after a legendary pre-INCA Sun king, from Collao, Peru, to Tuamotu Island in the South Pacific in 1947, spending 101 days adrift on the Humboldt Current.

heyoka NORTH AMERICA – GREAT PLAINS (*Dakota*)

A generic term used to refer to a group of spirits.

Hiawatha NORTH AMERICA – WOODLANDS (*Algonquian*)

With a name more correctly spelled HAIO-WATHA, Hiawatha was a legendary late sixteenth-century AMERINDIAN teacher and ONONDAGA chieftain. He is said to have brought together the six nations of the IROQUOIS into a confederation known as the LEAGUE OF THE LONG HOUSE in what is today upper New York State. He is perhaps best known as the eponymous hero of LONGFELLOW's epic poem THE SONG OF HIAWATHA. However, as the stories told in this famous poem do not relate to Hiawatha, but instead derive from the ALGO-NQUIAN myths from the HARE cycles, it is quite conceivable that Hiawatha was just a simplification of Haiowatha that was used by Longfellow to make the name easier for the Western tongue. As Longfellow's variant is the best known, the legends relating to Haiowatha are included here.

Hiawatha planned a peaceful union between all the various Iroquoian and Algonquian tribes, all of whom had been engaged in internecine warfare for a great many years. Though he did not fully succeed in what he set out to do, he did at least unite the six Iroquois nations into a federation.

Hiawatha's plans were bitterly opposed by ATOTARHO, a great warrior and SHAMAN whose head is reported to have been covered with serpentine hair, and whose anger was so fierce that anyone who was unfortunate to look at him immediately fell dead. During one tribal council it is reported that Atotarho called down a great white bird which pounced on Hiawatha's only daughter and killed her.

Hiawatha decided that he was wasting his time, for the time being, with Atotarho, and so left his tribal village in a magic white canoe and travelled to the settlements of the ONEIDA whose chief, DEKANAWIDA, became Hiawatha's great friend and staunchest ally. Together they converted the MOHAWK and CAYUGA peoples to Hiawatha's plan. Seeing that these people were now united, Atotarho changed his mind and joined the confederacy. Thus was the League of the Long House formed and Dekanawida became its law-giver.

With his work complete, Hiawatha stepped back into his magic white canoe and sailed away across the lake to the land of the souls in the far west.

Hide SOUTH AMERICA – LAKE LACAR, ARGENTINA

A flat, circular water-monster that is the embodiment of a mainly malevolent supernatural force. (cf. CUERO, IMAP IMASSOUR-SUA)

Hikuli CENTRAL AMERICA – MEXICO (*Tarahumare*)

The four-faced personification of the PEYOTE who is perceived as all-seeing.

Hino NORTH AMERICA – WOODLANDS
(*Iroquois*)
The THUNDERER, the guardian of the skies
who bears a huge bow and flaming arrows,
is the eternal enemy of evil, in which guise
he killed the horrific water-monster that
set about swallowing mankind. His wife
was RAINBOW[4] and among his many assis-
tants was the hero GUNNODOYAH.

Hînqumemen NORTH AMERICA –
BRITISH COLUMBIA (*Coeur-d'Alénes*)
A lake that is known as 'The Engulfer'.
The indigenous AMERINDIAN peoples who
live in the vicinity avoid it at all costs, for
whoever draws water from the lake is pursued by the lake itself which brings him
back and then drowns him.

Hisakitaimisi NORTH AMERICA –
WOODLANDS (*CREEK*)
THE GREAT SPIRIT who is responsible for
and controls all life on Earth.

Hobowakan NORTH AMERICA –
WOODLANDS (*Delaware*)
The name given to the peace-pipe that is
used in the CALUMET ceremony during
which gifts are distributed.

Hodag NORTH AMERICA – QUÉBEC
A water-monster with telescopic legs and
a snout that is shaped like a musket barrel
down which it shoots clay 'bullets' at sleeping prey.

Hogan NORTH AMERICA – SOUTHWEST
(*Navajo*)
The NAVAJO name for a lodge, the traditional home of the people as well as of the
gods.

Hoh CENTRAL AMERICA (*Maya*)
A crow, one of the four creatures said to
have brought maize to the gods so that
they could create mankind. The other
three animals who were thus responsible in

part for the creation of man were QUEL, a
parrot, UTIU, a coyote and YAC, a forest
cat.

Hoita NORTH AMERICA – GREAT PLAINS
(*Mandan*)
The spotted-eagle-spirit.

Hokewingla NORTH AMERICA – GREAT
PLAINS (*Dakota*)
The turtle-spirit who is said to live in the
Moon.

Hokhokw NORTH AMERICA –
NORTHWEST COAST (*Kwakiutl*)
A monstrous bird that has a very long beak
and which plays an important role in the
HAMATSU rituals.

Hokomata CENTRAL AMERICA – MEXICO
(*Mojave*)
The uncle of PUKEHEH, thus possibly the
brother of TOCHIPA, and the creator of the
flood that destroyed the Earth.

Holkan-Okot CENTRAL AMERICA
(*Maya*)
The 'Dance of Warriors' which is believed
to have formed a part of the PAX (May)
festival that was held in the honour of
NACON.

Homshuk CENTRAL AMERICA – MEXICO
(*Olmec*)
The personification and representation of
maize. He was discovered by an old couple
as he hatched from an egg. At birth his
hair was golden and as soft as the gossamer
threads that are to be found on ears of
maize. When just seven days old, his adventures began.

At first he was derided by other lesser
breeds such as the minnow and thrush, as
well as many other small creatures who
thought him ridiculous, though at this
stage they did not recognize his inherent
nobility and special attributes with which

he had been endowed. Enraged, Homshuk killed all those who sought to make fun of him, but his foster-parents became uneasy and convinced themselves that he intended to deal with them in the same way, so they plotted to kill him while he slept. However, the old couple also failed to recognize his divine nature, for only his mortal shape lay asleep when they came to kill him, his soul being outside on the roof. The foster-father was killed when the plan recoiled and afterwards the foster-mother persecuted little Homshuk.

Homshuk warned his foster-mother to leave him alone, warning her that he was very strong and could easily destroy her. He also added that he was destined to bring food to all mankind, but she paid him no attention and continued in her attempts to kill him. The final straw came when she surrounded Homshuk with a wall of flame and attempted to burn him to death. Homshuk escaped and made his way, after a great deal of wandering, to the seashore. There he sat down and began to beat on a drum, the sound of the drum carrying far away to the home of HURACÁN who sent a messenger to find out who was responsible for all the noise. Homshuk told that messenger, 'I am he who sprouts at the knees. I am he who flowers.'

Huracán thought that this reply was an attempt by Homshuk to conceal his true identity, and that he must, therefore, be a NAGUAL, an evil spirit, who desired to remain unknown and thus beyond harm. Huracán thus turned against Homshuk who enlisted the aid of a tortoise or turtle which carried him across the sea to Huracán's home.

Homshuk was immediately taken captive and thrown into three successive prisons. The first was filled with serpents, the second with ravenous tigers, and the third with arrows in constant flight, each prison being a representation of the three sides of man – his serpentine instincts, his dark tiger-like nature and his penetrating wickedness. When the captors came to the first prison after Homshuk had spent the night with the serpents, they found him seated on the back of one of the hungry vipers. The same thing happened after he had spent the night in the tiger prison. Finally, the arrows fell harmlessly at his feet and allowed themselves to be made into a bundle with which Homshuk might protect himself.

Huracán, however, still failed to understand the divine nature of Homshuk and now challenged him to a stone-throwing competition. Homshuk won this with the aid of a woodpecker who, when Homshuk cast his stone, hammered against a tree, the sound giving those listening the impression that Homshuk's stone was rebounding far away. Huracán then took his turn, but no one heard anything. Huracán grudgingly conceded to Homshuk.

Huracán then decreed that Homshuk should be swung out over the ocean. However, after Homshuk had gone no more than half way, he returned and reported that he could see how easy the journey was going to be, and that Huracán and his people should go first. Huracán and his people suffered many calamities on the voyage and finally accepted the true divine nature of Homshuk whom he offered to keep well watered – it appears as if by this stage he had taken on his true plant form – so that maize, which Huracán now recognized as being of supreme importance, should grow to feed mankind.

honga NORTH AMERICA – GREAT PLAINS (*Osage*)
Generic name used to refer to inhabitants of the UNDERWORLD.

honochenokeh NORTH AMERICA – WOODLANDS (*Iroquois*)
Generic name applied to benevolent spirits.

Hopi NORTH AMERICA – PUEBLO, SOUTHWEST
Indigenous North American AMERINDIAN people from the southwestern mountains of the USA, whose name means 'peaceful people', a role in which they have long been revered by other North American peoples. Today they number approximately 6,000 and live in the middle of the NAVAJO, or Dineh, reservation. Their language belongs to the Uto-Aztecan family. The Hopi see themselves as charged with maintenance of the balance between the upper and the lower worlds, a balance they keep through a series of elaborate festivals and rituals and thus ensure the continuance of life on Earth.

Hopop Caan CENTRAL AMERICA (*Maya*)
'He who lights up the sky', one of the alternative names for CHAAC, the MAYA rain-god.

Hoturu NORTH AMERICA – GREAT PLAINS (*Pawnee*)
The wind spirit.

houmfort HAITI (*Voodoo*)
The name given to a VOODOO temple that has a central post from which the loa is believed to descend to 'mount' the initiate, the particular loa being identifiable from the characteristic behaviour exhibited by the possessed worshipper.

houngan HAITI (*Voodoo*)
Name given to a cult priest.

Hozoni NORTH AMERICA – SOUTHWEST (*Navajo*)
A ritual chant, usually referred to as the Hozoni Chant, that recounts the tale of GLISMA and her marriage to the leader of the SNAKE PEOPLE, inhabitants of the UNDERWORLD. The myth itself suggests a fertility rite. However, like all other NAVAJO

chants whatever their original significance, the only known function of the Hozoni Chant is medicinal, as it was used by SHAMANs in healing rites and rituals.

huaca(s) SOUTH AMERICA (*Inca*)
A shrine or sacred cult object that is perceived as being possessed by a spirit, an especial category of these sacred items being the APACHITAS, piles of stones that were constructed at danger spots on roads, as well as on the summits of mountain passes. The huaca was the dominating concept of popular INCA religious belief, and included what would today be termed 'charms' or 'good-luck' emblems.

Huallallo Caruincho SOUTH AMERICA – PERU (*Quechua*)
A god or culture hero who was said to have expelled YANANAMCA INTANAMCA and taken his place. During his tyrannical reign no woman was allowed to bear more than two children, of which one had to be sacrificed to him. Eventually Huallallo Caruincho's people were liberated by PARIACACA and his sons.

Huana Cauri SOUTH AMERICA (*Inca*)
One of the CHILDREN OF THE SUN, the three or four brothers and their three or four sisters who emerged from a cave having three mouths at PACCARITAMBO ('Inn of Origin'), which is also sometimes called TAMBOTOCCO. While the Children of the Sun were to become the ancestors of the most important INCA clan, the people who emerged from the other two mouths of the cave were to become the ancestors of all the other, lesser Inca clans.

The names and numbers of brothers and sisters vary according to source. Pedro DE CIEZA DE LÉON says that the Inca nobility told him that there were three brothers named AYAR CACHI ASAUCA, AYAR MANCO, and AYAR UCHO (*ayar* apparently meaning 'male' or 'man'), and three sisters named

MAMA COYA, MAMA HUACO and MAMA RAHUA (*mama* apparently meaning 'female' or 'woman').

However, the accounts of Fray Martin DE MONIA differ. He had obviously heard a wide variety of renditions of the story of the Children of the Sun, for he says that he felt that the most 'plausible' version was that giving four brothers named, CUSCO HUANCA, Huana Cauri, MANCO CAPAC and TOPA AYAR CACHI, and four sisters named CORI OCLLO, IPA HUACO, MAMA COYA and TOPA HUACO. It is the version told by de Monia that is the most widely accepted due to the inclusion of Manco Capac as one of the brothers.

In this account Huana Cauri is the oldest brother who chose to stay in APITAY where he died, the mountain of HUANA-CAURI being named in his honour. The others proceeded to the city of ACAMAMA and occupied it with ease when they encountered no opposition. Cusco Huanca became the first Inca king of the city whose name he changed to CUZCO. He was succeeded by Manco Capac.

Huanacauri, Mount SOUTH AMERICA (*Inca*)

A mountain to the south of CUZCO that was, according to the version of the story of the CHILDREN OF THE SUN told by Fray Martin DE MONIA, named after HUANA CAURI who had died there. He additionally adds that it was the first resting place of the Children of the Sun on their journey from an island in the middle of Lake TITI-CACA, and says that it was near APITAY.

Pedro DE CIEZA DE LÉON adds that AYAR CACHI slung stones from the top of the mountain which caused the surrounding hills to split, an act that aroused such jealousy in his brothers that they lured him into a cave and imprisoned him there. Ayar Cachi's spirit then visited his brothers and sisters while they were camped at TAMBU QUIRU and told them to found a

city at CUZCO. He then turned himself into a cult stone on the top of Mount Huanacauri which was thenceforth revered as a god.

Huáscar SOUTH AMERICA – PERU (*Inca*)

(c.1495-1532). Son of HUAYNA-CAPAC and brother of ATAHUALPA. On the death of their father in 1525 the two brothers divided the INCA empire, Atahualpa receiving the northern half which he ruled from its capital at QUITO, and Huáscar the southern half which he ruled from CUZCO. Atahualpa overthrew and killed his brother in 1532 during the Spanish conquest.

Huastec CENTRAL AMERICA

Ancient civilization that once inhabited the southern reaches of Mexico along with the MIXTEC and ZAPOTEC peoples.

Huayanu Potosí SOUTH AMERICA – BOLIVIA AND PERU (*Aymará*)

Mountain of the Bolivian cordillera that was revered by the AYMARÁ as an ACHA-CHILA.

Huayna-Capac SOUTH AMERICA – PERU (*Inca*)

Historical king of the INCAs and father of ATAHUALPA and HUÁSCAR. Upon his death in 1525 the empire was split into northern and southern halves, the northern going to Atahualpa and the southern to his brother. A curious story says that CON-IRAYA VIRACOCHA gave Huayna-Capac a shining woman in a box which, when opened to release the woman, filled the world with light. This story would seem to suggest that there was considerable interaction between the QUECHUA and the Inca, and may have been one of the origins of the EL DORADO legend.

Huecuvu SOUTH AMERICA – ARGENTINA
AND CHILE (*Arauca*)
The name given to evil animation's of
spirits that have no particular form, but are
usually depicted as a HIDE, an embodiment
of a mainly malevolent supernatural force.
(cf. CUERO)

Huehuecóyotl CENTRAL AMERICA –
MEXICO (*Aztec*)
The god of mischief-making, thus a TRICK-
STER, and the tutelary deity of OTOMÍ.

Huehuetéotl CENTRAL AMERICA –
MEXICO (*Aztec*)
'Old God', a name sometimes given to
XIUHTECUHTLI, the fire-god, one of the
companions of NIGHT who is, in all probability, an early cult of the god that was later
to become known as QUETZALCÓATL.

Huehueteótl is one of the oldest of all
the ancient American deities whose ceremonies were of especial importance at the
end of every fifty-two-year cycle of time
when old fires were extinguished, and new
ones lit to perpetuate time itself. Not only
were all the fires dowsed. Wooden and
stone statues of the gods were thrown into
the water together with pestles and hearth
stones. Homes were swept clean and all
rubbish disposed of. At midnight, the
exact moment that the fifty-two-year cycle
came to an end, when time itself was
thought to have run out, the AZTEC priests
would kindle a new fire on the chest of a
captive, the victim being chosen due to his
noble birth. The heart of the victim was
thought to feed the fire which, if it did not
blaze well enough, was thought to herald
the moment when the sun itself would die
and the demons of the darkness that
would cover the land for all-time would
descend to devour men. Alternatively, it
was believed that men themselves would
become these demons and set upon each
other until they had all been destroyed.

When the future of mankind was seen
to be in limbo, women at this time were of
great importance. They were held in great
fear and were locked in granaries where
they were made to wear masks made of
maguey leaves. Children were also kept
awake, usually by being kicked, to save
them from being turned into mice. When
the dawn finally arrived, the people would
rejoice and prick their ears from which
they would sprinkle blood on the newly
kindled fire. From this fire a relay of run-
ners would take the new sacred flame to
every temple in the land.

Men and women put on new clothes
that had been set aside for this occasion,
redecorated their homes, made new votive
and ritual vessels and renovated the temples. Sacrifices were offered to the gods of
incense and quail, and amaranth seed
cakes covered in honey were eaten. However, nobody took a drink from the first
rays of dawn until noon, at which time
captives were ceremonially bathed and
then sacrificed by being thrown alive on to
the fire, after which their hearts would be
removed. Finally grains of maize were
cooked on the new fires and distributed by
the priests to all the people to eat.

Huemac CENTRAL AMERICA – MEXICO
(*Aztec*)
Even though some stories account for the
fall of the city of TOLLAN by saying that it
occurred when QUETZALCÓATL departed,
others say that it survived for a further 200
years, its last secular ruler in this instance
being Huemac. His disgrace and fall from
favour was engineered by TEZCATLIPOCA
who came to Tollan in the guise of a naked
Indian by the name of TOUEYO and began
to sell green peppers in the market-place
outside Huemac's palace.

Toueyo made sure that his presence
came to the attention of Huemac's beautiful daughter who, having never seen a
naked man before, became ill with desire

for him. Huemac summoned Toueyo to tell him that, as he was responsible for the princess's illness, he must cure her. Huemac thus married his daughter to Toueyo, a member of the lowest possible caste, and by so doing made him a prince of Tollan, an act which ensured catastrophic consequences and the eventual destruction of the city.

Huichol CENTRAL AMERICA – MEXICO
Ancient civilization that, along with the CORA people, once inhabited the most westerly portion of Mexico.

Huicton CENTRAL AMERICA – MEXICO (*Aztec*)
One of the leaders who journeyed from the ancestral homeland of AZTLAN, visited COATLICUE and then returned to Aztlan. His companions are named as ACACITLI, AHATL, AUEXOTL, OCELOPAN, TEÇACATETL, TENOCH and XOMIMITL. They were accompanied by the four guardians of HUITZILOPOCHTLI, the son of Coatlicue, who are named as CHIPACTONAL, OXOMOCO, TLALTECUIN and XOCHICAHUACA.

Huitaca SOUTH AMERICA – COLOMBIA (*Chibcha*)
The beautiful, amoral goddess of licentiousness and drunkenness who pursued NEMTEREQUETEBA, but, according to some accounts, he turned the goddess into an owl or the Moon. Other stories say that her transformation was down to BOCHICA. Sometimes she is identified with the Moon-goddess CHIÁ and is, in these instances, referred to as the wife of Bochica.

Huitzilihuitl CENTRAL AMERICA – MEXICO (*Aztec*)
The AZTEC leader who led his people into the COLHUACAN city of CHAPUTEPEC where

he was captured and put to death while the Aztecs were routed. See AZTLAN.

Huitzilopochtli CENTRAL AMERICA – MEXICO (*Aztec*)
The Sun-god and tutelary deity of the AZTEC people to whom ritual human sacrifices of prisoners were made. Sacrifices of Aztec citizens to Huitzilopochtli were also a common occurrence, their sacrifice being deemed as necessary to keep the Sun in the sky. These victims were painted white and were, after death, destined to become stars, so at least they were confident of immortality after a horrific death – small comfort to the countless young children who were drowned in waterholes, springs or special areas of Lake TEZCOCO to satisfy the water-gods. Described in some sources as a mortal, Huitzilopochtli was said to have been a magician, a 'disturber of life' and a 'terror', but these are actually more relevant to his aspect of TEZCATLIPOCA. His more benevolent qualities are more akin to CINTÉOTL, the god of corn with whom he is also identified.

Huitzilopochtli was one of the four sons of the dual god-above-all TONACATECUHTLI ('Lord Nourishment') and his consort TONACACÍHUATL ('Lady Nourishment') who lived in the ninth and highest heaven. The four appear to have originally been regarded as nature gods and protectors of the four cardinal points, but were later identified as the tutelary deities of the Aztec empire's different peoples. The four were QUETZALCÓATL, Green-Feathered Serpent, war-god and chief deity of the TOLTECS; black Tezcatlipoca, god of night and war-god of the great city of TEZCOCO; red CAMAXTLI, chief god of the TLAXCALA; and the Aztec Huitzilopochtli. This, however, is an anachronism as Huitzilopochtli and Quetzalcóatl are usually identified as one and the same, Quetzalcóatl being the earlier NAHUA name for the deity the Aztecs referred to as Huitzilopochtli. Other sources omit Tezcatlipoca, as Tezcatlipoca is actually an aspect of Huitzilopochtli, and replace him with the fearsome XIPE TOTEC, the flayed-god.

Huitzilopochtli, whose name means 'Hummingbird-of-the-Left' (derived from *huitzilin* – 'hummingbird', and *opochtli* – 'on the left'), was originally the guardian deity of the south, and appears to have already been elevated to the ranks of tutelary deity prior to the Aztec incursion into Central America. With the ascent of the Aztec people, the power of Huitzilopochtli was also increased so that he adopted the roles of both creator and war-god.

A relatively late account of his birth which says that Huitzilopochtli was the magically conceived son of COATLICUE illustrates this rise to pre-eminence, as it makes him the all conquering Sun who drives both Moon and stars from the sky. One day Coatlicue and her four sisters (whose names remain unrecorded) were doing penance for some unknown sin on a hill called COATEPEC. There Coatlicue, a virgin, gathered together some white feathers and placed them between her breasts, though an alternative version says that she swallowed an emerald. By this act she became pregnant and subsequently gave birth to Huitzilopochtli in the later Aztec versions of the story, or Quetzalcóatl in the earlier Nahua renditions. While Coatlicue was still pregnant, her daughter, COYOLXAUHQUI, disgusted by the revelation, instigated a plot to kill her mother, inciting Coatlicue's 400 sons, the CENTZONUITZNÁUA, to do the evil deed. However, as they approached to kill their mother, Huitzilopochtli was born armed with a blue shield and spear. His left leg was adorned with hummingbird feathers (as his name would suggest) and his head with plumes. He also carried his XIUHOCÓATL, a serpent made of turquoise or of fire, with a single blow of which he killed Coyolxauhqui. He then pursued the 400 Centzonuitznáua and killed almost all of them too. Only a small number managed to escape his fury and travelled south to HUITZLAMPA, the 'Place of Thorns'.

Huitzilopochtli also appears as a magician who joined forces with TITLACUHAN (a title of Tezcatlipoca) and his brother TLACAHUEPAN in a plot, mustered by fiends, against the great Quetzalcóatl. He was again used by Tezcatlipoca, this time unwittingly, in the downfall of the city of TOLLAN.

When the Aztec people journeyed from their ancestral homeland of AZTLAN, Huitzilopochtli went with them, his departure causing Coatlicue to enter a prolonged period of mourning, though he did promise her that when he had shown the Aztecs a new land he would return. Huitzilopochtli led the Aztecs to the COLHUACAn city of CHAPUTEPEC, but the Aztecs were routed and their lord, HUITZILIHUITL, captured and killed.

Huitzlampa CENTRAL AMERICA –
MEXICO (*Aztec*)
The 'Place of Thorns', the location to where the small remnant of the 400 CENTZONUITZNÁUA fled after HUITZILOPOCHTLI had killed their brothers.

Huixtocíhuatl CENTRAL AMERICA –
MEXICO (*Aztec*)
The goddess of salt.

Hun Came CENTRAL AMERICA (*Maya*)
One of the rulers of XIBALBA, the UNDERWORLD of MAYA belief. The other lords of this terrible domain were AHALCANA, AHALPUH, CHAMIABAK, CHAMIAHOLOM, CUCHUMAQIQ, PATAN, QUIQRE, QUIQRIXGAG, QUIQXIL, VUKUB CAME and XIQIRIPAT. The divine twins HUNAHPU and XBALANQUÉ were summoned before him and Vukub Came after they had survived the many horrors of Xibalba. At his own insistence he was burned by the twins as he

mistakenly believed them when they said that they could restore him; as soon as he was burned they simply spread his ashes around the underworld.

Hun Pic Tok CENTRAL AMERICA (*Maya*)
A symbolic war-god who was perceived as holding 8,000 spears.

Hunab Ku CENTRAL AMERICA – YUCATÁN, MEXICO (*Maya*)
King of the gods of the MAYA, god of the Sun, the inventor of weaving, the 'Great Hand', the 'God behind the Gods', the 'one and only God'. Invisible, impalpable, incorporeal and omniscient, Hunab Ku was the exact parallel of OMETÉOTL, or TLOQUE NAHUAQUE. He married IXAZA-LUCH, the goddess of water, by whom he had a son, ITZAMNÁ, a literate and cultured immortal who had the special ability of being able to bestow immortality.

Hunahpu CENTRAL AMERICA (*Maya*)
One of the semi-divine sons of HUNHUN AHPU and the maiden XQUIQ, his twin brother being XBALANQUÉ. The twins were conceived when their father's skull, hung in a calabash tree in XIBALBA after he had been killed for losing a ball game, had spat into Xquiq's hand as she stretched out to take a fruit from the tree. The two boys were at first persecuted by their brothers HUNBATZ and HUNCHOUEN, but that stopped when the twins turned them into monkeys. They then travelled to Xibalba and avenged their father before being translated to the heavens, one twin becoming the Sun, the other the Moon.

Hunbatz CENTRAL AMERICA (*Maya*)
One of the jealous brothers of HUNAHPU and XBALANQUÉ, and thus one of the sons of XQUIQ, as well as the brother of HUN-CHOUEN, Hunbatz and Hunchouen being

born before their father travelled to XI-BALBA and was killed there. He and his brothers at first persecuted the twins and plotted to kill them, but they were all turned into monkeys by the semi-divine twins.

Hunchouen CENTRAL AMERICA (*Maya*)
Son of XQUIQ by HUNHUN AHPU and the brother of HUNBATZ. He and his brother persecuted the semi-divine twins HU-NAHPU and XBALANQUÉ whom their mother had borne to Hunhun Ahpu after he had been killed in XIBALBA, but were turned into monkeys by the semi-divine pair before they could carry out their plot to kill the twins.

Hunger NORTH AMERICA – SOUTHWEST (*Navajo*)
One of the four ANAYE who were left alive after the assault of NAYANEZGANI and THO-BADZISTSHINI, and then by ESTANATLEHI, and then only after they had convinced Estanatlehi that they should be allowed to remain alive – otherwise man might not prize the good things in life, or even life itself. The other anaye who were allowed to survive were COLD, OLD AGE and POVERTY.

Hunhau CENTRAL AMERICA (*Maya*)
Also sometimes called AH PUCH or AH KINCHEL, this deity is identified in the *codices* simply as the god A. Hunhau is the god of death to the classical MAYA who rules over MITNAL, a realm that probably derives from the NAHUA land of the dead – MICTLÁN. Sometimes represented with a human body and the head of an owl, present-day Mexican AMERINDIANS believe that someone will die whenever the owl screeches. Hunhau is normally associated with the dog, the symbol of death and the bearer of lightning which is allied to the

Maya day of OC, the last day of the series that signifies the lowest point reached by the soul of a dead person on his long spiritual journey to the hereafter (see the AGES OF MAN). To the modern Yuacatec Maya he is YUM CIMIL.

Hunhun Ahpu CENTRAL AMERICA
(*Maya*)

The son of XPIYACOC and XMUCANÉ, brother of VUKUB AHPU and father of the flute players HUNBATZ and HUNCHOUEN who were skilled in all the arts, their mother being named as XQUIQ.

Hunhun Ahpu and his brother were fanatical players of the ball game TLACHTLI and willingly accepted the challenge of the lords of XIBALBA to play against them. The brothers immediately set out for the UN-DERWORLD and eventually came to a cross-roads where they were tricked by the guardian into taking the black road. All the brothers found at its end were en-throned statues. Travelling back to the cross-roads they were again tricked, this time into sitting on red-hot stones. Finally, having been given torches, they were led to the House of GLOOM in which they were placed with strict instructions that the torches must not be allowed to go out. Regrettably the torches burned even more fiercely inside the House of Gloom and soon went out. The next day the pair had to admit their defeat and were condemned to death.

Hunhun Ahpu's head was hung on a calabash tree to serve as a warning to any who dared to enter the UNDERWORLD. However, the calabash tree, which had until that time been barren, immediately bore fruit and was instantly venerated. Xquiq, Hunhun Ahpu's wife heard of this wondrous event and went to see for her-self, wondering aloud as she approached the tree if picking one of the fruits really would prove fatal. Hunhun Ahpu's skull spoke to her from its place among the branches and as she stretched out to grasp a fruit, he spat into her hand, thus impreg-nating her. Hunhun Ahpu then instructed her to return to the Earth, which she did with the lords of Xibalba hot on her heels. There she gave birth to the twins HU-NAHPU and XBALANQUÉ. However, the twins were instantaneously persecuted by their envious half-brothers who had, until that time, been models of good behaviour, but now became sullen and lazy, forcing the twins to gather food for them while they spent their days idling around and playing the flute. Eventually Hunahpu and Xbalanqué could stand this no longer and turned them into monkeys whose actions they were already mimicking. The twins then travelled to Xibalba, avenged their father's death, and were eventually trans-lated to the heavens where one became the Sun and the other the Moon.

Huracán CENTRAL AMERICA – MEXICO
(*Olmec*)

Ruler of an unidentified realm who heard the sound of HOMSHUK beating on a drum and sent a messenger to find out who was responsible for the noise. The reply Hom-shuk gave to the messenger led Huracán to suspect that Homshuk was a NAGUAL whose desire to remain unknown was to enable him to stay beyond harm. Huracán made a turtle or a tortoise carry Homshuk across the sea to his home so that he could challenge the nagual.

Homshuk was immediately taken cap-tive and thrown into three successive prisons. The first was filled with serpents, the second with ravenous tigers, and the third with arrows in constant flight, each prison being a representation of the three sides of man – his serpentine instincts, his dark tiger-like nature and his penetrating wickedness. When the captors came to the first prison after Homshuk had spent the night with the serpents, they found him seated on the back of one of the hungry vipers. The same thing happened after he had spent the night in the tiger prison. Finally, the arrows fell harmlessly at his feet and allowed themselves to be made into a bundle with which Homshuk might protect himself.

Huracán, however, still failed to understand the divine nature of Homshuk and now challenged him to a stone-throwing competition. Homshuk won this with the aid of a woodpecker who, when Homshuk cast his stone, hammered against a tree, the sound giving those listening the impression that Homshuk's stone was rebounding far away. Huracán then took his turn, but no one heard anything. Huracán grudgingly conceded to Homshuk.

Huracán then decreed that Homshuk should be swung out over the ocean. However, after Homshuk had gone no more than half way, he returned and reported that he could see how easy the journey was going to be, and that Huracán and his people should go first. Huracán and his people suffered many calamities on the voyage and finally accepted the true divine nature of Homshuk whom he offered to keep well watered – it appears as if by this stage he had taken on his true plant form – so that maize, whom Huracán now recognized as being of supreme importance, should grow to feed mankind.

Hurakan CENTRAL AMERICA (*Maya*)
The 'Heart of the Sky' whose signs are both sheet and fork lightning. When TEPEU and GUCUMATZ wanted to create mankind, he was consulted by them, but these – the first to attempt to create man – were destroyed by HUNAHPU and XBALANQUÉ. He again participated in the second, successful creation of man, though when these new men, named as BALAM AGAB, BALAM QUITZÉ, IQI BALAM and MAHUCUTAH, turned out to be so powerfully endowed that they threatened to become the equals of the gods, Hurakan breathed a cloud

over their eyes which reduced their eyesight to mortal levels, as well as reducing their levels of reasoning.

H'uraru NORTH AMERICA – GREAT PLAINS (*Pawnee*)
The Earth which is also called ATIRA (Mother).

Hurin Cuzco SOUTH AMERICA (*Inca*)
The lower of the two divisions of the city of CUZCO, the upper half being known as HANAN CUZCO. The divisions were made because so many people flocked to the city that had been founded by MAMA OCLLO and MANCO CAPAC, two of the CHILDREN OF THE SUN, which is why Cuzco is usually referred to as the City of the Sun.

Huron NORTH AMERICA – WOODLANDS
Indigenous North American AMERINDIAN people who inhabited one part of the huge WOODLANDS culture region in the vicinity of the Great Lakes. One of the IROQUOIS-speaking peoples, the Huron's linguistic neighbours were the CHEROKEE, MOHAWK, ONEIDA and SELISH, with whom, due to their characteristic internecine nature, they were frequently at war. Huron, however, is not the true name of these peoples, but is actually a French nickname meaning 'head of pig' or 'rough hair of the head'. A nomadic people who lived near lakes Huron (the second largest of the Great Lakes), Erie and Ontario, they were virtually wiped out by the Iroquois, their survivors forming a group known as the WYANDOT, a name that has become synonymous with the Huron, and believed by some to have been their original tribal name.

Huruing Wuhti NORTH AMERICA – PUEBLO, SOUTHWEST (*Hopi*)
The primordial women of the east and the west between whom the Sun would daily make its journey. Together they created

the Earth and all of its creatures, including mankind.

Hus Brothers NORTH AMERICA – SOUTHWEST COAST (*Wintun*)

As a prelude to the creation of man, OLELBIS ('The-One-Who-Sits-in-the-Sky') sent the two Hus ('Buzzard') Brothers down to the Earth to construct a stone ladder between it and OLELPANTI (heaven). The brothers began their work but were interrupted by SEDIT who, claiming great wisdom that challenged even that of Olelbis, poured scorn on the plan. He questioned what people would do when they grew old. Surely, he continued, they could simply climb the ladder to Olelpanti and then descend once more fully rejuvenated. He added that since they would be able to live forever, they would have no need for children and would therefore lead solitary and lonely lives. Surely, he finished, it would be far better for man to experience the joys of children and the grief of death.

So strong was Sedit's argument that the Hus Brothers dismantled the ladder, whereupon the younger of the two reminded Sedit that he too would die and be buried.

Huti Watsi Ya NORTH AMERICA – WOODLANDS (*Huron*)

The name given to the star-spirits that inhabit the PLEIADES[3].

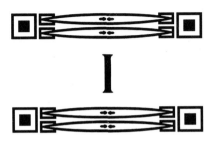

I Central America (*Maya*)
The goddess of war, floods and storms who is usually depicted wearing a knotted serpent on her head and a skirt decorated with crossed bones, and who has talons on her arms. She is simply identified as the I in the *codices* and is probably to be identified with IX CHEL.

Iatiku North America – Pueblo, Southwest (*Acoma*)
One of the two sisters who were responsible for the creation of mankind, the other being NAUTSITI.

Iavurê-cunha South America – Brazil (*Xingú*)
A minuscule spirit who lives in the dense Brazilian rain forests.

Ibo(-léle) Haiti (*Voodoo*)
One of the many LOA of the VOODOO religion, this particular handsome and friendly example, who is of secondary importance to cultists, having a name that derives from the Nigerian Igbo tribe.

Ibo loa Haiti (*Voodoo*)
Generic name given to VOODOO cult gods and spirits (LOA) that derive from the pantheon of the Nigerian Igbo tribe.

Iboroquiamio South America – Guyana
According to the accounts of the seventeenth-century missionary Ruiz BLANCO, Iboroquiamio was the personification of evil among the Guyanese people.

Ichpa Central America (*Maya*)
A name sometimes given to MAYAPAN, the name given to the MAYA New Empire which lasted between AD 987 and 1697. Mayapan means 'the Standard of the Not Many' from *maya* – ('not many') and *pán* – (standard). Ichpa itself means 'within the enclosure' which is an exact parallel to the NAHUA description of TLOQUE NAHUAQUE as 'Lord of the Ring'.

Idlirvirissong North America – Greenland (*Inuit*)
An evil spirit who was the cousin of the spirit of the Sun to whom he was opposed.

Igaluk North America – Alaska (*Inuit*)
The spirit of the Moon.

Igaranha South America – Brazil (*Xingú*)
An extremely powerful spirit who can manifest himself as a canoe in which form he cannot only help mankind, but can also do them great harm.

Iguagué, Lake South America – Colombia (*Chibcha*)
The lake, near TUNJA, from which the woman named either BACHUÉ or FURACHOGUÉ emerged soon after the creation of

the Moon, CHIÁ, and the Sun, ZUHÉ, carrying a young boy. She later married the boy when he had reached maturity, and their offspring populated the Earth.

Ik CENTRAL AMERICA (*Maya*)
The personification of the spirit of man which is also the second day of the MAYA spiritual pilgrimage known as the AGES OF MAN, on which man's spirit is bestowed on him although he has yet to be born. Ik is also the day sacred to the great KUKULCÁN. Ik appears in both the Ages of Man and the Maya CREATION[4] to symbolize events that affect the spirit. See MAN-IK, TWELVE-IK.

Ilamatecuhtli CENTRAL AMERICA – MEXICO (*Aztec*)
An alternative name for CIHUACÓATL which simply means 'The Goddess'.

Ilanyau, Mount SOUTH AMERICA – BOLIVIA (*Aymará*)
Mountain of the Bolivian cordillera that was regarded as an ACHACHILA by the AYMARÁ

Ilisitsok NORTH AMERICA – ARCTIC (*Inuit*)
The name given to an ANGAKOK who can propitiate evil and call down misfortune on his fellows.

Illampu SOUTH AMERICA – BOLIVIA (*Aymará*)
Mountain of the Bolivian cordillera that was regarded as an ACHACHILA by the AYMARÁ. Once a group of Aymará polluted the peak of this mountain, along with that of Mount ILLIMANI with the smoke from their fires. As a result KHUNO, the god of snowstorms, beset them with violent blizzards and landslides that forced the Aymará to hide in some caves. When the storm abated and they emerged, they found that there was nothing left to eat

apart from the brilliant foliage of a shrub that they had not seen before. Having eaten the leaves, they found themselves so elated that they were able to walk back to TITUANCO with no trouble at all. This shrub was the COCA.

Illimani, Mount SOUTH AMERICA – BOLIVIA (*Aymará*)
An ACHACHILA that was regarded as the guardian spirit of LA PAZ, the highest mountain in the Bolivian Andes that is situated to the east of the city and rises to a height of 21,004 feet. It is said that Mount Illimani was especially favoured by VIRACOCHA, a favouritism that made the neighbouring volcanic Mount MURURATA grumble in jealousy. Viracocha, in his annoyance, threw a stone at Mount Mururata which decapitated it, its peak flying through the air to form Mount SAJAMA when it landed.

Imap Imassoursua SOUTH AMERICA
A mythical water-monster that is the embodiment of a mainly malevolent supernatural force (cf. CUERO, HIDE).

Imaymana Viracocha SOUTH AMERICA – PERU (*Inca*)
According to one myth, one of the two sons of the Sun-god creator, the other being named TOCAPO VIRACOCHA. Imaymana Viracocha was sent by his father to cross the surface of the Earth naming the trees, flowers, plants and animals, and teaching mankind their properties and uses. Tocapo Viracocha was given a similar task, but he was told to cross the plains. Imaymana Viracocha was endowed with absolute power by his father whom he returned to in the skies after his task had been completed.

Imix CENTRAL AMERICA (*Maya*)
Coming from *Im* (womb), Imix is the first day of the MAYA spiritual pilgrimage – the

AGES OF MAN. On this day the new child is conceived and thus starts out on his long and perilous journey through life. Imix in this context is not to be confused with ELEVEN IMIX, the eleventh day of the Maya CREATION[4].

Inagi-utasunhi NORTH AMERICA – WOODLANDS (*Cherokee*)
One of the semi-divine twins, the malignant one. Such twins appear frequently throughout AMERINDIAN mythology from North America (cf. TASWISCANA).

Inca SOUTH AMERICA
Former ruling class of South American AMERINDIAN people whose empire was originally located almost exclusively in Peru. Their myths assert that the Incas originated in the area of Lake TITICACA, but it is still unknown whether this is a factual assertion of their origins, or simply a myth. It is, however, generally agreed that they first settled in the CUZCO valley sometime during the thirteenth century (c.1240). The first emperor of this new Inca Empire was MANCO CAPAC who was believed to be directly descended from the Sun. At first the new settlers encountered considerable resistance from neighbouring peoples, opposition that came to a head in the middle of the fifteenth century when the Incas were all but vanquished by a confederation of these neighbours, a confederation known as the CHANCA. Under the leadership of PACHACUTI the defeated Incas turned that defeat into an inspired victory and embarked on an expansionist policy that, within thirty years had given them an empire that covered most of Bolivia, Ecuador and Peru, along with significant areas of Argentina and Chile.

Throughout the entire Inca empire the myths, legends, folklore and history were orally preserved. The Incas, and the AYMARÁ-speaking peoples of Bolivia, employed a special class of learned men to preserve and transmit these traditions. However, even though the Incas – like the AZTECS – assimilated the beliefs and traditions of conquered peoples into their own, they– unlike the Aztecs – suppressed these stories to emphasize their own superiority. Thus they adapted the assimilated mythologies and traditions to place better emphasis on their own traditions which, without exception, always enhanced the prestige of their own theocratic rulers. Regrettably, such myths and legends that have survived this absorption have only done so in fragmentary and highly edited forms.

The civilization was destroyed by the Spanish conquest of the 1530s, though their descendants may still be seen in the QUECHUA. After the Spanish conquest a number of Inca converts set about recording what they knew of the Inca religion and tradition, but in many cases these converts seem to have been carefully selected by their new Spanish masters to emphasize those stories which were most akin to the Christian beliefs to which they had been converted, and to suppress those that did not comply. Two of the most important of these records, known as CODEX, are the illustrated *NUEVA CORONICA Y BUEN GOBIERNO* by Don Felipe GUAMÁN POMA DE AYALA who claimed royal Inca descent through his mother, and the *COMMENTARIOS RÉALES DE LOS INCAS* by the Metzio Garsilasco DE LA VEGA who, like his contemporary, also claimed royal Inca descent, but had in fact been brought up in Spain. Unlike Guamán Poma de Ayala, however, de la Vega was a highly educated man.

The second avenue for research is the records of the Spanish conquistadors and their missionary followers, though, as would be expected, these records are extremely biased, on the one hand to emphasize the glory of the empire they had conquered, and on the other by their own religious beliefs and dogmas. Even through all this confusion it is still possible to determine that the Incas had no organized pantheon of deities, either among themselves or among their subject peoples.

One cult did predominate over all others, that of INTI, the Sun-god from whom the Inca claimed their divine descent. Other deities were also of importance, but this importance seems to have followed a ritual cycle, so that when one came into the ascendancy, another declined. Apart from Inti, the most widely acknowledged and worshipped deity appears to have been VIRACOCHA, the creator, whose cult was developed by Pachacuti and combined many aspects of long-worshipped culture heroes.

It should be noted that when one refers to the Inca, one is not referring to an anthropological division, rather to the empire occupied by the people today referred to as Inca, who were in fact made up from a great number of different peoples, many of whom seem to have had the same line of descent as the Aztecs and the MAYA.

Inglésou HAITI (*Voodoo*)
A simple variant of L'INGLÉSOU.

Inktonmi NORTH AMERICA – GREAT PLAINS (*Dakota*)
'Spider', the TRICKSTER of the DAKOTA.

Inomème, Maîtresse HAITI (*Voodoo*)
One of the innumerable LOA of the VOODOO religion.

Insect Men SOUTH AMERICA – BOLIVIA (*Chamacoco*)
In the beginning men were incredibly small and lived underground. Gradually they climbed to the Earth's surface on a rope of *caraguata* (plant fibre). However, as there was very little food to be found on the Earth, a dog soon gnawed through the rope and thus prevented the remainder of

the people from following their relatives. The CHAMACOCO then tried to climb an incredibly tall tree up into the sky, but they all fell back to the Earth, many of them dying as a result. This is why, according to the Chamacoco, there were so few Chamacoco on the Earth.

Inti SOUTH AMERICA (*Inca*)
Also called APU-PUNCHAU, Inti was the personification of the Sun who, with his beautiful body and head circled by a great ball of gold, was the divine ancestor claimed by the INCA peoples. As the Incas claimed this descent, they also claimed the divine right that they alone should be allowed to pronounce his name, the penalty for a non-Inca transgressing this taboo being immediate and summary execution. Every night Inti plunged into the cold sea which he swam under through the night to emerge fully refreshed the following morning.

inu NORTH AMERICA – ARCTIC (*Inuit*)
Generic name given to celestial spirits that started their lives as mortals. See CREATION[3].

inua (pl. inue) NORTH AMERICA (*Widespread*)
'Owner', 'indweller', the all pervasive spirit(s) with whom the SHAMAN priests were able to communicate. Every object has its inua. Even air possesses one – the human inua is the soul. Normally invisible, the inue can sometimes manifest themselves as fire or light, the sight of such a manifestation being an omen of impending death. An inua who helps or protects a man is known, to the Inuit as a TORNAK. Inue of the seas are perceived as sorts of mermen, while those of the stars and planets are the displaced inue of people that now illuminate the night sky of which they are the

'owners' (cf. MANITOU, ORENDA, WA-KONDA).

Inuit NORTH AMERICA – ARCTIC
'Genuine People'. Possibly better known as the ESKIMO, though this term also encompasses the Aleut people of the Asiatic Arctic. The Inuit are the indigenous inhabitants of the Arctic coasts of North America, the eastern islands of the Canadian Arctic and the ice-free coasts of Greenland. They were first called Eskimos ('foul eaters of raw meat') by the ALGONQUIAN Indians, a term which today is only popularly used to refer to those nomadic people who, except in south Alaska and Labrador, live beyond the northern limit of trees, and thus in some of the most inhospitable and coldest regions of the Earth. Their language, Inuktitut, belongs to the Eskimo–Aleut grouping. The term Inuit is widely used today, as it is in this book, to encompass the KALAALLIT peoples of Greenland, the Inuit of northern Canada, the INUPIAT of northern Alaska, and the YUPIK of central Alaska, though this last people speak Yuk rather than Inuktitut.

Inupiat NORTH AMERICA – ALASKA
Indigenous ESKIMO people from the northern part of Alaska. Speaking one branch of Inuktitut, the Inupiat are referred to throughout this book as INUIT, a term that has come to encompass all of the indigenous peoples from the North American Arctic regions.

Iolokiamo SOUTH AMERICA – ORINOCO REGION, VENEZUELA
The TRICKSTER who is, in this region, opposed by CACHIMANA, the GREAT SPIRIT.

Iouskeha NORTH AMERICA (*Onondaga*)
The ONONDAGA variant of YOSKEHA.

Ipa Huaca SOUTH AMERICA (*Inca*)
According to Fray Martin DE MONIA, Ipa Huaca was one of the female members of the CHILDREN OF THE SUN. The other members of this divine grouping were the brothers CUSCO HUANCA, HUANA CAURI, MANCO CAPAC and TOPA AYAR CACHI, and the sisters CORI OCLLO, MAMA COYA, and TOPA HUACO. Ipa Huaca does not appear in the renditions of the myth of the Children of the Sun as recorded by Pedro DE CIEZA DE LÉON.

Iqi Balam CENTRAL AMERICA (*Maya*)
'Moon Jaguar', one of the four brothers created from the corn of ground yellow and white maize, which was then strengthened with nine broths brewed by XMUCANÉ. His brothers were BALAM AGAB ('Night Jaguar') BALAM QUITZÉ ('Smiling Jaguar'), and MAHUCUTAH ('Renowned Name'). However, the gods found that they had done their work too well, for the four brothers were so wondrously gifted that they threatened to rival their creators. HURAKAN therefore breathed a cloud over their eyes which reduced their vision and understanding to more mortal levels. The four were then made to fall into a deep sleep during which the gods created four women that were to become their wives.

At first everything was all right and the people lived in harmony. They all spoke the same language and prayed to their creators, those prayers asking for children and light for the Sun had yet to be created. Their first prayer was answered, but the second appeared to be overlooked. After a while the people became restless as they were being forced to live in perpetual darkness. The four brothers decided that they should leave their home in TOLLAN and go to TULAI ZUIVA, the PLACE OF SEVEN CAVES AND SEVEN RAVINES. There they were each given a tutelary deity to preside over their respective clans. Balam Quitzé received

TOHIL; Balam Agab was given AVILIX; Mahucutah – HACAVITZ; and Iqi Balam – NICAHTAGAH.

Tohil gave the brothers the gift of fire which he rekindled by striking his shoes together after the rain had extinguished it. Now at last the people had a source of light and heat, news of which quickly spread. Men from other tribes came, shivering, to ask for some of the sacred flame, but they were turned away. Finally Tohil interceded saying that they might have fire if they embrace him 'under the armpit and under the girdle', an expression that has been interpreted as meaning that he required human sacrifice in return for the fire.

Even though the people could now keep themselves warm, and had a source of light, they still prayed for the appearance of the MORNING STAR[3] which would herald the birth of the Sun. At length the four brothers decided that if the Sun were ever to be born they should resume their journey.

Having traversed many foreign lands they came, at last, to Hacavitz's mountain. There they burned incense and prayed to the gods, this time being answered when the Morning Star rose to be followed a short time later by the Sun. All the animals and birds greeted the Sun with loud cries, and all the people prostrated themselves on the ground. As the Sun grew in strength, the Earth began to dry out and his rays, touching the old animal gods (lion, tiger and viper), turned them all to stone along with the gods Avilix, Hacavitz and Tohil.

The brothers now lived in the warmth and the light of the Sun, but after a while their thoughts turned to their comrades who had remained in Tollan and who had yet to witness the wonder of the Sun. Thus they took leave of their wives and children to return to Tollan. This was the last anyone ever saw of them, but they left behind them a sacred bundle called MAJESTY ENVELOPED which they instructed should never be opened.

Iroquois NORTH AMERICA – WOODLANDS
Confederation of indigenous AMERINDIAN peoples of North America. The Confederation, which consisted of the CAYUGA, MOHAWK, ONEIDA, ONONDAGA and SENECA with the TUSCARORA joining in 1715, was traditionally founded by HAIOWATHA in 1570, though Haiowatha is not a personal name, but rather a priestly title.

Isakakate NORTH AMERICA – GREAT PLAINS (*Crow*)
The GREAT SPIRIT.

Isakawuate NORTH AMERICA – GREAT PLAINS (*Crow*)
'Old Man Coyote', the TRICKSTER of the CROW people.

Ishtinike NORTH AMERICA – GREAT PLAINS (*Ponca*)
The TRICKSTER-hero, the meaning of whose name is unknown.

Isitoq NORTH AMERICA – ARCTIC (*Inuit*)
'Giant Eye', a TORNAK whose thick, coarse hair stands on end. Each of his eyes is divided by a large mouth that contains a single long tooth at the top between two shorter ones. His purpose is to help to find people who have broken specific taboos.

Istepahpah NORTH AMERICA – WOODLANDS (*Creek*)
A man-eating monster about whom nothing else is known.

Itc Ak NORTH AMERICA – NORTHWEST COAST (*Tlingit*)
The impregnable rock after which YETL, the RAVEN, was named TAQLIKIC

('Hammer-father') as he was so tough and resilient.

Itsike NORTH AMERICA – GREAT PLAINS (*Osage*)
The TRICKSTER-hero, the meaning of whose name is unknown.

Itzá CENTRAL AMERICA (*Maya*)
The name of a family of usurpers who ruled over vast tracts of the MAYA lands for centuries. In the Maya tongue Itzá means 'yoke' which suggests that rather than being a family name, Itzá was actually a title conferred on the family by the Maya people who perhaps considered them to be enslaved by their rulers. The temple site of CHICHEN ITZÁ is named after this ruling family who were obviously highly cultured.

Itzamkabain CENTRAL AMERICA (*Maya*)
The alligator-footed whale who was fructified by AHU-UC-CHEKNALE during the Creation.

Itzamná CENTRAL AMERICA (*Maya*)
The god of resurrection and thus perceived as a great healer, Itzamná was also the inventor of all the visual arts and of writing. He introduced both maize and cocoa, and was the first to identify the many uses of rubber. The son of HUNAB-KU, Itzamná is thought to have been the head of the MAYA pantheon and has been identified by some with KUKULCÁN; through that association he has also been assimilated to the NAHUA deity QUETZAL-CÓATL. Itzamná is usually depicted as an old man with a Roman nose, and was married to IX CHEL. He was particularly revered by the priesthood as the patron of writing and learning, for these disciplines were confined to the priesthood.

Itzcuintli CENTRAL AMERICA – MEXICO (*Aztec*)
The tenth day of the twenty-day MONTH[1] employed by the AZTECs. The day was symbolized by a dog, represented the north, and was presided over by MICT-LÁNTECUHTLI.

Itzeecayan CENTRAL AMERICA – MEXICO (*Aztec*)
'The Palace of Cool Breezes', one of the three heavenly homes beyond the highest heaven that are said to be inhabited by XOCHIQUETZAL, her other homes being XO-CHITICACAN and TAMOANCHAN.

Itzlacoliohqui CENTRAL AMERICA – MEXICO (*Aztec*)
'Carved Obsidian Knife', the god of the obsidian knife, of ice, blindness, cold and obstinacy, who was the direct opposite of TEZCATLIPOCA for, whereas Itzlacoliohqui represented matter in its most lifeless state, Tezcatlipoca produced that life-giving spark. Itzlacoliohqui is, in fact, simply another aspect of Tezcatlipoca, and represents the duality of that deity, and his ability to serve both of the primeval forces – good and evil – simultaneously.

In the CODEX Itzlacoliohqui is illustrated making an offering to the powers of darkness. At the base of the temple there is a human heart that has been torn out, while inside the temple sits TLACOLOTL, the great horned owl, the omen of the very deepest evil.

Itzli(-Tezcatlipoca) CENTRAL AMERICA – MEXICO (*Aztec*)
'Stone Knife', god of the sacrificial knife, an aspect and symbol of TEZCATLIPOCA.

Itzpapálotl CENTRAL AMERICA (*Aztec*)
A stellar goddess of agriculture who appears to be a representation of the soul

that all things possess, and has been identified as the female counterpart of ITZLA-
COLIOHQUI.

Ix CENTRAL AMERICA (*Maya*)
The day of the jaguar and of obsidian, the
fourteenth day of the MAYA spiritual pilgrimage known as the AGES OF MAN on
which man emerges washed clean of all his
earthly sins. Deified, Ix was one of only
four gods who could start a New Year. The
other three were CAUAC, KAN the maize-
god and MULUC the rain-god. Ix and Cauac
were harbingers of disaster, while Kan and
Muluc would ensure good luck. Ix is not to
be confused with FOUR IX, the fourth day of
the Maya CREATION[4] when the heaven and
the Earth were complete and embraced
each other.

Ix Chel CENTRAL AMERICA (*Maya*)
'Rainbow Lady', the goddess of the rainbow and wife of ITZAMNÁ who is, by this
association, regarded as the mother of the
MAYA pantheon. Ix Chel is thought to be
an early Maya Moon-goddess, the patroness of childbirth, medicine and weaving,
though she is equally identified as a water-
goddess. However, in the DRESDEN CODEX
she is depicted with snaky locks and
clawed hands and feet which seems to
suggest that after the TOLTEC conquest she
became assimilated with COATLICUE. Ix
Chel is also sometimes called IX-
KANLEOM.

Ix Ch'up CENTRAL AMERICA (*Maya*)
The Moon-goddess from the TOLTEC
period who is possibly to be regarded as the
consort of AH KINCHIL. It seems as if she
took over the role of the Moon-goddess
from IX CHEL, the wife of ITZAMNÁ, who
after the Toltec conquest seems to have
become identified with COATLICUE.

Ix-huyne CENTRAL AMERICA (*Maya*)
A name applied to the Moon-goddess,
though whether to IX CHEL or IX CH'UP
remains unclear.

Ix-Kanleom CENTRAL AMERICA (*Maya*)
Variant name sometimes used to refer to IX
CHEL.

Ix Tub Tun CENTRAL AMERICA (*Maya*)
The patron goddess of those who worked
with jade and amethyst.

Ixazaluch CENTRAL AMERICA (*Maya*)
The goddess of water, wife of HUNAB KU
and mother of ITZAMNÁ.

Ixcozauhqui CENTRAL AMERICA –
MEXICO (*Aztec*)
Alternative name for XIUHTECUHTLI.

Ixcuina CENTRAL AMERICA – MEXICO
(*Aztec*)
'Four Faces', an aspect of TLAZOLTÉOTL.

Ixtab CENTRAL AMERICA (*Maya*)
Goddess of the noose or gallows to whose
paradisal realm it was thought all those
who committed suicide by hanging themselves went.

Ixtaccíhuatl CENTRAL AMERICA –
MEXICO (*Aztec*)
One of the three snow-capped volcanoes
that QUETZALCÓATL crossed after he had
left TOLLAN and was *en route* for TLILLAN-
TLAPALLAN, the others being POPOCATÉ-
PATL and CITLALTÉPETL. During the crossing of the two volcanoes all the dwarfs who
were accompanying Quetzalcóatl died of
the cold.

Ixtlilton CENTRAL AMERICA – MEXICO
(*Aztec*)
'Little-Black-Face', the god of healing,
fasting and games.

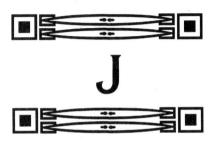

J

Jacques Majeur HAITI (*Voodoo*)
The Christian Saint James the Great who is regarded as a LOA by some VOODOO cultists.

Jacunâum SOUTH AMERICA – BRAZIL (*Xingú*)
The fish that every night swallows the Sun, swims around with it inside at night, and then regurgitates it the next morning.

Jaguar gods CENTRAL AND SOUTH AMERICA
The deification of the jaguar, or puma, is found in most of the ancient AMERINDIAN cultures of Central and South America. Its image is found in numerous carvings in both geographical regions, and archaeologists have deduced from this proliferation that the jaguar played an important role in many religious cults. However, even though the image may be widespread, the references to the jaguar in the myths of South America that have been recorded to date are extremely rare, except among the forest-dwelling tribes, and in eastern Bolivia where the jaguar is indigenous (cf. DUCÁ, PAITITI, TEPEYOLLOTL, TEZCATLIPOCA, ULÉ).

Jakuí SOUTH AMERICA – BRAZIL (*Xingú*)
An extremely important spirit who is said to live in a village at the bottom of rivers and streams, and not only manifests himself in ritual flutes, but is rather the flute itself.

Jakuí-katu SOUTH AMERICA – BRAZIL (*Xingú*)
A small wooden mask that is thought of either as a manifestation of JAKUÍ, or as a 'child'.

Jakuiaép SOUTH AMERICA – BRAZIL (*Xingú*)
A spirit that lives on the beds of rivers, and is thus closely related to JAKUÍ. It is also the name given to a ritual mask said to be a representation, or even a manifestation, of this spirit.

Jean, Sainte HAITI (*Voodoo*)
The Christian Saint John the Apostle who is regarded as a LOA by some VOODOO cultists to whom he is a stern, though somewhat nervous spirit who is always on the move, and thus rules over thunder and earthquakes.

Jean Baptiste HAITI (*Voodoo*)
Saint John the Baptist who is regarded as a LOA by some VOODOO cultists.

Jean Brigand HAITI (*Voodoo*)
One of the numerous LOA of the VOODOO cult who is the patron of robbers.

Jean Crabe, Maître HAITI (*Voodoo*)
One of the numerous LOA of the VOODOO religion.

Jean Délé HAITI (*Voodoo*)
One of the numerous LOA of the VOODOO
religion.

Jean Féro HAITI (*Voodoo*)
One of the numerous LOA of the VOODOO
religion.

Jeune Gens Direct HAITI (*Voodoo*)
One of the numerous LOA of the VOODOO
religion.

Jivaro SOUTH AMERICA
Indigenous South American AMERINDIAN
people of the tropical forests of southeast
Ecuador and northeast Peru. Traditionally, the Jivaro lived by farming, hunting,
fishing and weaving, and were once noto-
rious for preserving the hair and shrunken
skin of the heads of their enemies as battle
trophies. Their language belongs to the
Andean–Equatorial family.

jogah NORTH AMERICA – WOODLANDS
(*Iroquois*)
Generic name given to dwarf nature-
spirits who are divided into three tribes:
the GAHONGA ('stone-throwers') who inhabit rocks and rivers; the GANDAYAH who
maintain the fertility of the Earth; and the
OHDOWS who live in the UNDERWORLD and
control the monsters to be found there and
prevent them from achieving their goal of
reaching the Earth's surface so that they
might feel the warmth of the Sun.

Jupiter NORTH AMERICA – GREAT
PLAINS (*Blackfoot*)
The largest planet in the solar system that
is, worldwide, seen as the embodiment of
some deity or another. This personification, however, is uncommon among the
AMERINDIAN peoples. To the BLACKFOOT
people the planet was seen as symbolizing
POÏA, the son of MORNING STAR[6] and the
mortal SOATSAKI.

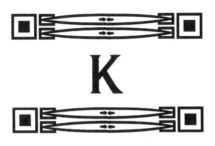

K

K CENTRAL AMERICA (*Maya*)
Deity depicted in the various CODEX with an abnormally long nose, some accounts describing it as elephantine in form – i.e. a trunk. He is possibly to be identified with KUKULCÁN, though it has also been suggested that the god K is simply a variant of the god B. Some authorities have sought to identify him as ITZAMNÁ. The god K is also known as LAKIN CHAN, 'serpent of the east', in which form he was said to have been the creator of not only mankind, but also every other form of organic life, as well as having founded the MAYA culture. He was the inventor of writing and books, had knowledge of herbs and medicine, and may have been a son of HUNAB-KU.

Kablunait NORTH AMERICA –
GREENLAND (*Inuit*)
The name given to a legendary race of white people who appear to be a memory of early Scandinavian settlers.

Kac-u-Pacat CENTRAL AMERICA (*Maya*)
A symbolic war-god who is usually depicted carrying a shield of fire.

Kadia-Bos(s)u HAITI (*Voodoo*)
A variant of the BAZO, a LOA who is also known as BOSU and BOSU-CESSÉ.

Kahit NORTH AMERICA (*Wintun*)
The primordial wind-god who is depicted as a huge bat that carries a whistle in its mouth.

Kalaallit NORTH AMERICA – GREENLAND
Indigenous ESKIMO people who inhabit the coastline of the frozen country of Greenland. Speaking one branch of Inuktitut, the Kalaallit are referred to throughout this book as INUIT, a term that has come to encompass all the indigenous peoples from the North American Arctic regions.

Kalasasaya SOUTH AMERICA – BOLIVIA
A huge platform complex within the city of TIAHUANACO that dates from the first century AD. Kalasasaya is entered through the Gateway of the Sun, and consists of a patio where Sun worship was obviously observed as indicated by the iconography of the attendant solar figures.

Kalinago CARIBBEAN (*Carib*)
Tiring of his life among the GALIBI, the name given to CARIBS who lived on the mainland, Kalinago set sail to find new lands, and eventually came to Santo Domingo where he settled, married and had many sons. These sons grew jealous of their father and poisoned him, after which his soul passed into ATRAIOMEN, a terrible fish-like monster, which pursued the murderers. They fled in all directions and were thus dispersed across a great number of islands. Each son killed all the men on the island he settled on and set up the dead men's heads in caves so that, in time, their own sons might be able to recognize and honour their martial prowess.

Kan CENTRAL AMERICA (*Maya*)
The god of maize and one of the four guardians of the divisions of the sacred 260-day CALENDAR, though also having links with the four winds and being symbolized as one of the four pillars that gave the world a firm support and held the sky in place after it had fallen on to the Earth during a great flood. Kan was associated with the colour yellow and the south. His colleagues were ED, CHAC and ZAC, the four deities being collectively referred to as the Four BACAB or the Four BALAM. During the years over which Kan presided, years that were perceived as being lucky, the statue of BOLON DZACAB was erected in the city centres whose gates were guarded by KAN-U-UAYEYAB. Kan is also the fourth day of the MAYA spiritual pilgrimage, the AGES OF MAN, the day on which man first realizes that there is evil in the world. Kan in this context is not to be confused with ONE KAN, the fourteenth day of the Maya CREATION[4].

Kan-u-Uayeyab CENTRAL AMERICA (*Maya*)
The deity whose statue was set up to guard the gates of cities during the KAN years which were governed by the southern BACAB, and during which time a statue of the god BOLON DZACAB was set up in the city centre. See also CHAC-U-UAYEYAB, EK-U-UAYEYAB, ZAC-U-UAYEYAB.

Kanati NORTH AMERICA – WOODLANDS (*Cherokee*)
The first man, husband of SELU, who was the ancestor of the CHEROKEE people.

Kanzibyúi CENTRAL AMERICA (*Maya*)
After the chaos and destruction caused by the FLOOD[7], Kanzibyúi was put on the Earth by CANTULTIKU to reorganize it. Kanzibyúi planted differently coloured trees at each of the four cardinal points which propped up the heavens, thus restoring the Earth and allowing the creation of mankind.

Karous, Maîtresse HAITI (*Voodoo*)
One of the numerous LOA of the VOODOO religion.

Karu SOUTH AMERICA – BRAZIL (*Kadevo*)
One of the two primordial beings, the other being Karu's son RAIRU. They stumbled about in the perpetual darkness until one day Rairu tripped over a bowl-shaped stone which his father told him to carry on his head. The stone grew and grew until it formed the sky. Rairu knelt to his father and honoured him as the sky-maker, but Karu perceived that his son was more knowledgeable than he was and grew so angry that Rairu was forced to flee and hide underground. Karu sought his son and, having discovered him, was just about to despatch him when Rairu reported that he had found people living beneath the Earth who would come and work for them. Rairu was spared and the first people emerged on to the Earth, being divided into tribes according to their colour and attractiveness as they came. The lazy people were turned into bats, birds, butterflies and pigs by Karu and Rairu.

kaspi SOUTH AMERICA – TIERRA DEL FUEGO (*Ona*)
Name given to the souls of the dead who go to TEMAUKEL.

Kastsatsi NORTH AMERICA – PUEBLO SOUTHWEST (*Acoma*)
The spirit of the rainbow.

ka(t)china NORTH AMERICA – PUEBLO, SOUTHWEST
1 *Zuñi*
  Generic term that appears to have been originally limited to a group of spirits

that personified the beneficent powers of nature. Each clan had its own katchina which visited the village annually where it was impersonated by men wearing appropriate costumes and masks. The masks worn by the imitators were highly revered and were often burned on the death of the owner.

2 *Hopi*

Although fairly similar to the katchina of the ZUÑI as described above, the katchina of the HOPI was singularly concerned with the beneficent powers of the Sun, particularly the medicinal quality of the Sun's light, as opposed to encompassing the entire beneficent powers of nature at large (cf. KATSINAS).

Katchina Mana NORTH AMERICA – PUEBLO, SOUTHWEST (*Hopi*)
One of the two spirits of the sprouting maize, the other being KERWAN.

Kathatakanave CENTRAL AMERICA – MEXICO (*Walapai*)
'Taught-by-Coyote', the first man who, along with COYOTE, the TRICKSTER, emerged on to the Earth from the Grand Canyon, some accounts saying that the canyon itself was formed by their emergence. Kathatakanave prayed to the sky deities to provide him with companions, but Coyote, in typical trickster style, interrupted the spell and thus spoiled it.

Katsinas NORTH AMERICA – PUEBLO, SOUTHWEST (*Acoma*)
The name given to the children of IATIKU who were revered as fertility and rain spirits.

katun CENTRAL AMERICA (*Maya*)
A period of time calculated as twenty cycles of the sacred division of 260 days, and thus equal to 7,200 days, which is roughly twenty years (19.71 to be exact), but is, quite remarkably, the exact time it takes

the planet VENUS to complete twelve and a half cycles. See CALENDAR.

Kchemnito NORTH AMERICA – WOODLANDS (*Potawatomi*)
A variant of KITSHI MANITOU.

Keckamanetowa NORTH AMERICA – GREAT PLAINS (*Fox*)
The creator who was perceived as a benevolent and gentle spirit.

Kelok NORTH AMERICA – SOUTHWEST (*Miwok*)
A winged giant monster that was responsible for killing WEKWEK with red-hot stones, but was himself disposed of by COYOTE, one of the few occasions when the TRICKSTER helped man. However, his corpse caught fire, that fire engulfing and destroying the first world.

Kemush NORTH AMERICA – NORTHWEST COAST (*Klamath*)
'The-OLD-MAN-OF-THE-ANCIENTS' whom the MORNING STAR[5] called upon to create the Earth from the ashes of the AURORA BOREALIS[2]. Kemush began by making the Earth as a great, flat plain. On this foundation he built the hills and mountains and scooped out the valleys and the river courses. In the valleys he planted grass, ferns and other vegetation, while on the hills and mountains he planted conifers and other trees and bushes.

Having created the Earth, Kemush set about making animals and man to people his new land. First he placed the white-tailed deer MUSHMUSH in the forests, together with the red fox WAN and its grey counterpart KETCHKATCH. On the sides of the mountains he put LUK, the grizzly bear, and KOIL, the sheep, while he placed GREY WOLF on Mount SHASTA.

Now the Earth was ready for mankind, everything in it newly created, except for the crescent-shaped rock in Lake KLA-MATH where the Sun and the Moon had their lodge for a long time. Kemush surveyed all he had done and then went away to rest in the lodge of the north wind. There he fell into a long and deep sleep, a sleep he remained in until he was awakened by SUN HALO who bade him follow the trail of SHEL, the Sun.

Together Kemush and Sun Halo trailed Shel to the very edge of darkness itself. Kemush and his daughter EVENING SKY, who makes an instantaneous appearance at this point of the myth, went to the lodges of the spirits in the PLACE OF THE DARK who all instantly turned to dried piles of bones. Kemush collected a sack full of these bones and carried it back to the Earth. Then he travelled over the Earth, scattering the bones as he went. Where they fell, they turned into the CHIPMUNK, MAIDU, MAKLAK and KLAMATH AMERINDIAN peoples.

Having finished his allotted task, Kemush followed Shel's trail to its very summit in the sky, and there built himself a lodge in which he still lives in the company of his daughter, Evening Sky, and Sun Halo.

Keneun NORTH AMERICA –
WOODLANDS (*Iroquois*)
The Golden Eagle, the chief of the THUNDERBIRDS. An invisible spirit with flashing eyes from which lightning emanated, and great wings whose beating caused the thunder. Keneun has guarded fire ever since MÄNÄBUSCH first collected it and passed it to his grandmother NOKOMIS who gave it to the THUNDERERS, or more particularly Keneun, for safe-keeping.

Keros SOUTH AMERICA – TIERRA DEL FUEGO (*Ona*)
The first man who has subsequently become the culture hero of the ONA people.

Kerwan NORTH AMERICA – PUEBLO, SOUTHWEST (*Hopi*)
One of the two spirits, possibly brothers, of the sprouting maize, the other being KATCHINA MANA.

Ketchimanetowa NORTH AMERICA – GREAT PLAINS (*Fox*)
The GREAT SPIRIT.

Ketchkatch NORTH AMERICA – NORTHWEST COAST (*Klamath*)
The grey fox who was, along with WAN, the red fox, placed in the forests during the Creation by KEMUSH. They were accompanied by MUSHMUSH, the white-tailed deer.

Ketqskwaye NORTH AMERICA – WOODLANDS (*Huron*)
'Grandmother Toad', the creatrix of the HURON people.

Ketsi Niousak NORTH AMERICA – WOODLANDS (*Abnaki*)
The personification of absolute goodness who is opposed, and directly contrasted, by MATSI NIOUSAK, the personification of absolute evil.

Khuno SOUTH AMERICA – BOLIVIA (*Aymará*)
The god of snowstorms who was held responsible for assailing a group of AYMARÁ, who had polluted the sacred peaks of ILLIMANI and ILLAMPU with the smoke from the fires they had built as they cleared land for farming. Khuno attacked the transgressors with violent snowstorms and landslides which forced the Aymará to hide in a group of nearby caves. When they emerged, they found that there was nothing left for them to eat, except for the brilliant foliage of a shrub they had not seen, or eaten before. When they ate they were filled with such euphoric energy that they were able to return to their home of TITUANCO. This shrub was COCA.

kia-pod SOUTH AMERICA –
BRAZIL (*Tupari*)
The name given to the heavenly spirits
with whom only the SHAMAN can communicate, and who give the shaman his magical yellow PAGAB seeds that he uses to
mesmerize, and thus kill his enemies.

Kiaklo NORTH AMERICA – PUEBLO,
SOUTHWEST (*Zuñi*)
A mythical culture hero who came to
PAUTIWAL[1] and warned the ASHIWI that
the gods were about to give them the
breath of life, a magical power that would
enable them to go to KOTHLUWALAWA, the
'dance-house-of-the-gods', before they
had to return to the UNDERWORLD from
whence they had originated.

Killer-of-Enemies NORTH AMERICA –
GREAT PLAINS (*Apache*)
The culture hero of the APACHE people as
well as being the personification of the
very principle of life itself.

Kina SOUTH AMERICA – TIERRA DEL
FUEGO (*Yahgan*)
The name given to a ritual from which
women are excluded as it was alleged that
women at first ruled over the men by
wearing spirit masks which frightened the
men into subserviency. The trick was discovered and all but one of the women
killed. Since that time men have owned
and worn the masks, and women have
become subservient to them.

kinchiltun CENTRAL AMERICA (*Maya*)
Ancient division of time calculated as
twenty CALABTUNS, or 1,250,000,000 days
– about three million years. See CALEN-
DAR.

Kinich Ahau CENTRAL AMERICA (*Maya*)
The fire bird, a solar deity, who is usually
identified with the god simply known as G
in the various CODEX. He is also sometimes
identified as QUETZALCÓATL, here in his
aspect as the Sun-god.

Kinich Kakmo CENTRAL AMERICA
(*Maya*)
The Sun-god, in this instance symbolized
as a brilliant macaw. Kinich Kakmo may
be an aspect or variant of KINICH AHAU,
which would, in turn, make Kinich Kakmo
an aspect of the god G, or of QUETZAL-
CÓATL.

kinno SOUTH AMERICA –
BRAZIL (*Tupari*)
The name given to the people who were
left stranded in the UNDERWORLD when
AROTEH and TOVAPOD dug out the first
men. It is said that they will finally emerge
and populate the Earth after all its present
inhabitants have been killed.

Kiousa NORTH AMERICA –
WOODLANDS (*Oumas*)
A variant of OKI.

Kisani NORTH AMERICA –
SOUTHWEST (*Navajo*)
Inhabitants, described as PUEBLO Indians,
of the fourth world together with the MI-
RAGE people. The Kisani had four gods -
BLACK BODY, BLUE BODY, WHITE BODY and
YELLOW BODY. See ASCENT OF THE
NAVAJO.

Kishá Manido NORTH AMERICA –
WOODLANDS (*Menominee*)
A variant of KITSHI MANITOU who is, like-
wise, also known as MASHA MANIDO.

Kisin CENTRAL AMERICA – YUCATÁN,
MEXICO (*Modern Maya*)
The evil earthquake-spirit who dislikes
and thus drives away the rain sent by
YUMCHAKOB by raising winds. Kisin inhabits and rules over purgatory in which
all souls, except those of soldiers killed in
battle or women who have died in childbirth, must spend some time. The souls of
those who have committed suicide are
fated to remain there for evermore.

Kitkaositiyiqa NORTH AMERICA –
NORTHWEST COAST (*Tlingit*)
The old man who was, according to some
accounts, the father of YETL who is more
usually said to have been created by NAS-
CAKIYETL. Kitkaositiyiqa gave Yetl the
strength he needed to create the world.
Yetl then transformed himself into a splinter of hemlock which was swallowed by
Nascakiyetl's daughter, and was thus reborn as her son. Yetl then stole the stars,
the planets and light from Nascakiyetl,
and so brought them out into the open.

Kitsawitsak NORTH AMERICA – GREAT
PLAINS (*Pawnee*)
One of the five houses that the NAHURAK,
animal-spirits, lived in, and the fourth in
importance. The others, in order of merit,
were PAHUK, NAKISKAT, TSURAPAKO and
PAHUA.

Kitshi Manitou NORTH AMERICA –
WOODLANDS (*Chippewa*)
The GREAT SPIRIT whose name translates
as 'Master-of-Life', or as 'Great Mystery'.

Kiva NORTH AMERICA – PUEBLO,
SOUTHWEST (*Zuñi*)
The generic name given to the six religious
societies or castes of the ZUÑI. These are
the Sun-Priests; the UWANAMI, rainmakers; the KATCHINA priests; the priests
of the war-gods; and the priests of the
animal-gods. The priests meet in their
communal temples, also known as Kiva, in
which the secret rites of the various cults
and fraternities are performed, and to
which women are only ever admitted
when the rites being performed call for
their attendance. After the CORN MAIDENS
had left the Zuñi and the people were
dying from the resulting famine, the
ASHIWI sat in their Kiva and fasted, thinking only of the Corn Maidens and of rain,
in an attempt to bring the Corn Maidens

back again, and thus restore the fertility of
the land.

Klamath NORTH AMERICA –
NORTHWEST COAST
Indigenous North American AMERINDIAN
people inhabiting the NORTHWEST COAST
culture region, together with the likes of
the BELLA COOLA, CHINOOK, HAIDA, KWA-
KIUTL, NOOTKA, SALISH and TSHIMSHIAN
Indians – tribes which speak six different
languages. They take their name from
Lake KLAMATH.

Klamath, Lake NORTH AMERICA –
NORTHWEST COAST (*Klamath*)
Eponymous lake from which the KLAMATH
people take their name and which appears
in the myth of the OLD MAN OF THE AN-
CIENTS as being the location of the
crescent-shaped rock that had been the
lodge of the Sun and the Moon long before
everything else in the world was created.

Klehonoai NORTH AMERICA –
SOUTHWEST (*Navajo*)
The name of the man who was appointed
as Moon-Bearer by ATSE HASTIN and ATSE
ESTSAN. He was one of the two men, the
other being TSHOHANOAI, who had found a
speck of soil from which the reed had
grown that had enabled the NAVAJO to
escape from a flood during their Ascent
(see ASCENT OF THE NAVAJO). Klehonoai
subsequently married YOLKAI ESTSAN.

Kloketen SOUTH AMERICA – TIERRA DEL
FUEGO (*Ona*)
An initiation rite that is comparable with
the KINA rite of the YAHGAN, and which
has its origin similarly explained.

Klukwala NORTH AMERICA –
NORTHWEST COAST (*Nootka*)
The Wolf Society whose rites resemble a
simplification of the HAMATSU of the
KWAKIUTL.

K'makamtch NORTH AMERICA – GREAT
PLAINS (*Klamath*)
'Old-Man', the creator and TRICKSTER of
the Plains KLAMATH (cf. KEMUSH).

Kobath NORTH AMERICA – WEST
COAST (*Skagit*)
The native name for Mount BAKER, one of
the two sacred mountains that were not
totally submerged in the great FLOOD[6], the
other being TAKOBAH (Mount RAINIER).

Koil NORTH AMERICA – NORTHWEST
COAST (*Klamath*)
The name given to the sheep that was
placed, along with LUK, the grizzly bear, on
the mountain slopes by KEMUSH while he
was populating the world he had newly
created.

Koko NORTH AMERICA – PUEBLO,
SOUTHWEST (*Zuñi*)
Generic name given to mask gods (those
who manifest themselves in ritual masks)
who are ruled over by the Sun.

Kokopelli NORTH AMERICA – PUEBLO,
SOUTHWEST (*Hopi*)
A fertility KATCHINA.

Koloowisi NORTH AMERICA – PUEBLO,
SOUTHWEST (*Zuñi*)
The plumed serpent who among the ZUÑI,
as it did among so many other AMERINDIAN
peoples, had a dual significance, being at
once both chthonic, and associated with
death, and celestial, and thus connected
with lightning and fertility. Called PALULU-
KOÑ by the neighbouring HOPI, Koloowisi
is depicted holding an ear of maize and has
water streaming from his mouth.

Komokwa NORTH AMERICA –
NORTHWEST COAST (*Kwakiutl and
Haida*)
The sea-god who lives in a great under-
water palace that is supported by sealions.

He rules over the killer whales who provide the food for his feasts, and at the very
highest of tides comes ashore accompanied by a host of his sea animal subjects.
Any mortal who was able to make, and
survive, the journey to Komokwa's home
would receive the right to use his masks,
dances and songs, a right that could be
passed on after death.

Kon-Tiki SOUTH AMERICA (*pre-Inca*)
The famous name of a legendary Sun king
and creator deity who ruled the country
that was later to be occupied by the INCA,
and was said to have led his people in a
migration out into the Pacific. The name
was most famously used by the explorer
and adventurer Thor HEYERDAHL for his
raft made of nine BALSA-wood logs on
which he sailed from Peru to the Pacific
Islands in 1947.

Konakadset NORTH AMERICA –
NORTHWEST COAST (*Tlingit*)
A mythical hero of renowned strength
who is usually depicted as an aquatic wolf
that has some features of the killer whale.
He is called WASCO by the HAIDA.

Koshari NORTH AMERICA – PUEBLO,
SOUTHWEST (*Sia*)
The name of the first men and thus the
ancestors of the SIA people.

koshpik SOUTH AMERICA – TIERRA DEL
FUEGO (*Yahgan*)
Generic name given to spirits of the dead
who fly away to their eternal kingdom in
the east.

Kothluwalawa NORTH AMERICA –
PUEBLO, SOUTHWEST (*Zuñi*)
The 'dance-house-of-the-gods', a paradisal
palace where the gods hold their councils.
The souls of all the dead men and those

few women who have, in life, been initiated into the KOTIKILI, have right of access to Kothluwalawa for a brief spell. See also ASHIWANNI.

Koti NORTH AMERICA – WOODLANDS (Creek)

The water-frog who is perceived as a helpful and benevolent spirit.

Kotikili NORTH AMERICA – PUEBLO, SOUTHWEST (Zuñi)

The name given to the KIVA who impersonate the KATCHINAS. The society includes all the ZUÑI men, and a few lucky women, and confers on those initiated the right to spend some time in KOTHLUWA-LAWA after their death.

Kowwituma NORTH AMERICA – PUEBLO, SOUTHWEST (Zuñi)

The twin brother of WATSUSII, the sons of the solar deity. They were responsible for the discovery of the CORN MAIDENS whom they brought to the ZUÑI on the instructions of the ASHIWI. After the Corn Maidens had fled, the ashiwi begged the twins to bring them back again as the land had become infertile, and many people were dying of starvation. They enlisted the help of BITSITSI, the musician employed by their father, who helped them to find the Corn Maidens, and then persuaded them to return to the Zuñi under his protection.

Koyemshi NORTH AMERICA – PUEBLO, SOUTHWEST (Zuñi)

'Mudheads', a title given to two of the KATCHINA priests who wear mud-smeared masks with monstrous bulging eyes, a gaping hole for the mouth and a face covered with warts. Licensed clowns who are believed to represent the offspring of an incestuous union, they are seen as the agents for the expression of hostility to the various ZUÑI ceremonies that would otherwise remain suppressed.

kuarup SOUTH AMERICA – BRAZIL (Xingú)

The name given to the complex funeral ritual of the XINGÚ people. See MATVUT-SINIM.

Kuku(l)cán CENTRAL AMERICA (Maya)

The wind-god who is thought to be identifiable with the god B, of the various CODEX, the equivalent of QUETZALCÓATL and the earlier ITZAMNÁ, and the most important deity in the MAYA pantheon. Some characteristics of Kukulcán link him with TLÁLOC. Kukulcán is usually depicted with a proboscis-like nose and has serpent's fangs on either side of his mouth. His chief symbol is a torch, which he is usually shown holding, but there are also four other symbols associated with him that appear to represent the four elements: maize – Earth; the fish – water; the lizard or salamander – fire; and the vulture – air. His heraldry contains four colours that also seem to represent the four basic elements: black – Earth, ; white – water; red – fire; and yellow – air. In his guise as the manifestation of fire, in which he is represented as a lizard-like figure, Kukulcán is identifiable with the god K of the codices, an aspect in which he is seen as the Sungod and is depicted with a snake-like forked tongue protruding from the side of his mouth. However, in this aspect, Kukulcán might also be identified with the god H whose spot or snake-scale on his forehead seems to connect him with Kukulcán in his serpent aspect. Kukulcán sits at the centre of a cross-shaped tree that is a representation of the four cardinal points, and the centre of the quincunx.

His association with the four elements is further demonstrated by the various guises in which he is perceived. Sometimes he traverses the Earth with a staff and bundle, armed with an axe and spear, planting maize as he goes, a perception of his connection to the Earth. On other occasions he is seen in his watery aspect, in which case he is enthroned in clouds or rides a canoe from which he fishes. Alternatively, he devours and is then devoured by a serpent, his chthonic aspects of both Earth and fire.

His sacred day is IK, the day of breath and life. As a result, he never, on any account, appears in any connection with any of the many death symbols of Maya mythology. Like Quetzalcóatl, Kukulcán is essentially the god of resurrection and rebirth. In his serpent aspect, Kukulcán's day is CHICCHAN which is associated with the serpent.

The priests of Kukulcán were at the very top of the caste system that the Maya employed in relation to their deities. Immediately below them were the caste of nobles who were known as the HALACH UINIC, 'true man', and the priestly caste AHUACAN, 'lord serpent'. The Halach uinic sat as judges on those rising through the caste system to determine who had the right to be called ALMENHENOB, 'those who had mothers and fathers'. It seems that this classification does not owe its origins to whether or not the individual's parents were married, but rather to the Halach uinic being the parents who looked to the individual to prove themselves worthy of being called their children. The key to this was knowledge and understanding of ZUYUA which was the sacred language of the XIU clan.

The Xiu were an important ruling clan of the MAYA who were centred in UXMAL. One member of this family, AH KUKUM XIU, helped Francisco MONTEJO the younger in his conquest of the Yucatán. However, it seems that the Xiu language may have been far older and more venerable than

the family that subsequently took their name from it.

The Halach uinic carried in their right hands, as a symbol of their office, a sceptre in the shape of a mannequin, one leg of which ended in a serpent that was the handle of the sceptre. In their left hands they carried yet another proof of their high status: a shield that depicted the Sun-god which was held to be manifest in it.

The Almenhenob had their parallel in the priestly hierarchy – CHILANES or diviners. Those who attained this rank could either be elected or reach there by hereditary inheritance. However, all the NACOM were elected for three years, during which time they were prohibited from having relations with women, not even their wives; neither could they eat red meat, get drunk, nor be attended by any women. They lived in isolation and had their own, sacred cooking utensils. The Nacom were the lowest level of the priestly hierarchy, but on the lay side there was a caste known as the AH HOLPOPOH, 'those at the head of the mat', who were in an intermediary position between the Halach uinic and the general populace. The name of the Ah holpopoh suggests that they perhaps presided at gatherings of the three lowest castes: the TUPILES, town constables; the common populace; and slaves. All these castes lived outside the towns and villages, demonstration of the fact that one's status within the Maya hierarchy might be determined by the distance of the individual's home from the central plaza.

Kukumatz CENTRAL AMERICA – MEXICO (*Mojave*)
One of the twin sons of the EARTH MOTHER, his brother being TOCHIPA. They were responsible, during the creation, for raising the sky, setting the cardinal points and generally organizing the land.

Kulimina CENTRAL AMERICA –
GUYANA (*Arawak*)
The creatrix of women who worked in conjunction with KURURUMANY, the creator of men.

Kumush NORTH AMERICA –
NORTHWEST COAST (*Modoc*)
The MODOC name for the character called KEMUSH by the neighbouring KLAMATH people. In the Modoc version of the OLD MAN OF THE ANCIENTS, Kumush travelled down the slopes of a very steep hill to the UNDERWORLD kingdom of the spirits where, because he felt extremely lonely on the world above, he decided to bring some of the spirit bones he found scattered around the Underworld back with him. Twice Kumush collected a basketful of bones and made his way back up the hill, but each time he reached the very summit he stumbled, the basket fell from his hands and the bones rolled back down the hill where they were once more transformed into the spirit people who ran home to their lodges.

The third time Kumush made the perilous ascent he was extremely careful and, as he reached the place where he had stumbled twice before, he threw the basket over the edge of the Earth, shouting 'Indian bones' as he did so. This time the bones were transformed into people.

Kumush then set about creating all the animals, fish and plants by simply calling out their names. He then organized his people's lives, telling the men that they should become hunters, fishermen and warriors, and the women that they should collect fire wood, draw water, gather berries and other edible plants, and do all the family's cooking. When all was complete, Kumush left, accompanied by his unnamed daughter. They travelled to the very eastern edge of the world, the point where the Sun rises, and followed the Sun's path to the very centre of the sky where he built his lodge in which he and his daughter live to this day.

Kururumany SOUTH AMERICA –
GUYANA (*Arawak*)
The creator of men, husband of EMISIWADDO and WUREKADDO, who worked in conjunction with KULIMINA, the creatrix of women, to populate the world. The origin of all goodness, Kururumany descended to Earth some time later and found that all the people he and Kulimina had created had become corrupt. Seeing that they could not be altered, he instead decreed that from that day forth they would die like snakes and other vermin, rather than enjoy the immortality he had originally intended that they should have.

Kutoyis NORTH AMERICA – GREAT PLAINS (*Blackfoot*)
A hero and wonderchild who was discovered by an old couple who had, having nothing else to eat, placed a clot of buffalo blood in a pot to cook. Turning away, they heard crying coming from the pot and when they looked to see who, or what, was making the noise, they found Kutoyis. Four days later he told his foster-parents that they should tie him to their lodge poles so that he might grow and become a man. They followed his instructions, and having been tied in turn to every lodge pole in the village, Kutoyis reached maturity.

Kwa-Gulth NORTH AMERICA –
NORTHWEST COAST
Alternative name for the KWAKIUTL people.

Kwakiutl NORTH AMERICA –
NORTHWEST COAST
Indigenous North American AMERINDIAN people inhabiting the NORTHWEST COAST

culture region, to either side of the northern entrance to the Queen Charlotte Strait in British Columbia, along with the likes of the BELLA COOLA, CHINOOK, HAIDA, KLAMATH, NOOTKA, SALISH and TSHIMSHIAN Indians, tribes which speak six different languages. The Kwakiutl, who are also known as the KWA-GULTH, are almost unique amongst North American Amerindian peoples for perceiving their cannibal spirit, the tongue-twisting BAXBAKUA-LANUCHSIWAE, to be male, whereas almost all other peoples saw this spirit as a CANNIBAL MOTHER. Like many other peoples of the region, the Kwakiutl placed great importance on their TOTEMic ancestry, the Totem poles of the Kwakiutl being among the most impressive of all North American Amerindian artefacts. Their language belongs to the Wakashan family.

Kwanyip SOUTH AMERICA – TIERRA DEL FUEGO (*Ona*)
A culture hero of the ONA, the subjugator and conqueror of the evil CHENUKE, after which he battled unceasingly against an invisible, black, man-eating giant who is, perhaps, a personification of death.

L

L CENTRAL AMERICA (*Maya*)

The identification used in the various CODEX for EKCHUAH, god of travellers, who is depicted as an old, black god with a sunken mouth.

La CENTRAL AMERICA – MEXICO (*Aztec*)

One dramatized version of the magical conception and birth by COATLICUE names that goddess as LA, a change of name that was perhaps brought about in the hope that the dramatist might hide the identity of the central player of the story from the wrath of the goddess herself. In this version she is a widow, her 400 sons having long since left and are now no more than a memory. One day a multicoloured feather appears, falling slowly from the sky. La places the feather in her bosom and then continues to sweep the heavens every day at twilight so that she might at least see her sons in the sky at night.

Having completed her chores, La sits down and remembers the feather, but when she looks for it, she finds that it has disappeared. Saddened by her loss, she suddenly feels a slight movement within her, and, remembering how she felt when her 400 sons had been gestating, she realized that she was pregnant, and all signs of her melancholy immediately lifted.

Her happiness is not to last for long for her 400 sons learn of their mother's condition, and demand to know who the father is, adding that no matter who he is, they

want him dead. However, La cannot answer the demands and so the sons begin to plot her death. However, before they can kill their mother, the baby is born, a boy who immediately declares himself to be HUITZILOPOCHTLI. He then sets out to kill the 400 who have plotted to kill their own mother. The actual number of sons need not be taken literally; indeed they are sometimes said to number 4,000, for this number is actually meant to represent the number of stars that the Sun extinguishes each morning.

La Dorada SOUTH AMERICA

A female statue, said to be the consort of the golden king EL DORADO, the statue being situated alongside that of her mate in the fabled city of gold.

La Paz SOUTH AMERICA – BOLIVIA

City of Bolivia that lies 12,400 feet above sea level in the Andes and was founded in 1548 by the Spanish. The city lies close to several important features of the Bolivian landscape, namely Lake TITICACA, Mount ILLIMANI (the mountain revered as an ACHACHILA by the AYMARÁ who regard the mountain as the guardian spirit of the city), and the River DESAGUADERO which the COLLAO believed had been formed by the rush boat carrying the body of THUNAPA across Lake Titicaca. An annual fair known as an ALACITA is held at La Paz, a fair which has become associated with the

QUECHUA cult of EKKEKKO. Since 1900 La Paz has been the seat of the Bolivian government.

La Silène-La Baliene HAITI (*Voodoo*)
One of the numerous LOA of the VOODOO religion.

Lacandone CENTRAL AMERICA – YUCATÁN, MEXICO
Indigenous Yuacatec AMERINDIAN people who appear to owe many of their beliefs to the MAYA culture, and thus may have originated from a common background.

Lacroix, Baron HAITI (*Voodoo*)
One of the numerous LOA of the VOODOO religion.

Lakin Chan CENTRAL AMERICA (*Maya*)
'Serpent of the east', a name sometimes applied to the god K. In this form he is said to have been the creator not only of mankind, but also of every other form of organic life, as well as founding the MAYA culture. He invented writing and books, and had knowledge of herbs and medicine, traits which have led some to speculate that he may have been a son of HUNAB-KU.

Lakone NORTH AMERICA – PUEBLO, SOUTHWEST (*Hopi*)
The two central female characters in the annual LALAKOÑTI ritual.

Lalakoñti NORTH AMERICA – PUEBLO, SOUTHWEST (*Hopi*)
A ritual performed in September that is conducted solely by women who invoke the goddess of growth and corn to ensure a good harvest. The participants in the rite carry baskets and dance around two girls who wear the fertility symbols of antelope horns and squash blossom, and throw gifts to the watchers, these two girls being known as LAKONE maidens.

Laloué-Diji, Maîtresse HAITI (*Voodoo*)
Possibly having origins in a West African goddess, this LOA is believed, by some authorities, to combine the two figures of ALAWE and DIJI, though this is by no means certain.

Lamallaka, Mount SOUTH AMERICA – PERU (*Quechua*)
Mountain to which the sons of PARIACACA returned after they had banished HUALLALLO CARUINCHO to the forests for all time, and where they gathered all the people together and established their father's cult.

Lamat CENTRAL AMERICA (*Maya*)
The sign of VENUS, the eighth day of the MAYA spiritual pilgrimage known as the AGES OF MAN on which the spirit of man descends into the lowest, infernal regions – purgatory – whose depravations he must overcome before he can progress along his way. Lamat is not to be confused with FIVE LAMAT, the eighteenth day of the Maya CREATION[4].

Lambeyeqye SOUTH AMERICA (*Chimu*)
The location, south of Cape Santa Elna, to which a fleet of BALSA craft came that were led by the great chief NAYMLAP.

Lances, House of CENTRAL AMERICA (*Maya*)
The first trial house that the divine twins HUNAHPU and XBALANQUÉ were sent into by the lords of XIBALBA to spend the night, having been given the instructions that they must emerge the following morning with four vases of flowers, or be killed. Inside the two brothers were attacked by the fiends that lived there, but they managed to tame them by promising them the flesh of all the animals of the Earth. They then persuaded the ants to gather the required flowers from the gardens of the

rulers of the UNDERWORLD, HUN CAME and VUKUB CAME.

Laoka HAITI (*Voodoo*)
One of the LOA of the VOODOO religion who is also called LOKO or LOKO ATTISO.

L'Arc en Ciel HAITI (*Voodoo*)
'Rainbow'. The personification of the rainbow as a LOA.

League of the Long House NORTH
    AMERICA (*Iroquois*)
The name given to the confederation of six IROQUOIS nations that was founded by HAIOWATHA during the sixteenth century in what is today upper New York State. The confederation was not formed without considerable opposition from other Iroquoian leaders, and was only started with five nations – the CAYUGA, MOHAWK, ONEIDA, ONONDAGA AND SENECA, the sixth nation, that of the TUSCARORA people did not join until some time later. Thus the frequent internecine warfare of the Iroquoian people was brought to an end, and the six nations lived in peace and worked for the common good.

Legba(ssou) HAITI (*Voodoo*)
An extremely important LOA who derives from the African deity of the same name, the messenger of the gods to the Fon people of Dahomey. Legba, also called PAPA LEGBA, is one of the two deities in the VOODOO religion who opens the road to souls as they travel from this life to the spirit world, the other being Maître CARREFOUR. See also GUÉDÉ.

Lenni-Lennapi NORTH
    AMERICA (*Delaware*)
The collective name given to the first-born people who were directly descended from the GREAT SPIRIT. See CALUMET.

Limba(-Zaho) HAITI (*Voodoo*)
A rough, male LOA who lives among the rocks and persecutes human beings on a

purely arbitrary basis. He also has an insatiable appetite which makes it extremely dangerous to be one of his devotees, for he is alleged to kill and eat them.

Limba-Zoau HAITI (*Voodoo*)
A variant of LIMBA-ZAHO.

L'inglésou HAITI (*Voodoo*)
Also simply known as INGLÉSOU, this fierce LOA lives in ravines and among boulders from where he ventures out to kill and devour all those who offend him.

Llampallec SOUTH AMERICA (*Mochica*)
'Figure of Naymlap', a carving made from green-stone, possibly jade, that was positioned in the temple called CHOT soon after the people led by NAYMLAP had landed at LAMBEYEQYE. It remained in position until it was removed by FEMPELLEC, the tenth king of CHIMOR after Naymlap.

Llapchilulli SOUTH AMERICA (*Mochica*)
The master of NAYMLAP's wardrobe who travelled with his master and landed with him and his people as they came ashore from their fleet of BALSA craft that landed at LAMBEYEQYE.

loa HAITI (*Voodoo*)
The name given to a god or spirit of the VOODOO religion that is at once singular and plural. The loa may be male or female (it is gender-independent), and include the likes of Maman BRIGITTE, the loa of death and cemeteries, and AIDA-WÉDO, the rainbow-snake. Initiates into the Voodoo cult are usually under the protection of a single loa, though they may actually worship many loa.

The multitude of loa that may be found within the Voodoo cult are divided into several distinct groupings. The most important of these groupings are the RADA LOA who derive from the gods of the West African Dahomey peoples. Others include the NAGO LOA, or YORUBA LOA, and the IBO LOA from Nigeria; the BUMBA LOA, MOUNDONGUE LOA and SOLONGO LOA that derive from the gods of the Congo regions of Africa; and the WANGOL LOA (Wangol being a corruption of Angola from whence they originate). Loa of native Haitian origin are less numerous, but include the PETRA LOA. In addition to all these groupings, there are a large number of figures derived from the saints of the Roman Catholic religion and who, in some areas, are believed to act as intermediaries who pass on the messages and prayers of man to God.

Locust NORTH AMERICA –
    SOUTHWEST (*Navajo*)
During the flood caused by TIEHOLTSODI that forced the NAVAJO to flee upwards from the multicoloured world, the people became trapped inside a great reed which saved them from the waters, but threatened to imprison them for all time. GREAT HAWK flew up to the sky and clawed at it until he glimpsed light filtering through from the world above. Locust then enlarged the tiny hole and climbed through to be met by four grebes, the guardians of the four cardinal points of the New World. Locust and the grebes engaged in a SHAMANistic contest of power which resulted in Locust gaining half the world for the Navajo people who now came up from below after BADGER had enlarged the hole Locust had made in the sky, arriving on an island in the middle of a lake. See ASCENT OF THE NAVAJO.

Loko (Attiso) HAITI (*Voodoo*)
A variant of LAOKA.

Lomi Ago HAITI (*Voodoo*)
With West African origins, this LOA is also called AGE.

Longfellow, Henry Wadsworth NORTH
    AMERICA
American poet (1807-82) born in Portland, Maine, who is responsible for the famous epic SONG OF HIAWATHA that was based on ALGONQUIAN mythology, and which used a metre borrowed from the Finnish national epic, the *Kalevala*.

loupgarou HAITI (*Voodoo*)
With a name that derives from the French *loup-garou* (werewolf), the loupgarou is a highly feared kind of witch that flies through the night air leaving a trail like a firework to fall on the thatch of a house, through which it wriggles in the form of a mosquito to suck away the life of any children it might find inside. Women have no control over whether or not they will eventually become a loupgarou – fate alone determines that matter. Men, on the other hand, do have a choice whether or not they formally join the male counterpart, the order of sorcerers known as the ZOBOP.

Louquo CARIBBEAN (*Carib*)
The name of the first man who descended from the sky, populated the world with his many children, and then returned from whence he had come. When his descendants die, they too ascend to the sky and there become stars.

Ludjatako NORTH AMERICA –
    WOODLANDS (*Creek*)
The spirit of the giant turtle.

Luk NORTH AMERICA – NORTHWEST
    COAST (*Klamath*)
The name of the grizzly bear that was, during the Creation carried out by KEMUSH, placed on the mountainsides together with the sheep KOIL.

lutin HAITI (*Voodoo*)
The name given to the ghost of a child that has died before it could be baptized.

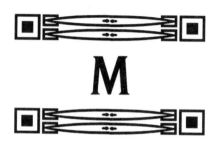

M

M CENTRAL AMERICA (*Maya*)
A deity who appears in the various CODEX, in association with the god F, as a black-faced god with red lips, the lower one of which is large, drooping and almost Negroid in form. He is possibly EK AHAU, the black lord, and may have had some connection with war though he was also the patron deity of merchants such as YIACATECUHTLI, the NAHUA deity.

Maasewe NORTH AMERICA – PUEBLO, SOUTHWEST (*Sia*)
The twin brother of UYUUYEWE, the sons of the Sun spirit who are the SIA counterparts of NAYANEZGANI and THOBADZISTSHINI, and have remarkably similar stories told about them.

Machu Picchu SOUTH AMERICA – PERU
Ruined INCA city that is located to the northwest of CUZCO. Built about AD 1500, it remained undiscovered until 1911 when Hiram Bingham ascended the 1,000 feet high cliffs on which the city is situated. Machu Picchu is remarkably well preserved and contains many fine houses and temple remains.

Mackonaima SOUTH AMERICA – GUYANA (*Ackawoi*)
The creator who is also called MAKANAIMA or MAKUNAIMA.

Macuilxóchitl CENTRAL AMERICA – MEXICO (*Mixtec*)
'Five Flowers', the god of games, music, dance and feasting who is an aspect of XOCHIPILLI, and who, with XIPE TOTEC, the flayed god, governs the southernmost regions of the world.

Madeleine, Maîtresse HAITI (*Voodoo*)
One of the numerous LOA of the VOODOO religion.

Madrid Codex CENTRAL AMERICA (*Maya*)
One of the three surviving CODEX, so named as it is today kept in Madrid, Spain.

maguey CENTRAL AMERICA
Indigenous plant from which the Mexican peoples (AZTECS, MAYA, etc.) brew tequila and PULQUE. The intoxicating qualities of the plant are said to have been discovered by MAYAHUEL

Mah Sish NORTH AMERICA – GREAT PLAINS (*Mandan*)
The spirit of the War-Eagle.

Maho Penekheka NORTH AMERICA – GREAT PLAINS (*Mandan*)
The GREAT SPIRIT.

Mahucutah CENTRAL AMERICA (*Maya*)
'Renowned Name', one of the four brothers who were created from the ground corn of yellow and white maize that was then

strengthened with nine broths which had been brewed by XMUCANÉ. His brothers were BALAM AGAB, BALAM QUITZÉ and IQI BALAM. He was later given HACAVITZ to be his clan's tutelary deity.

Maidu NORTH AMERICA – GREAT
    PLAINS (*Klamath*)
The name given to the AMERINDIAN peoples who were created from the bones of the spirits of the UNDERWORLD after KEMUSH had collected and then distributed them in pairs over the mountains and valleys of the newly created world.

Maiyun NORTH AMERICA – GREAT
    PLAINS (*Cheyenne*)
The GREAT SPIRIT.

maiyunahu'ta NORTH AMERICA – GREAT
    PLAINS (*Cheyenne*)
The name given to the guardian spirit of an individual, all of whom had their own maiyunahu'ta.

Majesty Enveloped CENTRAL
    AMERICA (*Maya*)
Sacred bundle left behind by the brothers BALAM AGAB, BALAM QUITZÉ, IQI BALAM and MAHUCUTAH who gave implicit instructions that the bundle was never to be opened.

Mak ~ anaima, ~ unaima SOUTH
    AMERICA – GUYANA (*Ackawoi*)
Alternative name(s) for MACKONAIMA.

Maklak NORTH AMERICA – NORTHWEST
    COAST
Indigenous North American AMERINDIAN people inhabiting a part of the NORTHWEST COAST culture region. Their neighbours, the KLAMATH say that their creator, KEMUSH, formed the Maklak, MAIDU and CHIPMUNK peoples at the same time as he

created the Klamath from bones he had brought up from the UNDERWORLD.

Makuri SOUTH AMERICA (*Collao*)
The father of an unnamed daughter, he killed THUNAPA after his daughter had been converted to, and baptized into the teachings of Thunapa.

Malinalli CENTRAL AMERICA –
    MEXICO (*Aztec*)
The twelfth day of the twenty-day AZTEC MONTH[1]. The day symbolizes grass and thorns, represents the south and is presided over by PATÉCATL.

Malsum NORTH AMERICA –
    WOODLANDS (*Micmac*)
The marten, the evil brother of GLOOS-CAP.

Mama Coya SOUTH AMERICA (*Inca*)
According to Fray Martin DE MONIA, one of the female of the CHILDREN OF THE SUN. De Monia named the four male members of this divine family as CUSCO HUANCA, HUANA CAURI, MANCO CAPAC and TOPA AYAR, and the four female members as CORI OCLLO, IPA HUACO, Mama Coya and TOPA HUACO. Mama Coya, whose prefix *mama* appears to mean 'woman' or 'female', is the only one of the Children of the Sun to be mentioned by both de Monia and Pedro DE CIEZA DE LÉON who names just six members of the family, the three brothers AYAR CACHI ASAUCA, AYAR MANCO and AYAR UCHO, and the three sisters Mama Coya, MAMA HUACO and MAMA RAHUA.

Mama Huaco SOUTH AMERICA (*Inca*)
According to Pedro DE CIEZA DE LÉON, one of the three female members of the divine

147

CHILDREN OF THE SUN, her sisters being MAMA COYA and MAMA RAHUA, and her three brothers AYAR CACHI ASAUCA, AYAR MANCO and AYAR UCHO. She is not mentioned in the writings of Fray Martin DE MONIA who names four brothers and four sisters. Her prefix *mama* appears to mean 'woman' or 'female'.

Mama Ocllo SOUTH AMERICA (*Inca*)
Called CORI OCLLO when this character is included as one of the four female members of the CHILDREN OF THE SUN as given by Fray Martin DE MONIA who names her sisters as IPA HUACO, MAMA COYA and TOPA HUACO, and her four brothers as CUSCO HUANCA, HUANA CAURI, MANCO CAPAC and TOPA AYAR. She does not appear in the writings of Pedro DE CIEZA DE LÉON. However, Mama Ocllo appears in a quite independent myth which says that it was just she and her brother Manco Capac who were the Children of the Sun sent by their father, the Sun, after he had taken pity on the people who were living like wild animals.

The Sun gave his children a long golden rod with which they were ordered to prod the Earth whenever they stopped to eat, drink, or sleep. When they came to a place where the rod sank completely into the ground, they were to found a city. There they would instruct the people in all the arts of civilization, bring them under the laws of the Sun, and organize their social and religious structure.

Mama Ocllo and her brother came down to the Earth on an island in the middle of Lake TITICACA from whence they travelled north. Every time they stopped they tested the Earth with the golden rod, but not once did it freely enter the ground. Finally they came to the hill or mountain named HUANACAURI where they stopped to eat. There the golden rod sank completely into the ground with consummate ease, so Manco Capac and Cori Ocllo set about the foundation of their city which they called CUZCO. The place they had rested the previous night, a village to the south, they called PACCARITAMBO – 'Inn of Dawn'.

Manco Capac and Mama Ocllo set out from Cuzco and summoned all the savage people who, impressed by the golden ornaments and clothes of the Children of the Sun, were only too willing to follow. Manco Capac and Mama Ocllo taught them the laws of the Sun. Manco Capac taught the men how to build their houses, to irrigate and tend the land, and to show themselves. Mama Ocllo taught the women how to spin, weave, sew and cook. News of this new paradise soon spread far and wide, and soon so many had come to Cuzco that the city had to be divided into two parts, the upper part being called HANAN CUZCO and the lower HURIN CUZCO.

This myth obviously owes a great deal to those recorded by both de Monia and de Cieza de Léon, but, due to the turbulent history of the INCAS, and of South America in general, it is now impossible to say which is the earlier, or whether this simplified version was simply the invention of the Spanish, their subjects, or the Christianized Inca people themselves.

Mama Quillo SOUTH AMERICA (*Inca*)
The sister and wife of INTI, the Sun, the goddess of the Moon and patroness of married women. It seems quite possible, though unverified, that Mama Quillo was the mother of the CHILDREN OF THE SUN in all their various guises.

Mama Rahua SOUTH AMERICA (*Inca*)
According to the writings of Pedro DE CIEZA DE LÉON, Mama Rahua was one of the three female members of the divine CHILDREN OF THE SUN, her sisters, in this case, being MAMA COYA and MAMA HUACA,

and her three brothers AYAR CACHI ASAUCA, AYAR MANCO and AYAR UCHO. She does not appear in the writings of Fray Martin DE MONIA.

mamaé SOUTH AMERICA –
BRAZIL (*Xingú*)
Generic name given to spirits of the dead.

Mama'sa'a NORTH AMERICA – GREAT PLAINS (*Fox*)
The first man.

Mamba Ya Djoni HAITI (*Voodoo*)
One of the numerous LOA of the VOODOO religion.

Mambo HAITI (*Voodoo*)
The name given to a VOODOO priestess.

Mambo La Salle HAITI (*Voodoo*)
One of the numerous LOA of the VOODOO religion.

Mambo Zacca HAITI (*Voodoo*)
Possibly having a West African origin, this LOA is also called AZAKA BAING-BAING, AZACA MEDE and AZACA-SI.

Man-Ik CENTRAL AMERICA (*Maya*)
The seventh day of the MAYA spiritual pilgrimage that comes from *Manzal-Ik* (pass through the spirit). On this day man overcomes his own death and enters the after-life. In this context Man-Ik is not to be confused with FOUR MAN-IK, the seventeenth day of the Maya CREATION[4], though the two are very closely linked because on that day the first man died and passed from Earth to heaven.

Manabozho NORTH AMERICA –
WOODLANDS (*Chippewa*)
The CHIPPEWA name, also MINABOZHO, for the more commonly used MENOMINEE name MÄNÄBUSCH – the Great HARE.

Mänäbus(c)h NORTH AMERICA –
WOODLANDS (*Menominee*)
The MENOMINEE name for the Great HARE, or RABBIT, the chief character of the ALGONQUIAN-speaking AMERINDIAN tribes of the North American forests to whom he is both culture hero and demi-urge, as well as the TRICKSTER. Various tribes give him a variety of names: GLOOSCAP – MICMAC; MANABOZHO or MINABOZHO – CHIPPEWA; MESSOU – MONTAGNAIS; NANABOOJOO or NANIBOZHO – POTAWATOMI.

The daughter of NOKOMIS bore twins but died during childbirth, together with one of the babies. Nokomis placed the surviving baby under a wooden bowl (a symbol of the heavens) to protect it. When she later removed the bowl, she found that the child had become a small white rabbit with long trembling ears. She named him Mänäbusch.

While still quite young, Mänäbusch decided to steal fire to keep his grandmother Nokomis warm, a plan that she begged him to drop. Deaf to her entreaties, Mänäbusch set off eastwards in his canoe to the island on which lived the old man who owned fire and his two daughters, one of whom discovered the cold and wet Mänäbusch outside their wigwam, and took him inside to warm him by the fire. Mänäbusch waited until all three were busy and then seized a brand from the fire and made off in his canoe, the old man and his daughters giving chase. Mänäbusch, however, rowed so fast that it seemed as if he were flying over the water, and soon outran the old man, while the brand burst into flame thanks to the rush of air past it. Arriving back at Nokomis's home, Mänäbusch gave her the burning brand. She, in turn, passed the brand on to KENEUN, the chief of the THUNDERERS, who has guarded it ever since.

Mänäbusch, in some versions of his story, had a brother named MOQWAOI, though whether this brother was his surviving twin, or another, younger, brother is not made clear. One day Moqwaoi was walking across the frozen surface of a lake when the ANAMAQKIU dragged him down. For four days Mänäbusch mourned the loss of his brother before, on the fifth, resolving to avenge him when he met his dead brother's shade whom he told to go to the far west, there to build a huge fire that would guide the souls of the dead to their eternal home, as well as keeping them warm on their long and arduous journey.

Mänäbusch now made war on the anamaqkiu and managed to trick their two BEAR chiefs to their deaths. The anamaqkiu retaliated by sending a FLOOD[3] to destroy the Earth. Mänäbusch climbed a huge pine growing on the summit of a mountain to escape the advancing waters, but they relentlessly chased after him. Mänäbusch made the tree grow to four times its original height, but still the waters advanced until they had reached Mänäbusch's armpits. Only then did the GREAT SPIRIT intervene and arrest the waters.

The entire surface of the Earth was now covered with water. Mänäbusch told the animals which had escaped with him that he could recreate the Earth if he had so much as a single grain of soil. Firstly OTTER, then BEAVER, and then MINK plunged down into the waters to look for some, but each of them died in their attempt. Finally MUSKRAT succeeded and Mänäbusch set about the recreation of the Earth.

In the Menominee Hare cycle, the name given to the series of stories surrounding Mänäbusch, a great fish-like, or multicoloured serpentine fiend, MASHENO-MAK, MESHEKENABEC or MISIKINEBIK, once caused havoc by devouring all the people on the Earth, so that there were very few Menominee left. Those who remained prayed to the gods for salvation from the fiend. Mänäbusch responded to these prayers by allowing himself to be swallowed by the fiend. Once inside the beast, he held a war dance in its stomach, stabbed it in the heart, and then proceeded to hack his way to freedom along with all its victims.

With his work on Earth at an end, Mänäbusch went away to the VILLAGE OF THE SOULS in the far west where he still lives with Nokomis, his grandmother, and MOQWAOI, his brother. There he is sometimes visited by braves. Once four braves (some say seven) were entertained by Mänäbusch, after which he offered each brave a boon. One asked to be a successful hunter while another asked to become a great warrior. The last of all asked for longevity so Mänäbusch turned him into a stone, or a tree, so that he would be visible for many generations.

Manco Capac SOUTH AMERICA (*Inca*)

One of the CHILDREN OF THE SUN who appears in a number of versions of that story. He is named as such in the writings of Fray Martin DE MONIA, but not in those of Pedro DE CIEZA DE LÉON. However, it is quite possible that the AYAR MANCO mentioned by de Cieza de Léon is simply his name for Manco Capac, for de Cieza de Léon says that Ayar Manco took the name Manco Capac after he and his sisters had founded the city of CUZCO, which had been named ACAMAMA before they had occupied it, and later succeeded his brother CUSCO HUANCA as its king. In these variants of the story there are either six or eight divine children, depending on which source is consulted. There is, however, one other variant which possibly predates either of these, and in this there are just two children – Manco Capac and his sister MAMA OCLLO.

In this interesting story, the Sun, the father of Manco Capac and Mama Ocllo, took pity on the people of the world who were living like wild animals. He sent them his children, hence the Children of the Sun, whom he gave a long golden staff which they were instructed to stick into the Earth every time they stopped to eat, drink or sleep. When the staff completely disappeared into the Earth, they were to found their city on that spot, bring the people under the laws of the Sun, their father, and instruct them in all the arts of civilization.

Manco Capac and his sister came down to the Earth on an island in the midst of Lake TITICACA from whence they travelled north. Every time they stopped they tested the Earth, but not once did it sink into the Earth more than a few inches. Finally they came to Mount HUANACAURI where they once again tested the Earth. This time the staff sank effortlessly into the ground with a single blow. They named the place they had set out from that morning before coming to Mount Huanacauri PACCARITAMBO, 'Inn of Dawn', as it was from there that they had set out on the final leg of their trek.

Manco Capac and Mama Ocllo went out from Mount Huanacauri to summon all the people to the city they were founding, and which they called Cuzco. The savage people were easily impressed by the golden ornaments worn by the Children of the Sun, and were thus willing to follow and believe them. At Cuzco Manco Capac taught the men to build their houses, to irrigate and tend the Earth, raise their crops, and to show themselves. Mama Ocllo taught the women how to spin, weave, sew, and look after their menfolk. Both taught them the rites and rituals of their father. So many people came to the new city that it had to be divided into two parts, the upper being called HANAN CUZCO and the lower HURIN CUZCO.

Mandan NORTH AMERICA – GREAT PLAINS
Indigenous SIOUX-speaking North American AMERINDIAN people who occupy a small part of the GREAT PLAINS culture region, sandwiched between, to the north, the ALGONQUIAN-speaking tribes, and to the south the SHOSHONEAN-speaking peoples. Their neighbours were the Sioux tribes of the ASSINABOIN, CROW, DAKOTA, OMAHA, OSAGE and WINNEBAGO, and the CADDO-speaking ARIKA, Caddo and PAWNEE.

Mani-Mani SOUTH AMERICA – BRAZIL (*Tupari*)
The river across which every PABID has to cross to reach the realm of the dead, to which it is welcomed by PATOBKIA.

mani ~ to(u), ~ do NORTH AMERICA – WOODLANDS (*Algonquian*)
The name given to the spirit or soul with which all things are possessed. It may be either good or evil in nature, but was generally used to refer to things that had supernatural powers (cf. INUA).

Manoa SOUTH AMERICA
A mythical land, also called OMOA, that was said to lie beyond the ORINOCO. In it, so it was alleged, one could discover Lake PARIMA, the lake that had become widely associated with the fabled EL DORADO until that association was disproved by VON HUMBOLDT.

Marassa Jumeaux HAITI (*Voodoo*)
This LOA, having a West African origin, and also simply known as MARISSA, is said to be the personification of the spirits of dead twins, and as such are the objects of a

special cult, for the birth of twins was considered a divine act.

Maria Madeleine, Sainte HAITI (*Voodoo*)

The Roman Catholic Saint Mary Magdalene who is regarded as a LOA by some VOODOO cultists.

Marinette bwa chèche HAITI (*Voodoo*)

One of the easily annoyed PETRA LOA grouping, her name may mean either 'Marinette dry arm' (*bras sèche*), or 'Marinette dry wood' (*bois sèche*).

Marissa HAITI (*Voodoo*)

Variant for MARASSA JUMEAUX.

Marocael CARIBBEAN (*Taïno*)

The night-watchman of the caves AMAIAUA and CACIBAGIAGUA from which mankind, under the leadership of GUAGUGIANA, was able to escape after he had tarried too long outside one morning and was caught in, and petrified by the rays of the Sun.

Martyr Anglerius, Peter

Sixteenth-century Italian historian (1459–1525) who became the bishop of Jamaica. He wrote several important works, the *De Orbe Novo* (1516) being relevant to Native American mythology and legend as it gave the first account of the discovery of America, and many of the customs, rites and beliefs of the native peoples, though on many occasions, as is the case with DABIABA, he omitted to name the people to whom the deity was connected.

Masha Manido NORTH AMERICA – WOODLANDS (*Menominee*)

A variant of KITSHI MANITOU and KISHÁ MANIDO.

Mashenomak NORTH AMERICA – WOODLANDS (*Menominee*)

Variant of MISIKINEBIK.

Matchi Manitou NORTH AMERICA – WOODLANDS (*Chippewa*)

Usually thought of as the benevolent 'medicine-spirit', one early commentator, Bacqueville de la Potherie (1753) reported that it was the personification of evil, a concept that is linguistically consonant with the similar forms for the evil spirit of the neighbouring ALGONQUIAN tribes (cf. MATSHEHAWAITUK, MATSI NIOUASK).

Matenino CARIBBEAN (*Taïno*)

The island on which GUAGUGIANA stranded all the women who had followed him, taking all their children off with him.

Matshehawaituk NORTH AMERICA – WOODLANDS (*Menominee*)

The personification of evil. See also MATCHI MANITOU.

Matsi Niouask NORTH AMERICA – WOODLANDS (*Abnaki*)

The personification of evil who is diametrically opposed by KETSI NIOUASK. See also MATCHI MANITOU.

Matvutsinim SOUTH AMERICA – BRAZIL (*Xingú*)

The creator who lived all alone at the source of the River XINGÚ. Tiring of his lonely existence he transformed a shell into a woman whom he took as his wife. She bore him a son whom Matvutsinim took away with him. Grief-stricken, the woman returned to the water and once more became a shell. The grandchildren of Matvutsinim's son became the Xingú people.

Some time later, Matvutsinim looked down on the people he had created via his son and saw that many of them had died (of old age). Saddened by their loss, he looked for a way to restore them to life. He cut three KUARUP logs which he decorated with feathers, necklaces and beautiful threads. He then called for the living people to celebrate a festival around the three logs. In this festival singers with gourd rattles implored the three kuarup logs to come to life.

However, around midday the singers switched to mourn the logs, whom they took to symbolize their dead, but Matvutsinim assured them that there was nothing to mourn, for these kuarup logs were going to come to life, as would all their dead. Gradually, through the second and third days of the festival, the kuarup logs started to stir into life, at which time Matvutsinim commanded his people not to look upon them. When they were nearly complete, Matvutsinim told his people to come out of their huts and celebrate near the kuarups, but told them that they must still not look upon them. He added that any man or woman who had had intercourse the night before must stay away.

However, one young man, in his enthusiasm, disobeyed, and as soon as he emerged from his hut, the kuarups turned back into logs. Thus the dead never came back to life, and all men must die. The kuarup simply became, from that day forth, a ceremony to commemorate the dead.

Matyavela CENTRAL AMERICA – MEXICO (Mojave)

The father of MUSTAMHO who was killed through the wickedness of FROG. His body was set upon a pyre ready for cremation but, before the fire was lit, the people sent COYOTE away as they feared his intentions. However, Coyote saw the smoke from the fire and hurried back to snatch Matyavela's heart from the flames. A similar story to this is told by the neighbouring DIEGUEÑO people.

Maya CENTRAL AMERICA

The name given to an AMERINDIAN civilization that originated in the Yucatán peninsula c.2600 BC, and which expanded, over the centuries, to cover sites in Mexico, Guatemala and Belize. It enjoyed a golden age between AD 325 and 925, after which it was in decline, though it did not fully disappear, for the Maya people, or rather their descendants, are still to be found in this area of Central America, especially in the Yucatán, Belize, Guatemala and west Honduras. Present-day Maya still speak their ancient language, a branch of the Totonac–Mayan (Penutian) family, though they also speak Spanish as a second language. The Maya are famous for their magnificent stone buildings and stepped pyramids which they built without the use of metal tools. They used an hieroglyphic system of writing, though only three contemporary Maya manuscripts now survive. They were also skilled potters, weavers and farmers, and regulated their rituals, as well as their warfare, by observations of the planet VENUS[2].

The history of the Maya presents many as yet unsolved problems, problems which are compounded by the diversity of their realm which can be conveniently split into three distinct regions. To the north was their ancestral homeland, the Yucatán peninsula, while to the south there were the highlands and coast of modern Guatemala. In between, in the unpropitious region that has been long covered by dense, tropical rain forest, the Maya civilization reached its peak.

The Maya city appears not to have been principally a place of residence, but was predominantly a centre of religion and learning that was confined to the priestly caste, though this is still to be conclusively proved one way or the other. The earliest known example of Maya architecture so far excavated lies in Guatemala and dates from c.300 BC.

The intellectual achievements of the Maya are astounding, and include one of the most complex calendars known, as well as wide-ranging mathematical and astronomical knowledge. Potentially the Maya are the most interesting of all the Central American civilizations for the student of myth and legend, but to date the few scripts they left behind remain largely undeciphered. Most of their manuscripts were burned by the invading and conquering Spanish. Of the three that remain, known from their present homes as the DRESDEN CODEX, PARIS CODEX and MADRID CODEX, little can be truly understood, nor are many of the numerous stone inscriptions the Spanish failed to destroy any more revealing. To date, the main source for the interpretation of the CODEX and the stone inscriptions is the information collected by Diego DE LANDA, the first Spanish bishop of Yucatán. Regrettably for the modern student, while de Landa was very interested in the Maya hieroglyphs, and asked the Maya scholars to explain them to him, he was also one of the most enthusiastic destroyers of the Maya texts. His data must therefore be treated with some caution, as he had a tendency to select both those who explained the Maya culture to him, and the stories he wrote about, for their Christian belief or content.

Coupled with the tentative interpretations of their surviving works, the modern student must also rely on three later works that were written after the Spanish conquest. Two of these, the POPUL VUH and the ANNALS OF CAKCHIQUEL, were compiled by the southern Maya peoples of Guatemala, and may possibly reflect rather more of the TOLTEC than the Maya culture and tradition. This assumption is made as it is historically recorded that by the time of the Spanish conquest the Maya of Guatemala knew very little about the builders of their great cities. It is also based on the fact that they told the Spanish their legend about their exile from TOLLAN, a story that resembles a story found among the central Mexican Toltec who certainly penetrated as far south as Guatemala, if not further. It seems perfectly reasonable, therefore, to assume that the Toltec and the southern Maya intermarried, and their traditions, myth and legends became assimilated and intermixed.

A further indication of possible Toltec influence among the southern Maya is the remarkable similarity between the concepts found in the *Popul Vuh*, and those to be found as the underlying theme of Toltec, AZTEC and North American Indian myth and legend. In this work, as in both the Aztec and the Toltec myths, there is a series of creations, each of which is destroyed by a great FLOOD[8]. Also, as in the myths of the North American Indians, great emphasis is placed on the adventures of the divine or semi-divine twins, the grandchildren of the SKY FATHER and the EARTH MOTHER. However, it might just be that these stories do not show outside assimilation, but rather that they were simply common among all the various cultures.

The final source is the fragmentary book of CHILAM BALAM OF CHUMAYEL, a sixteenth-century source that originates in the Yucatán, which was again conquered by the Toltecs, and is a collection of chronicles and miscellaneous information.

Mayahual CENTRAL AMERICA – MEXICO (*Aztec*)
Maiden with whom EHÉCATL fell in love, and by so doing brought the power of love

to mankind. Ehécatl found the maiden in the company of many others, all asleep, in the charge of an ancient guardian named TZIZIMITL who was also asleep. Ehécatl woke Mayahual who agreed to go with him. Their love was manifested in a beautiful tree that grew on the spot where they confirmed and consummated their passion for each other on the Earth. This great tree had two branches. One was known as the PRECIOUS WILLOW and belonged to Ehécatl. The other branch, the one that was covered in flowers, belonged to Mayahual.

In the meantime Tzizimitl had woken up and discovered that Mayahual was no longer where she should have been. Furiously she gathered together an army of young gods and set off in search of her wayward ward. On Earth they soon came to the tree in whose flowering branch Tzizimitl recognized the characteristics of Mayahual. Realizing that the maiden had been seduced, Tzizimitl broke the flowers from the branch and gave them to the gods who had accompanied her and who immediately ate them. Then she and her henchmen returned to the heavens.

After they had gone, Ehécatl resumed his proper shape and changed the other branch back into the now dead Mayahual whom he buried in a field. There her body brought forth a magical plant that provided man with an intoxicating drink which would induce in mankind the same feeling that Ehécatl had felt when he held Mayahual.

Mayahuel CENTRAL AMERICA – MEXICO (*Aztec*)
The wife of the farmer PATÉCATL, Mayahuel one day saw a mouse which she tried to kill, but it escaped and ran circles around her, laughing as it went. She investigated further and saw that the mouse had, moments before she had tried to kill it, been nibbling at the stem of a MAGUEY plant, and that some creamy sap had oozed out from the wound. She collected some of the sap in a gourd which she took home with her to share with her husband. As they drank it, they became extremely contented and loving towards each other, and decided that this must be the effect of the sap. For this discovery the gods, who also benefited from the effects of the drink, known as PULQUE, deified Mayahuel as the goddess of all intoxicating drinks, including the hallucinogens. Her husband became XOCHIPILLI, the Lord of Flowers, and patron of gamblers and gambling.

Mayapan CENTRAL AMERICA (*Maya*)
Also sometimes called ICHPA, Mayapan was the name given to the MAYA New Empire which lasted from AD 987 until 1697. Mayapan means 'the Standard of the Not Many' from *maya* ('not many') and *pán* ('standard'). Ichpa itself means 'within the enclosure' which is an exact parallel to the NAHUA description of TLOQUE NAHUAQUE as 'Lord of the Ring'.

Mayochina NORTH AMERICA – PUEBLO, SOUTHWEST (*Acoma*)
The spirit of the summer.

Mazatl CENTRAL AMERICA (*Aztec*)
The name given to the seventh day of the twenty-day MONTH[1] employed by the AZTEC people. Mazatl symbolized the deer, represented the west and was presided over by TLÁLOC.

Mchemnito NORTH AMERICA – WOODLANDS (*Potawatomi*)
The personification of evil (see also MATCHI MANITOU), though this spelling is

thought to be a variant of MITCHE MAN-ITOU.

Mearatsim SOUTH AMERICA – BRAZIL (*Xingú*)
A spirit that is closely associated by JAKUÍ, and represented in rituals by a mask un-remarkably known as a Mearatsim mask.

Medi Kenago NORTH AMERICA – GREAT PLAINS (*Fox*)
The spirit of the Great Snapping Turtle.

Melatha NORTH AMERICA – WOODLANDS (*Choctaw*)
The male Lightning-Bird.

Mem Loomis NORTH AMERICA – SOUTHWEST COAST (*Wintun*)
The primordial goddess of the waters who lives beneath the Earth and was, along with KAHIT, summoned by OLELBIS to ex-tinguish the fire that was destroying the Earth.

Membo-Delahi HAITI (*Voodoo*)
One of the many LOA of the VOODOO cult.

Men CENTRAL AMERICA (*Maya*)
The fifteenth day of the AGES OF MAN, the MAYA spiritual pilgrimage when man be-comes perfect but still has a long way to go until he reaches full consciousness. Men in this context is not to be confused with FIVE MEN, the fifth day of the Maya CREATION[4], the day on which things were first given life.

Menahka NORTH AMERICA – GREAT PLAINS (*Mandan*)
The spirit of the Sun.

Menominee NORTH AMERICA – WOODLANDS
Indigenous ALGONQUIAN-speaking, and mainly peaceable North American AMER-INDIAN people inhabiting just a small part of the vast WOODLANDS culture region. Their linguistic neighbours were the CHIP-PEWA, CREE, DELAWARE, MONTAGNAIS and POTAWATOMI peoples.

Meshekenabec NORTH AMERICA – WOODLANDS (*Menominee*)
Variant of MISIKINEBIK.

Messou NORTH AMERICA – WOODLANDS (*Montagnais*)
One of the many tribal names that is given to the Great HARE, his best known name possibly being MÄNÄBUSCH, the MENO-MINEE name for this character. Each tribe, however, had their own additions to the Hare cycle that was common amongst the ALGONQUIAN peoples. A MONTAGNAIS story tells how Messou gave a warrior a small packet of immortality, instructing him that it should never be opened. The man com-plied, but before long his inquisitive wife could not resist taking a look. As she undid the packet, the immortality flew away and ever since then man has been mortal.

Metztli CENTRAL AMERICA – MEXICO (*Aztec*)
The god of the Moon who is also called TECCIZTÉCATL, and sometimes identified with TEZCATLIPOCA.

Mexica CENTRAL AMERICA – MEXICO
Anthropological name for the many NAHUA peoples who moved into and estab-lished their homelands in Mexico, though in the main it is used to refer to the people more commonly known as the AZTECS, and which they appear to have used to refer to themselves collectively. It is perhaps more correct to refer to the early Aztec people as Mexica, for the term Aztec only appears to

have come into common usage after the Mexica had assimilated and confederated with other central Mexican peoples. However, for the sake of making the text more accessible, the term Aztec is used throughout this book to refer to both early and late Mexica.

mexólotl CENTRAL AMERICA – MEXICO (*Aztec*)

The name given to the MAGUEY plant into which XÓLOTL transformed himself. This was his second transformation, in his attempts to avoid being sacrificed, to vivify the Sun and the Moon; his first transformation being into the twin-stalked, and thus deformed, maize XÓLOTL. He was caught and sacrificed after his third transformation which was into the lava AX-ÓLOTL.

Michabo NORTH AMERICA – WOODLANDS

One of the many names given to the Great HARE by the ALGONQUIAN peoples. See MÄNÄBUSCH.

Michel HAITI (*Voodoo*)

Saint Michael, the Roman Catholic saint who is regarded as a LOA by some VOODOO cultists.

Micmac NORTH AMERICA – WOODLANDS

Indigenous IROQUOIS North American AMERINDIAN people inhabiting a relatively small part of the WOODLANDS culture region. They were closely allied to the AB-NAKI people, but, like all Iroquoian peoples, were frequently engaged in internecine wars.

Mictlán CENTRAL AMERICA – MEXICO (*Aztec*)

The UNDERWORLD, that dark realm that was ruled over by MICTLÁNTECUHTLI and his consort MICTLÁNTECUHTL. Mictlán was located at the very centre of the Earth and was a far less desirable place to be sent to after death than XOCHIQUETZAL, the cloudland realm of the souls of dead warriors whose death in battle, or by sacrifice, fed the Sun with whom they were said to go and live for all eternity. There they were joined by women who had died in childbirth, and were thus perceived to have sacrificed themselves for the sake of a potential warrior. Nevertheless, souls sent to Mictlán did not suffer, for Mictlán was not, unlike the Underworld of many other cultures, a purgatory, as it had no moral significance as a place of judgement to which the evil were condemned. Rather it was a place to where all souls went after death, and where there was neither pain nor pleasure, in which souls lived a dreary eternal existence.

To reach Mictlán, the travelling soul had to make a perilous four-day journey that passed between great trees which threatened to crush the soul, though some accounts say that rather than having to pass through a forest, the soul has to climb two mountains that threaten to crush it between them as they clash together. Having survived the forest (or the mountains), the soul had to evade a great serpent and a fearsome alligator, cross eight deserts and eight mountains during which time it had to endure a bitter wind that hurled stones and obsidian knives at them. Finally the soul would reach a great river, the limits of Mictlán, across which it would be carried by the red dog-soul that had accompanied it so far, this soul being that of the dog which was sacrificed in the dead person's grave. Having arrived in Mictlán, the soul would offer gifts to Mictlántecuhtli who would then allot the soul a place in one of the Underworld's nine regions. Some accounts say that the soul would not be immediately allotted a place, but would spend four probationary years in the outer regions, each region being separated from the next by a wide river, before that soul would be admitted to CHICUNAUHMICTLÁN – Mictlán proper.

Mictlánt ~ ecuhtl, ~ cehutl, ~ cihuatl CENTRAL AMERICA – MEXICO (*Aztec*)

'Lady of Death', the consort of MICTLÁNTE-CUHTLI, and thus the goddess of MICTLÁN, the UNDERWORLD.

Mictlán ~ tecuhtli, ~ cehutli CENTRAL AMERICA – MEXICO (*Aztec*)

'Lord of the Death', the consort of MICT-LÁNTECUHTL, god of the UNDERWORLD and ruler of MICTLÁN. The Lord of the North, he is sometimes, paradoxically, associated with the south, perhaps due to the aridity and inhospitality of that region.

Midewewin NORTH AMERICA – WOODLANDS (*Chippewa*)

The name given to the 'medicine' society, to which the SHAMANs belonged (cf. FALSE-FACE SOCIETY, HADIGANSO SHANO). Their sacred rites, rituals and teachings were said to have been introduced to them by the Great HARE.

Milky Way

1 NORTH AMERICA – NORTHWEST COAST (*Kwakiutl*)

The KWAKIUTL saw either the Milky Way or a RAINBOW[1] as the central pole of the home of their tongue-twisting deity BAXBAKUALANUCHSIWAE who lived in the Arctic at the exact north of the world.

2 CENTRAL AMERICA (*Aztec*)

Personified in the goddess CITLALINICUE, the Milky Way was perceived as the guardian of the dusk, the goddess Cit-lalinicue being the patron deity of the last hour of the day, though ILAMATE-CUHTLI is also sometimes seen in this role. The Milky Way was also seen as the personification of TONACATECUHTLI

in his aspect of CHICOMEXOCHTLI. A story concerning the birth of HUITZILO-POCHTLI says that the 400 sons of COAT-LICUE who plotted to kill their mother lived in the Milky Way.

3 NORTH AMERICA – GREAT PLAINS (*Cheyenne*)

EKUTSIHIMMIYO, the 'Hanging Road' that is suspended between, and links, heaven and Earth, and along which the TASOOM travels from Earth to the heavenly home of HEAMMAWIHIO.

Minabozho NORTH AMERICA – WOODLANDS (*Chippewa*)

A variant, along with MANABOZHO, of the more commonly used MÄNÄBUSCH, the ME-NOMINEE name for the Great HARE.

Mink NORTH AMERICA – WOODLANDS (*Menominee*)

One of the animals that found itself in the company of MÄNÄBUSCH during the flood that covered Earth's entire surface, and one which lost its life attempting to find a single speck of soil so that Mänäbusch could recreate the Earth. The required grain of soil was finally brought to the surface of the water by MUSKRAT.

mino NORTH AMERICA – GREAT PLAINS (*Cheyenne*)

Generic name given to horned, hairy water-spirits who were perceived as fearsome demons who would drag people down into the depths of the lake homes (cf. ANAMAQKIU). Their great foe is the THUNDERBIRD who would swoop down from the sky and release their victims moments before their death.

Miquiztli CENTRAL AMERICA – MEXICO (*Aztec*)

The deathshead day, the sixth day of the twenty-day MONTH[1] of the AZTECS which symbolized death, represented the west and was presided over by TECCIZTÉCATL.

Mirage NORTH AMERICA – SOUTHWEST
(*Navajo*)
A mythical people who inhabited the fourth world that the NAVAJO came to during their ascent to the present Earth (see ASCENT OF THE NAVAJO). They lived in this world along with the KISANI, and had four gods; BLACK BODY, BLUE BODY, WHITE BODY and YELLOW BODY.

Mirage Boy NORTH AMERICA –
SOUTHWEST (*Navajo*)
Semi-divine being who was married to the first woman, who had been made from an ear of yellow corn. The first man, who had been made from an ear of white corn, was married to GROUND-HEAT GIRL. The children of these two unions became the first NAVAJO. See ASCENT OF THE NAVAJO.

Misikinebik NORTH AMERICA –
WOODLANDS (*Menominee*)
Also known as MASHENOMAK and MESHE-KENABEC, Misikinebik was the monstrous, multicoloured serpent, that was swallowing all the people when MÄNÄBUSCH allowed himself to be swallowed in answer to the peoples' prayers for salvation. Once inside the monster, he held a war dance, stabbed Misikinebik in the heart and then hacked his way to freedom along with all the monster's other victims.

mistai NORTH AMERICA – GREAT PLAINS
(*Cheyenne*)
Generic name given to spirits that haunt dark woods and other equally gloomy places.

Mitche Manitou NORTH AMERICA –
WOODLANDS (*Potawatomi*)
The personification of evil, it is thought that Mitche Manitou might be the correct spelling or phrasing of MCHEMNITO.

Mitla CENTRAL AMERICA – MEXICO
(*Mixtec*)
Site of an important MIXTEC palace that dates from between the eighth and eleventh centuries AD. The elaborately and intricately decorated walls of the palace show motifs that also appear in the CODEX, but to date their application in architecture has not been determined with any degree of certainty.

Mitnal CENTRAL AMERICA (*Maya*)
The region of the UNDERWORLD that is best equated as a true hell, for here the wicked are tortured. As the name is linguistically similar to the AZTEC word MICTLÁN, it is quite possible that one gave rise to the other, but which derives from which remains uncertain. See also XIBALBA.

Mitsima NORTH AMERICA – ARCTIC
(*Inuit*)
A legendary hunter who became lost in a snowstorm. When the storm abated, his children saw him crawling across the ice like a dog as his hands and his feet had been blackened with frostbite. Realizing that their father was dying, they did not dare go near him, and so left him there. It is said that he may still be seen crawling over the ice floes after particularly bad storms in search of his treacherous offspring.

Miuisit, Baron HAITI (*Voodoo*)
One of the many LOA of the VOODOO religion.

Mixcóatl CENTRAL AMERICA – MEXICO
(*Aztec and Toltec*)
The Sky Father, 'Cloud Serpent', the father of QUETZALCÓATL. It is said that in the beginning the TOLTEC came from the north under the leadership of their great god Mixcóatl, conquered great tracts of central Mexico and built a great city there. Mixcóatl married CHIMALMAN, by whom he

became the father of CE ACTL TOPILTZIN who temporarily fled into self-imposed exile after his father had been murdered. He later returned, killed his father's murder, and then became the high priest of Quetzalcóatl, the tutelary deity of the city, whose name he adopted.

Mixtec CENTRAL AMERICA – MEXICO
A pre-colonial Mexican culture that eclipsed the earlier ZAPOTEC culture in the valley of Oaxaca. The Mixtec founded new towns such as TILANTONGO and Teozacualco, and partially rebuilt some of the earlier Zapotec cities. The most notable product of the Mixtec culture was the intricately decorated walls of the great palace at MITLA that dates from between the eighth and eleventh centuries AD. The motifs shown on these walls have a meaning that also appears in the CODEX, but their application in architecture has not so far been determined with any certainty. The Mixtecs left historical records that contained biographies of rulers and noblemen and traced their history back to AD 692.

Moan CENTRAL AMERICA (*Maya*)
The vulture-spirit who was perceived as the harbinger of death.

Moche SOUTH AMERICA – PERU (*Chimu*)
The central valley of the pre-INCA state of CHIMOR as well as of the MOCHICA civilization, the latter of which are sometimes referred to as Moche rather than Mochica.

Mochica SOUTH AMERICA – PERU
A pre-INCA classical civilization (c.AD 100–800) that followed the CHAVIN culture, was centralized around MOCHE valley, and gradually spread into the valleys of the North Peruvian coastline. The culture depended on a highly organized system of irrigation canals and aqueducts that were centred on the valleys of CHICAMA and Moche. The most important extant buildings are the great temple pyramids of the Sun and Moon in MOHIC valley. While both the Sun and Moon appear to have had great importance within the Mochica culture, it seems as if the Moon-god was the pre-eminent. Many subordinate deities, including a jaguar-god, possibly a war-god who demanded human sacrifices, were also worshipped, but regrettably very little else is known about this long lost, but once great civilization. Knowledge of the Mochica civilization was advanced in 1988 by the discovery of the tomb of a warrior-priest ruler who was given the nickname 'Great Lord of Sipan' after the village near the site of his tomb which contained a priceless hoard of treasure including a gold mask and ear pendants.

Modoc NORTH AMERICA – NORTHWEST COAST
Indigenous North American AMERINDIAN people from the NORTHWEST COAST culture region and neighbours of the KLAMATH whose creator KEMUSH is almost identical to the Modoc creator KUMUSH. The Klamath, however, say that Kemush created the Modoc and the Klamath, together with the CHIPMUNK and MAIDU peoples, from bones he brought up from the UNDERWORLD. The Modoc simplify this saying that Kumush only created their own race.

Mohawk NORTH AMERICA – WOODLANDS
Indigenous North American AMERINDIAN people who inhabited, and gave their name to, Mohawk Valley in New York State, a part of the WOODLANDS culture region. Their neighbours were the other IROQUOIS-speaking peoples, namely the CHEROKEE, HURON, ONEIDA, ONONDAGA, TUSCARORA and SELISH. The Mohawk language belongs to the Macro–Siouan group.

Frequently engaged in internecine war-fare, the Mohawk were one of the six Iroquois nations united by HAIOWATHA into the LEAGUE OF THE LONG HOUSE during the sixteenth century. Today those Mohawk who do not live within the general population live on reservations in Ontario, Québec and New York State.

Mohic SOUTH AMERICA – PERU
Valley that was once inhabited by the pre-INCA classical civilization of the MOCHICA that followed from the CHAVIN culture. The valley houses the most important artefacts of the Mochica civilization, the great temple pyramids to the Sun and the Moon, the Moon-god appearing to have been the pre-eminent deity.

Mojave CENTRAL AMERICA – MEXICO
Indigenous Central-American AMERIN-DIAN people who took their name from the Mojave Desert in Arizona before migrating southwards across the Mexican border.

Mombu, Maîtresse HAITI (*Voodoo*)
A stammering LOA who is said, when displeased, which he often is, to cause torrential rain storms.

Momu NORTH AMERICA – PUEBLO, SOUTHWEST (*Hopi*)
The spirit of the honeybee.

Mondamin NORTH AMERICA – WOODLANDS (*Chippewa*)
The corn-spirit who is thought of by the CHIPPEWA, quite exceptionally among North American AMERINDIAN peoples, as a youth. Originally sent from the sky, he was killed by a mortal and buried. From his grave sprang the maize plant, the first time

it had been seen on Earth, and a sign of his divine nature.

Montagnais NORTH AMERICA – WOODLANDS
Indigenous, mainly peaceful ALGONQUIAN-speaking North American AMERINDIAN people who inhabited a part of the WOODLANDS culture region. Their linguistic neighbours included the CHIPPEWA, CREE, DELAWARE, MENOMINEE and POTAWATOMI peoples.

Montejo, Francisco, the Younger CENTRAL AMERICA
Spanish conquistador who was helped in his conquest of the Yucatán peninsula by AH KUKUM XIU, a member of the ruling XIU family who were centred in UXMAL.

Montezuma I CENTRAL AMERICA – MEXICO (*Aztec*)
AZTEC emperor (c.1390–1464) from c.1437 who annexed Chalco and crushed the TLAXCALANs.

Montezuma II CENTRAL AMERICA – MEXICO (*Aztec*)
The last ruler (1466-1520) of the AZTEC empire who ascended in 1502. A distinguished warrior and legislator, he was imprisoned when CORTÉS invaded Mexico and was killed during the Aztec attack on Cortés' force as it tried to leave TENOCHTITLAN. One of his direct descendants was the Viceroy of Mexico (1697–1701), while the last of his descendants was banished from Spain for liberalism and died in New Orleans in 1816.

The legends made Montezuma II, the fifth ruler of TENOCHTITLAN, who decided to send emissaries to the AZTEC ancestral homeland of AZTLAN where, so he had heard, COATLICUE, the mother of HUITZI-LOPOCHTLI, was still alive. To determine just where Aztlan was, Montezuma called on the sage TLACAELEL who described Aztlan as being near a sea-girt mountain by the name of CULHUACAN.

Month

1 CENTRAL AMERICA – MEXICO (*Aztec*)
The AZTEC month was divided into twenty days, these days, their compass points and patron deities being as below:

1 CIPACTLI Water-serpent	East	TONACATECUHTLI – male creator
2 EHÉCATL Wind-god	North	QUETZALCÓATL – as wind-god
3 CALLI Temple	West	TEPEYOLLOTL – heart of the mountain
4 QUETZ-PALLIN Lizard	South	HUEHUECÓYOTL – god of dance
5 COATL Snake	East	CHALCHIUHTLICUE – water-goddess
6 MIQUIZTLI Death	North	TECCIZTÉCATL – Moon-god
7 MAZATL Deer	West	TLÁLOC – rain-god
8 TOCHTLI Rabbit	South	MAYAHUEL – goddess of drink
9 ATL Water	East	XIUHTECUHTLI – fire-god
10 ITZCUINTLI Dog	North	MICTLÁNTECUHTLI – god of death
11 OZMATLI Monkey	West	XOCHIPILLI – god of flowers
12 MALINALLI Grass/thorns	South	PATÉCATL – husband of Mayahuel
13 ACATL Arrow shaft	East	TEZCATLIPOCA
1 OCELOTL Mexican tiger	North	TLACOLTÉUTL – earth goddess
2 QUAUHTLI Eagle	West	XIPE TOTEC – the flayed god
3 COZCA-QUAUHTLI Vulture	South	ITZPAPÁLOTL – obsidian butterfly
4 OLLIN Movement	East	XÓLOTL – twin of Quetzalcóatl
5 TECPATL Stone knife	North	Tezcatlipoca
6 QUIAHUITL Rain	West	CHANTICO – fire-goddess
7 XOCHITL Flower	South	XOCHIQUETZAL – flower-goddess

The days of the month are also used to represent the hours of the day, the Aztec day having just twenty hours to the day, though another avenue of thought allocates twenty-two hours to the Aztec day (see CALENDAR). The first group of thirteen days represent the Companions of the Day, the last seven the Companions of the Night. Midday is, therefore, Mazatl (7), and midnight Ollin (4).

The compass points also represent the cycle of the years. Those starting with an eastern sign were supposed to be fertile; north signified a variable year; west signalled a good year for men, but a bad year for vegetation; while south meant hot and waterless, and thus a bad year for both men and crops.

2 CENTRAL AMERICA (*Maya*)
The first thing to be created during the CREATION[4]. MONTH then created the day, then the heavens and the Earth as a ladder – water first, then Earth, rocks, and trees – after which he created all things on Earth and in the sea.

Moon, Pyramid of the CENTRAL AMERICA – MEXICO (*Aztec*)

A pyramid at TEOTIHUACÁN that dates from before c. AD 200, and was supposedly constructed by the travellers from AZTLAN together with a similar structure that was dedicated to the Sun.

Moqwaoi NORTH AMERICA –
WOODLANDS (*Menominee*)
'Wolf', the brother of MÄNÄBUSCH, who
was, while walking across the surface of a
frozen lake one day, dragged down to his
death by the ANAMAQKIU, malignant UN-
DERWORLD spirits. For four days his brother
mourned him before, on the fifth, meeting
with Moqwaoi's shade, whom Mänäbusch
told to go to the far west where he was to
build a great fire, that would guide the
spirits of the dead to their eternal home,
and keep them warm on their journey.
Moqwaoi thus became revered as the lord
of the dead.

Moritama NORTH AMERICA – PUEBLO,
SOUTHWEST (*Acoma*)
The spirit of the spring who was believed
to chase away the spirit of the winter.

Morning Star
The personification of the planet VENUS
when seen in the sky shortly before sunrise
when the so-called Morning Star is perceived as the herald of the Sun. This
perception or personification was common
among not just the AMERINDIAN peoples,
but also around the world.
1 CENTRAL AMERICA – MEXICO (*Cora*)
CHULAVETE, one of the most important
of the CORA deities.
2 CENTRAL AMERICA – MEXICO (*Aztec*)
TLAHUIXCALPANTECUHTLI, an aspect of
QUETZALCÓATL in which he was perceived as the Lord of the House of
Dawn.
3 CENTRAL AMERICA (*Maya*)
The herald of the Sun whom BALAM
AGAB, BALAM QUITZÉ, IQI BALAM and
MAHUCUTAH saw rise for the first time at
HACAVITZ's mountain where they had
prayed and burned incense.
4 NORTH AMERICA – GREAT PLAINS (*Skidi
Pawnee*)
An alternative name for GREAT STAR.

5 NORTH AMERICA – NORTHWEST COAST
(*Klamath*)
An important deity to the KLAMATH
who say that the Morning Star existed
long before their creator KEMUSH, and
that Morning Star called upon Kemush
to create the Earth from the ashes of the
AURORA BOREALIS[2].
6 NORTH AMERICA – GREAT PLAINS
(*Blackfoot*)
The mother of POÏA by the mortal SOAT-
SAKI, her husband being perceived as the
personification of the planet JUPITER.

Moses NORTH AMERICA – OREGON
Historical SHAMAN who, c.1860, challenged SMOHALA and left him for dead
beside a river.

Mother Corn NORTH AMERICA – GREAT
PLAINS (*Arikara*)
The deity created by NESARU after he had
drowned on his first attempt at creating
mankind, for the explicit reason of travelling down into the UNDERWORLD where
mankind was imprisoned, and to lead
them to the surface, which she did.

Mouché Pierre HAITI (*Voodoo*)
'Peter Mouth', one of the innumerable
LOA of the VOODOO cult.

Moundbuilder NORTH AMERICA
Popular name given to any North American AMERINDIAN people of the midwest
and the south who built Earth mounds, the
earliest recorded example dating from
c.300 BC. These mounds were linear and
pictographic in form for tombs, such as the
Great Serpent Mound in Ohio, and trun-
cated pyramids and cones for the platforms
on which chief's houses and temples were
built. Under the rule of an elite, the
moundbuilders operated as group labour.
In decline by the time of the Spanish
invasion, traces of their culture live on in

the folklore of the CHOCTAW and CHERO-
KEE peoples.

Moundongue loa HAITI (*Voodoo*)
Name given to a group of LOA that derive
from the gods of the Congolese Moundongue people.

Mountain Chant NORTH AMERICA –
SOUTHWEST (*Navajo*)
A ritual that includes a masque of deities
that relates the adventures of a young
brave who climbed to the Eagle's home
that lay beyond the sky and there, helped
by SPIDER-WOMAN, overcame the Bumble
Bees and the Tumbleweeds, enemies of
Eagle. He then returned to Earth and
tricked the NAVAJO into gambling away all
their treasure, which he then took back to
the skies by means of ropes made out of
lightning.

Mpokálero SOUTH AMERICA – BRAZIL
(*Tupari*)
The male of the two giant SHAMAN rulers
of the village of the dead to which the
PABID come. Having been given sight by
PATOBKIA, the pabid is expected to have
ritual intercourse before it can be admitted
to the brotherhood of the village. Female
pabid have intercourse with Mpokálero,
while male ones carry out their obligation
with VAUGH'EH, the female counterpart of
Mpokálero.

Mudheads NORTH AMERICA – PUEBLO,
SOUTHWEST (*Zuñi*)
The popular name for KOYEMSHI, a pair of
the KATCHINA priests of the ZUÑI people.

Muluc CENTRAL AMERICA (*Maya*)
The ninth day of the AGES OF MAN, the
MAYA spiritual pilgrimage on which man is
rewarded for his efforts. Muluc in this
context is not to be confused with SIX
MULUC, the nineteenth day of the MAYA
CREATION[4] when the creation process was

completed. Deified Muluc was one of only
four gods who could start the New Year,
the other three being CAUAC, KAN and IX.
Ix and Cauac were harbingers of disaster,
while Kan and Muluc would ensure good
luck. During the years over which Muluc
presided, the gates of a city were guarded
by CHAC-U-UAYEYAB, while the god KINICH
AHAU had his statue erected in the centre
of the city and presided over it.

Mururata, Mount SOUTH AMERICA –
BOLIVIA (*Aymará*)
The volcanic neighbour of Mount ILLIM-
ANI who grew jealous of the favouritism
shown by VIRACOCHA towards Illimani and
grumbled. Viracocha, angered by this
show of annoyance, slung a stone at
Mount Mururata which decapitated it, its
peak flying through the air until it landed
to form Mount SAJAMA.

Mushmush NORTH AMERICA –
NORTHWEST COAST (*Klamath*)
The white-tailed deer that was set among
the forests by KEMUSH during the latter's
creation of the world.

Muskhogee NORTH AMERICA –
WOODLANDS
Indigenous, mainly peaceful North American AMERINDIAN people who inhabited a
part of the WOODLANDS culture region and
gave their name to just one family of the
many Indian languages spoken throughout
North America. Due to the fact that they
have given their name to a language, the
Muskhogee are sometimes commonly referred to as the CREEK people.

Muskrat NORTH AMERICA –
WOODLANDS (*Algonquian*)
Though the stories of the Great FLOOD[3]
differ widely amongst the various ALGO-
NQUIAN peoples, all stories agree that
Muskrat was the animal who successfully

brought back the speck of soil that the Great HARE used to recreate the Earth.

Mustamho CENTRAL AMERICA – MEXICO (*Mojave*)
The grandson of the Earth Mother and the Sky Father who became the creator of the first MOJAVE people. During the flood he held all the people he had created in his arms until the waters had receded.

Mutsoyef NORTH AMERICA – GREAT PLAINS (*Cheyenne*)
'Sweet-Medicine', the culture hero of the CHEYENNE who is credited with introducing to the people most of their rituals, rites and customs. As a youth he was described as handsome, but had a strange manner. Following his marriage, he and his wife travelled to the Sacred Mountains by the Black Hills where he became a pupil of MAIYUN, the GREAT SPIRIT, who gave him four arrows and taught him how to use and care for them. Two had mysterious powers over buffalo, while the other two had the same power over humans. The buffalo arrows only needed to be pointed at the buffalo for those animals to become confused and thus easy prey for the hunters. The human arrows had a similar effect on the Cheyenne's enemies.

Myths, House of NORTH AMERICA – NORTHWEST COAST (*Bella Coola*)
The kingdom where all the deities who are subordinate to QAMAITS live and which is governed by SENX, the creator and spirit of the Sun.

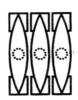

N

N CENTRAL AMERICA (*Maya*)
The unidentified deity who appears in the various CODEX wearing a head dress that bears the symbol of the 360-day year. He has, therefore, been identified as the deity who not only rules over the end of the year, but also over the greatly feared five inter-calendary days.

Naápatecuhtli CENTRAL AMERICA –
MEXICO (*Aztec*)
Named as a TLALOQUE.

Nacom CENTRAL AMERICA (*Maya*)
A lay caste on the same social level as the AH HOLPOPOH within the MAYA caste system. All Nacom were elected for a period of three years during which time they were prohibited from having relations with women, not even their wives, nor could they eat red meat, get drunk, or be attended by any women. They lived in isolation and had their own, sacred cooking utensils. The Nacom were the lowest level of the priestly hierarchy.

Nacon CENTRAL AMERICA (*Maya*)
The war-god who was honoured at a PAX (May) festival of which, it is assumed, the HOLKAN-OKOT (Dance of Warriors) formed an integral part. Nacon is associated with both AH PUCH and EK AHAU.

Nagai(t)cho NORTH AMERICA –
CALIFORNIA (*Kato*)
'The Great Traveller', the creator who, with the aid of the thunder-spirit, repaired the original sky, supported the heavens on four pillars and thus established the four cardinal points, and flooded the world. The Earth then appeared in the form of a vast, horned monster that is itself sometimes wrongly identified as Nagaitcho. This monster carried Nagaitcho between its horns, and on his order walked underground and every now and then paused and looked up, thus making the land rise above the floodwaters. When they reached the far south, Nagaitcho made the beast lie down. Nagaitcho then arranged its head, daubed clay over its eyes and horns, and on that lay successive layers of reeds and clay, until he had formed the Earth on which he planted trees and made mountains and valleys, and all the other features of the Earth.

Nago loa HAITI (*Voodoo*)
A group of LOA who have their origins in the gods of the Yoruba people of Nigeria.

Nago Shango HAITI (*Voodoo*)
An important and lively LOA who is derived from the thunder-god Shango of the Nigerian Yoruba people.

nagual (pl. naguales) CENTRAL AMERICA
Common to many Central American peoples, the nagual was a guardian spirit that took the form of an animal or bird and presided over the course of a man's life, and decided that individual's fate. The individual would receive his life-long nagual by going into the forest where he

would sleep, and in his sleep he would dream of one, or, when he awoke, he would be confronted by his nagual with whom he would have to make a lifetime contract. Some people, so it was thought, possessed the power to transform themselves into their nagual.

Naguales could become invisible and had the power to travel swiftly from place to place. If an individual prays to his nagual, then that nagual will do his bidding, but only if the individual knows the manner in which the prayers have to be made. A man and his nagual are not just spiritually linked, but also have a physical connection, for when the man dies so does his nagual, but if the nagual were to be killed, then the man would also die. Naguales were, therefore, treated with the utmost care and respect.

The concept of the nagual has persisted into modern times where it is believed that the first animal to cross the path of a newly born infant will become the nagual of that individual for their life. Ashes are sprinkled outside the place where the child has been born so that the footprints of the nagual may be captured and its correct identity determined. This animal then becomes a sort of second soul to the child whose physical appearance and psychic features are said to emulate those of the nagual. Thus a powerful man might have a thunderbolt as a nagual, while a seemingly humble, but in truth fierce, man might have the tiger as his guardian. The linking of birth and death to the nagual is pre-destination in its most rigid form. It is also alarmingly accidental, for it is impossible to foretell what animal will be the first to cross the new child's path.

Nahua CENTRAL AMERICA – MEXICO
Name generally applied to the warlike tribes that, from about the end of the eighth, or beginning of the ninth centuries AD, entered central Mexico from the north. The first of these peoples were the TOLTECS. They were followed by the CHICHIMECS and the MEXICA or AZTECS, all three of these people equally capable of being described as Nahuatlan.

nahurak NORTH AMERICA – GREAT PLAINS (*Pawnee*)
Generic name given to animal-spirits who lived in five houses: PAHUK (the most important), NAKISKAT, TSURAPAKO, KITSAWITSAK and PAHUA (the least important).

Naitaka NORTH AMERICA – BRITISH COLUMBIA
Water-serpent that inhabits Lake OKANAGAN and is said to resemble the HAIETLIK, as well as being akin to the PAL-RAI-YÛK of the INUIT.

Nakiskat NORTH AMERICA – GREAT PLAINS (*Pawnee*)
The name of one of the five houses inhabited by the NAHURAK or animal spirits, these five being, in order of importance: PAHUK, Nakiskat, TSURAPAKO, KITSAWITSAK and PAHUA.

Nambo-Nansi HAITI (*Voodoo*)
This LOA has its origins in the trickster-hero Anansi of the West African Fon and Ashanti peoples.

Nampanem SOUTH AMERICA – COLOMBIA (*Chibcha*)
The legendary divine king who was succeeded by his brother-in-law FIRAVITOBA.

Nanaboojoo NORTH AMERICA – WOODLANDS (*Potawatomi*)
The POTAWATOMI name, along with NANIBOZHO, for the Great HARE who is common among the ALGONQUIAN-speaking peoples, the most common and popular variant

167

being MÄNÄBUSCH, the MENOMINEE variant.

Each of the Algonquian peoples had slight differences to the Hare cycle. The Potawatomi version says that Nanaboojoo was the eldest of four brothers who had been born to a spirit father and a mortal mother. The second brother was CHIPIAPOOS, or CHIBIABOS, who was drowned by the evil, UNDERWORLD spirits, and became lord of the dead. The third was WABASSO who, as soon as he saw light for the first time, fled far to the north where he became a white rabbit and is revered as a great MANITOU. The fourth brother was CHAKEKENAPOK ('Flint') who killed their mother, her death being avenged by Nanaboojoo. The fragments of Chakekenapok's corpse were transformed into rocks and his intestines into vines, while patches of flint in the Earth mark the spots where the two brothers fought.

Nanaimo NORTH AMERICA – BRITISH COLUMBIA (*Nootka*)
Town on Vancouver Island, near which there is a site sacred to HAIETLIK where a group of three images have been found on a flat rock, while a huge horse-headed image, usually identified as Haietlik, has been discovered lying on its back, split by a fault, amid other designs of fish and game.

Nanautzin CENTRAL AMERICA – MEXICO (*Aztec*)
At the end of the fourth era of the creation, that known as FOURTH SUN, the gods met to discuss who should have the task of lighting the next era. At first there was only one volunteer, TECCIZTÉCATL, the god of the deathshead day MIQUIZTLI, who later became the Moon-god, who thought that he could raise his status by undertaking what at first glance was a simple task. The other gods were sceptical that Tecciztécatl

would carry out the allotted task, and so asked for a second volunteer. One by one the assembled gods made their excuses until there was just one god left, Nanautzin, a sorry sight as he was covered in scabs and tried to hide in the shadows.

It suddenly dawned on all the other gods that here they had the perfect volunteer, for no one would miss a god who was so gross to look upon. Therefore they volunteered Nanautzin who could do nothing other than accept. Tecciztécatl and Nanuatzin then spent four days in penance preparing themselves for the job ahead. Having completed their penance, the two lit a fire on a hearth of rock. Ritual sacrifices were then offered. Tecciztécatl, a proud god, offered rich feathers in place of the customary dead branches; nuggets of gold rather than hay; precious stones shaped like thorns instead of the thorns from the maguey cactus; thorns of red coral in place of those obligatory thorns that had to be tipped with blood; and the finest quality opals.

Nanautzin, though proud was very poor, and offered nine green reeds tied in bundles of three; hay; the thorns of the maguey cactus; thorns anointed with his own blood; but in place of opals he gave scabs that he removed from his own sores.

During this time the other gods had built a large tower, as high as a mountain beside the fire, and now the assembled company did a further four days' penance. Then they let the fire burn for another four days and then destroyed the receptacles into which the offerings had been placed. The gods then lined up and ordered Tecciztécatl to throw himself into the fire. Four times Tecciztécatl made ready, but always shied away at the last moment. As it had been decreed that no one was allowed to make more than four attempts, Nanautzin was then called forward to take his place.

Summoning all his courage and closing his eyes, Nanautzin rushed blindly forwards and leapt into the flames. Ashamed by his cowardice, Tecciztécatl followed Nanautzin's example and threw himself into the fire. Thus were the Sun, Nanautzin, and the Moon, Tecciztécatl born, the lowliest of all the gods showing the true way. The Sun, which was later to be made one of the central reasons for tearing the hearts out of living victims, owed its very existence to a much greater, voluntary sacrifice.

The story of Nanautzin represents the central idea and purpose of the myths of QUETZALCÓATL, for Nanautzin is, in fact, none other than Quetzalcóatl himself in embryonic form, the lowliest of all the manifestations of the great god whose self-sacrifice not only saves the cosmos from extinction, but also represents the opening up of all the latent possibilities for both men and the gods.

Nane Chaha NORTH AMERICA –
WOODLANDS (*Choctaw*)
A variant of NANIH WAYA.

Nanibozho NORTH AMERICA –
WOODLANDS (*Potawatomi*)
A variant of NANABOOJOO.

Nanih Waya NORTH AMERICA –
WOODLANDS (*Choctaw*)
The CHOCTAW name for the mound in Winston County, Mississippi, that is said to be the end of the tunnel from which the Choctaw emerged from their original home in the UNDERWORLD in the company of GRASSHOPPER. However, GRASSHOPPER MOTHER, who stayed behind, was killed by those Choctaw who had yet to emerge. Those who had already made their home on the Earth prayed to ABA, the GREAT SPIRIT, to close the entrance to the tunnel so that her murderers would be trapped in the Underworld where they were transformed into ants.

Nanook, Nanue NORTH AMERICA –
ARCTIC (*Inuit*)
The collective name given to the constellation of URSA MAJOR[3] and the PLEIADES[1] star cluster.

Naollin CENTRAL AMERICA – MEXICO
(*Aztec*)
'Four Movement', the name given to the FIFTH SUN whose birth was essential to make it possible for all the elements of creation to come together and form the Earth as it is known today.

Na'pi NORTH AMERICA – GREAT PLAINS
(*Blackfoot*)
'Old Man', the creator.

Nascakiyetl NORTH AMERICA –
NORTHWEST COAST (*Tlingit*)
'Raven-at-the-Head-of-Nass' and one of the main characters of the TLINGIT 'Raven cycle'. In the beginning everything was in darkness. Nascakiyetl lived in a lodge at the source of the River NASS where he kept all the planets, stars, and light itself. His daughter lived with him. She was attended by two manservants; ADAWULCANAK ('Old-Man-Who-Foresees-All-the-Troubles-of-the-World') and TLIEWATUWADJIGICAN ('He-Who-Knows-Everything').

Nascakiyetl created the very tall and very wise man HERON, and then YETL, the RAVEN, another good and wise man. Some versions of the story say that Nascakiyetl's sister had borne many sons, but that her brother had jealously killed them all. She sought the advice of Heron who told her to swallow a red-hot pebble. This she did and subsequently gave birth to Yetl who was named after the impregnable stone ITC AK and called TAQLIKIC ('Hammer-Father') as he was so tough and resilient. Nascakiyetl made him the head man of the world.

Others say that Yetl was neither created by Nascakiyetl, nor born to Nascakiyetl's sister, but was instead the son of the old man KITKAOSITIYIQA who gave him the strength he needed to create the world. Yetl then transformed himself into a splinter of hemlock which was swallowed by Nascakiyetl's daughter, and was thus reborn as her son. Yetl then stole the stars, the planets and light from Nascakiyetl, and so brought them out into the open.

Nass, River NORTH AMERICA –
NORTHWEST COAST (*Tlingit*)
Sacred river at whose source NASCAKIYETL was said to have had his lodge, in which he kept the stars, the planets and light prior to their being stolen from him by YETL.

Natchez NORTH AMERICA – GREAT
PLAINS
Indigenous North American AMERINDIAN people inhabiting that part of the GREAT PLAINS culture region that roughly covered what is the state of Mississippi today. They were one of the MOUNDBUILDER cultures and spoke the now extinct MUSKHOGEE language, though a few Natchez survive in Oklahoma. The Natchez were almost unique among North American tribes for their caste system which was developed to a very high level and headed by a ruler-priest. Members of the highest caste always married from the lowest caste, a system that lasted until French settlers colonized the area in 1731.

Nautsiti NORTH AMERICA – PUEBLO,
SOUTHWEST (*Acoma*)
One of the two sisters who created men, the other being IATIKU (cf. the story of ESTANATLEHI and YOLKAI ESTSAN).

Navajo NORTH AMERICA – SOUTHWEST
Indigenous North American AMERINDIAN people who are related to the APACHE and who refer to themselves as *Dineh* (people).

The creation myth of this people is told under the ASCENT OF THE NAVAJO, and is one of the most complete, beautiful and complex, of all the Amerindian creation myths. It describes not only the many worlds through which the Navajo passed before emerging on the Earth, but also illustrates how they learned from their mistakes *en route*, finally to emerge as the gods would have wanted, each UNDER-WORLD world being seen as a test that the people had to pass before being allowed to progress. The myth also introduces many of the Navajo deities and animal spirits.

In 1864 the Navajo nation was attacked by Kit Carson and US troops, rounded up, and exiled from their native homelands. Today there are approximately 200,000 Navajo people who live on the largest Indian reservation in the United States (created in 1868) that covers approximately 25,000 square miles, and is mainly located in northeast Arizona, but stretches into northwest New Mexico as well as southeast Utah. They speak one of the ATHAPASCAN languages that belongs to the Na-Dené family.

Nayanezgani NORTH AMERICA –
SOUTHWEST (*Navajo*)
Twin brother of THOBADZISTSHINI. According to some versions of the myths, these two were the sons of ESTANATLEHI and TSHOHANOAI, while in others these two were only the parents of Nayanezgani, Thobadzistshini being the son of YOLKAI ESTSAN and WATER.

Helped by NILTSHI, the wind-spirit, and by the SPIDER-WOMAN, the twins made a perilous journey to the HOGAN of Tshohanoai. Leaving home early in the morning, the twins set out along a sacred trail. Shortly after sunrise they noticed some smoke rising from the ground near DSIL-NAOTIL. Coming closer, they discovered that the smoke was coming from the fire of Spider-Woman who welcomed them to her underground home and asked them where they were going. Four times the twins evaded her question until Spider-Woman suggested that they were going in search of their father. The twins admitted that they were, and asked if Spider-Woman knew the way to his hogan. She warned them that the journey was incredibly dangerous, and, rather than welcoming them, their father might turn against them for their intrusion. The twins remained undaunted.

Spider-Woman, seeing that the twins fully intended to pursue their plan, told them of the four particular dangers that awaited them. First, they would come across a pair of clashing rocks that crushed travellers between them. Then they would encounter knife-sharp reeds that could, and probably would, cut them to shreds. Next, they would come to cane cacti that would likewise attempt to rend them into little pieces. Finally, they would find boiling sands that would engulf them. Still the twins would not be put off, so Spider-Woman gave them two life-feathers (feathers plucked from the tail of a living eagle) and joined them together into a talisman called 'feather of the anaye'. She also gave them another life-preserving feather and taught them this spell that would subdue their enemies:

Put your feet down with pollen.
Put your hands down with pollen.
Put your head down with pollen.
Your feet are pollen.
Your hands are pollen.
Your body is pollen.
Your mind is pollen.
Your voice is pollen.
The trail is beautiful.
Be still.

With the aid of Spider-Woman's charms and spells the two young men survived all the perils of their long and arduous journey and eventually came to Tshohanoai's hogan, a great, square house made of turquoise that was built on the shore of a vast tract of water. As they approached the entrance to the hogan, they were challenged firstly by a pair of huge bears, then by a pair of serpents, next by winds, and finally by lightning. They safely passed all these challenges by grasping the talismans given to them by Spider-Woman while chanting the soothing words that she had taught them.

As they entered the hogan, they saw a woman sitting in its western corner, two beautiful maidens in its southern corner, and two handsome youths in its northern. The two southern maidens stood up and came over to the twins and, without saying anything, wrapped them into a bundle with four 'sky-coverings' – of dawn, daylight, dusk and night – before placing them on a shelf where they lay quietly and waited.

Presently a rattle at the door shook four times before Tshohanoai entered carrying the Sun on his back. Taking it off, he hung it on the western wall of the hogan where it shook for a while before becoming still. Tshohanoai then asked his wife who the two visitors he had seen coming to his hogan were. She at first refused to answer, but finally said that they claimed to be his sons, a statement that had made her wonder about how faithful he had been to her and if he had visited anyone on Earth during his daily journeys.

Tshohanoai angrily took the bundle down from the shelf and shook the twins out on to the floor. He then picked them up and hurled them to every corner of the hogan, but the talismans of the Spider-Woman protected them. Next he tried to steam them to death in his sweat house, and then to poison them with doctored tobacco, but the twins not only smoked the poisoned pipe to its very end, but commented on its sweetness. Impressed, Tshohanoai at last acknowledged them as his sons, welcomed them to his home, and gave them gifts of magical weapons: arrows of lightning, sunbeams, rainbow, a huge stone knife and armour which flashed lightning from every joint.

Returning to Earth, the twins did battle with the monstrous ANAYE and killed a great number of them, but as they were unable to kill all of them, they once again sought the help of Tshohanoai. This time the Sun-Bearer gave them four magical hoops which the goddess Estanatlehi used to raise a terrible storm which not only destroyed all but four of the anaye, but also reshaped the Earth itself.

With their Earthly purpose at an end, the divine twins left to go to their mountain home where NAVAJO braves go to ask for success in battle.

Naymlap SOUTH AMERICA – PERU (Mochica)

Possibly historical leader of a great fleet of BALSA craft which landed at LAMBEYEQYE (to the south of Cape Santa Elena). He was accompanied by his wife CETERNI, and all his servants: PITAZOFI his trumpeter, NINACOLLA his throne-bearer, NINAGEN-TUE his cup-bearer, FONGASIDE who scattered powdered shells at his feet, OCHO-CALO his cook, XAN his make-up man, and LLAPCHILULLI the master of his wardrobe.

As soon as they had landed, the party immediately built a temple which they named CHOT, and in which they placed a green-stone carving of their king, this statue therefore becoming known as LLAM-PALLEC – 'figure of Naymlap'. At the end of his long reign Naymlap disappeared, some sources saying that he flew up into the sky followed by his grieving family and courtiers who left their children to inhabit the land.

The tenth king after Naymlap was FEM-PELLEC who decided to move the statue Llampallec, having been seduced by a fiend who assumed the guise of a beautiful woman. An unprecedented deluge followed and then a terrible famine. To appease the gods, the priests tied Fempellec hand and foot and threw him into the sea, thereby bringing to an end the line of rule by Naymlap's descendants. Without a leader the kingdom was invaded by the CHIMU under the leadership of CAPAC who made PONY MASSA its new ruler.

Neegyauks NORTH AMERICA – NORTHWEST COAST (Tlingit)

'Volcano-Woman', a frog spirit who is the TLINGIT version of DZERLARHONS, a HAIDU spirit.

Negakfok NORTH AMERICA – ALASKA (Inuit)

The spirit of cold weather who is represented in a ritual dance by a man wearing a sad-faced wooden mask, the expression on the mask being sad as the spirit must leave when spring reappears. These masks were carved from driftwood and burned each year at the end of the rite even though driftwood, the only wood available, was extremely scarce and therefore highly prized.

Nemterequeteba SOUTH AMERICA – BOLIVIA AND COLOMBIA (Chibcha)

A possibly historical culture hero who is said to have come from Venezuela 140 years before the Spanish conquest. He was depicted as an old, bearded and long-haired man who was similar to THUNAPA of whom he may be a version. He is also called SUGUMONXE or SUGUNSÚA ('Disappearer'), and CHIMIZAPAGNA ('CHIMINIGA-GUÉ's messenger'). He is sometimes, also, identified with the Sun ZUHÉ, or with the supreme being of the CHIBCHA – BOCHICA.

Nemterequeteba was pursued by the goddess HUITACA whom he changed, according to some stories, into either an owl or the Moon.

Nena CENTRAL AMERICA – MEXICO (Aztec)

Wife of TATA. At the end of the era of the FOURTH SUN the supreme god sent for the couple and told them to make a hole in a huge tree and hide in it. Thus they would be saved from the FLOOD, but only if they ate no more than a single cob of maize each. Tata and Nena followed the god's instructions and duly rode out the flood in complete safety. However, as the waters receded, they saw a fish which they caught and placed on a spit over a fire they built. The gods saw the smoke rising and were angry that their instructions should have been disobeyed. As a punishment they transformed both Tata and Nena into dogs and removed from them that portion of the brain which distinguishes man from the animals.

Nerrivik NORTH AMERICA – GREENLAND (Inuit)

'Food-dish', the GREAT GODDESS. A water-spirit who was known as SEDNA by the INUIT of Alaska, as well as ARNARKUSUAG-SAK ('Old Woman') and NULIAJOQ. According to the Inuit of Greenland, Nerrivik was not originally a cannibal giantess, but rather an ordinary Inuit woman who was carried off by a petrel to his home far across the sea, where she discovered that the petrel had tricked her.

She was rescued by her people, but the petrel raised such a storm that, in order to save their own lives, her relatives threw her overboard. However, Nerrivik clung on to the side of the boat, so they cut off her fingers. She sank into the depths of the ocean where she now reigns supreme. When Inuit hunters are unable to find any prey, their ANGAKOK sends his spirit down to plead with her in her underwater palace.

Nesaru NORTH AMERICA – GREAT PLAINS (Arikara)

The creator who, having made the Earth and peopled it with supermen, found that his created people were not only foolish, but also poured scorn on the gods. Nesaru therefore drowned them, though he made sure that all the animals, which he liked, and the maize plant were safely out of the way in a cave. He then created MOTHER CORN and sent her to the true people who were imprisoned in the UNDERWORLD, and told her to lead them up on to the Earth. This she did, and the world was once more populated, and this time the people were neither stupid nor did they shun the gods.

Nezahualcoytl CENTRAL AMERICA – MEXICO (Aztec)

Charismatic historical leader of TEZCOCO which, due to him, became the theological and cultural centre of the AZTEC empire, in which there was the only known active cult to the honour of TLOQUE NAHUAQUE.

Ngurvilu SOUTH AMERICA – CHILE

A water-god in the form of a wild cat having a claw at the end of his tail, though which people worshipped this feline deity remains a mystery.

Nhenebush NORTH AMERICA – WOODLANDS (Ojibway)

The TRICKSTER. Of human appearance, he marked the birch as his own by forming the delicate patterns on its bark that drew the respect of the THUNDERERS. The bark of the birch tree is not only waterproof but also highly resistant to fire, and thus is not easily set alight if the tree is hit by lightning.

Nicahtagah CENTRAL AMERICA (*Maya*)
The tutelary deity who was given to IQI BALAM at TULAI ZUIVA to preside over his clan.

Nicola, Lake NORTH AMERICA – BRITISH COLUMBIA (*Nootka*)
Small lake approximately 45 miles to the east of Lake OKANAGAN, above which an image of a serpent, thought to be a representation of HAIETLIK, is to be found. This image was avoided by fishermen at all costs since they believed that if they looked at it, an evil wind would spring up and capsize their canoe.

Night CENTRAL AMERICA – MEXICO (*Aztec*)
Companion of HUEHUETÉOTL and thought by some to be an early deity who was later to become known as QUETZALCÓATL. It is fully appropriate for Night to have been the companion of Huehuetéotl, a god of fire, for fire would only have provided light after darkness had fallen, and the two would have therefore gone hand-in-hand.

Night Chant NORTH AMERICA – SOUTHWEST (*Navajo*)
The most popular of all the NAVAJO rituals that can only be held in the winter during the hibernation period of snakes. The ritual lasts for nine days and nine nights and involves the preparation of sweat-houses, the sprinkling of sacred masks with life-giving pollen and water, and sand painting of the spirits. The ritual ends with a great masque of the spirits during which prayers to the 'dark bird who is lord of pollen' (i.e. the thunder cloud) are chanted.

Niltshi NORTH AMERICA (*Navajo*)
The spirit of the wind who guided the refugees from the BLUE WORLD into the YELLOW WORLD of the Grasshopper people during the ASCENT OF THE NAVAJO, and again from that world into the next, multicoloured world. He was also responsible for breathing life into the first man and the first woman.

Ninacolla SOUTH AMERICA – PERU (*Mochica*)
The throne-bearer of NAYMLAP who was aboard the fleet of BALSAS that brought Naymlap and his retinue to CHIMOR.

Nine Cauac CENTRAL AMERICA (*Maya*)
The ninth day of the CREATION[4] on which the first day was made to create a hell to which the first sinners were sent on TEN AHAU. Nine Cauac is not to be confused with CAUAC, the nineteenth day of the MAYA spiritual pilgrimage – the AGES OF MAN.

Nine Ollin, Lord CENTRAL AMERICA – MEXICO (*Mixtec*)
A boy would become Lord Nine Ollin when he was dedicated to the Sun, a dedication that would last until his fifty-second birthday when he would be voluntarily sacrificed, this sacrifice usually being made during the dedication of a TEMAZCALLI, a sweat-house that was used to cure the sick. After Lord Nine Ollin had been sacrificed, his body would be dressed as an Ocelot Chief, and then cremated. His spiritual brother EIGHT DEER, Lord of TILANTONGO, presided at the palace of the plumed serpent where he was seated on an ocelot skin cushion. The ashes of Lord Nine Ollin would be brought to Eight Deer who would adorn them with a feather head dress and a turquoise mask. Finally, a quail being a symbol of the sunrise, would

be sacrificed as the ashes were once more cremated.

Ningentue SOUTH AMERICA – PERU (*Mochica*)
The cup-bearer of NAYMLAP who accompanied the king and his retinue when they came to CHIMOR in a fleet of BALSAS.

Niparaya NORTH AMERICA (*Perico*)
The creator of the universe who married AMAYICOYONDI.

Nipinoukhe NORTH AMERICA – WOODLANDS (*Montagnais*)
The spirit of the spring who shares the world with PIPOUNOUKHE, the spirit of the winter. When their allotted time in any part of the world comes to an end, they reciprocally change places in a rite called AHITESCATONEH.

Noh Ek CENTRAL AMERICA (*Maya*)
The spirit of the GREAT STAR (the planet VENUS^2).

Nohochacyumchac CENTRAL AMERICA (*Maya*)
The god of all creation.

Nohochakyum CENTRAL AMERICA – YUCATÁN, MEXICO (*Lacandone*)
The chief deity of the LACANDONE people who probably derives from the ancient MAYA deity CHAC or NOHOCHACYUMCHAC. Nohochakyum lives in the eastern sky where he is served by all the stars and the planets, while his subordinate brothers rule the other quarters of the heavens, the most powerful of these brothers being USU-KUN. At the end of time Nohochakyum will enter into a fatal battle with the serpent HAPIKERN whose breath will kill all the people.

Nokomis NORTH AMERICA – WOODLANDS (*Menominee*)
The Earth goddess and grandmother of MÄNÄBUSCH, the Great HARE. Her daughter gave birth to twins but died in childbirth together with one of the babies. Nokomis placed the surviving twin under a wooden bowl, a symbol of the heavens, to protect it. When she removed the bowl some time later, she discovered that the child had become a little white rabbit with long, trembling ears. She named him Mänäbusch. Later Mänäbusch stole fire which he gave to Nokomis who, in turn, gave it to the THUNDERERS, or more particularly their chief KENEUN, who has guarded it ever since.

Nompanem SOUTH AMERICA – BOLIVIA AND COLOMBIA (*Chibcha*)
A legendary, possibly historical king to whom BOCHICA and the culture hero NEM-TEREQUETEBA taught all the arts of civilization, as well as all the rites and customs of religion. Nompanem was succeeded as the CHIBCHA king by his brother-in-law FIR-AVITOBA.

Noogumee NORTH AMERICA – WOODLANDS (*Micmac*)
The MICMAC name for NOKOMIS.

Noohlmahl NORTH AMERICA – NORTHWEST COAST (*Kwakiutl*)
The fool, a characterization that appears in the winter HAMATSU ritual.

Noohlum NORTH AMERICA – NORTHWEST COAST (*Kwakiutl*)
An annual masked rite in which the masked dancers were not, as in other KWA-KIUTL rituals, perceived as being possessed by the spirits whose faces were portrayed in the masks they wore.

Nootka NORTH AMERICA – NORTHWEST
COAST
Indigenous North American AMERINDIAN
people inhabiting a part of the NORTHWEST
COAST culture region. Situated mainly in
British Columbia, the Nootka spoke their
own tribal language and mainly lived on
the abundant fish in the numerous lakes
and rivers that flow through their traditional homeland.

Northwest Coast NORTH AMERICA
A geographical division of North America
used to describe the homelands of a number of indigenous AMERINDIAN peoples, including the BELLA COOLA, CHINOOK,
HAIDA, KLAMATH, KWAKIUTL, NOOTKA,
SALISH and TSHIMSHIAN Indians – tribes
who speak six different languages. The
basic region runs from Puget Sound and
Yukatat Bay where a warm offshore current assures a relatively mild climate. The
land is fertile and rich which assured the
Amerindian population easy sustenance.
This ease of survival left them with a great
deal of leisure time, which in turn led to
the development of a complex social structure where status depended, as in Mela-
nesia, upon ritual feasting and the pre-
sentation of gifts, the most valuable of
which were blankets and 'coppers' (sheets
of beaten copper). The settled nature of
the Amerindian peoples of the region
made them particularly sensitive to their
history and lineage. This was expressed in
elaborate ceremonies as well as the spectacular totem poles for which the region is
perhaps most famous, and which symbolized the clan's mythic theriomorphic ancestors.

Nowutset NORTH AMERICA – PUEBLO,
SOUTHWEST (*Sia*)
The sister of UTSET and, like her, created
by the primordial spider SUSSISTINNAKO.
Though Nowutset was stronger than her
sister, she was far less intelligent and lost a
riddle game to her, after which Utset killed
her and cut out her heart.

Nukuchyumchakob CENTRAL AMERICA
– YUCATÁN, MEXICO (*Modern Maya*)
Variant of YUMCHAKOB.

Nuliajoq NORTH AMERICA (*Inuit*)
A variant name for SEDNA or NERRIVIK.

Numokh Mukana NORTH AMERICA –
GREAT PLAINS (*Mandan*)
The name of the first man.

Nunhyunuwi NORTH AMERICA –
WOODLANDS (*Cherokee*)
A terrible man-eating giant made from
stone.

Nueva coronica y buen gobierno SOUTH
AMERICA
An illustrated CODEX of INCA records that
was compiled and written by Don Felipe
GUAMÁN POMA DE AYALA who claimed to
be of royal Inca descent through his
mother. It is an important, if somewhat
biased, source of information relating to
ancient Inca myth, legend and tradition.

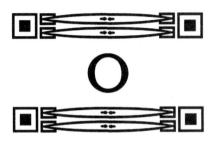

O

O CENTRAL AMERICA (*Maya*)
A goddess depicted in the various CODEX with wrinkles around the eyes and either with or working on a loom. It has been suggested that she is the goddess of fate.

Obtala HAITI (*Voodoo*)
A variant of 'BATALA.

Oc CENTRAL AMERICA (*Maya*)
The tenth day of the AGES OF MAN, the MAYA spiritual pilgrimage, and that on which the spirit of man becomes the lowest form of matter so that on the eleventh day, CHEUN, he may burn without flame and by so doing suffer the utmost agony. The day of Oc has been associated with both lightning and the dog, and by these associations with HUNHAU.

Ocelopan CENTRAL AMERICA – MEXICO
(*Aztec*)
Named as one of the original leaders of the AZTEC people who journeyed from their ancestral homeland of AZTLAN.

Ocelotanatiuh CENTRAL AMERICA –
MEXICO (*Aztec*)
The Jaguar Sun who ruled over the Age of Giants, the second age of the creation according to the AZTECS.

Ocelotl CENTRAL AMERICA – MEXICO
(*Aztec*)
The fourteenth day of the twenty-day MONTH[1] used by the AZTECS, and the one that symbolized the Mexican tiger (the ocelot), represented the North and was presided over by TLACOLTÉUTL.

Ochocalo SOUTH AMERICA – PERU
(*Mochica*)
The cook of NAYMLAP whom he accompanied, together with all his retinue, to CHIMOR.

Ockabewis NORTH AMERICA –
WOODLANDS (*Chippewa*)
The culture hero of the CHIPPEWA people.

Ocpatli CENTRAL AMERICA – MEXICO
(*Aztec*)
The name given to the PEYOTE from which a sacred intoxicating drink is made and over which PATÉCATL has governorship.

Ogoun (Tonnère) HAITI (*Voodoo*)
Deriving from the West African war-god of the Yoruba people, this LOA is regarded by VOODOO cultists as both warrior and blacksmith. Being especially fond of rum and tobacco, Ogoun is also called AGOMME TONNÈRE and is sometimes depicted in the likeness of Saint George, this association stemming from the fact that the thunder and warrior-god is especially associated among almost every culture with the slayer of the monster dragon-serpent.

Ogu HAITI (*Voodoo*)
A warrior LOA who corresponds to the Roman Catholic Saint James the Great.

Ogun ~ Balanjo, ~ Ferraille HAITI
(*Voodoo*)
Variants of OGOUN TONNÈRE.

Ohdows NORTH AMERICA –
WOODLANDS (*Iroquois*)
One class of JOGAH, dwarf nature-spirits,
and the ones that live in the UNDERWORLD
and control the monsters to be found
there, preventing them from reaching the
Earth's surface. The other classes of jogah
are the GAHONGA and the GANDAYAH.

Ohoyo-osh Chishba NORTH AMERICA –
WOODLANDS (*Chibcha*)
The goddess of corn and patroness of the
harvest.

Oí SOUTH AMERICA – BRAZIL (*Xingú*)
A peculiar, legendary people who were
very tall and always sang in chorus as they
walked or spied on the XINGÚ, which they
did incessantly. Even though the Oí always carried a great club slung over their
right shoulder, they simply watched people
and never attacked them.

Okanagan, Lake NORTH AMERICA –
BRITISH COLUMBIA
Lake approximately 150 miles to the east
of Vancouver that is said to be inhabited
by the water-monster known as the NAI-
TAKA, a monster that appears to be a
variant of the HAIETLIK.

Oke Hede NORTH AMERICA – GREAT
PLAINS (*Mandan*)
The evil one of the first born twins.

Oki NORTH AMERICA – WOODLANDS
(*Oumas*)
The spirit of the Sun, also called KIOUSA,
whose image watched over the bodies of

dead chiefs who were alleged to be his
direct descendants.

Oklatabashih NORTH AMERICA –
WOODLANDS (*Choctaw*)
'Mourner-of-the-People', the sole survivor
of the flood that wiped out mankind.

Old Age NORTH AMERICA – SOUTHWEST
(*Navajo*)
One of four of the ANAYE who survived the
assaults of THOBADZISTSHINI and NAYANEZ-
GANI, and then the terrible storm raised by
ESTANATLEHI. Old Age and his compat-
riots, COLD, HUNGER and POVERTY, were
only allowed to live after they had convinced Estanatlehi that if they did not
exist, mankind would no longer prize the
good things in life, or even prize life itself.

Old Man Acorn NORTH AMERICA –
SOUTHWEST COAST (*Wintun*)
After the Earth had been recreated by
OLELBIS following the flood, Old Man
Acorn refertilized it.

Old Man of the Ancients NORTH
AMERICA – NORTHWEST COAST
(*Klamath and Modoc*)
The term of reverence by which the KLA-
MATH and the MODOC referred to the crea-
tor (KEMUSH to the Klamath and KUMUSH
to the Modoc).

Olelbis NORTH AMERICA – SOUTHWEST
COAST (*Wintun*)
'He-Who-Sits-in-the-Sky', the creator who
was first known of living in OLELPANTI,
though it is said that he came from elsewhere. In Olelpanti he lived with two old
women, his grandmothers who helped him
to build a paradisal sweat-house that was
roofed with the entwined branches of six
oak trees and walled with screens of the
most fragrant flowers. The first world was

destroyed by a fire that was started by BUCKEYE BUSH, FIRE DRILL and SHOOTING STAR in revenge for the theft of FLINT. Olelbis viewed all this with dismay and then sought the advice of his grandmothers. Following the advice they gave him, Olelbis had the sky propped up, and then summoned KAHIT, the spirit of the wind, and MEM LOOMIS, the water-goddess to extinguish the fire. This they did by raising a great flood. Olelbis then set about recreating the Earth which was then fertilized by OLD MAN ACORN.

Prior to creating man, Olelbis sent the two HUS brothers down to the newly created Earth with instructions to build a ladder between it and Olelpanti. The two brothers began to build the stone ladder but were interrupted by SEDIT who, professing wisdom on a par with Olelbis himself, openly scoffed at the plan. He asked the Hus brothers what use such a ladder would be if all man had to do, when he reached old age, was to climb the ladder to heaven, from which he would later descend fully rejuvenated. Surely, he argued, it was far better that mankind should experience the joys of parenthood and the grief of bereavement. The two Hus were finally convinced and disassembled the ladder, though the younger reminded Sedit that he too would now die.

Too late Sedit realized his mistake and in desperation made himself a pair of wings from sunflowers, as sunflowers follow the course of the Sun, and tried to fly up to Olelpanti. However, as he rose, the flowers wilted and he fell to his death. Viewing all this from the heavens, Olelbis decreed that as a result of Sedit's trickery, all those who lived on the Earth, both man and beast, would lead a finite life.

Olelpanti NORTH AMERICA –
SOUTHWEST COAST (*Wintun*)
Heaven, the domain and home of OLELBIS, the creator.

Ollin CENTRAL AMERICA – MEXICO
(*Aztec*)
The seventeenth day of the twenty-day MONTH[1] used by the AZTEC people. Ollin symbolized movement, represented the east and was presided over by XÓLOTL.

Olmec CENTRAL AMERICA
Ancient civilization about which very little is known. Archaeological finds that can be attributed to the Olmec culture to date span the period 1200–400 BC, and locate its centre of development in the coastal zone to the south of Vera Cruz and in adjacent Tabasco. The Olmecs built a large clay pyramid and several smaller mounds at La Venta (located just inland from the Gulf of Mexico near Coatzalcoalcos). Some gigantic stone heads, remnants of their religious beliefs, also survive. Some scholars have sought to link the Olmec civilization with the ancient CHAVIN culture, but these links are tenuous to say the least. Current thinking makes the Olmec culture the oldest of the Central-American civilizations, and in all probability the mother of the MAYA civilization.

Omacatl CENTRAL AMERICA – MEXICO
(*Aztec*)
'Two Reeds', a fairly late aspect of TEZCATLIPOCA that appears to have derived after that deity had absorbed many lesser deities.

Omaha NORTH AMERICA – GREAT
PLAINS
Indigenous SIOUX-speaking North American AMERINDIAN people who lived in Nebraska, which falls within the GREAT PLAINS culture region. They have given their name to the city of Omaha that lies on the banks of the Missouri River. Their linguistic neighbours, all Sioux-speakers, included the ASSINABOIN, CROW, DAKOTA, MANDAN, OSAGE and WINNEBAGO tribes.

Omecíhuatl CENTRAL AMERICA –
MEXICO (*Aztec*)

The goddess of heaven, wife of OMETE-
CUHTLI, and one half of the dual OME-
TÉOTL. She is also called CITLALINICUE, in
which case her husband is called CITLAL-
TONAC. Omecíhuatl gave birth to an obsidian knife which she threw down to the
Earth, and from it 1,600 heroes were born,
the very first beings to inhabit the Earth.
At first they were all alone, many of them
dying as the result of the not infrequent
calamities which befell the newly created
Earth. Finally, the remnants of these
people sent an emissary to their mother to
ask her to create man to serve them and
the gods. She replied by sending a hawk
that told them that, if they could make
their thoughts and deeds nobler, then they
would be worthy of living with her in
heaven for all eternity.

However, they decided that they would
prefer to stay on Earth. Thus they sent
XÓLOTL, the twin of QUETZALCÓATL, to the
UNDERWORLD to bring back a bone which
they intended to sprinkle with their blood,
and thus create a man and a woman whose
children would populate the Earth. Xólotl
safely secured the bone but was pursued
back to the Earth by the god of the Underworld. As Xólotl neared the surface, he
tripped and broke the bone into two unequal parts. Nevertheless Xólotl managed
to escape. The two halves of the bone were
duly doused with blood. Four days later a
male child emerged from the larger half of
the bone, followed three days later by a
female from the smaller half. The children
were entrusted to Xólotl who raised them
on the milk of the thistle, and in time their
children populated the Earth.

Ometecuhtli CENTRAL AMERICA –
MEXICO (*Aztec*)

The husband of OMECÍHUATL, the Lord of
Duality, an important if somewhat remote
god, the equivalent of TONACATECUHTLI,
and one half of the dual OMETÉOTL.

Ometéotl CENTRAL AMERICA – MEXICO
(*Aztec*)

The omnipotent creator of the universe
who has dual aspects in OMETECUHTLI and
OMECÍHUATL, or in CITLALTONAC and his
consort CITLALINICUE. Ometéotl stands on
the very topmost rung of the thirteen-rung
ladder that joins heaven to Earth. The
creator is a true example of duality, for
Ometéotl is at once both god and goddess,
'god of the near and far', 'he who is at the
centre or within the ring [of life]', 'he to
whom mankind owes the existence of life',
self-inventing and self-creating, lord of all
heaven and Earth, and the land of the
dead.

The duality of Ometéotl was a duality in
quality. It stands for the negative and the
positive, the male and female principles of
the universe, light and shadow, yes and no,
and so forth. It was not, however, a duality
that arose from polytheism, as the concept
is monotheistic and can be seen to represent the equilibrium of Creation, rather
than the diversity of that divine act.

Ometochtli CENTRAL AMERICA –
MEXICO (*Aztec*)

'Two Rabbit', one of the CENTZONTOTOCH-
TIN, and an important PULQUE god.

Omeyocan CENTRAL AMERICA – MEXICO
(*Aztec*)

'Place-of-the-Twofold', the home of OME-
TECUHTLI and OMECÍHUATL and thus, as
these deities are aspects of the androgynous creator OMETÉOTL, also the home of
that deity. It is from Omeyocan that souls
descend to be born as has been predes-
tined since the time of the Creation, when
all souls were created to be sent down to
Earth as and when a new child was to be
born, the fate of the resulting individual
also following a long destined path.

Omoa SOUTH AMERICA
An alternative name for MANOA, the mythical land in which Lake GUATAVITA, the lake that has been associated with the legends of EL DORADO, was said to lie – that is, until VON HUMBOLDT disproved this theory.

Ona SOUTH AMERICA – TIERRA DEL
   FUEGO
Indigenous AMERINDIAN people whose descendants still live in this inhospitable region of South America.

Onatah NORTH AMERICA – WOODLANDS
   (*Iroquois*)
The spirit of the corn, the daughter of EITHINOHA who was once captured by the spirit of evil when she went out to collect dew. She was imprisoned in the darkness of the UNDERWORLD, but the Sun-spirit came looking for her and eventually found and rescued her.

Ondoutaete NORTH AMERICA –
   WOODLANDS (*Huron*)
The god of war.

One Cheun CENTRAL AMERICA (*Maya*)
The first day of the MAYA CREATION[4] on which MONTH[2] created infinity, the heavens and the Earth. One Cheun should not be confused with CHEUN, the eleventh day of the AGES OF MAN, the Maya spiritual pilgrimage.

One Kan CENTRAL AMERICA (*Maya*)
The fourteenth day of the MAYA CREATION[4] on which MONTH[2] was sickened by the evil things he had created. One Kan should not be confused with KAN, the fourth day of the AGES OF MAN.

Oneida NORTH AMERICA – WOODLANDS
Indigenous North American AMERINDIAN people from the WOODLANDS culture region who spoke one branch of the IROQUOIS language and were frequently involved in internecine warfare. The Oneida were one of the peoples to be united into the LEAGUE OF THE LONG HOUSE by HAIOWATHA during the sixteenth century.

Onodja Tree NORTH AMERICA –
   WOODLANDS (*Iroquois*)
Tree beneath which the celestial chief lived and whose blossom lit up the world. Following his marriage to AWENHAI, the celestial chief became jealous when she started to show her pregnant state, and suspected her of having had an affair with AURORA BOREALIS[3] as well as with FIRE DRAGON WITH A BODY OF PURE WHITE COLOUR. He uprooted the Onodja Tree and pushed both Awenhai and the two he suspected through the resulting hole in the sky, though their ghosts remained with him in heaven.

Onondaga NORTH AMERICA –
   WOODLANDS
Indigenous IROQUOIS-speaking North American AMERINDIAN people who inhabited a northeastern part of the WOODLANDS culture region and were habitually engaged in internecine warfare with their Iroquoian neighbours. As a result of this continual bloodshed, an Onondaga leader by the name of HAIOWATHA sought to unite the Iroquois and ALGONQUIAN peoples, an ideal to which he partly succeeded with the formation of the LEAGUE OF THE LONG HOUSE which united six Iroquois nations, and so brought peace to their homelands.

Oraji Brisé HAITI (*Voodoo*)
An extremely powerful LOA who shares his status with GRAND BOIS even though both represent far more primitive forms of the

181

loa than those of West African derivation.

orenda NORTH AMERICA – WOODLANDS (*Iroquois*)
An indwelling spirit, the quintessence of all that is good, of life and vitality, as contrasted by the OTKON. The orenda is believed to survive after death so that nothing evil, not even the otkon, can harm it in any way at all.

Orinoco, River SOUTH AMERICA
Flowing for about 1,500 miles through Venezuela, and forming the boundary with Colombia for about 200 miles, this mighty river of northern South America is navigable for 700 miles from its Atlantic delta, the upper reaches of the river being obstructed by rapids.

Orizaba, Mount CENTRAL AMERICA – MEXICO
Mountain some 18,700 feet high slightly to the northwest of the town of Orizaba. Orizaba is the Spanish name for the mountain originally known as CITLALTÉPETL which QUETZALCÓATL crossed *en route* from TOLLAN to TLILLAN-TLAPALLAN.

Oruro SOUTH AMERICA – BOLIVIA
Town to the southeast of LA PAZ, and southwest of COCHAMBAMBA, all three hosting an annual ALACITA, a fair that has become associated with the QUECHUA cult of EKKEKKO.

Osage NORTH AMERICA – GREAT PLAINS
Indigenous nomadic, SIOUX-speaking North American AMERINDIAN people inhabiting a portion of the central GREAT PLAINS culture region. The Osage are linguistically linked with the ASSINABOIN, CROW, DAKOTA, MANDAN, OMAHA and WINNEBAGO peoples.

Oshadagea NORTH AMERICA – WOODLANDS (*Iroquois*)
'Dew Eagle', one of the warriors of HINO, he lives in the western sky and carries a pond of dew in a hollow in his back. When the evil fire-spirits attack the Earth, Oshadagea flies over the land sprinkling the life giving dew from his back on to the scorched land, and thus restores its fertility.

Oterongtongnia NORTH AMERICA – WOODLANDS (*Iroquois*)
One of the twin sons of the daughter of AWENHAI, his sibling being TAWISKARON. Oterongtongnia and his brother were bitter enemies even before they were born, Oterongtongnia actually causing the death of his mother by being born through her armpit. Tawiskaron, however, appeared in the more normal manner. Awenhai, greatly displeased by the death of her daughter, immediately expelled Oterongtongnia, and placed the dead body of her daughter on a tree, where it became the Sun. The head she placed in the branches of another tree where it became the Moon. Oterongtongnia made the Earth and all the good and beautiful things, while Tawiskaron jealously did his utmost to obstruct the good deeds of his brother, and managed to spoil several perfectly good projects before Oterongtongnia built an immense fire and frightened him off. Then he pursued him with such fury that he shattered to pieces and formed the Rocky Mountains.

The latter part of this story should be compared with the story of ATAENTSIC, TASWISCANA and YOSKEHA, as it is simply a variant of that legend.

otkon NORTH AMERICA – WOODLANDS (*Iroquois*)
An indwelling spirit, the quintessence of all that is evil, of death and decay, as contrasted to the ORENDA.

Otomí CENTRAL AMERICA – MEXICO
(*Aztec*)
One of the various non-AZTEC peoples who had left AZTLAN with the Aztec people, but left them at the PLACE OF SEVEN CAVES to travel to COATEPEC.

Otonteuctli CENTRAL AMERICA –
MEXICO (*Otomí*)
The supreme deity of the OTOMÍ people, a dual god who is regarded as the parents of five different nations, the Otomí being just one of these five. Otonteuctli is usually depicted with a head dress that represented an obsidian butterfly, and is sometimes shown in the company of XOCHIQUETZAL, the goddess of flowers and of the obsidian butterfly.

Otter NORTH AMERICA (*Algonquian*)
The first of the animals who dived into the FLOOD[3] waters and attempted to bring back the single grain of soil MÄNÄBUSCH required so that he could recreate the Earth. Otter died in the attempt, as did BEAVER, the second to try, and MINK, the third. The required speck of earth was finally retrieved by MUSKRAT.

Owasse NORTH AMERICA – WOODLANDS
(*Menominee*)
The name of one of the two BEAR chiefs of the ANAMAQKIU.

Oxheheon NORTH AMERICA – GREAT
PLAINS (*Cheyenne*)
The god of the SUN DANCE, an important CHEYENNE ritual, whose name can be roughly translated as 'New-Life-Lodge'.

Oxlahuntiku CENTRAL AMERICA (*Maya*)
'Thirteen Gods', though it remains uncertain whether this was simply the title of a single deity, or the generic name for thirteen gods, or even for a single deity with thirteen faces or aspects. In the eleven AHAU, AHMUCENCAB covered the faces of Oxlahuntiku who was then captured by BOLONTIKU. Fire, salt, stones and trees were then brought down to Earth during which time Oxlahuntiku was knocked about before his serpent and TIZNÉ, his symbols of power, were taken away from him, which thus rendered him impotent and unable to spoil the Creation.

Oxomoco CENTRAL AMERICA – MEXICO
(*Aztec*)
The first man who was created along with CIPACTONAL, the first woman, by the deities TONACATECUHTLI and TONACACÍHUATL after they had rested for 600 years after the creation of the Earth. However, PILTZINTECUHTLI, his son by Cipactonal, is usually referred to as the first man, Oxomoco being demoted to a role whereby he was simply created to become the progenitor of mankind.

Oxomoco was one of the four AMOXAOQUE, the four guardians of HUITZILOPOCHTLI, who remained at TAMOANCHAN during the journey from AZTLAN, the other three who remained there with him being named as CHIPACTONAL, TLALTECUIN and XOCHICAHUACA. There they invented the CALENDAR so that the AZTEC people might have a means by which to organize their lives, both pastoral and religious.

Ozmatli CENTRAL AMERICA – MEXICO
(*Aztec*)
The eleventh day of the twenty-day MONTH[1] employed by the AZTECS. Ozmatli symbolized the monkey, represented the west and was presided over by XOCHIPILLI.

Ozoun Elou Mandja, Maître HAITI
(*Voodoo*)
A variant of OGOUN TONNÈRE.

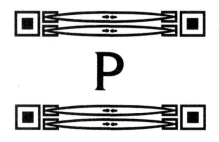

P

P Central America (*Maya*)
Popularly known as the frog god, this deity has been connected with the god N as, in the various CODEX, he, like N, wears a head dress that contains the sign for the 360-day year.

pabid South America – Brazil
(*Tupari*)
The name given to the soul of the dead which emerges through the pupils of the deceased before travelling across the land of the dead over the backs of two crocodiles and two enormous snakes. *En route* great jaguars try to frighten it, and thus catch it, but they are powerless to cause it any harm. Eventually the pabid reaches the River MANI-MANI which it crosses to enter the realm of the dead where it is welcomed by PATOBKIA, the chief SHAMAN of the kingdom. Having completed the necessary initiation rites, the pabid joins its comrades who live in great circular huts where they sleep standing up, do no work as Patobkia magically produces all they require, and spend much of their time dancing adorned with feathers.

Paccaritambo South America (*Inca*)
'Inn of Origin' or 'Inn of Dawn', a village to the south of CUZCO that was the penultimate resting place of MANCO CAPAC and MAMA OCLLO on their mission to discover the correct place to found their city. Paccaritambo is also called TAMBOTOCCO, 'Place of the Hole', for it was from here that the CHILDREN OF THE SUN emerged

from a three-mouthed cave at dawn to set out on the final leg of their long trek.

Pachacamac South America
(*Quechua*)
1 The creator, father of the gods, a fire-god, who was so great that he could not be represented in any tangible form. The son of the Sun and the Moon, Pachacamac expelled CON and transformed all his people into monkeys before creating a new race, the people of today, whom he provided with all the things they needed to survive. In gratitude the people worshipped Pachacamac and established a temple to him near Lima, where his cult survived into INCA times when he became a god of the Sun, and which was the site of an oracle and became a centre for pilgrimage. Archaeologists have established that the QUECHUA felt it a great honour to be interred nearby, the closeness to the temple perhaps being regarded as easing their journey into the after-life.
2 The coastal location to which CAVILLACA fled from the attentions of CONIRAYA, and where she transformed herself, and her child by Coniraya, into rocks.

Pachacuti South America (*Inca*)
An historical leader of the INCA whose inspiration turned near defeat into resounding victory, and thus saved the Inca people from being exterminated. He then embarked on a thirty-year campaign of

expansion that finally gave the Inca an empire that covered most of Ecuador, Bolivia and Peru, together with parts of Argentina and Chile.

Pachamama SOUTH AMERICA – BOLIVIA AND PERU
The goddess of the Earth to whom COCA was offered in order to ensure good crops, and to obtain her blessing whenever a new house was erected.

Pachayachachic SOUTH AMERICA (*Inca*)
The creator who, according to one source, was the father of IMAYMANA VIRACOCHA and TOCAPA VIRACOCHA. He is said to have appointed MANCO CAPAC as king and told him that from that day forth he was to regard him as his father.

pagab SOUTH AMERICA – BRAZIL (*Tupari*)
The name given to magical yellow seeds that the SHAMAN receives from the KIAPOD, and then uses to mesmerize and thus kill his enemies.

Pah NORTH AMERICA – GREAT PLAINS (*Skidi Pawnee*)
The spirit of the Moon who was set in the west by TIRAWA so that he might shine at night. When summoned by Tirawa, Pah united with SAKURU, the spirit of the Sun, their union producing a son who was set on the Earth together with the daughter born to BRIGHT STAR and GREAT STAR, these two children being the progenitors of the SKIDI PAWNEE people.

Pahua NORTH AMERICA – GREAT PLAINS (*Pawnee*)
The least important of the five houses occupied by the NAHURAK, animal-spirits. The other four, in order of importance, are PAHUK, NAKISKAT, TSURAPAKO and KITSAWITSAK.

Pahuk NORTH AMERICA – GREAT PLAINS (*Pawnee*)
The most important of the five houses occupied by the NAHURAK, animal-spirits. The other four, in order of importance, are NAKISKAT, TSURAPAKO, KITSAWITSAK and PAHUA.

Paititi SOUTH AMERICA – PARAGUAY (*Guaraní*)
The land of gold that was ruled over by EL GRAN MOXO and which was said to be located in Lake CUNI-CUNI where it was guarded by the jaguar-lizard TEYÚ-YAGUÁ. This curious tale undoubtedly owes its origins to exploratory raids made against outposts of the INCA empire.

Paiute NORTH AMERICA – SOUTHWEST
Indigenous North American AMERINDIAN people occupying the California–Nevada border regions. Their particular claim to fame is the origination of the GHOST DANCES led by the prophet WODZIWOB.

pajé SOUTH AMERICA – BRAZIL (*Xingú*)
The name given to a SHAMAN who was also a powerful medicine-man.

Pakoc CENTRAL AMERICA (*Maya*)
The frightener, a symbolic war-god and a tutelary deity of the usurping ITZÁ dynasty.

Pal-Rai-Yûk NORTH AMERICA – ARCTIC (*Inuit*)
A lake-dwelling water monster that has been likened to the HAIETLIK of the NOOTKA of British Columbia.

Palenque CENTRAL AMERICA – MEXICO (*Maya*)
Site of an ancient MAYA city that was said to have been founded by the mysterious

VOTAN who had left his village of VALUM CHIVIM to travel up the River USUMACINTA to found the city. The ruins of the city are rich in Mayan artefacts, and are notable for the stone portraits which show the flattened forehead favoured by the Maya aristocracy that is said to represent an ear of maize, the source of all nourishment, as well as being the profile with which YUM CAAX is usually portrayed.

Palulukoň NORTH AMERICA – PUEBLO, SOUTHWEST (*Hopi*)
The great plumed serpent who is identifiable with KOLOOWISI of the neighbouring ZUŇI people.

Panotlan CENTRAL AMERICA – MEXICO (*Aztec*)
'Place-of-Arrival-by-Sea', the name given by the travellers from AZTLAN, an island, to the place where they first landed on the mainland.

paqok CENTRAL AMERICA – YUCATÁN, MEXICO (*Modern Maya*)
Generic name given to fiends that wander through the night attacking women.

Pariacaca SOUTH AMERICA – PERU (*Quechua*)
One of the five men who were born from golden eggs that lay on Mount CONDORCOTO after the great FLOOD[9], that destroyed the world. A great lord of both wind and storm, Pariacaca expelled HUALLALLO CARUINCHO who had to flee into the forest where he turned himself into a bird and hid on Mount TACILLUKA. Pariacaca saw this and bade his sons attack the mountain with thunderbolts. Huallallo Caruincho had to flee again, this time hiding behind a great two-headed snake, but Pariacaca petrified the snake, and Huallallo Caruincho returned to the forests where he has remained ever since. Pariacaca's sons then returned to Mount LAMALLAKA and, having summoned all the people to that place, established their father's cult.

Parichata, Mount SOUTH AMERICA – BOLIVIA (*Aymará*)
One of the two peaks, the other being Mount TATI-TURQUI, that were honoured as the tutelary ACHACHILAS of POTOSÍ. It is said, the story still being orally transmitted, that when the AYMARÁ were forced to work under their Spanish overlords in the silver mines of Mount Parichata, they called upon the spirit of the mountain to help them. At night the spirit turned all the beetles in the mine into mules which carried all the silver away. Thus the mines had to be closed, and the Aymará were no longer worked to their deaths.

Parima, Lake SOUTH AMERICA
Mythical lake said to lie beyond the River ORINOCO in a land named either MANOA or OMOA, and which has become associated with the legends of EL DORADO.

Paris Codex CENTRAL AMERICA (*Maya*)
The name given to one of the three surviving CODEX that, though difficult to decipher, remain the main sources of ancient MAYA culture. The *codex* is so named as it is today housed in Paris, France. The other two *codex* are similarly known by the names of the cities where they are housed: Madrid and Dresden.

Pasikola NORTH AMERICA – WOODLANDS (*Creek*)
'Rabbit', the TRICKSTER of the CREEK people.

Patan CENTRAL AMERICA (*Maya*)
One of the eleven terrible lords of XIBALBA, who was subordinate to HUN CAME and VUKUB CAME, but of the same standing as

AHALCANA, AHALPUH, CHAMIABAK, CHA-
MIAHOLOM, CUCHUMAQIQ, QUIQRE, QUIQ-
RIXGAG, QUIQXIL and XIQIRIPAT.

Patécatl CENTRAL AMERICA – MEXICO
(*Aztec*)
An important PULQUE god, the husband of
MAYAHUEL and the god of medicine.

Patobkia SOUTH AMERICA – BRAZIL
(*Tupari*)
The chief SHAMAN of the PABID (souls of
the dead). When the pabid first comes to
the village of the dead, it is blind. Patobkia
sprinkles the juice of a pepper in its eyes so
that it might see, and then gives it CHICHA
(unfermented beer) before leading it to
VAUGH'EH and MPOKÁLERO, the giant shaman rulers of the village. Male pabid have
to have ritual intercourse with Vaugh'eh,
female ones with Mpokálero, before they
are finally admitted to the brotherhood of
the village that will be their home for all
time.

Pauahtuns CENTRAL AMERICA (*Maya*)
Collective name for four deities whose
significance is, to date, unknown.

Pautiwal NORTH AMERICA – PUEBLO,
SOUTHWEST
1 (*Zuñi*)
The lord of the dead and ruler of the
UNDERWORLD.
2 (*Hopi*)
The spirit of the Sun.

Pawnee NORTH AMERICA – GREAT
PLAINS
Indigenous CADDO-speaking North American AMERINDIAN people who lived within
the central portion of the GREAT PLAINS
culture region where they were linguistically linked with the ARIKA and the Caddo
tribes.

Pax CENTRAL AMERICA (*Maya*)
The MAYA name for the time of year that
roughly corresponds to the month of
May.

Payatami NORTH AMERICA – PUEBLO,
SOUTHWEST (*Zuñi*)
The butterfly god whose thoughts, as he
watched the CORN MAIDENS dance and
became enchanted by their leader
YELLOW-CORN MAIDEN, frightened them so
that, when Payatami fell asleep, they fled
to SHIPOLOLO spring where they hid under
the wings of a duck. They were eventually
persuaded to return to the ZUÑI, who were
suffering a terrible famine, and once more
danced for the good of the people, this
time to the singing of a choir and the music
of Payatami's flute.

Paynal CENTRAL AMERICA – MEXICO
(*Aztec*)
The messenger of HUITZILOPOCHTLI.

Pek CENTRAL AMERICA (*Maya*)
The dog of lightning and of the UNDER-
WORLD, whose AZTEC equivalent was XÓ-
LOTL.

Pelado Peak NORTH AMERICA –
SOUTHWEST (*Navajo*)
The easternmost sacred mountain of the
NAVAJO upon which ATSE ESTSAN and ATSE
HASTIN placed ROCK-CRYSTAL BOY and
ROCK-CRYSTAL GIRL during the final phases
of the ASCENT OF THE NAVAJO.

Petalsharo NORTH AMERICA – GREAT
PLAINS (*Pawnee*)
A late nineteenth-century hero who was
said to have stopped the ritual sacrifice of a
COMANCHE maiden just as she was, according to the correct PAWNEE ritual, about to
be torn into pieces and then buried in the
fields to honour and satisfy the fertility
spirit MORNING STAR[4].

Petén CENTRAL AMERICA (*Maya*)
The city of TA-ITZÁ where the high chief of that name showed the princess SAC-NICTÉ to his people, having abducted her after she had been betrothed to ULMIL ITZÁHAL. Sac-Nicté, however, did not love Ta-Itzá and so drowned herself in nearby PETÉN ITZÁ lake.

Petén Itzá, Lake CENTRAL AMERICA
(*Maya*)
Lake named after both the no longer extant city of PETÉN that was supposedly located nearby, and after ITZÁ, the usurping ruling family whose member TA-ITZÁ was once the ruler of Petén. The lake was that in which SAC-NICTÉ drowned herself to save herself from marriage to Ta-Itzá who loved her, but whom she did not care for. The lake is to be found in northern Guatemala approximately 100 miles south-southwest of Belize City.

Petra loa HAITI (*Voodoo*)
The name given to a group of LOA whose rites are said to have been introduced from San Domingo by one DON PEDRO (hence the name). The emblem of the Petra loa is the whip which tends to suggest that these spirits originated in response to imposed slavery. Easily annoyed and then malign, these loa have red eyes and possess initiates whom they make writhe and grimace in an ugly fury, this possession usually being caused by the initiate's failure to make prompt payment for their services. The Petra loa are in strong contrast to the benevolent and dignified RADA LOA with whom they compete.

Petrel NORTH AMERICA – NORTHWEST
COAST (*Tlingit*)
The owner of fresh water who had it stolen from him by YETL who sprinkled it over the barren land to make rivers and streams. Petrel lit a fire underneath Yetl as he was flying away with the water, the smoke of which changed the colour of his feathers from white to the black which they retain to this day. When the two later met again, they argued over who was the older. At last Petrel put on his fog hat so that Yetl became lost and had to admit defeat, but he did persuade Petrel to let his hat travel freely around the world.

Peyote NORTH AMERICA
A ritual, organized in the Native American Church, that is a blend of traditional AMERINDIAN and Christian belief, and involves the hallucinogen peyote.

Philomène, Maîtresse HAITI (*Voodoo*)
The Roman Catholic Saint Philomena who is regarded as a LOA by some VOODOO cultists.

pictun CENTRAL AMERICA (*Maya*)
Ancient period of time used by the MAYA that was calculated as twenty BAKTUNS, or 2,880,888 days which is roughly 8,000 years.

Pie, Papa HAITI (*Voodoo*)
Saint Peter as a LOA. Very powerful and the cause of all floods, Papa Pie is depicted as a soldier who lives at the bottom of ponds and rivers.

Pié Anfalo HAITI (*Voodoo*)
One of the numerous LOA of the VOODOO religion.

Pié Damballa HAITI (*Voodoo*)
A variant of DAMBALLA.

Pillan SOUTH AMERICA – CHILE
(*Arauca*)
The god of storms.

Piltzintecuhtli CENTRAL AMERICA –
MEXICO (*Aztec*)
'Young Prince', the first man and son of OXOMOCO and CIPACTONAL, though some

authorities state that Piltzintecuhtli is simply a title of TONATIUH. His wife, by whom he had an unnamed son, was born from a hair of XOCHIQUETZAL, though some have suggested that this simply infers that Piltzintecuhtli and Xochiquetzal were lovers.

Piltzintecuhtli-Tonatiuh CENTRAL
   AMERICA – MEXICO (*Aztec*)
A Sun-god, the amalgamation of the deities PILTZINTECUHTLI and TONATIUH, and guardian of the second hour of the night during the twenty-two-hour AZTEC day.

Pinga NORTH AMERICA – ARCTIC (*Inuit*)
A female spirit whose home is a secret, and who appears only in times of great need. A strict housekeeper, Pinga watches carefully over the actions of men, paying particular attention to the way they treat hunted animals.

Pipounoukhe NORTH AMERICA –
   WOODLANDS (*Montagnais*)
The spirit of winter who shares the world with NIPINOUKHE, the spirit of spring. They periodically reciprocally change places when their time in one part of the world has come to an end, in a ritual called AHITESCATONEH.

Pishumi NORTH AMERICA – PUEBLO,
   SOUTHWEST (*Acoma*)
The spirit of disease, decay and ultimately death.

Pitazofi SOUTH AMERICA (*Mochica*)
The trumpeter of NAYMLAP who accompanied that great king as he, and his retinue, sailed to CHIMOR on a fleet of BALSA craft.

Pizzaro, Francisco
Spanish conqueror (c.1475–1541) of Peru. In 1526 Pizzaro and Diego de Almagro sailed for Peru and, after many adventures

and delays, reached its port of Tumbes where they collected information about the INCA empire. Pizzaro then returned to Spain to gain the authority to undertake the conquest which he did in 1529, being made captain-general of the invasion forces. Pizzaro returned to Panama from which he sailed in 1531 with just 183 men and 37 horses. Landing at Tumbes, they moved inland from May 1532, and in November entered Cajamarca near where Pizzaro captured ATAHUALPA, whom he had put to death in 1533 after extracting a truly enormous ransom. Pizzaro then marched to CUZCO where he was created a marquis by the Emperor Charles V. Pizzaro then went on to found Lima and other coastal cities. During an insurrection both Cuzco and Lima fell back into the hands of the Incas, but were both recaptured by Almagro. Pizzaro had no intention of letting Almagro retain Cuzco, so sent his forces to attack him, which they did, duly defeating him. One of Almagro's followers called Juan de Rada avenged the death of his comrade by leading an attack on Pizzaro's home in Lima and murdering him.

Place of Emergence NORTH AMERICA –
   SOUTHWEST (*Navajo*)
The name by which the NAVAJO people quite naturally referred to the location where they said they first came to this world, having ascended through numerous other UNDERWORLD worlds. See ASCENT OF THE NAVAJO.

Place of Seven Caves CENTRAL
   AMERICA (*Aztec*)
The place where all the peoples who had left the ancestral homeland of AZTLAN went their separate ways. It seems quite likely that the Place of Seven Caves is the same as TULAI ZUIVA, the PLACE OF SEVEN CAVES AND SEVEN RAVINES mentioned in the MAYA myth of BALAM AGAB and his

189

three brothers, though this has never been proved one way or the other.

Place of Seven Caves and Seven Ravines CENTRAL AMERICA (*Maya*)

The way in which TULAI ZUIVA is referred to, possibly reflecting the geographical lie of the land at that particular place.

Place of the Dark NORTH AMERICA – NORTHWEST COAST (*Klamath*)

The UNDERWORLD. During the Creation, the spirits that lived in this world were visited by KEMUSH and EVENING SKY who danced with the spirits around a great fire until SHEL called them back to the world. As Kemush and Evening Sky left, the spirits of the Underworld, who were as numerous as the stars of the MILKY WAY, all turned to dry bones, bones that were later to be used by Kemush in the creation of mankind.

Place of the Division of Waters CENTRAL AMERICA (*Maya*)

Unidentified location where the gods discovered that yellow and white maize grew, maize that they ground into flour and mixed with the nine broths brewed by XMUCANÉ to form the four brothers, BALAM AGAB, BALAM QUITZÉ, IQI BALAM and MAHUCUTAH.

Pleiades

Famous star formation of the northern celestial hemisphere that has, throughout time, been identified by different cultures in the northern hemisphere with deities or heroes. The common name for the cluster is the 'Seven Sisters' which refers to the seven stars within the group that are visible to the naked eye.

1 NORTH AMERICA – ARCTIC (*Inuit*)
    This star cluster is said, by the INUIT, to be some hunters and their dogs who, having chased a bear out on to an ice floe, continued to chase it after it had risen into the air. The bear became the constellation URSA MAJOR[3] (the Great Bear) which the Pleiades nightly chase across the sky.

2 NORTH AMERICA – WOODLANDS (*Cherokee*)
    The CHEROKEE believe the Pleiades star cluster is the home of the ANITSUTSA.

3 NORTH AMERICA – WOODLANDS (*Huron*)
    The HURON believe that the Pleiades is the home of a group of spirits called the HUTI WATSI YA.

pochteca CENTRAL AMERICA (*Maya and Aztec*)

A member of a society of followers of QUETZALCÓATL who, though apparently humble, formed a guild with the material purpose of trade, but which had a central set of ethical principles that they held more dearly than actually making money. From their centre in CHOLULA, near the Mexican capital, they travelled down into the Gulf lands and on into MAYA territory to the south, carrying not only goods for sale but also ideas. It has been suggested that they were wholly responsible for the spread of the cult of Quetzalcóatl who is, perhaps, the most widely and diversely worshipped of all the NAHUA deities.

The pochtecas were a curious breed of men who formed what could be best described as a secret society. They were very definitely hard-headed business men, but if they ever accumulated too much wealth, they quickly organized a religious banquet, often as not in honour of YIACATECUHTLI, in order to dispose of their riches. In an ancient land where so much depended on ostentatious displays of wealth, the pochtecas preferred to work behind the scenes, silently influencing through their humility, rather than openly and forcibly converting the populace.

Poïa NORTH AMERICA – GREAT PLAINS
   (*Blackfoot*)
'Scarface', the son of MORNING STAR[6] and
the mortal SOATSAKI who is a personification of the planet JUPITER. While still a
youth he fell in love with the daughter of a
chieftain, but she repulsed his advances on
account of his scarred face. Despondent,
Poïa travelled to the home of the Sun
whom he asked to remove the blemishes,
and *en route* killed seven evil birds who
were threatening his father's life. The Sun
duly rewarded Poïa by removing the scars,
and also gave him a flute which he was to
play and then sing a song the Sun taught
him in order to bewitch his beloved. Before he departed, the Sun also taught Poïa
the rites of the sacred Sun Dance which he
was ordered to teach to the BLACKFOOT.
This he did before going on to enchant and
subsequently marry the chieftain's daughter who had earlier rejected him.

Polik Mana NORTH AMERICA – PUEBLO,
   SOUTHWEST (*Hopi*)
The butterfly KATCHINA[2].

Polisson, Monsieur HAITI (*Voodoo*)
One of the many LOA of the VOODOO
cult.

Pollen Boy NORTH AMERICA –
   SOUTHWEST (*Navajo*)
During the final phase of the ASCENT OF
THE NAVAJO, Pollen Boy was placed, along
with GRASSHOPPER GIRL, on the northern-
most sacred mountain of the NAVAJO,
Mount SAN JUAN, by ATSE ESTSAN and ATSE
HASTIN.

Pony Massa SOUTH AMERICA (*Chimu*)
The first CHIMU ruler of the valley that had
been formerly ruled over by NAYMLAP and
his descendants, this line of descent coming to an end with the deposing of FEMPEL-
LEC. The valley was then left without a
ruler and easily conquered by CAPAC, the
Chimu leader who installed Pony Massa as
the new ruler.

Pookonghoya NORTH AMERICA –
   PUEBLO, SOUTHWEST (*Hopi*)
The brother of BALONGAHOYA, one of the
twin sons of the Sun-spirit who are the
HOPI equivalents of MAASEWE and
UYUUYEWE, as well as of NAYANEZGANI and
THOBADZISTSHINI.

Poopó, Lake SOUTH AMERICA – BOLIVIA
A lake that was sacred to the Moon and
revered as the original parent of the native
peoples of this region. The lake is situated
to the south of ORURO and is fed by the
River DESAGUADERO.

Popocatépatl CENTRAL AMERICA –
   MEXICO (*Aztec*)
'Smoking Mountain', one of the three
snow-capped volcanoes that QUETZAL-
CÓATL climbed *en route* from TOLLAN to
return to TLILLAN-TLAPALLAN. The others
were IXTACCÍHUATL and CITLALTÉPETL. Popocatépatl is located to the west of Puebla,
30 miles southeast of Mexico City and
approximately 100 miles to the southwest
of Citlaltépetl. It rises to a height of 17,526
feet. Popocatépatl last erupted in 1920.

Popul Vuh SOUTH AMERICA –
   GUATEMALA (*Maya*)
Compiled by the southern MAYA living in
Guatemala, this important source details
what limited information remains regard-
ing the Maya civilization.

Poshaiyangkyo NORTH AMERICA –
   PUEBLO, SOUTHWEST (*Zuñi*)
The first man, and thus the culture hero of
the ZUÑI people.

191

Poshaiyanne NORTH AMERICA –
PUEBLO, SOUTHWEST (*Sia*)
A great SHAMAN, the son of a virgin, and a
skilful gambler who won all of the SIA
people from their chief and subsequently
proved a benevolent and wise ruler, who
brought his people an abundance of riches
and game. Eventually he left the Sia, but
promised to return. As he travelled, he was
killed by some jealous enemies, possibly
the previously defeated chief and his followers, but he was revived by the touch of
a downy eagle's feather. He never returned, but the Sia believe that one day he
will, and when he does a new Golden Age
will be inaugurated. Some authorities see
this story as a northern version of the
QUETZALCÓATL legend, but the theme is, of
course, common in many parts of the
world.

Potawatomi NORTH AMERICA –
WOODLANDS
Indigenous, mainly peaceful, ALGONQUIAN-
speaking North American AMERINDIAN
people inhabiting the far northern part of
the WOODLANDS culture region. The Potawatomi are linguistically linked with the
CHIPPEWA, CREE, DELAWARE, MENOMINEE
and MONTAGNAIS peoples.

Potosí SOUTH AMERICA – BOLIVIA
City to the southeast of Lake POOPÓ
which, according to the AYMARÁ people
had two mountains, PARICHATA and TATI-
TURQUI as its tutelary ACHACHILAS.

Poverty NORTH AMERICA – SOUTHWEST
(*Navajo*)
One of the four ANAYE who survived the
assault of NAYANEZGANI and THOBADZIST-
SHINI and then the terrible storm raised by
ESTANATLEHI. The other three anaye were
COLD, HUNGER and OLD AGE. These four
were only allowed to survive after they had
successfully argued that if they were to be

destroyed, mankind would no longer prize
the good things of life, or even life itself.

Ppiz Hiu Tec CENTRAL AMERICA
(*Maya*)
The god of poetry and poets who is also
called AB KIN XOC.

Precious Flower CENTRAL AMERICA –
MEXICO (*Aztec*)
Goddess who lay with a prince in a cave
and gave birth to a divine child named
WELL-BELOVED who immediately died and
was buried. From the body of the dead
infant there grew many of the plants that
were to satisfy man's needs. Cotton grew
from his hair; seed-bearing plants (such as
corn) grew from his ears; a herb used to
cool a fever grew from his nostrils; the
sweet potato grew from his fingers; maize
from his finger-nails; and so on until his
body had brought forward around 1,000
different varieties of fruit and grain.

Precious Tree CENTRAL AMERICA
(*Aztec*)
The name given to QUETZALCÓATL when
he, at the start of the era of the FIFTH SUN,
helped to prop up the heavens along with
TREE OF MIRRORS (a name for TEZCATLI-
POCA in this role), and the four giants,
FALLING EAGLE, RESURRECTION, SERPENT OF
OBSIDIAN KNIVES and THORNY FLOWERS.

Precious Willow CENTRAL AMERICA
(*Aztec*)
One of the two branches of the great tree
that grew on the spot where EHÉCATL consummated his passion for MAYAHUAL.

Pueblo, Indians of the NORTH AMERICA
– SOUTHWEST
The style of agriculture practised in the
Southwest led to settlement in closely knit
villages of cliff and cave dwellings and
adobe houses that are known as *pueblos*.
The extreme aridity of the area makes the

people that live there especially dependent upon the careful use of their scant water resources, a practice that fosters close-knit communities. The closeness of these communities is also fostered by the inaccessibility of one valley to the next, especially along the coast, and it is almost certainly due to the cohesive independence of the AMERINDIAN peoples that inhabited this region that they have been able to preserve and maintain so much of their traditional culture.

Like other purely agricultural societies, the Pueblo Indians have a close and intimate relationship with their environment, and a highly conservative sense of history. This is expressed in their myths and legends by precise reference to local features – the mountain homes of the gods, and the caves and islands from which they believe their ancestors emerged from the UNDERWORLD, that dark region being the source of all life and fertility.

Pukeheh CENTRAL AMERICA – MEXICO
(*Mojave*)
The daughter of TOCHIPA by whom she was sealed in a hollow log when her uncle, HOKOMATA, flooded the Earth. After the waters had receded, Pukeheh crawled out of the log and gave birth to two children, a boy fathered by the Sun-spirit, and a girl fathered on her by a waterfall, these two going on to become the progenitors of mankind.

pukwudjie NORTH AMERICA – WOODLANDS (*Algonquian*)
The name given to a dwarf, nature-spirit.

pulque CENTRAL AMERICA – MEXICO
An hallucinatory drink that is made from the fermented sap of the MAGUEY plant, and is widely used in rituals (cf. PEYOTE).

Purrunaminari SOUTH AMERICA – GUYANA (*Maipuri*)
The creator, the husband of TAPARIMARRU and father of SISIRI.

puskita NORTH AMERICA – WOODLANDS (*Creek*)
The correct name for the festival that is more commonly known as the anglicized BUSK FESTIVAL.

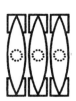

Q

Qalanganguase NORTH AMERICA –
ARCTIC (*Inuit*)
A crippled orphan who was left alone
when his entire village went hunting. The
spirits of his dead parents and younger
sister came to visit him, leaving moments
before the hunters returned. His younger
sister, however, left slightly too late and
was seen by the villagers who challenged
Qalanganguase to a SHAMANistic singing
duel which he lost, so they bound him to
the house posts where they left him dan-
gling in mid-air. Seeing the distress of their
son, his parents came and took him away
with them, and the villagers never saw him
again.

Qamaits NORTH AMERICA –
NORTHWEST COAST (*Bella Coola*)
The chief deity of the BELLA COOLA who
are unique among the AMERINDIAN peoples
of the Northwest Coast in conceiving their
Supreme Being to be feminine. Qamaits is
perceived as a great warrior who reduced
the mountains to more manageable pro-
portions at the very beginning of time,
after they had rendered the Earth uninhabitable. Qamaits lives at the eastern end
of the uppermost heaven beyond a vast,
bleak prairie, in a house that is located in
front of the pool of SISIUTL. Qamaits is not
offered any prayers by the Bella Coola, to
whom the subordinate spirits led by SENX
are the more important, and rarely visits
Earth, though when she does sickness and
death are the result.

qentilis SOUTH AMERICA (*Quechua*)
Generic name given to the spirits of dead
ancestors who live in caves, or other dark
places, which they had found during life
and nominated to be their resting place. If
a person was to approach one of these
places, he would see his skin wrinkle before his eyes. Shortly afterwards he would
die.

Quauhtli CENTRAL AMERICA – MEXICO
(*Aztec*)
The fourteenth day of the twenty-day
MONTH[1] of the AZTEC people which sym-
bolized the eagle, represented the west and
was presided over by the terrible XIPE
TOTEC.

Qu ~ echua, ~ ichua SOUTH AMERICA
Indigenous South American AMERINDIAN
people of the Andean regions whose ancestors include the INCAS who established
the Quechua language in the region. The
Quechua language, which belongs to the
Andean–Equatorial family, is the second
official language of Peru and is also spoken
in Ecuador, Bolivia, Colombia, Argentina
and Chile. The Quechua are the largest
indigenous Amerindian grouping in South
America.

Quel CENTRAL AMERICA (*Maya*)
The name of a parrot who brought the
gods the maize grain they needed to create
mankind. He was helped by three other
animals: HOH, a crow; UTIU, a coyote; and
YAC, a forest cat.

Querrana NORTH AMERICA – PUEBLO,
SOUTHWEST (*Sia*)
The second man (cf. KOSHARI).

quetzal WIDESPREAD
A long-tailed bird whose feathers symbolize the spring vegetation, the use of these
feathers being common among many
AMERINDIAN peoples, from the HOPI and
the ZUÑI in the north, to as far south as the
Andes Mountains. They are usually combined with a serpentine figure such as in
QUETZALCÓATL, the great AZTEC deity. The
quetzal bird is properly the *Pharomachus
mocinno* of the *trogon* family. The male is
about 4 feet 4 inches in length, including
its tail, and is brightly coloured with red,
green, blue and white feathers. The female
is smaller and lacks both the plumage and
tail of the male. The national emblem of
Guatemala, the quetzal bird is coming
under increasing threat from the destruction of its natural habitat, and from man
who hunts it as a trophy.

Quetzalcóatl CENTRAL AMERICA –
MEXICO (*Toltec and Aztec*)
'Green-Feathered-Serpent', the god of
wind who represented spirit freed from
matter, the god of fertility, and, on a
deeper level, the god of regeneration, SHA-
MAN, priest-king, and culture hero. He was
worshipped as the bestower of all the arts
of civilization on mankind by the TOLTECs,
and later by the AZTECs of central Mexico
who saw themselves, in some ways, as the
upholders and heirs of the Toltec culture.
Quetzalcóatl was perceived as presiding
like the wind over all space. He is the soul
that ascends to heaven, and he is matter
descending to Earth as the serpent. He is
waking and dreaming; angel and demon,
though in the latter he is TEZCATLIPOCA.
He represents daylight and, when he journeys to the UNDERWORLD, he represents
night. He is love and carnal desire, and yet
he is purity and chastity. Quetzalcóatl is all

this and more – he is the true representation of the omnipotent god on Earth who,
with his coming, brings all the possibilities
of the miracle of life.

Quetzalcóatl was depicted as a plumed
serpent – a snake with QUETZAL feathers
instead of scales, and as such became commonly known as the plumed-serpent god.
He is, up to a point, interchangeable with
EHÉCATL. Quetzalcóatl has a dual principle: he is XOCHIQUETZAL as well, this duality being born out of the basic element of
water. His exact MAYA equivalent is KU-
KULCÁN, but he is also identical to the
earlier ITZAMNÁ, the son of HUNAB-KU.
The representation of Quetzalcóatl as a
bird symbolizes the god's associations with
the heavens. Besides being obviously associated with his own bird, the elusive quetzal, Quetzalcóatl is often portrayed in the
company of a hummingbird, the tiny bird
which represented, to the NAHUA, the
human soul released from its bodily bond-
age to alight on whichever flower will provide it with the honey it so adores.

The stories of Quetzalcóatl's birth are
somewhat confused, as one would expect
for a deity whose origins are far earlier than
either the Toltec or Aztec cultures. In one
he is the son of MIXCÓATL ('Cloud Serpent'), though one of the most widely
known versions makes him one of the four
sons of TONACATECUHTLI ('Lord Nourishment') and TONACACÍHUATL ('Lady Nourishment') who lived in the ninth and highest heaven. The four brothers originally
appear to have been nature deities who
represented the four cardinal points,
though later they came to be identified as
the tutelary deities of the empire's four
different peoples. The four were red CA-
MAXTLI, the chief deity of the TLAXCALA;
black Tezcatlipoca, god of night and the
war-god of TEZCOCO (some variants make
this brother the flayed god XIPE TOTEC);
HUITZILOPOCHTLI of the Aztec, and Quetzalcóatl of the Toltec. All four brothers are

in fact, to some degree, aspects of Quet-zalcóatl.

From his parents Quetzalcóatl received four temples, one of which was that of the MORNING STAR, his symbol as VENUS[4] in the morning sky. Another belongs to the Moon and is round in plan like the famous observatory at CHICHEN ITZÁ. The third was for medicine – the priests of Quetzal-cóatl being referred to as healers or physi-cians. The last was the temple of Xipe Totec which was only accessible by people of true Toltec descent. His parents also gave him the gifts of seed; a conch shell and a wind mask; a spear-thrower and an arrow; a jewel and feather-fringed shirt as worn by high-priests; a black feather with a pair of eyes; and Quetzalcóatl's distinctive conical hat which is echoed in the internal structure of the conch. This spiral symbol-izes Quetzalcóatl's role as the wind-god as well as a fertility deity. The conch repre-sents the rushing wind (which may be heard captured within if the shell is held to the ear), while the spiral contained within represents the complex nature of birth and the many turns man's life will take. In Nahua philosophy the shell represented the end of one era and the start of the next, so that even time itself becomes ephemeral.

From his heavenly home Quetzalcóatl came to Earth down a ladder knotted in the form of a sacrificial lash, though this seems a misnomer as he (in his earthly incarnation) would have nothing to do with human sacrifice. He was followed by two gods who came to help him in his earthly tasks – the civilization of mankind. In his hands he held a staff sprouting life itself as well as the spear that signified the Morning Star.

During the age of the FIRST SUN, Tezcat-lipoca ruled, but after 676 years he was struck down by Quetzalcóatl who trans-formed him into a jaguar which ate the giants that were at the time populating the Earth. Afterwards Quetzalcóatl threw him into the sea, an act he goes through nightly as the constellation URSA MAJOR[1] is seen falling towards the water.

Quetzalcóatl then recreated mankind and ruled over the second era of the crea-tion, the era known as the SECOND SUN. This era also lasted 676 years until TLÁLOC, the great wind-god, struck down Quetzal-cóatl and raised a huge storm that blew away almost all the people, those who managed to survive doing so by climbing and clinging on to the trees. Tláloc thus transformed those who had survived into monkeys.

At the end of the fourth era of the creation, that era known as the FOURTH SUN, the gods created four men who helped Tezcatlipoca and Quetzalcóatl to lift up the heavens to their present posi-tion. The two gods then became the rulers of the skies that lay between heaven and Earth. Quetzalcóatl then threw his son by the goddess CHALCHIUHTLICUE into a fire from which he emerged as the FIFTH SUN.

Tláloc followed suit and threw his son into the cinders of the fire. He emerged as the Moon which emitted a lesser light as the fire had significantly cooled. Quetzal-cóatl's son in this instance is the humble NANAUTZIN, all covered in sores and scabs, but he is, in fact, none other than Quetzal-cóatl himself in embryonic form. The Fifth Sun was the Sun of movement whose per-petual round in the heavens creates night and day, and which is represented by the passage of Quetzalcóatl as an eagle across the sky, his disappearance into the Under-world as an ocelot every evening, and his re-emergence the following dawn. This pe-riodic passage from the sky to the Under-world, and back again, is yet another rep-resentation of the duality of the deity, a concept that seems to have preoccupied the ancient Toltecs and Aztecs. Quetzal-cóatl's connection to the planet Venus echoes this periodic symbolism, though here the connection is specifically with the planet when it dips beneath the horizon to enter the Underworld. Thus Quetzalcóatl proved that he was still a god in the making, for every night, he had to prove himself worthy of resurrection in the Underworld.

Later legends augment this story by saying that Tezcatlipoca was sacrificed in recognition of the Sun's superiority, but soon after the rituals he appeared to Quetzalcóatl, here depicted as his subordinate and one of Tezcatlipoca's grieving devotees. Tezcatlipoca commanded him to go to the home of the Sun, from which he was to fetch musicians to make a feast in his honour. Quetzalcóatl set off, singing as he went, but the Sun warned his people not to listen. However, some of them disobeyed and became so captivated by Quetzalcóatl's singing that they followed him back to Earth, bringing with them the musical rites of the gods.

In many of the known and surviving myths, Quetzalcóatl is the bitter adversary of Tezcatlipoca, both apparently at one time, as the story above illustrates, being regarded as superior to the other. It appears as if this enmity may reflect the struggle for supremacy among the various NAHUAtlan tribes. This hypothesis is supported by the fact that Tezcoco, the city of which Tezcatlipoca was the tutelary deity, was, until the very end of the Aztec empire one of its most powerful allies, while Quetzalcóatl himself was the principal deity of the earlier, and already assimilated Toltec civilization.

The underlying theme of Quetzalcóatl's continuing struggle with Tezcatlipoca is illustrated by yet a further variant on his birth. In this he is the son of COATLICUE who, while doing penance for some unrecorded sin on Mount COATEPEC with her four unnamed sisters and while still a virgin, gathered some white feathers to her bosom, though in another version she

swallows an emerald. By this act she becomes pregnant and subsequently gives birth to Quetzalcóatl, if one is talking in ancient Nahua terms, or Huitzilopochtli in later Aztec terms.

In one version of the story the goddess is called LA, a widow who has had 400 sons who have gone to live elsewhere. Thus she is alone. As she ponders her loneliness, a feather drops from the sky, a feather that she places in her bosom before sweeping the heavens in the hope that her sons might return to her. All this seems to happen around twilight when her husband – the Sun, so one surmises – has departed and her sons – the stars – have yet to appear. As she sets aside the broom and sits down, she remembers the beautiful feather but she cannot find it. Sadness quickly turns into joy as she realizes that she is pregnant.

Her sons then return and insist on being told who has made their mother pregnant, demanding his death for the dishonour he has done their mother and themselves. While they plot, La gives birth to her son, Huitzilopochtli, who is fully armed and proceeds to kill the 400, or 4,000. This number need not be taken literally, for it simply symbolizes the number of stars in the night sky. A variant of this story says that the battle did not take place until the child was nine years old, by which time the 400, who lived in the MILKY WAY[2], were consumed with hatred for the Sun, the child's father, though in one sense Quetzalcóatl is also the Sun. The legend clearly demonstrates the mythological concept of reality, for every day the Sun kills the stars who retaliate every night and duly kill the Sun. Thus the 400 killed the Sun, Quetzalcóatl's father, and buried him in the sand. News of his death was brought to Quetzalcóatl by a vulture, and with the help of a coyote, an eagle, a wolf, and an army of moles, Quetzalcóatl dug up the bones of his father's skeleton.

The feathered-serpent is the most powerful figure in Central-American mythology, his symbol being found widely among AMERINDIAN peoples, from the ZUÑI and HOPI to the north, as far south as the Andes mountain range. From TEOTIHUACÁN on the high plateau of CHICHEN ITZÁ, his is the dominant motif on ancient monuments. This possibly denotes that Quetzalcóatl was originally conceived of as a fertility deity of rainclouds, for the feathers of the quetzal bird symbolize the fresh spring vegetation, while the serpent is both the fertility and lightning symbol among peoples from all parts of the American continent south of the Arctic.

Perhaps the most dazzling example of the artistic representation of this great deity is his pyramid at Teotihuacán which dates from the eighth century AD. Here the great size of the motifs, combined with the sheer number of them, produces an aggressive effect that belies the true compassionate and gentle nature of Quetzalcóatl. Though the pyramid is usually named after the plumed serpent, it was in fact shared with Tláloc, whose symbolic representation alternates with that of Quetzalcóatl on the façade of the pyramid. Regrettably, the temple that once surmounted the great pyramid no longer survives, nor do the obsidian eyes of the serpent motifs.

Legend records that Quetzalcóatl, in his manifest self, was originally white-skinned. This belief was later to stop the Aztec people from adequately defending themselves against CORTÉS whom they believed to be the returning god, thus opening up the empire for easy Spanish conquest. However, artistically the god is usually shown with a dark body that has been taken to symbolize the rain cloud, but one legend recounts how Tezcatlipoca and Quetzalcóatl challenged each other to a ball game, the victor, in this case Tezcatlipoca, banishing his rival to the far east where the Sun burned him. Another version of this story says that the game was played between Quetzalcóatl and Tláloc and his children. In this instance Quetzalcóatl was the winner. Tláloc offered him maize as his reward, but Quetzalcóatl would have nothing less than exquisite feathers and fine jade which Tláloc gave him, though he warned him that jade and feathers could not compare in value with maize which would feed mankind.

Quetzalcóatl's physical attributes are recorded in some detail. He was tall, robust, broad-browed with large eyes and a fair beard, though one account says that his beard was black. His face was smeared with soot (perhaps to cover the true fairness of his skin), and he wore a necklace of shells and a quetzal bird on his back. His jacket was cotton, while on his feet he wore anklets, rattles and foam sandals. His head dress is adorned with flowers that serve two purposes: representing growth and life, and also serving as a reminder that life is ephemeral, and everything that has been created must perish.

The story of the celestial ball-game, in which – as is common in ancient Central-American myths – the game echoes the journey of the Sun across the sky, is also a version of the legendary expulsion of Quetzalcóatl from the city of TOLLAN, an expulsion that was allegedly masterminded by Tezcatlipoca and intertwines myth and legendary history. This story is basically as follows.

The Toltecs originally came, so it is said, from the north under the leadership of their great god MIXCÓATL and conquered large parts of central Mexico where they built a great city. Mixcóatl married CHIMALMAN and by her became the father of CE ACTL TOPILTZIN. Ce Actl Topiltzin is, without doubt, an historical person living sometime during the latter part of the tenth century AD. He temporarily fled into exile following his father's murder, but later returned to avenge his father's death. Having done so, he became the last king of the Toltecs as well as the high priest of the city's god, Quetzalcóatl whose name he adopted, thus suggesting that Ce Actl Topiltzin was regarded as the earthly manifestation of the god. No one actually knows where the historical Quetzalcóatl came from, or who he really was, his divine lineage simply being an attempt to ratify his position as priest-king. It is almost certain that there was more than one historical Quetzalcóatl, for the name was given in ancient times to any priest who was supposed to have reached enlightenment. It seems equally likely, therefore, that the legends of the historical Quetzalcóatl refer to a line of priest-kings, and not just the priest-king who claimed his descent from Mixcóatl.

Under the inspired leadership of their god-priest, the people built a new city at Tollan. The architecture of the new city was remarkable. Some of the houses were built from green stone, some from silver, some of white shells, some of coloured shells, some of turquoise, and some of exquisite feathers. Under Quetzalcóatl's leadership everything prospered. From a hill in the centre of Tollan his voice was said to have carried for a distance of at least ten leagues. The maize (the god of maize CINTÉOTL is simply an aspect of Quetzalcóatl) grew to such size, some accounts saying that the plants grew as tall and as robust as men themselves, and that the cobs were not just used for food but also for fuel. Cocoa, pumpkins and cotton grew naturally and abundantly, the pumpkins growing to a man's height and the cotton in red, yellow, blue, green, brown and orange, as well as white. Quetzalcóatl was a great law-giver and civilizer who introduced writing and the CALENDAR, or Book of Fate. His people lived in Utopia, for only snakes and other animals were

sacrificed, Quetzalcóatl steadfastly refusing to sacrifice humans, though he was continually pestered by evil spirits to do so.

Eventually, at the instigation of these fiends, a plot was hatched against Quetzalcóatl by the magicians Huitzilopochtli, TITLACUHAN (a title of Tezcatlipoca, thus introducing an earthly version of the heavenly contest between the two gods) and their brother TLACAHUEPAN. Tezcatlipoca showed Quetzalcóatl his image in a mirror. Quetzalcóatl was astonished to see that his eyelids were inflamed, his eyes sunken back into their sockets, and his skin wrinkled like the most ancient of living men – a face that appeared non-human. Quetzalcóatl feared that if his subjects saw him, they would destroy him, and so went into hiding, thus conceding the advantage to Tezcatlipoca. Tezcatlipoca then decked out his great rival in a garment of quetzal feathers and a turquoise mask. He coloured Quetzalcóatl's lips with red dye and painted small squares on his forehead with yellow dye. A wig and a beard of red and blue guacamaya feathers completed the effect which, when Quetzalcóatl again looked in the mirror, made him appear as a handsome youth so that he was persuaded to come out of hiding.

Titlacuhan then disguised himself as a doctor and offered to cure Quetzalcóatl who had become ill as a result of the incessant torments of the fiends. Titlacuhan tricked Quetzalcóatl, along with all his retinue, into drinking a goblet of wine, thus breaking one of his priestly vows. One version says that he and his retinue drank so much wine that, in his drunken state, he seduced a maiden, some sources saying that he laid with his sister QUETZALPETLATL, and so also lost his priestly chastity. Having recovered, he repented and ordered that a stone coffin should be built. In this he spent four days doing penance for his sins before he built his own funeral pyre, on to which he threw himself, his ashes rising into the heavens as a flock of birds bearing his heart which became the planet Venus. The stone coffin is, in most cases, taken to symbolize the Underworld into which he had to descend before he could ascend to heaven, and into which the planet Venus dips periodically, thus showing that Quetzalcóatl still has to prove his worth on a regular basis.

Some versions say that Quetzalcóatl was banished from Tollan, though others say that he left of his own free will, or had to flee when he was attacked by his enemies. Before he left for his former home of TLILLAN-TLAPALLAN (the Yucatán), he burned all the beautiful houses he had built and buried all his treasure. He promised to return to Tollan in 1519, the year of the Spanish conquistadors' arrival, a fact that was to ultimately lead to the conquest of the Aztec empire by Cortés and his men. On his journey eastward all his retinue died from the cold, but finally he reached the coast and set off on his serpent raft for Tlillan-Tlapallan.

Even though the majority of the stories equate the fall of Tollan with the departure of Quetzalcóatl, some sources say that it survived for a further 200 years, its last secular ruler being HUEMAC whose disgrace and fall were also engineered by Tezcatlipoca who seems to have had a hatred for the city. Whatever the truth, the downfall of Tollan and of Quetzalcóatl seems to be, at least partially, legendary, for the Aztecs were great preservers of tradition.

Quetzalcóatl, that is the first priest to take that name, must have been a truly extraordinary person whose insight and rectitude made him stand head and shoulders above the general population. His morality in refusing human sacrifice is just one example of his remarkable nature, and proof, perhaps, that he lived many centuries before the Aztecs rose to power, for

the degeneration of the high principles of civilization engendered by this form of Quetzalcóatl, to the barbarity of the later culture would have taken a long time. It was not something that would happen overnight, though the legends conveniently compress the time scale and say that once Quetzalcóatl had been overthrown, the society degenerated very quickly.

Historically speaking, the remaining facts are meagre in the extreme. That the legends of Quetzalcóatl, both god and man, exist at all tells us one important thing – someone must have created them. The name is important in determining the truth. It is made up of quetzal, a rare bird with bright green feathers which lives in the highlands of Chiapas and Guatemala where it inhabits the very tops of the trees and is thus seldom seen. It is easily distinguished from other birds in that it only has two front toes and almost no claws. The second part of the name, cóatl, is the NAHUA word for a snake, but it might equally have been a combination of co, the MAYA generic term for a serpent or snake, and atl, the Nahua word for water.

This would seem to suggest that the Mayas and the plateau-living Nahua were in close contact by the time of the first incarnation of Quetzalcóatl, for which the Maya had their own equivalent deity – Kukulcán. It is interesting to note that the quetzal bird which is symbolically included in the name Quetzalcóatl is common to the Maya lands, but is not found anywhere that would have been inhabited by the Nahua-speaking peoples. It might simply be that the deity was common to both people at one time, the Maya retaining the name Kukulcán, while the Nahua took his title Quetzalcóatl. In this manner both Maya- and Nahua-speaking peoples had erected a consistent, meaningful and cosmically complete mythological figure who was simultaneously water, Earth (the serpent) and air (the quetzal bird).

Quetzalcóatl is thus a representation of a ladder between the heavens and the Earth, a ladder that he himself established and climbed. His name also has a secondary meaning: precious twin. His mythical twin was the dog XÓLOTL, the planet Venus as the EVENING STAR. This concept may have originated with a CHICHIMEC king and explorer of that name, but the twinship possibly has a more profound meaning, for the spiritual companionship of a dog is extended into Aztec belief as the soul that guides the human soul to the Underworld. His twinship is actually a very complex affair; as Venus, his twin is Xólotl but, as the Sun, his twin is a tiger or an ocelot. While the dog would accompany the soul into the Underworld forever, the ocelot would accompany the Sun and Venus through the Underworld to re-emerge again. As the ocelot is a nobler creature than the dog, it can easily be assumed that this is why the ocelot was allotted the higher task. At dawn, when Quetzalcóatl reappears, the ocelot characteristically howls in welcome.

The two Quetzalcóatls blend history, both legendary and actual, and mythology in a confusing manner, where the outer limits of the heavens blend almost imperceptibly into the tangible Earth. There is evidence that at least one of the earthly Quetzalcóatls was king of TULA, ruler of the Toltecs, sometime during the tenth century AD, but this is far too late for that character to have been the discoverer of corn, and much later than the earliest images of the god-man. By that time Quetzalcóatl had already become a generic name for the priest-kings. Anyway, the name derives from the symbolism of myth and not from history, no matter how tempting the evidence to suggest otherwise.

One apparently humble band of Quetzalcóatl's followers had a profound impact on the society of ancient Central-America. These were the POCHTECA, 'merchants who lead', a guild of itinerant merchants who formed a central set of ethical principles that were to establish the cult of Quetzalcóatl wherever they went. Even though these merchants were hard-nosed business men, they readily disposed of all their riches at religious banquets. Their main purpose in travelling was not to accumulate wealth but rather to convey their own ideas, ideas that stemmed from their single aim – to search for the Land of the Sun, the domain from which Quetzalcóatl originated, and to which he had later returned. Though they openly worshipped Quetzalcóatl, their patron deity was YIA-CATECUHTLI.

Quetzalpetlatl CENTRAL AMERICA (Aztec)

The sister of QUETZALCÓATL, the earthly incarnation who was, according to some stories, meant to have been seduced by her brother during his torment in TOLLAN at the hands of TEZCATLIPOCA, this seduction being one of the reasons why Quetzalcóatl had to leave the city. Other accounts simply say that Quetzalcóatl seduced a maiden and make no reference to whether or not this maiden was related.

Quetzpallin CENTRAL AMERICA (Aztec)

The fourth day of the twenty-day MONTH[1] that was used by the AZTEC people. Quetzpallin symbolized the lizard, represented the south and was presided over by HUE-HUECÓYOTL.

Quiahuitl CENTRAL AMERICA (Aztec)

The nineteenth day of the AZTEC twenty-day MONTH[1] which symbolized the rain, represented the west and was presided over by CHANTICO.

Quiqre CENTRAL AMERICA (*Maya*)
One of the eleven terrible lords of XI-
BALBA.

Quiqrixgag CENTRAL AMERICA (*Maya*)
One of the eleven terrible lords of XI-
BALBA.

Quiqxil CENTRAL AMERICA (*Maya*)
One of the eleven terrible lords of XI-
BALBA.

Quito SOUTH AMERICA – ECUADOR
   (*Inca*)
City in Ecuador that was the capital of the
northern half of the INCA empire after it
had been split between ATAHUALPA and
HUÁSCAR following the death of their father HUAYNA-CAPAC in 1525. Atahualpa
ruled from Quito and sought to reunite the
Inca empire when he overthrew his
brother in 1532, but his dominion was to
be cut short by the arrival of the Spanish

who overthrew the kingdom and killed
Atahualpa.

Quiyauhtonatiuh CENTRAL AMERICA –
   MEXICO (*Aztec*)
'Rain Sun', the ruler of the third era of the
creation known as the THIRD SUN, which
ended in a deluge of fire and red-hot
stones (perhaps a remembrance of violent
volcanic activity) in which only one pair of
humans survived.

Qumoqums NORTH AMERICA (*Modoc*)
The creator who dived into the depths of
Lake TULE in an attempt to bring up a
handful of soil with which to create the
world. On his fifth dive he succeeded and
laid the handful of silt next to the lake. He
proceeded to spread it out until it covered
the entire world. Then he formed the
mountains and the rivers before finally
pulling the trees and the plants out of the
ground.

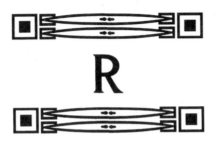

R

Rabbit NORTH AMERICA
An alternative for the Great HARE in many cultures.

Rada loa HAITI (*Voodoo*)
The generic name given to the chief group of VOODOO deities which originate from Benin (Dahomey) on the West African coast. In direct contrast to the PETRA LOA, the Rada loa are dignified and benevolent, and are organized in a manner reflecting the hierarchical organization that existed in the ancient kingdom of Dahomey.

Raimondi SOUTH AMERICA – PERU
(*Chavin*)
The name given to a representation of an anthropomorphic deity found in the ancient CHAVIN kingdom on the Peruvian coast. It shows a man having serpentine locks and feline features. Another stele, called EL LANZÓN, has also been discovered, though to date its true purpose, other than as a religious idol, has not been accurately determined.

Rainbow

1 NORTH AMERICA – NORTHWEST COAST (*Kwakiutl*)
The rainbow is sometimes named as the central pole of the Arctic home of the CANNIBAL MOTHER[3] – BAXBAKUALA-NUCHSIWAE.

2 CENTRAL AMERICA – MEXICO (*Aztec*)
Said to have been invented by CHAL-CHIUHTLICUE to be used as a spiritual bridge between heaven and Earth without which mankind could not survive.

3 SOUTH AMERICA – COLOMBIA (*Chibcha*)
The incarnation of BOCHICA in answer to the prayers of mankind to be saved from the flood raised by CHIBCHACUM who had grown tired of mankind's petty bickering. Bochica as the rainbow struck the rocks which split open. As they did so, the waters flowed away, thus creating the great waterfall TE-QUENDAMA.

4 NORTH AMERICA – WOODLANDS (*Iroquois*)
The wife of HINO.

Rainier, Mount NORTH AMERICA – WEST COAST (*Skagit*)
The centre of Mount Rainier National Park in Washington State, rising to 14,000 feet. Mount Rainier was known as TAKO-BAH to the SKAGIT who say that, together with KOBATH (the native name for Mount BAKER) these were the only two sacred mountains not to be totally submerged in the great FLOOD[6].

Rairu SOUTH AMERICA – BRAZIL (*Kadevo*)
The son of KARU who, together with his father, stumbled about in the darkness in the earliest days of the creation. Rairu tripped over a bowl-shaped rock which his father told him to carry on his head where it grew and grew until it formed the sky. Rairu honoured his father as the sky-maker, but Karu became aware that his son was more knowledgeable than himself and turned against him, so Rairu had to flee and hide in the UNDERWORLD.

Karu sought out his son and was about to dispose of him when Rairu told his father that he had discovered people in the Underworld who would come and serve them. Karu spared his son who led the first people up on to the Earth where they were divided into tribes according to the colour of their skin and their looks. Those who were lazy were transformed into bats, pigs, butterflies and birds.

Raphaél HAITI (*Voodoo*)

The Roman Catholic Saint Raphael who is regarded as a LOA by some VOODOO cultists.

Ravagé HAITI (*Voodoo*)

One of the many LOA of the VOODOO religion.

Raven NORTH AMERICA

The TRICKSTER who is common among a great many North American AMERINDIAN peoples. He is perhaps best known as YETL. Raven also appears in the HARE cycle of the MONTAGNAIS where he is the first to make the attempt to recover a single speck of soil so that MÄNÄBUSCH might recreate the Earth after the FLOOD[3].

Red World NORTH AMERICA –
SOUTHWEST (*Navajo*)

One of the subterranean worlds encountered by the NAVAJO during their ascent through a number of worlds before emerging on to the Earth (see ASCENT OF THE NAVAJO). In this world four streams flowed from the centre of the Earth to the four cardinal points, and thence into the surrounding seas. The people who began life in this world were mostly insects, though bats flew through the air and, according to some versions, the first man ATSE HASTIN, the first woman ATSE ESTSAN, and COYOTE, the TRICKSTER, were also created in this world.

revenant HAITI (*Voodoo*)

A spirit of the dead who, feeling neglected for whatever reason, returns to plague their living relatives. A revenant is not, regardless of the similarity, to be confused with a ZOMBIE.

Resurrection CENTRAL AMERICA –
MEXICO (*Aztec*)

One of the four giants who were placed at the four corners of the Earth to hold the heavens up at the start of the FIFTH SUN era, the other three giants being called FALLING EAGLE, SERPENT OF OBSIDIAN KNIVES and THORNY FLOWERS. QUETZAL-CÓATL and TEZCATLIPOCA also lent a hand, the former becoming the PRECIOUS TREE, and the latter the TREE OF MIRRORS.

Rhpisunt NORTH AMERICA –
NORTHWEST COAST (*Haida*)

'Bear-Mother', the wife of DZARILAW.

Rock-Crystal Boy NORTH AMERICA –
SOUTHWEST (*Navajo*)

During the creation (see ASCENT OF THE NAVAJO), Rock-Crystal Boy was set on the easternmost sacred mountain of the NAVAJO, PELADO PEAK, along with ROCK-CRYSTAL GIRL, by ATSE HASTIN and ATSE ESTSAN after they had formed the land. Rock-Crystal Boy later gave minds to the first man, formed from the ears of white corn, and the first woman, formed from the ears of yellow corn.

Rock-Crystal Girl NORTH AMERICA –
SOUTHWEST (*Navajo*)

The companion of ROCK-CRYSTAL BOY with whom she was set on PELADO PEAK, the easternmost of the sacred mountains of the NAVAJO, by ATSE HASTIN and ATSE ESTSAN after they had created the Navajo land (see ASCENT OF THE NAVAJO).

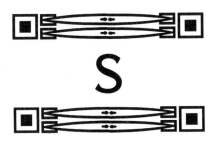

S

Sac-Nicté CENTRAL AMERICA (*Maya*)
Princess who was loved by, but did not
love, TA-ITZÁ. After he had abducted her,
following her betrothal to ULMIL ITZÁHAL,
and had shown her to his people in PETÉN,
she drowned herself in nearby Lake PETÉN
ITZÁ.

Saiyamkoob CENTRAL AMERICA –
YUCATÁN, MEXICO (*Modern Maya*)
The generic name for the 'adjusters',
dwarfs who lived at the start of time and
built the cities that now lie in ruins. They
were nourished by food that was sent down
to them via a living rope that stretched
from Earth into the heavens. However,
one day the rope was cut, from which
blood freely flowed, and Earth and heaven
were separated. At this time everything
was still in darkness but when the Sun
appeared, shortly after the living rope had
been cut, its rays turned the Saiyamkoob
to stone, their petrified figures still being
visible among the ruins of their cities.

Sajama, Mount SOUTH AMERICA –
BOLIVIA (*Aymará*)
The mountain that was formed when VIR-
ACOCHA flung a stone at Mount MURUR-
ATA for grumbling in jealousy over Vir-
acocha's apparent favouritism towards
Mount ILLIMANI. The stone decapitated
Mount Mururata, its peak flying through
the air to form Mount Sajama as it fell
back to Earth.

Sakuru NORTH AMERICA – GREAT
PLAINS (*Skidi Pawnee*)
The spirit of the Sun who was set in the
eastern sky to give light and warmth to the
Earth by TIRAWA. Later Sakuru impregnated PAH, the spirit of the Moon, at Tirawa's beckoning. Their union produced a
son who was set on the Earth together
with the daughter of BRIGHT STAR and
GREAT STAR, these two children becoming
the progenitors of the human race.

Salish NORTH AMERICA – NORTHWEST
COAST
One of the indigenous North American
AMERINDIAN peoples who inhabited a part
of the NORTHWEST COAST culture region,
together with the BELLA COOLA, CHINOOK,
HAIDA, KLAMATH, KWAKIUTL, NOOTKA and
TSHIMSHIAN Indians, tribes which speak
different languages. The Salish should not
be confused with the SELISH.

Samedi, Baron HAITI (*Voodoo*)
'Baron Saturday', an important LOA of the
cemetery.

San Francisco, Mount NORTH AMERICA
– SOUTHWEST (*Navajo*)
One of the sacred peaks of the NAVAJO
land that was formed by ATSE ESTSAN and
ATSE HASTIN, upon which they set WHITE-
CORN BOY and YELLOW-CORN GIRL.

San Juan, Mount NORTH AMERICA –
SOUTHWEST (*Navajo*)
One of the sacred peaks that were formed
by ATSE HASTIN and ATSE ESTSAN when
they created the NAVAJO land, and the one
upon which they set POLLEN BOY and
GRASSHOPPER GIRL.

Santeria CUBA
The name given to the worship of African
deities on Cuba, deities that predominantly originate with the Yoruba people of
Nigeria.

Second Sun CENTRAL AMERICA –
MEXICO (*Aztec*)
The second era of the creation, the Sun of
Air that represented that era of pure spirit
that might, at some later date, become
incarnate. The era came to an end as the
redeeming principle of life was absent, and
those people who had been created were
turned into monkeys. One account of the
FIVE SUNS says that a single couple were
able to escape the cataclysmic end to this
era, and took the gift of fire forward into
the THIRD SUN era, though that fire was
ultimately to bring about the end of that
era.

Sedit NORTH AMERICA – SOUTHWEST
COAST (*Wintun*)
COYOTE, the TRICKSTER. He appears in the
story of the HUS brothers who were sent
down to Earth by OLELBIS to prepare the
Earth for the creation of man. The two
Hus started to build a stone ladder
between the Earth and OLELPANTI
(heaven), but were interrupted in their
work by Sedit who, professing great wisdom, asked them who had come up with
such a stupid idea. Surely, he said, mankind would only have to climb the ladder
when they grew old to once again become
young. They would have no need for children and no purpose to life. Perhaps it
would be better, he added, if mankind

should have to suffer the grief of bereavement, but also experience the joy of children.

The Hus brothers took some convinc-
ing, but finally tore down the ladder,
though the younger of the two reminded
Sedit that he too would now have to suffer
death. Too late, Sedit realized his mistake
and in desperation made himself a pair of
wings from sunflowers and tried to fly up to
Olelpanti, but the Sun withered the flowers and he crashed to Earth and was killed.
From that day to this, mankind and all the
living things on the Earth have a finite life
span.

Sedna NORTH AMERICA – ALASKA
(*Inuit*)
Known as NERRIVIK to the INUIT of Greenland, and also called ARNARKUSUAGSAK or
ARNAKUAGSAK, and NULIAJOQ, Sedna is
the GREAT GODDESS of the Inuit. Unlike
most peoples, where the Great Goddess is
the Earth Goddess, to the Inuit, whose
survival depends on the sea, Sedna is a
water-spirit. However, she shares all the
archetypal aspects of the Great Goddess,
and has an ambivalent nature, being simultaneously the source of all life and
ruler of the dead.

Sedna was born to two giants and immediately proved to have an insatiable
appetite, an appetite that manifested itself
one night when she started to chew her
sleeping parents. Aghast, they snatched up
the infant and carried her to their *umiak*
(hunting canoe), and paddled far out to
sea where they threw her overboard.
Sedna clung on to the sides of the canoe,
so her parents cut off her fingers and she
sank beneath the waves. There she became the ruler of the ocean depths, governing both the sea and all its creatures
who were born from her severed fingers.

When Inuit hunters are unable to find
any prey, their ANGAKOK sends his spirit
down to plead with the goddess. To reach

her home, the ankgakok's spirit must firstly pass through the land of the dead; then it must navigate an icy whirlpool which threatens to engulf him. Next the spirit must pass a massive cauldron full of boiling seals, evade the fierce guard-dog of Sedna and then cross an abyss on a knife-edge before arriving at Sedna's beautiful palace. There the spirit dances for Sedna. Finally, induced into helping, Sedna either tells the angakok's spirit that his people must move and build a new settlement, or she agrees to send them seals and other prey.

Selish NORTH AMERICA – WOODLANDS
One of the indigenous IROQUOIS-speaking North American AMERINDIAN peoples who inhabited a small part of the Great Lakes area within the WOODLANDS culture region together with their linguistic neighbours, the CHEROKEE, HURON, MOHAWK and ONEIDA. The Selish were frequently involved in internecine warfare with these tribes – warfare that ended during the sixteenth century with the foundation of the LEAGUE OF THE LONG HOUSE at the instigation of HAIOWATHA. The Selish are one of the oldest of all the North American tribes and should not be confused with the SALISH.

Selu NORTH AMERICA – WOODLANDS
(*Cherokee*)
The wife of KANATI, the first man, and thus, with him, the ancestor of the CHERO-KEE people.

Seneca NORTH AMERICA – WOODLANDS
One of the indigenous North American AMERINDIAN peoples who, along with the CAYUGA, MOHAWK, ONEIDA and ONON-DAGA, was one of the founder nations of the LEAGUE OF THE LONG HOUSE. This confederation was traditionally founded in 1570 by HAIOWATHA and was strengthened in 1715 when the TUSCARORA tribe, who had previously opposed the formation of the confederation, joined the league.

Senotlke NORTH AMERICA – NORTHWEST COAST (*Squawmish*)
The serpentine monster that is an important TOTEM of the Northwest Coastal region.

Senx NORTH AMERICA – NORTHWEST COAST (*Bella Coola*)
'Sacred One' or 'Our Father', the creator and spirit of the Sun who rules the House of MYTHS in the lower heaven where all the gods who are subordinate to QAMAITS live. He is helped in his role as the creator by ALKUNTAM.

Seqinek NORTH AMERICA – ARCTIC (*Inuit*)
The spirit of the Sun who is of extreme importance to a people who spend a great deal of their lives in darkness.

Serpent of the Obsidian Knives CENTRAL AMERICA – MEXICO (*Aztec*)
The name given to one of the four pillars, at the world's cardinal points, that support the heavens, and which symbolizes the principle of sacrifice that is needed for incarnation – a perpetual cycle that cannot be escaped except through resurrection and the growth of flowers. However, even flowers can have thorns, thorns that illustrate that nothing in creation can escape the duality of matter: suffering and beauty. The Serpent of Obsidian Knives was originally perceived as a giant, the other three being called FALLING EAGLE, RESURRECTION and THORNY FLOWERS. Set in position at the start of the era of the FIFTH SUN, they were assisted in their task by QUETZALCÓATL and TEZCATLIPOCA who,

in this context, became known as the PRE-CIOUS TREE and the TREE OF MIRRORS respectively.

serviteur HAITI (*Voodoo*)
The name given to an initiate who is possessed by a LOA during cult rites.

Seven C'Haban CENTRAL AMERICA
(*Maya*)
The seventh day of the MAYA CREATION[4] on which MONTH[2] created the Earth itself. Seven C'Haban should not be confused with C'HABAN, the seventeenth day of the AGES OF MAN.

Shakanli NORTH AMERICA –
WOODLANDS (*Choctaw*)
The serpent-monster (cf. SENOTLKE).

Shakuru NORTH AMERICA – GREAT
PLAINS (*Pawnee*)
The spirit of the Sun.

shaman WIDESPREAD
The name given to priestly magicians and seers who practise a form of what is now popularly known as 'charismatic religion', and is possibly one of the world's oldest religious doctrines. The word shaman (feminine: *shamanka*) means 'one who is excited' or 'one who is raised up'. The shaman, or more rarely shamanka, is thought to have the power of entering the spirit world at will where he, or she, can either elicit the help of the spirits, or even command them. In some cases the journey taken by the spirit of the shaman is symbolized by his climbing a ladder or a tree. In others he flies, either in bird form, or even on a flying horse. He has the power to send his own spirit forth in any form he chooses to summon other spirits, and to exorcise those who cause illness or other harm.

Many North American Indian myths concern the powers and exploits of the shaman. While in some cases the shaman inherits his role, it is more common for him to be summoned by the spirits, usually against his will, who drive him out into the wilds in great anguish until he undergoes an ecstatic experience, best described as enlightenment. He then accepts his vocation, having had all the secrets of the universe revealed to him, and having acknowledged his particular spiritual aids and guides.

The idea of shamanism is not confined to the AMERINDIAN peoples, among whom the principle is almost universal, but can be found among many cultures worldwide. African 'doctors' and Haitian VOODOO priests have a similar role to play, as do the spiritual healers and exorcists of western Christian and spiritual cults.

Shango HAITI (*Voodoo*)
An important LOA whose origins lies with the Yoruba (Nigerian) god of lightning.

Shasta, Mount NORTH AMERICA –
NORTHWEST COAST (*Klamath*)
The mountain that was created by KEMUSH who set GREY WOLF on its slopes.

Shel NORTH AMERICA – NORTHWEST
COAST (*Klamath*)
The Sun who was followed by KEMUSH and SUN HALO right to the edge of darkness from whence Kemush and his daughter, EVENING SKY, went to the lodges of the spirits that lived in the PLACE OF THE DARK. There, for five days and five nights, Kemush and Evening Sky danced with the spirits in a circle around their fire until Shel was called into the world. As his light flooded into the Place of the Dark, all the spirits turned into dried bones.

Kemush collected a sack full of these bones and then followed Shel back to the very edge of the world, scattering pairs of bones as he went over the mountains, valleys and seashore. These bones turned into the various peoples of the region, the CHIPMUNK, the MAIDU, the MAKLAK and the KLAMATH, and thus the world was populated. With the creation now complete, Kemush followed Shel's trail to the very summit of the sky where he built his lodge, and there he still lives, with Sun Halo and his daughter Evening Sky.

shilup NORTH AMERICA – WOODLANDS (*Choctaw*)
An indwelling spirit of a type similar to the MANITO.

Shilup Chito Osh NORTH AMERICA – WOODLANDS (*Choctaw*)
The GREAT SPIRIT.

Shipololo NORTH AMERICA – PUEBLO, SOUTHWEST (*Zuñi*)
The 'Place of Mist and Cloud' where the ten CORN MAIDENS hid for four years until they were discovered by the two witches, who had been the last of the ZUÑI to emerge from the UNDERWORLD. The two witches presented the Corn Maidens with gifts of seeds of maize and squash before going on to tell their people of them. Having been presented to the people, the Corn Maidens were scared by the thoughts of PAYATAMI and fled back to Shipololo. Here they were hidden in a spring under the wings of a duck until they were persuaded to return to the people for one last time, after which they went back to Shipololo where they lived in a cedar bower roofed with clouds.

Shiwanni NORTH AMERICA – PUEBLO, SOUTHWEST (*Zuñi*)
A primordial being, the husband of SHIWANOKIA. He existed long before AWONAWILONA, the GREAT SPIRIT, and either the Sun or the Moon. After Awonawilona had created the clouds and the oceans, Shiwanni thought that he too would like to create something of beauty and decided to make

a myriad of lights for the night sky. Thus he blew multicoloured bubbles from his saliva into the sky where they became the stars.

Shiwanokia NORTH AMERICA – PUEBLO, SOUTHWEST (*Zuñi*)
The primordial wife of SHIWANNI who, after her husband had created the stars, herself created AWITELIN TSITA, the EARTH MOTHER, from her saliva.

Shooting Star NORTH AMERICA – SOUTHWEST COAST (*Wintun*)
One of the three beings who, along with FIRE DRILL and BUCKEYE BUSH, set the world on fire to avenge the theft of FLINT, and thus destroyed the first attempt at the creation by OLELBIS.

Shoshone NORTH AMERICA – GREAT PLAINS
Indigenous North American AMERINDIAN people from the GREAT PLAINS culture region. The most famous of the Shoshonean-speaking peoples were the COMANCHE of Texas.

shtabai CENTRAL AMERICA – YUCATÁN, MEXICO (*Modern Maya*)
Generic name given to demons who may take either male or female form, in the latter being blamed for enticing men to their ruin.

Sia NORTH AMERICA – PUEBLO, SOUTHWEST
PUEBLO-dwelling indigenous North American AMERINDIAN people from the southwest of the country. They are closely related to the ZUÑI and share many of their customs, rites and beliefs.

Sibu CENTRAL AMERICA – PANAMA (*Bribri and Borcua*)
The GREAT SPIRIT.

Sicasica, Mount SOUTH AMERICA –
BOLIVIA (*Aymará*)
One of the two ACHACHILAS of SUCRÉ, the
other being Mount CHURUQUILLA. The
pair are sometimes said to embody a male
and a female spirit, that of Sicasica manifesting itself at times as a seductive, yet
unapproachable young woman.

Sila Inua NORTH AMERICA – ARCTIC
(*Inuit*)
'Lord of Power', a personification of the
mythical animistic power which SHAMANS
can call upon and command.

Simba-La Source HAITI (*Voodoo*)
This LOA is most probably a variant of
SIMBI LAOKA.

Simbi (Laoka) HAITI (*Voodoo*)
One of the many LOA of the VOODOO cult
who have their origins in the Congo region
of Africa, this loa possibly deriving from
the similarly named Congolese deity
Simbi.

Sinaa SOUTH AMERICA – BRAZIL (*Xingú*)
The heroic son of DUCÁ.

Sinchi Roca SOUTH AMERICA (*Inca*)
The legendary second ruler of the INCAS
whose mother was said to have dressed
him magnificently and placed him in a
cave mouth, after she had started the ru-
mour that the Sun was about to send the
people a leader. When the people encountered Sinchi Roca, they were so impressed
by the finery in which he was decked that
they readily accepted him. The story possibly refers to an earlier rite, and is sometimes told of the great MANCO CAPAC.

Sio Calako NORTH AMERICA – PUEBLO,
SOUTHWEST (*Hopi*)
A mythical giant about whom nothing else
is known or recorded. It is possible that Sio

Calako was a rain-spirit due to the similarity of his name and that of SIO HUMIS.

Sio Humis NORTH AMERICA – PUEBLO,
SOUTHWEST (*Hopi*)
The name of a rain-spirit, and possibly the
brother of SIO CALAKO.

Sioux NORTH AMERICA – GREAT PLAINS
Famous indigenous North American
AMERINDIAN people who were the principal group of the DAKOTA family, who entered the GREAT PLAINS from c. AD 800
from the northwest, and are today to be
found in South Dakota and Nebraska. The
Sioux are possibly most famous for their
defeat of General George Custer at Little
Bighorn, Montana, under their chiefs
Crazy Horse and Sitting Bull. As a result of
this, Congress abrogated the Fort Laramie
treaty of 1868, a treaty that had given the
Sioux a large area of the Black Hills of
Dakota. In 1980 the Sioux nation was
awarded $160 million in compensation.

Sipapu NORTH AMERICA – PUEBLO,
SOUTHWEST (*Zuñi*)
The name given to the hole through which
the ZUÑI emerged on to the Earth from the
UNDERWORLD.

Sisiri SOUTH AMERICA – GUYANA
(*Maipuri*)
The son of the creator PURRUNAMINARI
and TAPARIMARRU.

Sisiutl NORTH AMERICA – NORTHWEST
COAST (*Kwakiutl*)
One of the most important of the TOTEMIC
beings of the KWAKIUTL, and other AMER-
INDIAN peoples of the Northwest Coast of
North America. Sisiutl, a water-spirit, is
represented as a serpent-monster, a common characterization among Amerindian
peoples, having three heads, a human one
in the middle of two snakes heads. His skin
is so tough that not even the sharpest knife

can mark it, and yet it can be pierced with ease by a holly leaf. Sisiutl had the ability to change himself into a poisonous fish at will, though conversely he was a powerful friend to whosoever he might favour, particularly the tribal SHAMANS who would make potent medicine from 'pieces' of its body. The BELLA COOLA, the neighbours of the KWAKIUTL, say that Sisiutl's home is to be found in a lake situated behind the home of QAMAITS.

siudleratuin NORTH AMERICA (*Inuit*)
The name given to the spirits of the dead, i.e. ghosts.

Six Cib CENTRAL AMERICA (*Maya*)
The sixth day of the CREATION[4] on which MONTH[2] created the first candle and thus brought light into the world for the first time, as neither the Sun nor the Moon had yet been formed. Six Cib should not be confused with CIB, the sixteenth day of the AGES OF MAN.

Six Muluc CENTRAL AMERICA (*Maya*)
The nineteenth and penultimate day of the CREATION[4] on which MONTH[2] brought everything he had created to life. Six Muluc should not be confused with MULUC, the ninth day of the MAYA spiritual pilgrimage known as the AGES OF MAN.

Skagit NORTH AMERICA – WEST COAST
Indigenous AMERINDIAN people who came from the west coastal regions of North America, anywhere from the Canadian borders down to the north of present-day California.

Skidi Pawnee NORTH AMERICA – GREAT PLAINS
Indigenous North American AMERINDIAN people from the state of Nebraska which lies in the GREAT PLAINS culture region. The Skidi Pawnee are just one tribe of the people collectively known as the PAWNEE,

though the Skidi Pawnee exhibit beliefs and customs that are unlike the rest of the Pawnee nation.

skoyo NORTH AMERICA – PUEBLO, SOUTHWEST (*Sia*)
Generic name given to mythical man-eating monsters.

Sky-Elk NORTH AMERICA – WOODLANDS (*Iroquois*)
Spirit who came down to Earth to graze but was chased back up into the highest heaven by SOSONDOWAH.

Sky Father WIDESPREAD
A common concept among all the AMERINDIAN peoples, whether from north, south, or central America. The Sky Father was not necessarily the creator, though in a good many cases he was, but was the deity whose domain was the sky and who had overlordship over the Sun, the Moon, the stars, the wind, the rain, and anything and everything else that could possibly be connected with the sky. Usually the Sky Father and the EARTH MOTHER united, a union that in almost all instances produced TWIN HEROES.

Sky Youth NORTH AMERICA – WOODLANDS (*Kwakiutl*)
The killer of TSONOQUA, the CANNIBAL MOTHER[1] who had fallen in love with his reflection. Obviously Sky Youth did not reciprocate Tsonoqua's feelings.

Skyamsen NORTH AMERICA – NORTHWEST COAST (*Tlingit*)
The THUNDERBIRD.

Smohala NORTH AMERICA – OREGON
Born c.1820, this historical SHAMAN led the DREAMERS, a cult that was based on a mixture of Roman Catholicism and AMERINDIAN beliefs. In c.1860 he was challenged by a rival shaman called MOSES who

left him for dead beside a river. Smohala was carried downstream on the flood waters and was rescued by a white farmer. He then wandered extensively through the Southeast and into Mexico before he returned to Oregon. There he claimed to have actually drowned in the river, his spirit conversing with the GREAT SPIRIT who had rebuked him for abandoning the 'old ways' on favour of white man's religion. Smohala's 'miraculous' return convinced many people that he had been chosen by the Great Spirit to be his spokesman, and that he was speaking the words of the Great Spirit when he said that the Indians had owned the Earth long before white men appeared and therefore had a responsibility to take it back again. The cult, which at one stage had a very large following, proved a major obstacle to US government policy, and took its name from the trance-like state the shamans entered when they conversed with and sought the advice of the gods.

Snake NORTH AMERICA – SOUTHWEST (Navajo)

One of the four animal spirits that appear in the myth of the HOZONI chant. Along with BEAR, FROG and TURTLE, Snake went to an undersea village to capture two of its young women, Frog and Turtle actually entering the village to carry out the abduction. However, they were surprised in their attempt and had to kill the unfortunate maidens whom they quickly scalped, the hair of the older girl being decorated with white shell jewellery and that of the younger with turquoise. Frog and Turtle only just escaped the village, having survived the villagers' attempts to roast and then to drown them. Rejoining Bear and Snake, all four set off for home.

En route they met eight men from their own village who saw the scalps and wanted them for themselves. As the animals would not give them up, two of the men

suggested holding a shooting match, offering their own daughters as the prizes to the victors. Both Bear and Snake protested that they were far too old to participate, but when forced to do so, they not only won the shooting match but also every other contest that was subsequently suggested. However, not one of the men was willing to give up his daughter, so they all set off for the village to hold a scalp dance.

Bear and Snake did not attempt to keep up with their younger companions, nor did they enter the village to join the dance. Instead they built themselves a shelter outside the village where they sat down to smoke, the delicious aroma of their tobacco wafting into the village, the perfume of which enticed the two girls who were their rightful prizes, to seek out its source. When they came to the shelter, the two girls found two handsome youths – Bear and Snake in disguise – Bear being dressed all in black, and Snake in the colours of the rainbow. The girls consented to stay with the men and soon fell asleep amid the intoxicating smoke of the tobacco.

The next morning, much to their horror, they found that the handsome youths of the previous night had become old men. The younger girl, GLISMA, tried to escape, but found the door guarded by serpents which seemed to grow more excited the more afraid she became. However, when she feigned disinterest, the snakes ignored her and let her pass unharmed. Knowing that her family would kill her if she returned to the village, Glisma instead waded downstream in order to hide her trail from the people of her village, and from Bear and Snake.

Eventually she came to a lake near the PLACE OF EMERGENCE where she was met by the SNAKE PEOPLE who asked her where she had come from and what her purpose was. She told them all what had befallen and they, rewarding her honesty, took her down into their UNDERWORLD home where they assured her that she would be safe. However, some time later Snake once again came to her in the guise of a handsome youth, and Glisma once again fell for him. Snake then taught her all the painting rituals and words of the Hozoni chant and, after two years when she began to feel homesick, Snake told her to return to her village and teach the Hozoni to her brother so that he might become a powerful healer.

Snake Dance NORTH AMERICA – PUEBLO, SOUTHWEST (*Hopi*)
A biennial fertility and rain dance that alternates with the FLUTE DANCE. The Snake Dance includes both public and secret rites that involve live snakes, the celebrants belonging to two societies – the Snake Priests and the Antelope Priests. The main ritual involves the celebration of the marriage of SNAKE YOUTH (possibly a sky-god) to SNAKE GIRL, an UNDERWORLD inhabitant whose offspring included both reptiles and the human ancestors of the HOPI Snake Clan. At the conclusion of the rites the snakes are taken out into the fields where they are released to carry the prayers of the Hopi for rain and good harvests to the spirits of the Underworld.

Snake Girl NORTH AMERICA – PUEBLO, SOUTHWEST (*Hopi*)
An UNDERWORLD fertility spirit whose marriage to SNAKE YOUTH is celebrated in the biennial SNAKE DANCE. She is said to have been the mother of both reptiles and the human ancestors of the HOPI Snake Clan.

Snake People NORTH AMERICA – SOUTHWEST (*Navajo*)
The name given to an UNDERWORLD race who gave sanctuary to GLISMA after she had escaped from SNAKE. However, Snake

found her and taught her all the rites and rituals of the HOZONI chant.

Snake Youth NORTH AMERICA – PUEBLO, SOUTHWEST (*Hopi*)
Possibly a sky-spirit, Snake Youth is celebrated every other year in the SNAKE DANCE which celebrates his marriage to SNAKE GIRL, an UNDERWORLD fertility spirit.

Sneneik(ulala) NORTH AMERICA – NORTHWEST COAST (*Kwakiutl*)
The CANNIBAL MOTHER[1] who is also called BAXBAKUALANUCHSIWAE, but is most commonly known as the KWAKIUTL goddess TSONOQUA.

Soatsaki NORTH AMERICA – GREAT PLAINS (*Blackfoot*)
'Feather-Woman', the mother of POÏA.

Sobo-si HAITI (*Voodoo*)
Possibly deriving from a West African deity, this LOA is portrayed as a handsome soldier.

Solongo loa HAITI (*Voodoo*)
Generic name given for VOODOO spirits, who derive from the gods of the Congolese Solongo people.

Solophine HAITI (*Voodoo*)
One of the numerous LOA of the VOODOO religion.

Song of Hiawatha, The
Famous epic poem by Henry Wadsworth LONGFELLOW that purports to tell the story of HIAWATHA, but is in fact based on the HARE cycle of the WOODLANDS tribes. The poem relates little to the actual historical facts behind the life of Hiawatha, the name itself being suspect (the true spelling is HAIOWATHA). It is, however, essential reading for any student of the myths of the North American AMERINDIAN peoples, and

not just those of the Woodlands culture region, for it introduces and explains – albeit poetically – many of the customs, doctrines and beliefs that were common to almost all native North American peoples.

Sosondowah NORTH AMERICA –
  WOODLANDS (*Iroquois*)
'Great-Night', a hunter who chased the spirit SKY-ELK, who had come down to Earth to graze, right back up into the highest heaven, way beyond the Sun. There Sosondowah was caught by DAWN who made him her watchman, from which position he looked down on the Earth, and one day caught sight of the beautiful GLEN-DENWITHA with whom he was immediately smitten. In the spring Sosondowah took the form of a bluebird and descended to Earth to woo her. In the summer he assumed the guise of a blackbird; and in the autumn he became a night-hawk, and carried her off. Dawn found out about Sosondowah's trips to the Earth and angrily tied him to her door-posts and transformed Glendenwitha into a star which she then placed in Sosondowah's forehead, forever beyond his reach.

Sousson-Pannan HAITI (*Voodoo*)
An extremely ugly LOA who lives in the air and is covered with weeping sores. Sousson-Pannan is both wicked and pitiless, and is especially fond of drinking both alcohol and blood.

soyoko NORTH AMERICA – PUEBLO,
  SOUTHWEST (*Hopi*)
Generic term applied to a host of mythical monsters.

Spider-Woman NORTH AMERICA –
  SOUTHWEST (*Navajo*)
An UNDERWORLD being whose existence was discovered by the twins NAYANEZGANI

and THOBADZISTSHINI who saw the smoke rising from her home near DSILNAOTIL. She welcomed the twins to her home soon after they had set out to travel to the home of their father TSHOHANOAI. She diligently tried to dissuade the twins from undertaking their intended journey, warning them that the trail was both long and hazardous. When she realized that they would not be persuaded otherwise, she gave them a spell and talismans to protect them from the dangers that lay ahead. The spell she told them to chant whenever they were in danger was:

Put your feet down with pollen.
Put your hands down with pollen.
Put your head down with pollen.
Your feet are pollen.
Your hands are pollen.
Your body is pollen.
Your mind is pollen.
Your voice is pollen.
The trail is beautiful.
Be still.

With the aid of this spell and the talismans that Spider-Woman gave them, the twins survived all the trials of the journey, as well as all the tests their father put them through before accepting them as his children.

Spirit Star NORTH AMERICA – GREAT
  PLAINS (*Pawnee and Delaware*)
The spirit placed in the southern sky by TIRAWA so that he would only be seen at irregular intervals on the Earth. It has never been established to any degree of certainty just which celestial object can be identified with Spirit Star.

Spirit World WIDESPREAD
The concept of the Spirit World is common to all AMERINDIAN peoples, whether from the North, the South, or the central regions. In almost all cases it is neither heaven nor hell, but simply a place to

which the spirits of the dead go, and where they will remain for all eternity. Several stories illustrate that man once did not consider death final, but through a variety of means, death became eternal, there never being any hope of return.

A PAWNEE story illustrates this point. A man who had lost his wife and son wandered across the prairie hoping that he soon would die and so join his dead spouse and their child. As he wandered, the spirits beseeched TIRAWA to take pity on him and allow the dead to return. Tirawa consented but set the condition that the living and the dead must live together for four days, neither touching the other, though they could communicate. This was agreed and all the Pawnee people gathered on the prairie to await the return of their loved ones. Across the vast expanse of the prairie a great cloud of dust drew near, out of which the spirits of all the dead Pawnee appeared. However, as soon as the man saw his wife and son, he could not contain his joy and seized them both to him, vowing silently that he would never let them go. All the other people screamed and in an instance the spirits of the dead disappeared. Thus, so the Pawnee say, death continued.

Another story, this time told by the Shahaptian Klickitat people of British Columbia, again illustrates that the spirits once decided that the dead could return, but later reversed their decision. In this story a young chief had died and was buried, as was the custom, on the island of the dead in the middle of a river. However, separated from his beautiful wife his spirit could not rest, so he appeared to her in a dream and told her to come to him. She paddled across the river at dusk and was welcomed by her husband. However, when she woke the next morning she found herself in a charnel-house in the arms of a skeleton. Disgusted, she immediately paddled home but her people

would not let her land, so she was forced to paddle back again. There she enjoyed the company of her husband every night. In due course she gave birth to a beautiful child, whom she completely swaddled and sent to her own mother with the instructions that she must not look at the child for ten days. The grandmother could not resist looking at the child who had been so miraculously born to her daughter, but as soon as she loosened the swaddling, the child died. The spirits decided then that the souls of the dead should no longer be allowed to return.

Star Creator SOUTH AMERICA – TIERRA DEL FUEGO (*Ona*)
Long ago, before the birth of mankind, the Earth was inhabited by white, bearded giants, and the Sun and Moon lived among them as husband and wife. Then the giants began to fight among themselves, so the Sun and Moon left the Earth and the creator sent down the red star (the planet Mars) who killed all the giants. Then Star Creator fashioned a man and a woman out of two lumps of clay, these people becoming the ancestors of the ONA.

Star-That-Does-Not-Move NORTH AMERICA – GREAT PLAINS (*Pawnee and Delaware*)
The personification of the Pole Star that was placed in the sky by TIRAWA, who made him the chief of all the star spirits. They included the four that had been specifically positioned as guardians of the four cardinal points whose task was to support the heavens.

Sucré SOUTH AMERICA – BOLIVIA (*Aymará*)
City of Bolivia, situated to the southeast of Lake POOPÓ and to the north of POTOSÍ, that the AYMARÁ said was guarded by the ACHACHILAS of Mount CHURUQUILLA and

Mount SICASICA, mountains that they said embodied two spirits, Churuquilla being male and Sicasica female.

Sugumonxe SOUTH AMERICA –
COLOMBIA (*Chibcha*)
'Disappearer', a variant name for NEMTEREQUETEBA.

Sugunsúa SOUTH AMERICA – COLOMBIA (*Chibcha*)
A variant name for NEMTEREQUETEBA that might in itself be a variant of SUGUMONXE, or vice versa.

Sun, City of the SOUTH AMERICA (*Inca*)
The popular name for CUZCO, the city founded by the CHILDREN OF THE SUN. The city had to be divided into two distinct regions as so many flocked to live there, the upper part being named HANAN CUZCO, and the lower part HURIN CUZCO.

Sun, Pyramid of the CENTRAL AMERICA – MEXICO (*Aztec*)
The unremarkable name by which a pyramid built at TEOTIHUACÁN to the worship and glorification of the Sun is known.

Sun-Bearer CENTRAL AMERICA – MEXICO (*Aztec*)
The title given to the deity that was considered the incarnation or personification of the Sun during any of the eras of the FIVE SUNS, the five stages of the AZTEC creation. It should be noted that this title was not solely confined to the Aztec people, and can be found used widely to both the north and the south.

Sun Dance NORTH AMERICA – GREAT PLAINS
The chief ritual of many of the AMERINDIAN peoples of the Plains region of North America. This annual festival usually lasted for eight days, though the length varied from tribe to tribe, and culminated in the building of a symbolic lodge that represents mankind's home. The central pole of the lodge denoted the distance between Earth and heaven and was decorated with symbols of the elemental powers. Warriors who had vowed their lives to the spirit of the Sun then led a dance around the pole, to which they were attached by ropes that were skewered under their pectoral and shoulder muscles. This ritual torture was not essential among all the Plains tribes; in fact, in some tribes this aspect was expressly forbidden as to these people the sight of even a single drop of blood during a ritual was an dire ill omen. The Sun Dance would finish with prayers to the Sun Father, Earth Mother, and the fertility spirit MORNING STAR to bless the celebrants.

Sun Halo NORTH AMERICA –
NORTHWEST COAST (*Klamath*)
Sky-spirit who summoned KEMUSH to follow the trail of SHEL, the Sun, right to the edge of darkness itself, Sun Halo accompanying him and his daughter EVENING SKY on the journey. Later, after Kemush had finished the creation of mankind, Sun Halo, Kemush and Evening Sky once again followed Shel, this time to the summit of the sky where Kemush built a lodge in which he, his daughter and Sun Halo live to this very day.

Sun of Earth CENTRAL AMERICA – MEXICO (*Aztec*)
Title by which the fourth era of the AZTEC creation, that of the FOURTH SUN, is sometimes known.

Sun of Water CENTRAL AMERICA – MEXICO (*Aztec*)
Title by which the fourth era of the AZTEC creation, that of the FOURTH SUN, is sometimes known.

Sussistinnako NORTH AMERICA – PUEBLO, SOUTHWEST (*Sia*)
'Spider', the first being who created the mothers of mankind as two sisters: UTSET who became the mother of the SIA, and

NOWUTSET who became the mother of everyone else, man and beast. Sussistinnako also created rain, thunder, lightning and the rainbow.

Sutalidihi NORTH AMERICA – WOODLANDS (*Cherokee*)
The spirit of the Sun.

Swaikhway NORTH AMERICA – NORTHWEST COAST (*Cowicha*)
A ritual that enacts the myth of a boy who, upon diving into a lake, discovered the spirits who lived there. They entertained the boy, gave him magical powers and sent him back to his people with a mask, known as the Swaikhway Mask, which the tribal elder would wear during the ritual.

Swaixwe NORTH AMERICA – NORTHWEST COAST (*Cowicha*)
A sky-spirit who descended from heaven to live in terrestrial lakes. It seems highly probable that Swaixwe was the spirit that the boy remembered in the SWAIKHWAY ritual, that came across at the bottom of the lake he dived into.

Swallow People NORTH AMERICA – SOUTHWEST (*Navajo*)
The inhabitants of the BLUE WORLD with whom the NAVAJO people lived for just twenty-four days before one of the Navajo committed adultery with the wife of the Swallow People's chief and were expelled. See ASCENT OF THE NAVAJO.

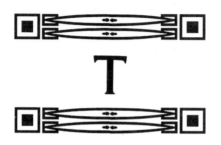

T

Ta-Itzá CENTRAL AMERICA – MEXICO
(*Maya*)
A high chief of the usurping ITZÁ family
that ruled over a large part of the MAYA
lands for centuries. He caused the death of
his beloved princess SAC-NICTÉ after she
had been betrothed to ULMIL ITZÁHAL. Ta-
Itzá abducted the princess and presented
her to his people in PETÉN, but she did not
love him and so drowned herself in nearby
PETÉN ITZÁ lake.

Taapac SOUTH AMERICA (*Collao*)
A variant of THUNAPA.

Tacanaymo SOUTH AMERICA (*Chimu*)
One of the names given to NAYMLAP.

Tacilluka, Mount SOUTH AMERICA –
PERU (*Quechua*)
Peruvian mountain on which HUALLALLO
CARUINCHO took refuge, after he had been
expelled from the forests by PARIACACA.

Tacuilla SOUTH AMERICA – BOLIVIA
(*Aymará*)
Chieftain whom, some say, brought the
URUS as slaves from the coast.

Tahit NORTH AMERICA – NORTHWEST
COAST (*Tlingit*)
The god of fate who determines the course
of man's life and lives in the northern
heaven.

tahmahnawis NORTH AMERICA –
NORTHWEST COAST (*Chinook*)
Name given to supernatural power, such
as the powers a SHAMAN would exhibit.

Taikomol NORTH AMERICA –
SOUTHWEST COAST (*Yuki*)
'He-Who-Goes-Alone', the creator.

Tajín CENTRAL AMERICA (*Totonac*)
The TOTONAC name for TEZCATLIPOCA in
his aspect as the rain-god.

Takobah NORTH AMERICA – WEST
COAST (*Skagit*)
The SKAGIT name for Mount RAINIER, one
of the two peaks that were not fully submerged in the great FLOOD[6], the other
being KOBATH, the Skagit name for Mount
BAKER.

Takuskanskan NORTH AMERICA –
GREAT PLAINS (*Dakota*)
The TRICKSTER and spirit of the wind.

Tamacauí SOUTH AMERICA – BRAZIL
(*Xingú*)
A legendary chief of immense physique
and strength who routed his people's enemies single-handed until all the hostile
tribes formed a confederacy against him.
Tamacauí fought on, even though all his
people were massacred. A long time later,
when his enemies were running short of
arrows, they rushed Tamacauí and tried to
crush him, but he fought them off and
killed them. As evening drew on, his

strength began to fail him and he sank slowly into the marshy ground. He was then easily overpowered and killed, and yet he still had the final victory, for his flesh was poisonous and those who ate him all died in agony.

Tambotocco SOUTH AMERICA (*Inca*)
The 'Place of the Hole' that is also called PACCARITAMBO, the 'Inn of Origin'. It was at this place from a cave with three mouths that the CHILDREN OF THE SUN were said to have emerged on to the Earth.

Tambu Quiru SOUTH AMERICA (*Inca*)
A place where the CHILDREN OF THE SUN camped and where they were visited by the spirit of AYAR CACHI, who told them to complete their journey and found their city at CUZCO.

Tamoanchan CENTRAL AMERICA – MEXICO (*Aztec*)
Place that was visited by the travellers from AZTLAN, and where all but four of the AMOXAOQUE who had left with them departed. From Tamoanchan the travellers journeyed on to TEOTIHUACÁN.

Tamosi(kabotano) SOUTH AMERICA – GUYANA (*Carib*)
'Ancient One', the supreme being whose variant of Tamosikabotano means 'Ancient-One-in-the-Sky'.

Tancanaymo SOUTH AMERICA – PERU (*Mochica*)
A giant who was said to have come to MOCHE valley, possibly from Ecuador, and there to have founded the CHIMOR civilization, though other accounts credit the foundation of this pre-INCA civilization to NAYMLAP.

tapacu SOUTH AMERICA (*Inca*)
Name given to the beautiful woollen tabards and cloaks that were the royal regalia of the INCAS.

Taparimarru SOUTH AMERICA – GUYANA (*Maipuri*)
The wife of the creator PURRUNAMINARI and the mother, by him, of SISIRI.

Taperinha SOUTH AMERICA – BRAZIL
Archaeological site on the AMAZON[1] river to the east of Santarem, Brazil, the discovery of which in 1991 provided evidence that an ancient 'New World' civilization existed between 6,000 and 8,000 years ago, and thus predated any of the Mexican or Andean cultures known to date.

TAqlikic NORTH AMERICA – NORTHWEST COAST (*Tlingit*)
'Hammer-Father', the name given to YETL, the RAVEN, who was so named after the impregnable rock ITC AK, because he was so tough and resilient, properties he shared with the rock.

Tarascan CENTRAL AMERICA – MEXICO
Indigenous Central-American AMERINDIAN people inhabiting what is today referred to as central Mexico, an area they shared with the ZACATECan people.

Tarhuyiawahku NORTH AMERICA – WOODLANDS (*Iroquois*)
The giant who holds up the skies.

tasoom NORTH AMERICA – GREAT PLAINS (*Cheyenne*)
The spirit of the individual (the soul). After death the tasoom separates from the body and journeys to the sky home of

219

HEAMMAWIHIO by travelling along the EKUTSIHIMMIYO, the 'Hanging Road' (the MILKY WAY[3]), that is suspended between and links heaven and Earth.

Taswiscana NORTH AMERICA –
WOODLANDS (Onondaga)

'Flint', one of the twin sons, the malevolent one and a personification of the OTKON, of GUSTS-OF-WIND and the WIND-RULER, whose fighting with his brother YOSKEHA while they were still in the womb caused the death of their mother. Taswiscana, obviously not wanting to be blamed for the death, managed to persuade their grandmother ATAENTSIC that Yoskeha was totally responsible for the death of Gusts-of-Wind. Ataentsic banished Yoskeha from the Earth, so he went to seek his father Wind-Ruler who gave him a bow and arrows and some maize, these gifts signifying Yoskeha's lordship of all the animals and plants of the Earth.

Taswiscana and Yoskeha then embarked on a life of bitter jealousy. Firstly, at Taswiscana's instigation, Ataentsic sprinkled ashes over the maize that Yoskeha had planted to feed mankind, and thus spoiled it. Then Taswiscana entered the fray himself by imprisoning all the animals his brother had created in a cave. Yoskeha managed to free the majority of them, but those that remained were transformed into the evil creatures that inhabit the UNDER-WORLD. Taswiscana then called on his ally HAIDU the hump-backed source of all disease and decay. Yoskeha, however, managed to overcome this formidable foe and in so doing obtained the secret lore of medicine and the rites of the tobacco ceremony that he later taught mankind.

Seeing all his attempts to thwart his brother were coming to nothing, Taswiscana, again with the help of Ataentsic, buried the Sun and Moon that had been created from the body of Gusts-of-Wind. Yoskeha managed to dig up the Sun with the help of the animals he had created. Taswiscana and Ataentsic pursued him, but Yoskeha managed to evade them by passing the Sun to the animals who ran a relay and thus saved the Sun so that it could provide light for the Earth.

Yoskeha next created man, and Taswiscana tried to emulate his brother, but all he managed to create were vile monsters. Having had enough of his brother, Yoskeha now banished him together with the monsters he had created, to the Underworld where he remains.

Tata CENTRAL AMERICA – MEXICO
(Aztec)

The husband of NENA. As the era of the FOURTH SUN drew to an end, the gods sent for Tata and Nena and told them to make a hole in a huge tree and hide in it. Thus they would be saved from the flood, but only if they ate no more than a single cob of maize each. Tata and Nena followed the gods' instructions and duly rode out the flood in complete safety. However, as the waters receded, they saw a fish which they caught and placed on a spit over a fire they built. The gods saw the smoke rising and were angry that their instructions should have been disobeyed. As a punishment they transformed both Tata and Nena into dogs and removed from them that portion of the brain which distinguishes man from the animals.

Tati-Turqui, Mount SOUTH AMERICA –
BOLIVIA (Aymará)

One of the two peaks, the other being Mount PARICHATA, that were honoured as the tutelary ACHACHILAS of POTOSÍ.

Tatu-Karaiá SOUTH AMERICA – BRAZIL
(Xingú)

A legendary race of people who were discovered by ancient XINGÚ explorers who were led to their underground homes by the columns of smoke that rose from their fires. Having been discovered, the Tatu-Karaiá came up to the Earth, but were all killed by the Xingú as they emerged.

Taureau HAITI (*Voodoo*)
'Bull', one of the numerous LOA of the VOODOO religion.

Tawiscara NORTH AMERICA – WOODLANDS (*Onondaga*)
A little used variant of TASWISCANA that appears to be simply a misspelling.

Tawiskaron NORTH AMERICA – WOODLANDS (*Iroquois*)
The brother of OTERONGTONGNIA and thus the grandson of AWENHAI. He and his brothers were enemies even before they were born, an enmity that continued after they had been delivered – Tawiskaron being born in the normal manner while his brother emerged through his mother's armpit which killed her.

Greatly displeased at the death of her daughter, Awenhai threw Oterongtongnia out and placed the dead body of her daughter on a tree, where it became the Sun. The head she placed in the branches of another tree where it became the Moon. Oterongtongnia made the Earth and all the good and beautiful things, while Tawiskaron jealously did his utmost to obstruct the good deeds of his brother and managed to spoil several perfectly good projects before Oterongtongnia built an immense fire and frightened him off. Then he pursued him with such fury that he shattered to pieces and formed the Rocky Mountains.

This story should be compared with the story of ATAENTSIC, YOSKEHA and TASWIS-CANA, as it is simply a variant of that legend.

Taxet NORTH AMERICA – NORTHWEST COAST (*Haida*)
'House Above', a god of the sky who receives the spirits of those who die violent deaths.

Taylor, Mount NORTH AMERICA – SOUTHWEST (*Navajo*)
The southernmost of the sacred mountains of the NAVAJO land that was created by ATSE HASTIN and ATSE ESTSAN, and on which they set TURQUOISE BOY and CORN GIRL.

Tchakabech NORTH AMERICAN – WOODLANDS (*Algonquian*)
A dwarf whose parents were eaten by a bear-chief from the UNDERWORLD and the Great HARE. Wanting to escape the same fate, Tchakabech climbed a tall tree into the sky where he was enchanted by the beauty of the heavenly realm, and so returned to Earth to fetch his young sister, for whom he built houses in the trees for her to rest in *en route*. During their long climb his sister's child broke off the branches below them so that no one could follow them, nor would they ever be able to return to the Earth. Once in the heavens, Tchakabech caught the Sun, some accounts saying that he used a noose made out of his sister's hair to do so. From that day, until a mouse nibbled through the noose and released the Sun, there was no light on Earth.

Tcochkut NORTH AMERICA – PUEBLO, SOUTHWEST (*Hopi*)
Semi-latinized variant of TCÜCHKUTI.

Tcolawitze NORTH AMERICA – PUEBLO, SOUTHWEST (*Hopi*)
The spirit of the fire.

Tcüchkuti NORTH AMERICA – PUEBLO, SOUTHWEST (*Hopi*)
The glutton-priest, a KATCHINA.

Teçacatetl CENTRAL AMERICA – MEXICO
(*Aztec*)
One of the AZTEC leaders who left their
ancestral homeland of AZTLAN to travel to
a new realm on the mainland, Aztlan
being described in the myths as an offshore
island.

Tecciztécatl CENTRAL AMERICA –
  MEXICO (*Aztec*)
'He-Who-Comes-From-the-Sea-Snail', a
title of METZTLI, though Tecciztécatl is
sometimes identified as the god or personification of the Moon who rules over the
drunken man while he is asleep, and also
when he awakens. The ancient NAHUA
observed Tecciztécatl in all his contra-
dictory states. They observed that when he
first appeared, he was 'like a bow, like a
bent straw lip ornament, a very tiny one.
He did not yet shine'. Every night he was
seen to grow larger until, after fifteen days,
they recorded that he was 'quite plump'.
When the sky darkened, he would appear
'like a large earthen skillet, very round and
circular, seeming to be a bright, deep red.
And after this, when he was already some
way on his travels, when he had risen, he
became white'. The Nahua then said 'Now
he puts out moonbeams'.
  A later story tells how the humble god
NANAUTZIN leaped into the fire and became the Sun. He was followed by Teccizt-
técatl who became the Moon as the fire
had died down in the interim and thus
became a lesser source of light. A variant
says that the two were both Suns at first,
but while the gods were playing with them,
one of the gods struck Tecciztécatl in the
face with a rabbit, an act that maimed and
dimmed him, so that he became the
Moon.
  The powers of the Sun and the Moon
were so feared by both the Nahua and the
AZTECs that eclipses of either were times of
profound fear, lest the powers of darkness
should forever consume them and throw
the world into perpetual darkness. Eclipses
of the Moon were especially feared by the
women, who thought that their unborn
children might be changed into mice.
Thus they placed obsidian in their mouths
so that they would not bear deformed
children.

Tecpatl CENTRAL AMERICA (*Aztec*)
The eighteenth day of the twenty-day
MONTH[1] employed by the AZTEC people
and which symbolized the stone or obsidian knife, represented the north and was
presided over by TEZCATLIPOCA.

Tecumbalam CENTRAL AMERICA (*Maya*)
One of the four great birds that were sent
by TEPEU and GUCUMATZ to attack and tear
to pieces the wooden people whom they
had created, people who lacked intelligence and refused to do honour to their
creators. The other three birds sent to
destroy this first attempt at the creation of
mankind were CAMALOTZ, COTZBALAM and
XECOTCOVACH.

Tehabi NORTH AMERICA – PUEBLO,
  SOUTHWEST (*Hopi*)
The clown of the Mudhead ceremony. See
KOYEMSHI.

Tehuelcho SOUTH AMERICA –
  PATAGONIA
Indigenous South American AMERINDIAN
people inhabiting the geographical division of South America known as Patagonia, an area lying to the south of latitude
40° that was sighted by Magellan in 1520
and claimed by both Argentina and Chile
until it was divided between them in
1881.

Teicu CENTRAL AMERICA – MEXICO
(*Aztec*)
The second oldest of the four sisters, aspects of TLACOLTÉUTL who appear to make
that deity the corollary of TEZCATLIPOCA.

Teicu's sisters were TICAPAN, TLACO and XOCUTIN. The four were not usually perceived of as separate entities, but rather the four faces of a witch who, in true pan-European style, rides through the air on a broomstick wearing a peaked hat, though, unlike her European counterparts, Tlacoltéutl rides naked.

Telpochtli CENTRAL AMERICA (*Aztec*)
'Youth', an aspect of TEZCATLIPOCA that evolved after that deity had absorbed many lesser deities.

Temaukel SOUTH AMERICA – TIERRA
  DEL FUEGO (*Ona*)
The supreme being who, like WATAUI-NEIWA of the neighbouring YAHGAN, is a disembodied spirit who symbolizes the sustenance of the universe and its cosmic and moral order. The KASPI, the souls of the dead, go to live with him in his home among the stars.

Temazcalli CENTRAL AMERICA – MEXICO
  (*Mixtec*)
A sweat-house used to cure the sick, the dedication of which would usually happen during the voluntary sacrifice of Lord NINE OLLIN.

Temazcalteci CENTRAL AMERICA –
  MEXICO (*Aztec*)
'Grandmother-of-the-Sweatbath', an aspect of CIHUACÓATL.

Ten Ahau CENTRAL AMERICA (*Maya*)
The tenth day of the CREATION[4] on which the first sinners were sent to hell. Ten Ahau is not to be confused with AHAU, the twentieth and final day of the AGES OF MAN, the MAYA spiritual pilgrimage.

Tenoch CENTRAL AMERICA – MEXICO
  (*Aztec*)
One of the original leaders of the AZTEC people who left their ancestral homeland of AZTLAN in search of a new kingdom on the mainland, Aztlan being described as an offshore island.

Tenochtitlan CENTRAL AMERICA –
  MEXICO (*Aztec*)
A marshy island that is today located in the centre of Mexico City. The myths record that it was to this island that the travellers from AZTLAN finally came and settled, and from where they gradually came to dominate the entire region. MONTEZUMA II is also recorded as having sent emissaries from here to revisit the ancestral homeland of Aztlan.

Teocipactli CENTRAL AMERICA –
  MEXICO (*Aztec*)
Variant name sometimes used to refer to COXCOX.

Teotihuacán CENTRAL AMERICA –
  MEXICO (*Aztec*)
The place where the gods came together and built a great fire on to which one of their number was to throw himself to be reborn as the Sun. It is also named as the location where the travellers from AZTLAN built pyramids to both the Sun and Moon, to honour the earlier events that were said to have taken place there. It was also the place where the AZTEC people elected their first kings, who were thought of as the incarnation of the gods and who were subsequently buried at Teotihuacán.

Teoyaomqui CENTRAL AMERICA –
  MEXICO (*Aztec*)
The god of dead warriors whose spirits he entertained.

Tepanaguaste CENTRAL AMERICA
  (*Maya*)
The guardian of the TEPANAGUASTE, a sacred hollow wooden instrument that is

similar to the TEPONAZTLI, the AZTEC ceremonial drum.

Tepeu CENTRAL AMERICA (*Maya*)

The creator who, together with GUCU-MATZ, consulted HURAKAN about the creation of the Earth in a time when the whole world was covered by water. The three commanded the waters to part, which they did, and the Earth rose from the depths with mountains already covered with pine trees.

Gucumatz and Tepeu then created all the animals and placed them on the Earth, but before long the gods realized that the creatures they had given life to fell far short of perfection, for they had no language with which they might praise and glorify their creators. Thus the two gods made the first men from damp soil. These too proved to be highly unsatisfactory, for they were blind and lame and, although they could speak, they lacked the necessary intelligence to recognize their creators. Gucumatz and Tepeu raised a flood and washed them away.

Next the two gods consulted Hurakan, XPIYACOC and XMUCANÉ, and the Sun. This time, having divined with maize kernels and the red berries of the TZITÉ plant, they decided to carve men from wood. Again these new people failed to live up to the expectations of the gods, for they lacked intelligence and remembered nothing of their creators. Thus the gods sent a heavy rain against them together with four mighty birds to tear them to pieces. These four birds were named CAMALOTZ, COTZ-BALAM, TECUMBALAM and XECOTCOVACH, each bird attacking a different part of the wooden people's bodies. When they saw their masters were being attacked, all their animals and fowls – and even their household utensils – turned against the wooden people, for they had been cruel masters. When they tried to seek refuge in the forests, the trees drew away from them, and when they sought refuge inside caves, the mouths of the caves shut. Thus all the wooden people and their descendants, save the monkeys, were destroyed.

During the next stage of the Creation process it appears as if the world was inhabited by the giant VUKUB CAKIX and his sons. They were defeated by the twin heroes, HUNAHPU and XBALANQUÉ.

Again the gods came together to discuss how they might successfully populate the world. They travelled to the PLACE OF THE DIVISION OF WATERS where white and yellow maize grew, and which they ground into a flour that was strengthened with nine broths that were brewed by Xmucané. Thus the gods formed the four brothers, BALAM AGAB, BALAM QUITZÉ, IQI BALAM and MAHUCUTAH.

This time the gods discovered that they had done their work a little too well, for the four brothers were so intelligent that they were likely to rival their creators. Thus Hurakan breathed a cloud over their eyes to reduce their vision to mortal levels, and also to lessen the level of their intelligence. The gods then sent the four brothers into a deep sleep while they created four women – who remain unnamed – to be their wives. Thus mankind came to the Earth.

Tepeyollotl CENTRAL AMERICA – MEXICO (*Zapotec*)

'Heart of the Mountain', a jaguar god, and one of the Lords of Night who was said to be the cause of earthquakes.

Teponaztli CENTRAL AMERICA – MEXICO (*Aztec*)

The sacred ceremonial drum that is akin to the TEPANAGUASTE of the MAYA people.

Tepoztécatl CENTRAL AMERICA –
MEXICO (*Aztec*)
The tutelary deity of the city of TEPOZTLAN
who was allegedly born to a virgin.

Tepoztlan CENTRAL AMERICA (*Aztec*)
Ancient AZTEC city of which the goddess
TEPOZTÉCATL was the tutelary deity.

Tequendama SOUTH AMERICA
(*Chibcha*)
The great waterfall that was created when
BOCHICA manifested himself as the rain-
bow, in answer to the prayers of mankind
after CHIBCHACUM had flooded the Earth.
The Earth split and the water rushed into
the chasm forming the waterfall.

Teteoinnan CENTRAL AMERICA –
MEXICO (*Aztec*)
'Mother-of-the-Gods', an aspect of TLA-
ZOLTÉOTL, though sometimes also consid-
ered as an aspect of CIHUACÓATL.

Teyú-Yaguá SOUTH AMERICA –
PARAGUAY (*Guaraní*)
The jaguar-lizard said to guard PAITITI, the
fabled land of gold, which is situated in
Lake CUNI-CUNI and ruled over by EL GRAN
MOXO.

Tezacatzontécatl CENTRAL AMERICA –
MEXICO (*Aztec*)
'Straw-Covered-Mirror', an important PUL-
QUE god who is possibly to be identified
with the CHAC MOOL figures of the TOL-
TECS. Tezacatzontécatl was one of the CEN-
TZONTOTOCHTIN, the collective name for
the pulque gods.

Tezcatlipoca CENTRAL AMERICA –
MEXICO (*Aztec and Toltec*)
'Smoking-Mirror', a solar deity and tutelary deity of TEZCOCO whose name comes
from his emblematic mirror that has a
spiral of smoke ascending from it. Tezcatlipoca represented the phenomenal world
and was patron of the knightly order of
ocelots – an ocelot being a South American big cat similar to the tiger. At one
stage, before differentiation and diversification, all the AZTEC deities who stood at
the four cardinal points were all Tezcatlipocas of various colours. In his northern
aspect he was black, red in his eastern,
blue in his southern and white in his western. It is interesting to note that these
colours do not tally with the normally
accepted Aztec colours for the cardinal
points: north = white, east = red, south
= yellow, and west = black. Tezcatlipoca was also associated with TLAZOL-
TÉOTL, the goddess of luxury and illicit
love, an ideal partner for such a deity as
Tezcatlipoca.

Later, following the diversification of
the Aztec culture, these four Tezcatlipocas
became differentiated. The blue Tezcatlipoca of the south became TLÁLOC, the god
of rain. The red Tezcatlipoca of the east
became XIPE TOTEC, though sometimes this
aspect, which represented the point at
which the Sun rose every day, became
TONATIUH, the Sun itself. The white Tezcatlipoca of the west, the point associated
with the sunset, became QUETZALCÓATL,
while Tezcatlipoca himself retained his
northern black aspect. Later Quetzalcóatl
remained as the sole deity, having conquered the three Tezcatlipocas of the
other cardinal points, each cardinal point
representing an aspect of nature itself.

The MAYA had their equivalent in the
Four BACAB who also represented the four
cardinal points, but the Aztec seem to
have developed the concept to a much
higher and more complex level. Other
accounts, that obviously date from the
Aztec rather than the TOLTEC period, say
that Tezcatlipoca was one of the four sons
of TONACATECUHTLI and TONACACÍHUATL.
In this case his brothers were the red
CAMAXTLI, tutelary deity of the TLAXCALA;
HUITZILOPOCHTLI, the god of the Aztecs;

Quetzalcóatl, chief deity of the Toltecs; and black Tezcatlipoca, god of the night and war-god of the great city of TEZCOCO.

This later version of events fits nicely into the order of the Creation as told in the myth of the FIVE SUNS. In this cycle of five evolutionary eras, Tezcatlipoca was the ruler of the first era, unremarkably known as that of the FIRST SUN. Some 676 years later the era of Tezcatlipoca came to an end when he was struck down and deposed by Quetzalcóatl who threw him into the sea. It is said that Tezcatlipoca, as the constellation URSA MAJOR[1], may still be seen falling towards the waters into which he was thrown. This is just another aspect of the long-standing struggle between the two deities which Quetzalcóatl won in this instance. In a later era of the Creation, the two warring deities were helped by four men to lift the heavens to their present position, after which the two became rulers with neither having precedence over the other.

The most important of the four cardinal points was the east, as this was the place where the Sun rose every day, that place where the UNDERWORLD, through which the Sun travelled at night, merged with the land of the living – Earth. At this point two deities stood facing each other: ITZLI, the god of the cutting-stone, and Quetzal-cóatl in his aspect as god of the rising Sun. At the northern cardinal point, the land of souls to which all go after death, stands the maize-god CINTÉOTL who faces MICTLÁN-TECUHTLI, the Lord of the Dead, this pairing representing resurrection in the face of death. XOCHIPILLI, goddess of flowers, stands at the western point facing an unnamed goddess of witchcraft and drunkenness (the latter being thought of as the result of witchcraft), a pairing in which beauty is offset by ugliness. Finally, at the southern point stands Tláloc, god of rain, who faces another unnamed deity, this one

being thought to be a god of the Underworld.

Between the four cardinal points that all started life as an aspect of Tezcatlipoca, are various signs of the CALENDAR. The sign ACATL is carried by a QUETZAL bird that feeds on a white plant on which there is another bird with a seed in its beak. TECPATL is carried by a red parrot, CALLI by a falling eagle, and TOCHTLI by a parrot. This representation of Tezcatlipoca as the omnipotent god of the compass illustrates the quite amazingly complex concept that the Aztecs had of the four cardinal points and the importance they placed on each direction.

Another aspect of Tezcatlipoca is that of Xipe Totec, the god of the spring, represented at horrific ceremonies by a priest wearing the freshly flayed skin of an initiate, a ritual symbolization of his own agony as he allowed his skin to be flayed in order that the growing principle that was locked away within him might be freed. Through his agony he redeemed mankind by bringing fertility to the Earth and allowed man to grow the divine gift of maize to sustain themselves.

The symbol of the growth of the maize is one of the most important in ancient Mexican religion. In the Maya culture, in which many parallels may be found, the creators were supposed to have needed the maize so that they could create mankind itself, the grain itself being brought to the gods by HOH, a crow; QUEL, a parrot; UTIU, a coyote; and YAC, a forest cat (possibly an ocelot).

Both Xipe Totec and Cintéotl, the corn or maize-god, are important figures in both the early NAHUA and the later Aztec pantheons, as the importance of the sustenance of mankind clearly illustrates, for without either deity mankind would not have been able to survive. Tláloc, the rain-god, is also to be included at the same level of importance, for without his life-giving waters, the efforts of Xipe Totec and Cintéotl would be fruitless. He is, perhaps, the most benign of the four aspects of Tezcatlipoca, though he, like that deity of which he is essentially an aspect, also has a variety of aspects and roles. In his purely agricultural aspect he causes trees and flowers to bud and ripen. His representation showed him with a black face on to which amaranth seeds had been encrusted. His jacket was a net that symbolized the clouds and his crown was made of heron feather. He wore a green necklace and foam sandals and carried rattles that created thunder as well as a braided rain pendant. Stylized portrayals of Tláloc show him with large circular eyes giving the impression that he is wearing spectacles, which has led to this aspect of Tezcatlipoca sometimes being known as the spectacled god. He appears under various names throughout Central-American mythology. To the Maya he was CHAAC; to the MIXTEC – TZAHUI; to the TOTANAC – TAJÍN; and to the ZAPOTEC – COCIJO.

Not only did the Aztecs and Toltecs differentiate between the deities of the four cardinal points, they also gave Tezcatlipoca a great number of different aspects that reflected his role as a god of the all-encompassing sky, though some of these aspects undoubtedly came through his absorption of lesser deities. Thus Tezcatlipoca became OMACATL ('Two Reeds', the 'Ruler of Feasts'), TELPOCHTLI ('Youth'), YAOTL ('the warrior') or YOALLI EHÉCATL or YOALTL EHÉCATL ('Night Wind').

Tezcatlipoca was, as can be clearly seen, an incredibly complex character, but in his simplest form he was perceived of as Quetzalcóatl's greatest enemy, though not principally a personification of evil. His favourite disguise was that of a turkey, one of whose feet was amputated by the Earth Monster to be replaced by a mirror. Some accounts, however, simplify the loss of his foot, saying that it was simply caught in a door that led to the Underworld. Having aspects that reflect both the struggle and necessary suffering of nature, and the reviving rain, it can be seen that Tezcatlipoca becomes a personification of the uncertainty of matter itself, rather than the personification of evil. This is further supported by the fact that his mirror-foot is shaped like a rabbit, that animal being the symbol of unpredictability.

Some accounts say that Tezcatlipoca dropped down to Earth on a spider's web. He was the god of sin and feasting who rewarded righteous men, but made evil men ill through a variety of means, though most usually through disease. He was invisible and impalpable, born out of the sky, but he bestowed on mankind the gifts of intelligence and understanding. He could, with a single glance, pierce stones and trees, and even the hearts of men so that he could read mankind's innermost thoughts. With a single thought he could create and by the same means destroy. He was held in such reverence that the Aztec people placed seats for him to rest on, at the corners of all their roads down which they believed he was perpetually travelling. They also believed that men were simply put on Earth to entertain Tezcatlipoca who could snuff out their existence if they failed to keep him amused, or to honour him correctly.

The culmination of a year-round cycle of festivals to the honour of Tezcatlipoca – the only deity to be continuously celebrated in an attempt to placate all the contrasting forces of nature – was the sacrifice of a virgin youth who went to his death of his own volition. This youth was taken to be the earthly image of the god, and for the year prior to his sacrifice was the centre of extraordinary reverence, cherished and treated with the greatest respect – respect that only stopped slightly short of actual worship. He was taught how to play the flute, music being an important part of the iconography of Tezcatlipoca, as well as how to carry himself with a demeanour befitting the incarnation of a god, to be courteous and gently spoken, and to fetch and carry the flowers that were required for offerings. Those who met him during this year bowed in reverence and kissed the Earth. Dressed like a god, he was free to roam by day or by night, but was always accompanied by eight servants dressed as palace lackeys.

Twenty days (one Aztec month) before the date on which the youth was to be sacrificed, his keepers changed his clothes for those in which he would meet his death. They then married him to four virgins who had been specifically raised for that moment, and who were then given the names of four goddesses. Five days before the appointed date, a great feast was held in the honour of the youth who was now regarded by all as a god. On the actual day of the ceremony the youth and his four wives were placed in a canoe with a canopy which carried them to a low hill where the wives were abandoned, though whether left there to die or simply to make their own way is not certain. Then only the youth and his eight servants were left in the canoe which continued to a small and poorly equipped temple where the sacrifice was to take place.

As the youth climbed the steps to the temple, he broke a flute on each step until he reached the temple proper where the priests were assembled and waiting to kill him. Standing in pairs, they bound his hands and feet and lifted him on to the sacrificial table. There a stone knife was plunged into his breast and his heart gouged out to be offered immediately to the Sun. On this occasion Tezcatlipoca would be incarnate as ITZLI-TEZCATLIPOCA, the personification of the sacrificial knife.

This ceremony was the enactment of a myth in real life, the myth concerning man himself who must learn to glorify the gods through sensual things such as fine clothes, music and dance, before he is worthy of breaking the senses one by one, as symbolized by the breaking of the flutes on the temple steps, and then losing his life in order to gain it.

The story of the eternal struggle for supremacy between Quetzalcóatl and Tezcatlipoca demonstrates that the latter was a wayward god who possessed enormous, yet unbridled, power and was able to control much of the fate of men, animals and all other forms of organic life. Although this story contains much that concerns Quetzalcóatl incarnate, it is given here as it is the story of the conflict started by Tezcatlipoca.

Tezcatlipoca, as has been mentioned, is said to have descended to Earth on a rope of cobweb, though some accounts say that he was so light that he simply alighted on a single gossamer strand. Having reached the Earth, he transformed himself into an ocelot while playing a game of ball with Quetzalcóatl. In that form he drove Quetzalcóatl from TULA, and then pursued him from city to city until they came to CHOLULA, a city which stands close to Puebla on the road from Mexico City, and which was one of the chief centres of the Quetzalcóatl cult. This story clearly shows a remembrance of some terrible storm in which the wind-god, Quetzalcóatl, swept over the land, abating as it reached Cholula, an event that would no doubt have strengthened the cult of Quetzalcóatl.

A curious variant on the theme of the supremacy struggle says that Tezcatlipoca was sacrificed by the gods to the glory of the Sun. Later he appeared to one of his grieving devotees, none other than Quetzalcóatl, whom he commands to travel to the home of the Sun and bring back some musicians. Tezcatlipoca gave specific instructions to Quetzalcóatl and then sent him on his way. At the seashore Quetzalcóatl enlisted the help of Tezcatlipoca's servants, as per his instructions, whom he ordered to form a bridge across which he might travel to the house of the Sun. When the Sun saw him approaching, he ordered his musicians not to make a sound, for any who did would have to travel back to Earth with the wind-god. All the musicians, clad in red, white, green and yellow, did as they had been told until at last one of them could no longer resist the temptation, and, by breaking into song, had to return to Earth with Quetzalcóatl, thus bringing music to the Earth. In this story it is quite obvious that Tezcatlipoca is pre-eminent, though this is not the usually accepted order of things.

Yet another example of the struggle between the two deities has a TOLTEC origin, though it was later to appear in Aztec mythology as the story of the Earthly Quetzalcóatl's ultimate downfall. In this it is said that the Toltec people became slothful and thus easy prey to the schemes of demons who were sent to ensure their destruction. These demons are clearly all Tezcatlipoca who was said to have first appeared as an stooping old man with white hair. Tezcatlipoca offered Quetzalcóatl a drink, saying that this would ease Quetzalcóatl's heart and banish all thoughts of death. Quetzalcóatl asked Tezcatlipoca, knowing that his time on Earth was coming to an end, where he should go next. Tezcatlipoca told him to travel to TLILLAN-TLAPALLAN where he said that he would be rejuvenated by another old man. Quetzalcóatl accepted the drink which is said to have been made from the juice of the maguey cactus, a plant that still provides the Mexicans with tequila and PULQUE.

Even though Quetzalcóatl had allowed himself to be tempted, he had not been altogether fooled by the disguise of Tezcatlipoca who now had to resort to a more indirect deception, though in later Aztec accounts this portion of the story is said to have occurred some 200 years after Quetzalcóatl had left Tollan, HUEMAC being the last secular ruler who was deposed by the trickery of Tezcatlipoca. Quetzalcóatl was the father of a daughter after whom all men lusted, but which her father would give to no man. One day, as she looked out of the palace, she saw a naked man with an erect phallus selling green chilli in the market – Tezcatlipoca in the guise of the peasant TOUEYO, though the name Toueyo is usually confined to the stories that concern the downfall of Huemac. Sick with desire she soon became weak, so Quetzalcóatl, having discovered the reason for her malaise, ordered that the chilli-seller be found. The search was unproductive, but, just as it was called off, the man reappeared in the market-place, from where he was brought to Quetzalcóatl who told him that, as he had caused his daughter's illness, he must cure her.

Quetzalcóatl ordered his valets to make the man presentable. They bathed and anointed him, dressed his hair and gave him a loincloth. Then he was presented to the princess and lay with her, later being acknowledged as Quetzalcóatl's son-in-law, though this greatly angered the Toltec people. Quetzalcóatl, even though he had allowed the stranger to become a member of his own family, was certain that he was in fact an enemy and did nothing to stop his people from declaring war on the man and his people. At first, much to Quetzalcóatl's delight, the Toltecs appeared to have the upper hand, but finally the army of Tezcatlipoca were victorious. Quetzalcóatl reluctantly admitted defeat and went out to greet the young man who was now firmly admitted to the family.

Repeatedly Tezcatlipoca caused the Toltecs almost to destroy themselves, but each time stopped short of wiping them out. Tezcatlipoca, on one occasion, took the form of a warrior and called all that remained of the Toltec army to assemble in Quetzalcóatl's field of flowers. The Toltecs did as they were asked without question, whereupon Tezcatlipoca and his army descended on them and began to massacre them. Many were killed and many others trampled to their deaths as they tried to flee. This section also appears in the later stories concerning Huemac, though here, rather than the people being killed by Tezcatlipoca's army, they fell to their deaths over the edges of ravines in a drunken orgy of delight that was arranged to celebrate their recent victory over a neighbouring culture.

Once again adopting a new disguise, Tezcatlipoca went into the market-place in front of the palace where he entertained the people by holding a dancing figure of the god HUITZILOPOCHTLI (a later form of Quetzalcóatl) in the palm of his hand. Many crowded around to see the sight. Tezcatlipoca then persuaded the assembled throng that he was only able to do this through witchcraft, whereupon the people stoned him to death. His body quickly putrefied and started to smell so badly that wherever the wind carried the stench, people died. Tezcatlipoca, who was in true mythical fashion still alive despite the temporary form he had adopted, persuaded the people that the body must be removed. They put a rope around the festering remains and tried to drag them out of the city, but they were so heavy that, no matter how many joined the line, they could not move them. This portion also appears in the story of Huemac's downfall, though now all who touched the rope slung around the corpses – for here it is the bodies of Tezcatlipoca and Huitzilopochtli that have to be removed – fell dead.

Next Tezcatlipoca made a white kite whose head had been pierced by an arrow fly back and forth as a bad omen. Then, really going to town, he caused a local volcano to erupt. Next Tezcatlipoca took the guise of an old woman and sat in the market-place selling little paper flags. Those who sought to buy one from her were immediately taken off to the sacrificial stone. Then Tezcatlipoca turned all the food bad and soon the people were close to starvation. Seizing on this opportunity, Tezcatlipoca once again assumed the guise of an old woman who entered Tula and began to roast maize, the delicious smells soon drawing all the surviving Toltec people to see if they could beg some of the mouth-watering maize. With the entire population milling around him, Tezcatlipoca simply wandered among the throng and killed them all, though the later Huemac version says that the city of Tollan was vanquished by its enemies who killed all that remained of the severely decimated population.

Now that Quetzalcóatl had no subjects left to rule, he decided to abandon Tula. He burned all the houses of gold and coral and then buried his treasure in caves, canyons and the mountains, before changing the cacao trees into dry mesquite fit only for the desert and sending away all the animals and the birds that lived there. Having destroyed Tula and made it uninhabitable, Quetzalcóatl and his surviving retinue set out for ANÁHUAC, the 'place at the centre, in the midst of the circle', the holiest place of the Toltec people, the source of their very existence. En route the entourage came to a place where a single sturdy tree grew. There Quetzalcóatl called for his mirror, but when he saw his reflection showed a decrepid old man, he, in a fit of pique, threw stones so hard at the tree that they remained buried within its trunk.

Some distance further on Quetzalcóatl sat down to rest on a rock and started to weep great floods of hailstones that rolled down his cheeks and gouged great holes in the rock, which also received an impression of his hands and buttocks. From there the party travelled on until they came to a broad river which Quetzalcóatl crossed by throwing boulders into the water to act as stepping-stones. However, no sooner had he reached the opposite bank than he was approached by a horde of demons (Tezcatlipoca up to his old tricks again) who urged him to return from whence he had come. Quetzalcóatl refused, telling him that he had to travel to Anáhuac.

The demons told Quetzalcóatl that they would only let him pass if he gave them all his gifts and treasures. Thus Tezcatlipoca wrested all Quetzalcóatl's skills from him: the casting of gold; the cutting of precious stones; the carving of wood; the sculpting of stone; the knowledge of the scribes; and the intricate art of feather work. Seeing that he was being stripped of everything he still possessed, Quetzalcóatl ripped off his personal jewellery and threw it into the river. Satisfied, the demons let Quetzalcóatl continue on his journey. Later he was to encounter some more demons (again Tezcatlipoca) who this time demanded that he must become drunk if he wished to pass. Quetzalcóatl accepted their wine, fell into a drunken stupor and snored like thunder.

Awaking, he set off and climbed the two snow-capped volcanoes POPOCATÉPATL and IXTACCÍHUATL, leading a great host of dwarfs and hunchbacks until they all eventually died of the cold, a loss which must have greatly saddened Quetzalcóatl. Dwarfs were held in great esteem as far as the Yucatán, where a small temple at UXMAL is known locally as the Dwarf's House. As the last of the dwarfs died, Quetzalcóatl wept and sang to him as he gazed across at a third snow-capped mountain, the one that was then known as CITLALTÉPETL but is now called ORIZABA.

Elsewhere along the tortuous route of his journey, in locations that have been forgotten over the ensuing years, Quetzalcóatl planted maguey, built a ball court and shot at two silk-cotton trees which he pierced. He also built a house in MICTLÁN and then proved his strength by pushing a rock with his little finger that no man had been able to move. Finally, he came to the coast and set off on his serpent raft for an unknown destination that is usually referred to as Tlillan-Tlapallan.

It was this final act that was to prove that Tezcatlipoca, though visibly perhaps the victor, had in fact lost his struggle with Quetzalcóatl who had, throughout all the trials he had experienced, proved that the force of spirit would always win against that of illusion. The later versions of this story greatly simplify it. In these, the demons are sent by Tezcatlipoca in an attempt to persuade the earthly Quetzalcóatl to perform human sacrifices, but he steadfastly refuses. Eventually a plot is hatched against him by the magicians Huitzilopochtli, TITLACUHAN (a title of Tezcatlipoca) and their brother TLACAHUEPAN.

Titlacuhan, disguised as a doctor, offered to cure Quetzalcóatl of the malaise that had been brought about by the continual pestering of the demons. Quetzalcóatl accepted the treatment, that consisted of drinking great quantities of wine. By getting drunk, he broke one of his priestly vows. An addition to this story says that Quetzalcóatl also lost his virginity, another priestly condition, while drunk, some versions saying that he had an incestuous union with his sister. Quetzalcóatl then left Tollan, either through banishment or of his own free will, but he first destroyed the city. However, before he left for Tlillan-Tlapallan, he said that he would return in the year 1519, the exact year when the Spanish invaders arrived, a reason put forward by some for why the Aztecs put up so little resistance to CORTÉS whom they believed to be the returning Quetzalcóatl.

Tezcatlipoca, elusive, sprightly and ever-changing, wore black sandals of obsidian to show that, although he was a shape-changer, he was firmly rooted in matter. However, Quetzalcóatl wore white sandals which have been taken to signify that he purified the Earth wherever he set down his foot. In modern parlance, a more basic comparison may be made between the colours of the respective sandals worn by these two warring deities. Black, in modern usage, is usually taken as a representation of something bad or evil, whereas white usually represents something good or godly. Thus, by showing the two gods with these particularly coloured sandals, it can be assumed that even the ancient Toltecs and Aztecs had a firm understanding of this principle, and the war between Tezcatlipoca and Quetzalcóatl can be seen as simply another of the many variants of the eternal struggle between the forces of good and those of evil. Yet again good is the victor.

This concept appears to have been carried over into the iconography of Tezcatlipoca, for it is recorded that there was once a statue to the god made of black stone which was covered with gold and silver sequins. It is quite normal, in many cultures and religions, to depict a bad spirit as a black figure adorned resplendently, the fine clothing apparently being an attempt to hide the true nature of the being. This particular statue is further described. From the lower lip hung a glass bead, inside which was a green and blue feather which, at first sight, resembled a jewel. His hair was tied back with a gold band and he wore a head dress of quail feathers, together with golden earplugs tinted with smoke that represented the prayers of the afflicted. From his neck a golden pectoral hung, and on both arms he wore gold bracelets. An emerald was positioned in his navel while in one hand he held a shield and four arrows, and in the other a fly-whisk made of precious feather, or else a spear. He gazed into a disc that had been burnished like a mirror, and in which it was believed that he could see all that was going on in the world. His stone was obsidian as his name betrays, for *tezcat* means 'obsidian'.

Sometimes this extremely complex deity was represented seated in front of a red curtain that was decorated with skulls and bones. He ruled over the night and was, in one aspect, the Moon. The jaguar was his anvil and he sometimes called out a warning like a bird to its fellows.

Tezcatlipoca presided over the school of plebeians (the common, unrefined people), while his great adversary Quetzalcóatl presided over the school of the nobles – army leaders, priests and judges. There rests the immediate popularity of Tezcatlipoca who was more human, not aloof like Quetzalcóatl whose popularity was more defined. Having some affinity with the Maya deity HURAKAN, Tezcatlipoca was a deity of the world of noumena, that clouded world of half-truth and half-perception.

Tezcatlipoca sowed dissension, though in a mischievous rather than malevolent manner. He stimulated sexual desire and excess, but also listened to the confessions of lovers and others. He was lord over all the material possessions of the world and could, at will, either withhold or dispense them. Tezcatlipoca was a friend to both the slave and the powerful. Even more significantly, those born under his sign were not ruled by fate alone but could be happy or accursed depending on what they themselves were able to make of their birth.

Tezcatlipoca was, therefore, a representation of the natural energy of all things, rather than a satanic figure who used that energy solely for his own gain. If man could tap that energy, then the individual would prosper but if it was left unfettered, it could destroy with equal ease. In Tezcatlipoca's breast were two little doors that met at the centre. A brave man might dare to open these and take hold of Tezcatlipoca's heart, whereupon that individual would be able to ask him for whatever ransom he so desired. Any weakling who dared to challenge Tezcatlipoca in such a way, and then failed to reach his heart, would die instantly.

Tezcatlipoca is also sometimes referred to as the god of fire, as fire possesses the same attributes as the god himself – it can consume with consummate ease or it can, if confined, provide life-giving warmth and light. However, there was another fire-god in his own right – XIUHTECUHTLI, also called IXCOZAUHQUI, of the yellow face. Tezcatlipoca fell in love with XOCHIQUET-ZAL, the goddess of flowers and love, who lived on the top of a mountain where she was surrounded by an entourage of dwarfs, musicians and dancing maidens, and who had the power to entice all men. Tezcatlipoca snatched her away from her husband Tláloc. Xochiquetzal and her male counterpart XOCHIPILLI were closely associated with Huitzilopochtli, the later Aztec representation of Quetzalcóatl. During the Aztec period, at a feast in the honour of the flower deities, a bower of roses was built in Huitzilopochtli's temple where Xochiquetzal was enthroned, and where youths masquerading as butterflies and birds danced around her and climbed artificial trees.

One version of the flower-goddess story says that a flood destroyed all the creatures except a god called COXCOX, or TEOCIPACTLI, and the goddess Xochiquetzal. The story does not say who caused the flood, but the blame is usually placed with Tezcatlipoca. Coxcox and Xochiquetzal had many children, but they had no voice until a dove landed in a high tree and gave them each a voice and a different language.

A further connection can be made between Xochiquetzal and Tezcatlipoca, as butterflies were particularly connected

with the latter, transmuted, in other words, with Quetzalcóatl. Tezcatlipoca is best summed up as a neutral though always lively deity, on the one hand linked with song, flowers and butterflies, but on the other with sin. He is the direct contrast of ITZLACOLIOHQUI, the god of the curved obsidian knife, a knife that is also a symbol of Tezcatlipoca, thus sometimes leading to the identification of Itzlacoliohqui as an aspect of Tezcatlipoca.

Tezcoco, Lake CENTRAL AMERICA – MEXICO (*Aztec*)
Lake in central Mexico that was the centre of the ancient AZTEC culture. An early myth records how the travellers from the ancestral homeland of AZTLAN came to the lake, where they received a divine sign and founded the city of TENOCHTITLAN on a marshy island in the midst of the lake. Tenochtitlan today is situated right in the heart of Mexico City. Another myth says that the Aztec people founded the lakeside city of Tezcoco, named after the lake, after the city of TOLLAN had fallen to the CHICHIMECS, their fortunes in that place depending on their dominance of the lake's salt pans. The tutelary deity of the city of Tezcoco was the great TEZCATLIPOCA.

Theelgeth NORTH AMERICA – SOUTHWEST (*Navajo*)
A hairy, headless, man-eating monster that numbered amongst the ANAYE, those monsters born to virgins who indulged in inhuman acts. See ASCENT OF THE NAVAJO.

Third Sun CENTRAL AMERICA – MEXICO (*Aztec*)
The name given to the third era of the creation, the 'Sun of the Rain of Fire'. The era came to an end when the Earth and all living things, except for the birds which took to the air, perished in a fire. This

either rained down from the heavens, hence the name given to the era, or was started by the man and the woman who had survived the previous era, that of the SECOND SUN, from which they brought the gift of fire. The Third Sun was, quite logically, followed by the era of the FOURTH SUN.

Thirteen Akbal CENTRAL AMERICA (*Maya*)

The thirteenth day of the CREATION[4] when MONTH[2] modelled the first true men out of clay. Thirteen Akbal should not be confused with AKBAL, the third day of the AGES OF MAN, though that day is a direct parallel for on it man is born.

thlawe NORTH AMERICA – PUEBLO, SOUTHWEST (*Zuñi*)

A beautiful UNDERWORLD plant with a plume that was carried by the CORN MAIDENS, who brought it up from the Underworld with them.

Thobadzistshini NORTH AMERICA – SOUTHWEST (*Navajo*)

The twin brother of NAYANEZGANI. According to some versions, these twins were the sons of ESTANATLEHI and TSHOHANOAI, while others say that only Nayanezgani was the son of these parents, his brother – though her in a spiritual sense – being the son of YOLKAI ESTSAN and WATER.

Helped by the wind-spirit NILTSHI and the SPIDER-WOMAN, the twins made a long and hazardous journey to the HOGAN (lodge, or home) of Tshohanoai, whose confidence and acceptance they eventually won having survived many trials. Tshohanoai gave them magical weapons: arrows of lightning, sunbeams, a rainbow, a huge stone knife which some have identified with a thunderbolt, and armour from which lightning flashed from every joint.

Having returned to Earth, the brothers battled with the monstrous ANAYE and managed to kill a great number of them. However, as they had been unable to overcome them all, they once again sought the help of their father. This time Tshohanoai gave them four magical hoops with which the goddess Estanatlehi raised a great storm that not only destroyed all but four of the remaining anaye, but also reshaped the very Earth itself. The four anaye who survived were COLD, HUNGER, OLD AGE and POVERTY.

With their allotted tasks on Earth completed, the twin heroes returned to their mountain home to which NAVAJO braves go to ask for victory in battle.

Thorny Flowers CENTRAL AMERICA – MEXICO (*Aztec*)

One of the four giants who were placed at the four corners of the Earth to hold the heavens up at the start of the FIFTH SUN era, the other three giants being called FALLING EAGLE, SERPENT OF OBSIDIAN KNIVES and RESURRECTION. QUETZALCÓATL and TEZCATLIPOCA also lent a hand, the former becoming the PRECIOUS TREE and the latter the TREE OF MIRRORS.

Three Ben CENTRAL AMERICA (*Maya*)

The third day of the CREATION[4] on which MONTH[2] made the whole diversity of the creations, the things in heaven, in the sea, and on the Earth. Three Ben should not be confused with BEN the thirteenth day of the MAYA spiritual pilgrimage, the AGES OF MAN.

Three Cimi CENTRAL AMERICA (*Maya*)

The sixteenth day of the CREATION[4] on which death was created. Three Cimi should not be confused with CIMI, the sixth day of the AGES OF MAN, though the two are parallels of each other as Cimi is the day on which man dies in the MAYA spiritual pilgrimage.

Thunapa SOUTH AMERICA (*Collao*)
A culture hero who is also called TONAPA and TAAPAC. The stories that survive concerning this character are muddled. The tale of Thunapa was to be assimilated with that of the origins of the INCA people, as well as with the tale of VIRACOCHA, while the Augustinian fathers who recorded the legend were prone to identify Thunapa with prominent Christian saints, particularly Saint Thomas. The best that can now be done is to take the legend as recorded and attempt to strip out any post-Christian influences.

It was said that Thunapa came from the north a long time ago, either in the company of five comrades, or alone, carrying a large wooden staff (this staff later became the crucifix). Wherever he went, he preached peace, sobriety and monogamy but was killed for his convictions by MAKURI, a chief who resented the fact that his daughter had been converted by Thunapa. Thunapa's body was placed in a rush boat on Lake TITICACA, the boat swiftly moving away even though the lake has no current. The boat crossed the lake quickly and struck the shore at COCHAMARCA so forcibly that it created the River DESAGUADERO, on whose waters the body of Thunapa was carried away to the coast of Africa.

Thunder ~ bird, ~ er NORTH AMERICA
Common amongst the AMERINDIAN peoples of North America is the Thunderbird, a mythical bird who is the creator of all the terrible storms that sweep the countryside. He is a particularly important TOTEM figure among the Indian peoples of the Northwest Coastal regions and the Great Plains. In the northwest it is said that lightning flashes from his eyes, and

that he feeds on monstrous killer whales. Like the Aryan thunder-gods (Indra, Thórr, Zeus and so on), the North American Thunderbird is an embodiment of the life force that strikes down the man-eating monster or serpent. He is also regarded as the guardian of fire, particularly amongst the IROQUOIS who name the chief of the Thunderers as KENEUN, to whom NOKOMIS entrusted fire after it had been stolen by MÄNÄBUSCH, the Great HARE. Another Iroquoian leader of the Thunderers is OSHADAGEA. To the TLINGIT, the Thunderbird is SKYAMSEN.

Ti Jean Quinto HAITI (*Voodoo*)
An insolent LOA who lives under bridges and appears in the form of a policeman.

Ti(a)huanaco SOUTH AMERICA –
BOLIVIA
The first great Andean highland civilization appears to have been centred on Tiahuanaco, a city 15 miles south of Lake TITICACA on the Bolivian plateau 13,000 feet above sea level. Radiocarbon tests carried out on the main buildings of the city have indicated that they date from around the first century AD. These buildings include four pyramids and a great complex that is known as KALASASAYA – a huge platform containing a patio that is entered through the Gateway of the Sun. At the centre of this gateway is a head surrounded by Sun-rays, some of the rays beginning as pumas. Around it, attendant deities hold staffs that are possibly Sun-ray emblems which end in condor heads. These subordinate deities obviously represent various animal gods as they wear animal and birds masks – jaguar, condor, and other predators.

Art that can be traced back to the city of Tiahuanaco appears to have been disseminated across the whole of the Andean region between AD 600 and 1000, but whether this dissemination was a result of trade or war is not known. Likewise, the end of this obviously highly advanced civilization remains a mystery. No signs exist of either emigration or conquest. It simply seems to have abruptly come to an end, one possible explanation being a plague against which the inhabitants had no defence. By the time of the INCAS, the city was already lying in ruins and was thus talked of as a legendary city whose origins were unknown, its founders being regarded as mysterious giants who built the city in a single night.

Tiahuanaco was said to have been the location at which CON TICCI VIRACOCHA made the Sun, the Moon and the stars, and then made stone models of people of all ages and from all walks of life, which were then brought to life to populate the world.

Tiamuni NORTH AMERICA – PUEBLO, SOUTHWEST (*Acoma*)
The name of the first man.

Ticapan CENTRAL AMERICA – MEXICO (*Aztec*)
The second oldest of the four sisters, aspects of TLACOLTÉUTL, who appear to make that deity the corollary of TEZCATLIPOCA. Ticapan's sisters were TEICU, TLACO and XOCUTIN. The four were not usually perceived of as separate entities, but rather the four faces of a witch who, in true pan-European style, rides through the air on a broomstick wearing a peaked hat, though, unlike her European counterparts, Tlacoltéutl rides naked.

Ticci Viracocha SOUTH AMERICA (*Collao*)
A shortened version of CON TICCI VIRACOCHA.

Tieholtsodi NORTH AMERICA – SOUTHWEST (*Navajo*)
The water-monster who dragged down to his watery kingdom the last two of the NAVAJO women, who crossed the stream that divided the territory of the men and women who had been living apart for some time following a disagreement. A man and a woman went down into Tieholtsodi's realm to rescue them, but were secretly followed by COYOTE who abducted two of Tieholtsodi's children. When the monster discovered his loss, he flooded the world in which the Navajo were living, thus making them flee upwards into the next world – the Earth as we know it today. However, the flood waters began to escape into the upper world and threaten that world as well. Fortunately the abduction was discovered just in time and the two children thrown back into the world below, whereupon the waters receded. See ASCENT OF THE NAVAJO.

Tigers, House of CENTRAL AMERICA (*Maya*)
One of the trial houses into which the lords of XIBALBA threw the twins HUNAHPU and XBALANQUÉ who had to survive until the following morning. They did so by throwing bones to the jaguars all night long, thus distracting them.

Tilantongo CENTRAL AMERICA – MEXICO (*Mixtec*)
Spiritual realm over which EIGHT DEER, the spiritual brother of Lord NINE OLLIN, presided.

Tirawa (Atius) NORTH AMERICA – GREAT PLAINS (*Pawnee and Delaware*)
The GREAT SPIRIT whose creation of the world is celebrated in the HAKO ritual. The husband of ATIRA and ruler of TIRAWAHUT, Tirawa sat in council with the other spirits at the start of time and appointed each of

the great spirits to their relevant places in the sky as the stars, giving each in turn the special powers they would require to help and care for the people he proposed to create, and by doing so actually giving away a large proportion of his own powers.

Firstly he positioned SAKURU, the spirit of the Sun, in the eastern sky with the single purpose of giving light and warmth, together with the warrior GREAT STAR (the planet VENUS[1] as the MORNING STAR[4]). Then he set PAH, the spirit of the Moon, in the west so that he might light the Earth at night when Sakuru was not visible. In the west, Tirawa also placed BRIGHT STAR (the planet Venus as the EVENING STAR), the 'Mother-of-all-Things'. In the south he placed SPIRIT STAR who would only be seen at irregular intervals on the Earth. In the north he placed the STAR-THAT-DOES-NOT-MOVE, the pole star, whom he made the chief over all the other star-spirits, including those four that he specifically positioned as guardians of the four cardinal points with the task of supporting the heavens, and to whom Tirawa gave the power to create people and to give them their sacred bundles.

Tirawa then told Bright Star that he was going to send her wind-, lightning- and thunder-spirits whom she was to position between herself and her garden (the Earth). These spirits would then be transformed into people, each of whom would be wearing a downy feather in his hair (a symbol of the breath of life), a buffalo robe and moccasins. Each would hold, in their right hand, a rattle symbolizing Bright Star's garden. To these transformed spirits would be given the task of creating the Earth itself.

The wind-spirit blew hard while the clouds came together and an almighty storm ensued. Into the midst of it Tirawa tossed a pebble which rebounded around it until the storm abated to reveal, when the clouds drew apart again, a huge waste of water. Then Tirawa commanded Bright Star to pass on his instructions to the four guardians of the cardinal points who struck the water with their clubs. The water divided and the Earth appeared, but as yet it had no features. Bright Star thus commanded the four guardian spirits to sing of the shaping of the Earth. As they sang, the great storm reformed and formed the features of the Earth. In a similar fashion the Earth was next clothed with trees and grass, its water purified and the first seeds germinated.

Tirawa now called on Sakuru to mate with Pah and from their union a son was born. Next Bright Star and Great Star united and from their union a daughter came. These two children were placed on the newly created Earth, but there they lay, inert. Tirawa then commanded the storm once more to form and in the torrential rains that fell the children received life and understanding. Upon reaching maturity, the couple united and bore a son, CLOSED MAN, for whom they toiled hard to feed and clothe. Tirawa, however, watched over them and regularly sent them spirits to help them, each spirit either bearing a useful gift, or some piece of teaching that they could use for their benefit. The woman was given seeds and moisture so that she might grow food. She was also given a lodge, a fireplace and the power of speech. They taught her how to use and guard the fire, and gave her the land that surrounded the lodge, as well as command over the materials from which sacred ritual pipes are made.

Through Bright Star, Closed Man received the instructions of Tirawa that, when he died, his skull was to be placed on top of a sacred bundle, which it duly was, and by so doing his spirit remained with the PAWNEE, his descendants.

Tirawahut NORTH AMERICA – GREAT
PLAINS (*Pawnee*)
The 'heaven's circle', the domain of TIR-
AWA and his wife ATIRA.

Tiri SOUTH AMERICA – BOLIVIA
(*Yuracare*)
The son of ULÉ. His mother stumbled into
the lair of a jaguar family before he was
born. There she had her obedience tested
by the mother jaguar, who had taken pity
on her, and the four jaguar sons who wanted to kill her. The latter told her that she
must eat the poisonous ants which infested
the lair and caused the jaguars untold
discomfort. The young woman deceived
three of the jaguars by replacing the ants
she picked from their bodies with seed, but
the fourth had eyes in the back of his head
and saw what she was doing. He killed
her.

From her body Tiri was born whom the
jaguar mother cared for in secret. Having
reached maturity, he went hunting but
was scolded by the animals he shot at, for
hunting them while he still lived with his
mother's killers. Tiri ambushed the four
jaguar brothers and managed to kill the
first three, but the fourth, the killer of his
mother, leaped into a tree where it beseeched the Sun, the Moon, and the stars
to help it. The Moon reached down out of
the sky and took the jaguar up to the
heavens where it may still be seen on the
Moon's surface.

Titicaca, Lake SOUTH AMERICA –
BOLIVIA AND PERU
Famous lake situated on the Bolivian plateau in the Andes mountain range, 12,500
feet above sea level and 4,000 feet above
the tree line. The largest lake in South
America, Lake Titicaca covers an area of
3,200 square miles and is divided between
Bolivia and Peru. The first great civilization of the Andes appears to have been
centred on the ruins of TIAHUANACO
which are situated nearby. The lake features in several myths of the INCAS, and
their ancestors.

1 A COLLAO myth says that the Sun rose
suddenly from an island in the midst of
the lake. The Collao say too that CON
TICCI VIRACOCHA also emerged from this
lake to create the Earth, and then rose
from the lake at a later date with a large
number of attendants before travelling
to Tiahuanaco where he created the
Sun, the Moon, and the stars.

2 An Inca myth of their origins talks of a
god who rose from the lake, and of
MANCO CAPAC and MAMA OCLLO coming
down to the Earth on an island in the
lake. It is possible that, due to their
similarities, these myths are simply later
versions of the earlier Collao myths.

Titlacuhan CENTRAL AMERICA –
MEXICO (*Aztec*)
A title of black TEZCATLIPOCA, by which he
was referred to in the story of the plot
hatched by him, HUITZILOPOCHTLI and
TLACAHUEPAN to overthrow the earthly
QUETZALCÓATL.

Disguised as a doctor, Titlacuhan went
to Quetzalcóatl who had grown ill from
the perpetual torments of demons who
wanted him to conduct human sacrifices,
something he steadfastly refused to do.
Titlacuhan offered to cure him, his cure
consisting of copious quantities of wine.
Quetzalcóatl accepted the treatment and
by so doing broke one of his priestly vows,
that of sobriety. Some accounts also say
that in his drunken state Quetzalcóatl seduced and lay with a maiden, some say his
sister, and thus also broke another of his
vows – chastity. Having been degraded,
Quetzalcóatl left TOLLAN, some accounts
saying that he went of his own accord,
while others say that he was banished.

Tituanco SOUTH AMERICA – BOLIVIA
(*Aymará*)
The home of the AYMARÁ who survived the onslaught of KHUNO for their despoiling of Mounts ILLIMANI and ILLAMPU with the smoke from their fires.

Tiuh Tiuh CENTRAL AMERICA –
GUATEMALA (*Cakchiquel*)
A hawk that killed a COYOTE while that animal was cleaning his maize field. The hawk then obtained the blood of a tapir and a serpent which he kneaded with the flour of the ground maize, and thus created man. In total Tiuh Tiuh created thirteen men and fourteen women who soon united and multiplied. The humans then separated into seven tribes and thirteen divisions.

All the warriors of the seven tribes set out under the command of Tiuh Tiuh and reached the coast, but found themselves unable to cross the sea. The two eldest warriors, named GAGAVITZ and ZACTE-CAUH, fell asleep on the seashore and were drowned. However, they had in their possession a red staff that they had brought with them from TULAN ('The Place of the Sun'). The other warriors drove this staff into the sea which caused the waters to part so that they could cross to the far shore by walking on the sea bed.

Tizapan CENTRAL AMERICA – MEXICO
(*Aztec*)
During the journey from their ancestral homeland of AZTLAN the travellers were said to have been welcomed to this city of the COLHUACA. Some time later they fought alongside the Colhuacan people against XOCHIMILO, whom they defeated, but were driven out shortly afterwards for the barbarity they showed when asked to prove how many they had killed.

Tizné CENTRAL AMERICA – MEXICO
(*Maya*)
Symbol of the power of AHMUCENCAB and of OXLAHUNTIKU without which either would have been rendered impotent, a situation that the latter had to face.

Tizoc CENTRAL AMERICA – MEXICO
(*Aztec*)
Historical ruler of the AZTEC people who ascended to the throne in AD 1481.

Tlacaelel CENTRAL AMERICA – MEXICO
(*Aztec*)
A philosopher who told the AZTECS that their ancestral homeland of AZTLAN was located near a sea-girt mountain named CULHUACAN when the fifth ruler of the Aztecs, MONTEZUMA II, decided to send emissaries to Aztlan. This was where, so he had heard, HUITZILOPOCHTLI's mother COATLICUE was still alive.

Tlacahuepan CENTRAL AMERICA –
MEXICO (*Aztec*)
One of the participants in the plot hatched by TEZCATLIPOCA to dishonour and thus overthrow the earthly QUETZALCÓATL. He was accompanied by HUITZILOPOCHTLI and TITLACUHAN. When Tezcatlipoca, in the guise of the peasant TOUEYO, went into the market-place at TOLLAN with Huitzilopochtli dancing on his hand (or head), Tlacahuepan went with them. After the people had apparently killed Tezcatlipoca and Huitzilopochtli, he suggested tying ropes to the two corpses so that they might be dragged over the edge of a nearby ravine. This the people did, but whoever picked up the rope died instantly.

tlachtli CENTRAL AMERICA
1 (*Maya*)
A ball-game of which the brothers HUNHUN AHPU and VUKUB AHPU were

devoted players, and of which they accepted a challenge to play against the lords of XIBALBA. The twins HUNAHPU and XBALANQUÉ were similarly keen players of the game, and were also challenged to a game against the lords of Xibalba, a challenge which they gladly accepted and won.

2 (*Aztec*)

The AZTEC played a ball-game having this name that was apparently the same as that played by the MAYA (see 1 above). The game was governed by the solar deity XÓLOTL who was also a keen player who played on a magical court in the skies.

Tlacale CENTRAL AMERICA – MEXICO (*Aztec*)

Division of Mexico that was the home of the TLAXCALA whose tutelary deity was CAMAXTLI.

Tlaco CENTRAL AMERICA – MEXICO (*Aztec*)

The second oldest of the four sisters, aspects of TLACOLTÉUTL, who appear to make that deity the corollary of TEZCATLIPOCA. Tlaco's sisters were TEICU, TICAPAN and XOCUTIN. The four were not usually perceived of as separate entities, but rather the four faces of a witch who, in true pan-European style, rides through the air on a broomstick wearing a peaked hat, though, unlike her European counterparts, Tlacoltéutl rides naked.

Tlacoltéutl CENTRAL AMERICA – MEXICO (*Aztec*)

The goddess of childbirth and mother of XOCHIQUETZAL and CINTÉOTL, though she was also, in another aspect, the goddess of vice and carnal sin, an aspect that she countered as the 'Eater of Filth' who consumed the sins of mankind and received their confession. This confession, which could only be made once in a lifetime, was guaranteed absolution.

She appears to be a corollary of TEZCATLIPOCA for, like that deity, there were also four sisters who were all aspects of Tlacoltéutl. These sisters were, in order of age, TICAPAN, TEICU, TLACO and XOCUTZIN, though they were not usually perceived of as separate entities, but rather the four faces of a witch who, in true pan-European style, rides through the air on a broomstick wearing a peaked hat, though, unlike her European counterparts, she rides naked. Her iconography, Tlacoltéutl riding a broomstick, was the AZTEC symbol for sex. This fearsome figure was believed to hover at the turning points in the life of man, ready, so it is assumed, to divert them from their appointed destiny. To protect themselves from their evil influence, men used to go as penitents to Tezcatlipoca, thus showing that he, though the opponent of QUETZALCÓATL, whom he frustrates at every opportunity, is not a totally malevolent figure.

Tlacotecuhtli CENTRAL AMERICA (*Aztec*)

Water-god to whom CHALCHIUHTLICUE was said to have been married, though this goddess was usually associated with her brother TLÁLOC.

Tlacolotl CENTRAL AMERICA (*Aztec*)

The great horned owl, the omen of the very deepest evil who sits within the temple of ITZLACOLIOHQUI.

Tlaelquarni CENTRAL AMERICA (*Aztec*)

'The cleansing one', a title applied to TLAZOLTÉOTL, under which this goddess was perceived as the patroness of steam-baths known as TEMAZCALLI.

Tlahuixcalpantecuhtli CENTRAL AMERICA – MEXICO (*Aztec and Toltec*) 'Lord of the House of Dawn', the god of dawn, QUETZALCÓATL as the MORNING STAR[2] and patron of the twelfth hour of the twenty-two-hour AZTEC day. Tlahuixcalpantecuhtli was the culture hero of the TOLTECs who dominated southern Mexico before the arrival of the Aztecs.

Tlaik NORTH AMERICA – NORTHWEST COAST (*Comox*)
The sky-chief who was conquered by the two sons of FAIR WEATHER and then eaten by the serpent monster of the sky (cf. SISIUTL).

Tláloc CENTRAL AMERICA – MEXICO (*Aztec*)
Though not a major deity within the AZTEC pantheon, Tláloc was the god of rain and the mountains, and thus of considerable importance in the hot and very dry climate of Mexico. He married his sister CHALCHIUHTLICUE, the goddess of fresh water, although he was also associated with UIXTOCIHUATL, the goddess of salt water and the sea, and with MIXCÓATL ruled the eastern sky. His cult was one of the most horrible of all the Aztec gods, one that even outdid that of XIPE TOTEC. Tláloc was propitiated at a festival in his honour through the sacrifice of as many babies and young children as possible, preferably babies that were not yet weaned. They were then cooked and eaten by the cult priests. If the children cried it was a good omen, a sign of rain to come – the greater the noise they made, the better the rain that would ensue.

Tláloc has very ancient origins, possibly even dating from the early OLMEC period. His hilltop home was TLALOCAN which was abundantly supplied with food and was inhabited by the corn-goddesses. In his role as the god of rain he was said to have poured water on the Earth from four jars that had four very different effects. The first was benevolent and brought forth good crops. The second brought cobwebs and blight, the blight coming from the spiders that inhabited the cobwebs. The third brought frost, while the fourth ensured a poor harvest. As god of the mountains, it was believed that every mountain had its own Tláloc, and he thus also became associated with volcanic eruptions. His symbol was the double-headed serpent, which adorns his blue mask, his eyes being encircled by its coils.

Tláloc struck down QUETZALCÓATL at the end of the era of the SECOND SUN, after which he raised a great storm that blew away almost all the people, those who survived being transformed by him into monkeys. Though Tláloc was clearly of great ritual importance, he is to be found in very few of the narratives, possibly due to his bloodthirsty nature which would not have suited the Christians who recorded the myths and legends of the Aztec following the Spanish conquest.

Tlalocan CENTRAL AMERICA – MEXICO (*Aztec*)
The home of TLÁLOC, the rain-god, and the lowest of the three heavens to which the earliest NAHUA were said to have gone after death. Tlalocan is described as a land of water and mist, a paradise where happiness seemed almost earthly, but was purer and less susceptible to change. Here the dead played leapfrog, chased the butterflies and sang incessantly. Happiness in this sensual world was conceived of in a simple-minded, materialistic manner, a state of mind that was furnished by the abundance of food – maize, peppers, tomatoes, beans and flowers that the corn-goddesses who lived there supplied.

Tláloc did not preside over the realm directly, but instead employed the TLALOQUES, benign mannequins as his ministers, as well as his spies. After a four-year period in this paradisal kingdom that was not much removed from the Earth itself, the souls of the dead were supposed to have been reborn as mortals. The cycle of events would then repeat itself unless man could reach a higher level of enlightenment, in which case he might be considered worthy of entry into TLILLAN-TLAPALLAN.

Some sources delineate between the types of souls of the dead that would find entry to Tlalocan. In these instances the realm was only open to the souls of those who had been sacrificed to Tláloc, thus ensuring that the realm was always full of children whose laughter would fill the air. They were joined, surprisingly, by those who had died of dropsy or skin disease, or had been struck by lightning, though the latter may have been considered as having been chosen by Tláloc himself and thus worthy of reaching this paradise.

Tlaloctecuhtli CENTRAL AMERICA – MEXICO (*Aztec*)
A variant of TLÁLOC that is possibly an earlier name for that deity, in the era before that of the FIRST SUN when Tláloc was thought of as a water-god rather than the rain-god.

Tlaloque CENTRAL AMERICA – MEXICO (*Aztec*)
Generic name given to numerous minor rain-gods who are usually described as mannequins and who acted as TLÁLOCS ministers in TLALOCAN.

Tlaltecuhtli CENTRAL AMERICA – MEXICO (*Aztec*)
The lord of the Earth, a personification of the Earth in opposition to the Sun, and thus associated with death. Tlaltecuhtli was usually depicted as a huge toad with a gaping mouth that had to be kept full with the blood of sacrificial victims.

Tlaltecuhtli is sometimes considered, having undergone a change in gender, as an aspect of the goddess CIHUACÓATL in her aspect ILAMATECUHTLI, an aspect in which she is depicted as the toad Tlaltecuhtli swallowing a knife.

Tlaltecuin CENTRAL AMERICA – MEXICO (*Aztec*)
One of the four guardians of HUITZILO-POCHTLI and thus AMOXAOQUE, the other three being CHIPACTONAL, OXOMOCO and XOCHICAHUACA. They were said to have left AZTLAN with the travellers who set off to find a new homeland, and to have been the only four amoxaoque to have remained with the travellers all the way, after the others had left at TAMOANCHAN.

Tlanuwa NORTH AMERICA – WOODLANDS (*Cherokee and Natchez*)
The magical GREAT HAWK.

Tlascaltec CENTRAL AMERICA
An ancient Central-American people who either lived prior to the AZTECS or co-habited with them. They are recorded as having placed the present era as the fourth era of evolution.

Tlaxcala CENTRAL AMERICA – MEXICO (*Aztec*)
Ancient race within the general constraints of the AZTEC empire whose tutelary deity was CAMAXTLI.

Tlazoltéotl CENTRAL AMERICA – MEXICO (*Aztec*)
The EARTH MOTHER and goddess of lasciviousness who was also known as TLAEL-QUARNI, 'the cleansing one', in which guise she was the patroness of steam-baths known as TEMAZCALLI. Tlazoltéotl was depicted as a young girl wearing a rubber mask with a crescent-shaped ornament on

her nose. Spindles were entwined in her hair to symbolize her patronage of spinners. Though Tlazoltéotl was the goddess of lust, and thus responsible for all man's infidelities, she was also able to grant a person complete absolution. This ritual, which freed the person making the confession, was preceded by a number of penances after which the confessor would give a letter of confession to the priest of the goddess. Upon delivery of the confession, the person would be pardoned from all the sins they had committed throughout their lives, but more importantly, it would also release them from any legal consequences. Perhaps it was for this reason that the AZTECS would only allow each person one such confession in a lifetime.

As the goddess of renewal, Tlazoltéotl demanded an annual human sacrifice. For this purpose a handsome young man would be chosen. Having been killed, his skin would be flayed and then draped around a statue of the goddess. Tlazoltéotl was also worshipped under various aspects as IXCUINA, TETOINNAN and TOCI.

Tlecuil CENTRAL AMERICA (*Aztec*)
The brazier that was the hearth in every home and which was the representation of XIUHTECUHTLI or HUEHUETÉOTL, the god of the year and of the centre.

Tliewatuwadjigican NORTH AMERICA (*Tlingit*)
'He-Who-Knows-Everything', one of the two manservants of NASCAKIYETL, together with ADAWULCANAK.

Tlillan-Tlapallan CENTRAL AMERICA – MEXICO (*Aztec*)
The former home of QUETZALCÓATL to which he returned after leaving TOLLAN.

The realm was obviously offshore as the myths relate that they set off from the coast on his serpent raft to reach it. The realm was referred to as the land of black and red, the two colours together signifying wisdom. This was the paradisal kingdom to which those initiates who had found some practical application for the teachings of Quetzalcóatl went after death. Often celebrated in AZTEC poetry, and a realm to which many desired to go, it was a land of the fleshless – in other words, it was open to those who had learned to live outside the physical constraints of the human body. Tlillan-Tlapallan was the second highest of the three Aztec heavens. Beneath it was TLALOCAN and above it TONATIUHICAN.

Tlingit NORTH AMERICA – NORTHWEST COAST
Indigenous North American AMERINDIAN people from the NORTHWEST COAST culture region who spoke one of the ATHA-PASCAN languages, and placed great emphasis on animal spirits, whose images they carved on their TOTEM poles. Living in South Alaska and northern British Columbia, their neighbours included the BELLA COOLA, CHINOOK, HAIDA, KLAMATH, KWAKIUTL, NOOTKA, SALISH and TSHIMSH-IAN Indians – tribes which speak different languages.

Tloque Nahuaque CENTRAL AMERICA – MEXICO (*Aztec*)
The alternative name for OMETÉOTL, the dual god-above-all. Even though he is referred to as the 'god of the near and close' in his title of 'Lord-of-the-Close-Vicinity', he remains somewhat remote to the ordinary man, the ineffable supreme being. Tloque Nahuaque is described as 'invisible as night, impalpable as wind', which would

not have brought him into immediate favour with the common man who liked to see a more clearly defined image of his god than the hand and footprints that sometimes appear in some TEOTIHUACÁN frescoes to represent this deity. No statue to Tlogue Nahuaque was ever erected. As far as present knowledge of the ancient AZTECs indicates, the only active cult in his honour was at TEZCOCO which, under the charismatic leadership of NEZAHUALCOYTL, became the theological and cultural centre of the Aztec empire.

Tlotli CENTRAL AMERICA – MEXICO (Aztec)

The name of the hawk that was sent, by the other gods, to see why the Sun had stopped moving across the sky, and to ask it to resume its travels once more. The Sun refused until all the gods sacrificed themselves, which they did once they had recognized that the Sun was their superior.

Tocapo Viracocha SOUTH AMERICA – PERU (Inca)

The younger son of the creator PACHAYACHACHIC, and brother of IMAYMANA VIRACOCHA. During the Creation Tocapo Viracocha was given the task of traversing the plains, naming the trees, plants and rivers as he went, as well as teaching all the people the properties and uses of them all. After he had completed his journey, he ascended to the heavens with his brother.

Tochipa CENTRAL AMERICA – MEXICO (Mojave)

The sibling of KUKUMATZ, though some sources give him this relationship to HOKOMATA. Tochipa saved his daughter from the flood raised by Hokomata by sealing her inside a hollow log, an act that ensured the survival of mankind.

Toci CENTRAL AMERICA – MEXICO (Aztec)

'Our Grandmother', an aspect of TLAZOLTÉOTL.

Tochtli CENTRAL AMERICA (Aztec)

The eighth day of the twenty-day MONTH[1] employed by the AZTEC people, which symbolized the rabbit, represented the south and was presided over by MAYAHUEL.

Tohil CENTRAL AMERICA (Maya)

The deity that was given to BALAM QUITZÉ at TULAI ZUIVA to become the tutelary deity of his clan. Tohil gave the clansmen fire and, when the rain extinguished it, he rekindled the sacred flame by striking his shoes together. When men from other tribes came to beg some of the fire, they were at first repulsed but Tohil told them that he would allow them this gift if, in return, they would embrace him 'under the armpit and under the girdle' – a phrase meaning they should acknowledge his presence with human sacrifices. Tohil was turned to stone when the Sun first appeared, its rays petrifying the god.

Tollan CENTRAL AMERICA – MEXICO (Aztec and Toltec)

The city governed over by the earthly QUETZALCÓATL, though early myths credit the foundation of the city to the godly Quetzalcóatl in a time long before it fell to the CHICHIMECs. The exact location of this legendary city has never been fully established, though many authorities site it at modern TULA. The city plays a significant part in early myths, but is not often mentioned in later stories.

The city was allegedly the home of the brothers BALAM AGAB, BALAM QUITZÉ, IQI BALAM and MAHUCUTAH, who left its confines to witness the birth of the Sun. From this cursory mention, the city later develops into a sort of earthly paradise, a city that would have been fitting for the incarnate Quetzalcóatl. The houses were made from green stone, or precious metals, or shells, or turquoise and exquisite feathers. It was also an extremely prosperous city. The people never went hungry because the harvests were always good, the abundance of food leading to the largest maize cobs not being eaten but rather burned as fuel. Cocoa and various shades of cotton – red, green, yellow, blue, brown, orange and the usual white – grew and the people wanted for nothing. Quetzalcóatl also introduced to his subjects writing and the CALENDAR.

Quetzalcóatl loved his subjects so dearly that he would not allow human sacrifice within the city. Instead birds, snakes and butterflies were offered in sacrifice, a fact that angered black TEZCATLIPOCA who plotted to destroy both Quetzalcóatl and his paradisal city. After Quetzalcóatl had succumbed to the evil machinations of Tezcatlipoca, he left Tollan, some sources saying that he was banished, others that he left of his own volition. Before he left he utterly destroyed the city, though some accounts say that the city survived for a further 200 years until its last secular king, HUEMAC, was destroyed, once again by the evil plans of Tezcatlipoca. In this instance the king did not destroy the city but rather it was overrun by its enemies as the population had been almost wiped out by Tezcatlipoca's schemes.

Toltec CENTRAL AMERICA – MEXICO
A Central-American AMERINDIAN people who ruled much of MAYAn central Mexico between the tenth and the twelfth centuries AD. They were alleged to have come from the north, the first of the NAHUA peoples to arrive in Mexico, a statement supported by the similarity of many of their legends to those of the North American Indians who lived in the southern part of that country. The Toltecs were followed

south by the CHICHIMECs and then the MEXICA or AZTECs. They were legendarily led south by MIXCÓATL who founded their capital at TULA, a city that has been cited as a possible location for the legendary city of TOLLAN. Their religious and cultural centre was at TEOTIHUACÁN where there are temples to the Sun and the Moon, as well as to their serpent god QUETZAL-CÓATL. The Toltecs are usually referred to in the same breath as the Aztecs, though this is not strictly true. Certainly both the Aztecs and the Toltecs were Nahua peoples, but there were distinct cultural differences between them. None the less, the two were almost completely assimilated during the rise of the Aztec empire.

Tomsivsi NORTH AMERICA – GREAT
PLAINS (*Cheyenne*)
'Erect Horns', the culture hero of the CHEYENNE who is credited with the introduction of the SUN DANCE.

tona CARIBBEAN (*Taïno*)
The name given to a dwarf-like being, into which the children who were abandoned by GUAGUGIANA were said to have been transformed.

Tonacacíhuatl CENTRAL AMERICA –
MEXICO (*Aztec*)
'Lady-of-our-Being' or 'Lady Nourishment', the mother of the gods and the consort of TONACATECUHTLI with whom she lived in the ninth and highest heaven. She had four sons by her husband, these four seemingly originating as nature deities and guardians of the four cardinal points. They later came to be identified with the tutelary deities of the AZTEC empire's different peoples. They were red CAMAXTLI, chief deity of the TLAXCALA; HUITZILO-POCHTLI of the Aztecs; QUETZALCÓATL, wind-god and chief deity of the TOLTECS; black TEZCATLIPOCA, god of the night and war-god of the city of TEZCOCO.

Tonacatecuhtli CENTRAL AMERICA – MEXICO (*Aztec*)
'Lord-of-our-Being' or 'Lord Nourishment', the consort of TONACACÍHUATL with whom he lived in the ninth and highest heaven. The creator and food provider, Tonacatecuhtli is symbolized by a crown filled with the staple food of the AZTECS – maize. He was also called CHICOMEXOCHTLI ('Seven Flowers'), in which guise he was identified with the MILKY WAY[2]. There were no temples built to his honour and glorification, and he had no cult because, so it was said, he was regarded as being far elevated above these things. He and his wife had four sons who were some of the greatest of the Central-American deities. They were CAMAXTLI, HUITZILOPOCHTLI, QUETZALCÓATL and TEZCATLIPOCA.

Tonalpohualli CENTRAL AMERICA (*Aztec*)
The sacred division of 260 days that equates to the TZOLKIN of the MAYA. The Tonalpohualli was divided into five parts that were seen as corresponding to the four cardinal points and the centre, and has an exact parallel in the fifty-two-year cycle at which the Sun had to be revived, or the world would come to an end.

Tona(n)tzin CENTRAL AMERICA – MEXICO (*Aztec*)
'Our Mother', the goddess of motherhood, though strictly this role is taken by CIHUACÓATL for whom this name is thought to be an alternative.

Tonapa SOUTH AMERICA – PERU (*Collao*)
A simple variant of THUNAPA.

Tonatiuh CENTRAL AMERICA – MEXICO (*Aztec*)
The god of the Sun, the heavenly warrior who was perceived as an eagle. Also called PILTZINTECUHTLI and closely associated with the deities HUITZILOPOCHTLI and TEZCATLIPOCA, Tonatiuh had a much greater cult following than the theologically superior gods OMETECUHTLI, TLOQUE NAHUAQUE and TONACATECUHTLI. His home, TONATIUHICAN, was originally thought of as the highest heaven, even higher than that of Tonacatecuhtli and TONACACÍHUATL, a place for those who had achieved in life. The AZTECS, however, later made it the place to which dead warriors went after death, either in times of peace or of war.

Tonatiuhican CENTRAL AMERICA – MEXICO (*Aztec*)
The abode of TONATIUH, that was originally thought of as being the highest heaven to which the souls of those who had fully achieved in their mortal lives would go after death. Later the realm became the abode of dead warriors, though this may be a misinterpretation of the NAHUA holy-war, which has been described as an earthly war against mortal enemies, though, while the war was fought on Earth, the combatants were certainly not mortal men.

Topa Ayar Cachi SOUTH AMERICA (*Inca*)
One of the four brothers of the CHILDREN OF THE SUN according to Fray Martin DE MONIA, the other three being CUSCO HUANCA, HUANA CAURI and MANCO CAPAC. Their four sisters are named by de Monia as CORI OCLLO, IPA HUACO, MAMA COYA and TOPA HUACO. The name Topa Ayar Cachi does not appear in the accounts of Pedro DE CIEZA DE LÉON who also recorded the story of the Children of the Sun. He names three brothers as AYAR CACHI ASAUCA (possibly to be identified with Topa Ayar Cachi), AYAR MANCO (possibly identifiable with Manco Capac) and AYAR UCHO, and three sisters named

MAMA COYA, – the only name common to both accounts, MAMA HUACO and MAMA RAHUA.

Topa Huaco SOUTH AMERICA (*Inca*)
According to Fray Martin DE MONIA, Topa Huaco was one of the four sisters who made up the CHILDREN OF THE SUN together with their four brothers. Her sisters are named as CORI OCLLO, IPA HUACO and MAMA COYA, and her four brothers as CUSCO HUANCA, HUANA CAURI, MANCO CAPAC and TOPA AYAR CACHI. Her name does not appear in the writings of Pedro DE CIEZA DE LÉON who also recorded the legends of the Children of the Sun.

tornak (pl. tornait) NORTH AMERICA – ARCTIC (*Inuit*)
The name given to an INUA after it has become the guardian spirit or helper of an individual. The most powerful inue that might become a tornak are those of bears and stones. If a bear inua becomes a tornak, then it might swallow the individual and subsequently regurgitate him as an ANGAKOK. The INUIT of Greenland have a vague belief in a ruler of the tornait named TORNASUK (literally 'Great Tornak') who is said to have enabled the SHAMANS to control their individual tornait.

Tornasuk NORTH AMERICA – GREENLAND (*Inuit*)
'Great Tornak', the leader of the tornait (see TORNAK) who is vaguely believed in by the INUIT of Greenland. They say that he was responsible for giving SHAMANS the ability to control their tornait.

Torngasoau NORTH AMERICA – ARCTIC (*Inuit*)
The immortal god of the INUIT who reigns supreme over all the other spirits.

Tornit NORTH AMERICA – GREENLAND (*Inuit*)
'Inlanders', a mythical people who, though taller and stronger than the INUIT, were not as skilled at handling boats or hunting. They fled after an Inuit youth killed one of them by boring a hole in his head with a crystal drill. From that day to this, the Tornit have been the enemies of the Inuit, though they pose no real threat, occasionally stealing an Inuit woman when there is a thick fog, but they always hide from the Inuit men and are terrified of their dogs.

Totem(ic) WIDESPREAD
Totemism was widespread throughout all the native AMERINDIAN peoples from all parts of the continent. The name is ALGONQUIAN and means 'mark of my family', though some sources claim that it comes from the Ojibway *ototeman*, meaning 'he is my relative'. Totemism is the belief in kinship, either individually or as a clan, with animals, plants, or any other object, animate or inanimate. It is also the symbol of the clan or individual's theriomorphic ancestors (those having animal form), and as such represents the metamorphical expression of man's relationship to his fellows and to the rest of the world. This totem is sacred to those concerned and they are forbidden to eat or desecrate it. Additionally, marriage within the clan is usually forbidden. The familiar, and sometimes spectacular totem poles of the North American Indian tribes are perhaps the best-known icons of their cultures. These were carved and painted to represent the totems of the clan or tribe and acted either as a symbol of the people or as commemoration of the dead.

Totonac CENTRAL AMERICA – MEXICO
Ancient civilization that inhabited the Gulf coastline of Mexico together with the OLMEC people and who adopted some of

the AZTEC beliefs and deities, though they gave their own names to the latter.

Toueyo CENTRAL AMERICA – MEXICO (Aztec)

The name used by TEZCATLIPOCA when he assumed the guise of a naked peasant who came to the market-place outside the palace at TOLLAN. He was seen there by HUEMAC's virgin daughter who had never seen a naked man before. She fell ill out of her desire for the unidentified peasant who could be found nowhere when Huemac's men searched for him. Yet, as soon as Huemac called off the search, Toueyo reappeared in the market-place.

He was brought before Huemac who told him to cure the sickness he had caused in this daughter. Thus Toueyo, a man from the lowest social class, was married to the princess. Catastrophe followed. The city was firstly stricken by drought, followed, as would be expected, by a terrible famine. With the people severely weakened by the effects of these blights, the city of Tollan was easily overrun and destroyed by its enemies. Tezcatlipoca thus finally destroyed the city from which 200 years before he had driven out the earthly QUETZALCÓATL.

Toussaint, Monsieur HAITI (Voodoo)

One of the numerous LOA of the VOODOO religion.

Tovapod SOUTH AMERICA – BRAZIL (Tupari)

He and his companion, AROTEH, primitive VAMOA-POD, lived together in a tent, from which they had their food stolen by the first men who, at that time, lived in the UNDERWORLD. Tovapod and Aroteh sought out the thieves and tracked them to a hole at which they began to dig. Streams of the Underworld dwellers rushed forth until the two could fill in the hole. These primitive beings were tusked and had webbed hands and feet. Forgiving the people for having stolen their food, Tovapod removed their tusks and webbing, thus giving them their beautiful hands, feet and teeth.

Toxint NORTH AMERICA – NORTHWEST COAST (Kwakiutl)

A masked ritual dance that mimics the ritual decapitation of a woman.

Tracas HAITI (Voodoo)

One of the numerous LOA of the VOODOO religion.

Tree of Mirrors CENTRAL AMERICA (Aztec)

The name given to TEZCATLIPOCA when he helped to support the heavens at the start of the FIFTH SUN era. His adversary QUETZALCÓATL also helped and became known as the PRECIOUS TREE. This pair lent their assistance to the four giants, FALLING EAGLE, RESURRECTION, SERPENT OF OBSIDIAN KNIVES and THORNY FLOWERS who had been specifically positioned at the four cardinal points to keep heaven and Earth apart.

Trelque Huecuvu SOUTH AMERICA – CHILE AND ARGENTINA (Arauca)

Little used variant of HUECUVU, though it is conceivable that this is the full name of that character whose name has been shortened over time.

Trickster NORTH AMERICA

A characterization that is common to all AMERINDIAN peoples of North America, though the concept, under slightly different guises, may also be found in Central-American traditions. The concept of the Trickster is related to that of the twin heroes, either or both of whom are shown to embody some of the Trickster's aspects. A changeable character, neither god nor man, the Trickster is both a creator and a destroyer, though neither good nor evil, cunning, devious, spiteful and sometimes, as in the case of SEDIT, too clever for his own good. Trickster is a very apt name for a character whose chief role seems to have been a sort of mythical practical joker, though often as not the joke would back-fire. In many cases the Trickster was at the root of all mankind's joy, as well as all his sorrows.

The Trickster appears in both mytho-logy and folklore. He helped to form the first world, helped to recreate it after the FLOOD, obtained fire, defeated monsters, created mankind, and then caused man to lose his immortality though, as he realized a little too late, by making man mortal, he had also caused his own mortality. The Trickster does not always appear in a crea-tive role, and in these instances he is given the role of an adventurer. He is usually perceived in theriomorphic terms: on the Great Plains and in the Southwest he is COYOTE (a characterization that is also to be found in Central-American mytho-logy); on the Northwest Coast he is YETL, the RAVEN or CROW; in the Woodlands he is the Great HARE or RABBIT, a figure who appears again in the folklore of the south-ern Negro as Brer Rabbit, an amalgam of the Trickster and West African animal heroes.

Tsanta SOUTH AMERICA – ECUADOR (Jivaro)
The name of a ritual that was performed after a head-hunting raid. The successful warrior was washed in chicken's blood and the tsanta, (the head that has been shrunken) stuck on a lance around which, at the height of the ritual, men dance flourishing their spears in a re-enactment of the kill. The idea of the ritual is to gain victory over the spirit of the dead man, perceived of as evil, and by so doing trans-form it into a benevolent and helpful spirit. A Jivaros man is not considered mature

until he has captured the soul of an enemy which was then said to enable the souls of his loved ones to end their sad wanderings and rest at peace forever.

Tsegihi NORTH AMERICA – SOUTHWEST (Navajo)
The name of a sacred place, location un-known, that is referred to in the great NIGHT CHANT.

Tsenta NORTH AMERICA – WOODLANDS (Huron)
The HURON equivalent of YOSKEHA.

Tsetseka NORTH AMERICA – NORTHWEST COAST (Kwakiutl)
The winter, a supernatural season, when everything is changed – names, chants and the ways of singing them. The BAKOOS (summer names) of the clans and tribal ranks are also changed so that they relate to the winter spirits.

Tshanahale NORTH AMERICA – SOUTHWEST (Navajo)
A feathered, man-eating monster who was one of the terrible ANAYE.

Tshimshian NORTH AMERICA – NORTHWEST COAST
Indigenous North American AMERINDIAN people of the NORTHWEST COAST culture region whose neighbours include the likes of the BELLA COOLA, CHINOOK, HAIDA, KLA-MATH, KWAKIUTL, NOOTKA and SALISH In-dians – tribes which speak different lan-guages.

Tshohanoai NORTH AMERICA – SOUTHWEST (Navajo)
One of the two men who had, together with KLEHONOAI, found the soil and grown the reed that enabled the NAVAJO people to escape from the flood waters that threatened to engulf them, and so arrive

on the present Earth (see ASCENT OF THE NAVAJO). As a reward Tshohanoai was appointed Sun-Bearer by ATSE HASTIN and ATSE ESTSAN, while Klehonoai was made the Moon-Bearer.

Some accounts say that he was the father, by the goddess ESTANATLEHI, of the twins NAYANEZGANI and THOBADZIST-SHINI, though other accounts say that they were simply the parents of Nayanezgani, and that Thobadzistshini was the son of YOLKAI ESTSAN and WATER, though how this could make the two boys twin brothers is uncertain.

Nayanezgani and Thobadzistshini, helped by SPIDER-WOMAN and NILTSHI, made a tortuous and perilous journey to visit their father in his HOGAN. At first he refused to believe who they were, but as they had been armed with magical chants by Spider-Woman, they survived all his tests and by doing so won his confidence and acceptance. He gave the twins magical weapons: arrows of lightning; sun-beams; a rainbow; a huge stone knife that possibly symbolized a thunderbolt; and armour from every joint of which lightning flashed. Later, after the twins had been unable to kill all the ANAYE, Tshohanoai gave them four hoops that were used by ESTANATLEHI to raise a terrible storm that not only killed all but four of the anaye (COLD, HUNGER, OLD AGE and POVERTY), it also reshaped the Earth.

Tsichtinaka NORTH AMERICA – PUEBLO, SOUTHWEST (*Acoma*)
The name of the leader of the UNDER-WORLD people who brought them up to the Earth's surface.

Tsiskagili NORTH AMERICA – WOODLANDS (*Cherokee*)
The Red Crayfish who got both his colouring and his inedible flesh, when the primordial animals first set the Sun in the sky,

but set it too low so he was badly scorched.

Tsolb CENTRAL AMERICA – YUCATÁN, MEXICO (*Modern Maya*)
'Offenders', the inhabitants of the second world that was, like that of the SAIYAM-KOOB (the inhabitants of the first era), destroyed by a FLOOD[7]. The Tsolb were followed by the MAYA, but their world was also destroyed by a flood, and so the present era began, an era inhabited by many races.

Tson(o)qua NORTH AMERICA – WOODLANDS (*Kwakiutl*)
The CANNIBAL MOTHER[1], an important TOTEM figure in clan rituals. Tsonoqua lived in the woods where she fed on the corpses of the dead as well as on children she stole. She was eventually killed by SKY-YOUTH with whose reflected image she had fallen in love. Neighbouring tribes called her SNENEIKULALA and the tongue-twisting BAXBAKUALANUCHSIWAE, the latter also being a KWAKIUTL deity, but this time from the NORTHWEST COAST dwelling Kwakiutl.

Tsotil NORTH AMERICA – SOUTHWEST (*Navajo*)
One of the sacred mountains of the NAV-AJO people. See ASCENT OF THE NAVAJO.

Tsurapako NORTH AMERICA – GREAT PLAINS (*Pawnee*)
One of the five houses inhabited by the NAHURAK. These five houses, in order of importance, were the PAHUK, NAKISKAT, Tsurapako, KITSAWITSAK and PAHUA.

ttlaya NORTH AMERICA – GREAT PLAINS (*Fox*)
Generic name for a spirit or a ghost.

Tuapaca SOUTH AMERICA (*Collao*)
The COLLAO name for CON TICCI VIRA-
COCHA.

Tuchaipai CENTRAL AMERICA – MEXICO
(*Diegueño*)
Killed through the wickedness of FROG.
His body was set upon a pyre ready for
cremation but, before the fire was lit, the
people sent COYOTE away as they feared his
intentions. However, Coyote saw the
smoke from the fire and hurried back to
snatch Tuchaipai's heart from the flames.
A similar story to this is told by the neighbouring MOJAVE people.

Tula CENTRAL AMERICA – MEXICO
Ancient TOLTEC city, near modern Tula de
Allende, 40 miles northwest of Mexico
City which flourished *c*.750–1168 and had
a population estimated at about 40,000.
Tula is thought by some to have been the
site of the legendary city of TOLLAN.

Tulai Zuiva CENTRAL AMERICA (*Maya*)
The PLACE OF SEVEN CAVES AND SEVEN
RAVINES where each of the Four BACAB
were given a tutelary deity to preside over
their respective clans. BALAM AGAB gained
AVILIX; BALAM QUITZÉ received TOHIL; IQI
BALAM was given NICAHTAGAH and MAHU-
CUTAH obtained HACAVITZ.

Tule, Lake NORTH AMERICA –
NORTHWEST COAST (*Modoc*)
Lake from the depths of which QUMO-
QUMS, at his fifth attempt, managed to
bring up a handful of soil with which to
create the world.

Tun CENTRAL AMERICA (*Maya*)
The basic MAYA year which was measured
as a period of 360 days, the remaining five
days of the year being outside the normal

course of events, and thus much feared by
the Maya people.

Tunja SOUTH AMERICA – COLOMBIA
(*Chibcha*)
City to the northeast of Bogota, the capital
of the Andean department of Boyacá that
was formerly the seat of the CHIBCHA kings,
and near which BACHUÉ was said to have
emerged from Lake IGUAGUÉ carrying a
young boy whom she subsequently married
and set about populating the world.

Tupilak NORTH AMERICA – ARCTIC
(*Inuit*)
A magical animal, usually in the form of a
seal, under the command of an ILISITSOK
who would use it to attack his victims.

tupile CENTRAL AMERICA (*Maya*)
The name given to a town constable, a
member of one of the three lowest castes
within the MAYA social hierarchy.

Turquoise Boy NORTH AMERICA –
SOUTHWEST (*Navajo*)
Tutelary deity of the NAVAJO who was set
on Mount TAYLOR, along with CORN GIRL,
by ATSE HASTIN and ATSE ESTSAN after they
had created the Navajo land. See ASCENT
OF THE NAVAJO.

Turtle NORTH AMERICA – SOUTHWEST
(*Navajo*)
One of the four animal spirits that travelled to an undersea village with the intention of taking two of its young women
captive. He was accompanied by BEAR,
SNAKE and FROG. He and Frog were elected
to enter the village and kidnap the two
maidens, but they were spotted as they
tried to leave with the young women
whom they killed and quickly scalped. The
villagers then tried to roast the kidnappers
and, having failed, attempted to drown
them. Frog and Turtle made good their

escape with the girls' scalps, rejoined their comrades and all four set off for their home. See HOZONI.

Tuscarora NORTH AMERICA –
   WOODLANDS
Indigenous North American AMERINDIAN people inhabiting a northern part of the WOODLANDS culture region. At first violently opposed to the confederation of IROQUOIS nations proposed by HAIOWATHA, the Tuscarora people joined that confederation, known as the LEAGUE OF THE LONG HOUSE in 1715, thus bringing an end to the frequent internecine warfare between the Iroquoian peoples.

Twelve Ik CENTRAL AMERICA (*Maya*)
The twelfth day of the CREATION[4] when the wind blew for the first time, the wind thenceforth being known as IK, for the wind is alone on Earth as an immortal.

Twin Heroes NORTH AMERICA
A common concept among AMERINDIAN peoples of North America, the twins are usually the grandsons of the EARTH MOTHER and play a particularly important role in many of the creation myths. In the southwest the twins are thought of as war-gods, but further north they adopt a very familiar role, that of the eternal struggle between good and evil – one twin being benevolent, the other most definitely malevolent.

Two Chicchan CENTRAL AMERICA
   (*Maya*)
The fifteenth day of the CREATION[4] on which evil first made its presence known to man. Two Chicchan is not to be confused with CHICCHAN, the fifth day of the MAYA spiritual pilgrimage, the AGES OF MAN.

Two Eb CENTRAL AMERICA (*Maya*)
The second day of the CREATION[4] on which MONTH[2] formed the first ladder so that god could travel between heaven and Earth. Two Eb is not to be confused with EB, the twelfth day of the AGES OF MAN, though both days are parallel as Eb is the day on which the spirit begins its long ascent of the ladder to heaven.

Tzahui CENTRAL AMERICA (*Mixtec*)
The MIXTEC name for TEZCATLIPOCA, in his aspect as TLÁLOC the rain-god.

Tzinteotl CENTRAL AMERICA – MEXICO
   (*Aztec*)
The goddess of procreation and the birth of all things organic or inorganic, spiritual or material.

tzité CENTRAL AMERICA (*Maya*)
Plant whose red berries were used by GUCUMATZ and TEPEU, together with the kernels of maize, to determine how they should proceed with the creation of mankind. The result of this divination was to carve men from wood, but this proved disastrous, and the gods destroyed them.

tzizhui NORTH AMERICA – GREAT
   PLAINS (*Osage*)
Generic name given to spirits of the sky.

Tzizimime CENTRAL AMERICA – MEXICO
   (*Aztec*)
'The-Monsters-Descending-From-Above', the generic name given to malevolent stellar deities.

Tzizimitl CENTRAL AMERICA (*Aztec*)
Guardian of MAYAHUAL (and other maidens) who was asleep when EHÉCATL came to her and persuaded her to leave with him.

Tzolkin CENTRAL AMERICA (*Maya*)
The divine division of 260 days that was the equivalent of the TONALPOHUALLI of the AZTECS.

Tzontemoc CENTRAL AMERICA – MEXICO (*Aztec*)
'He-of-the-Falling-Hair', a title of MICT-LÁNTECUHTLI.

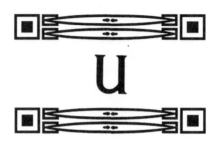

U

Uchtsiti NORTH AMERICA – PUEBLO, SOUTHWEST (Acoma)
'Nothing-Lacking', the omnipotent father of the gods.

Uixtocihuatl CENTRAL AMERICA – MEXICO (*Aztec*)
The goddess of salt water and the sea who became the wife of TEZCATLIPOCA in his aspect as TLÁLOC.

Ulala NORTH AMERICA – NORTHWEST COAST (*Haida*)
Mythical man-eating ogress.

Ulé SOUTH AMERICA – BOLIVIA (*Yuracare*)
Having been killed and torn to shreds by a jaguar, Ulé's wife gathered together all the pieces of his body she could find and successfully brought him back to life. However, when Ulé saw his reflection in a forest pool, he reeled back in disgust as a large part of the flesh on his face was missing. Despite his wife's pleas, Ulé decided to leave and spend the remainder of his life alone. His wife, in her distraction lost her way in the forest and, heavily pregnant, stumbled into a jaguar's lair where the mother jaguar took pity on her, though her four sons wanted to kill her. However, they promised not to hurt her if she would eat the poisonous ants that infested both the lair and their backs. She managed to trick three of the jaguar cubs by exchanging the ants for seeds, but the fourth had eyes in the back of his head and

saw what she was doing. He killed her, and from her body the boy TIRI was born who was later to avenge her death.

Ulmil Itzáhal CENTRAL AMERICA (*Maya*)
A member of the usurping ITZÁ family who was betrothed to the princess SAC-NICTÉ. However, she was loved by TA-ITZÁ who abducted her, but she drowned herself.

umiarissat NORTH AMERICA (*Inuit*)
The boats of phantom women of the sea which are crewed by transformed seals.

Underworld WIDESPREAD
The concept of the Underworld, that is a world below the Earth, is common to all North, Central and South American AMERINDIAN peoples. However, while the concept might be common, different peoples have different perceptions of the exact purpose of this region. To some it is the classic dark, foreboding realm that may be equated with the Christian hell, or the classical Greek Hades. It is a land of the dead from which there is no return, though some myths do indeed show heroes travelling to the Underworld from which they later return, but only after they have, in some way or another, defeated the lords of the Underworld.

Equally the Underworld is, to the majority of Amerindian peoples, not a place of death, but rather a place of creation. The NAVAJO, for example, travelled up through several such Underworlds (see ASCENT OF THE NAVAJO) before they came to the Earth itself. A number of South American peoples, including the INCA, believed that either they or their divine ancestors came up from the Underworld, which they consider as the source of all life. However, it is the stories of the realm of the dead that stick in most people's minds when they refer to the Underworld as, perhaps, these are the easiest to equate to Christian and classical beliefs. It is better regarded as an ambivalent realm, for, even if it is a land of the dead, it is not necessarily hell, but rather an undefined realm to which all the dead go. It is only those who have been evil on Earth who would find their eternal after-life one of torment.

Unelanuki NORTH AMERICA – WOODLANDS (*Cherokee*)

'The Appointer', the goddess of the Sun whose brother, the god of the Moon, became her lover, visiting her once a month. As they always met in the dark, Unelanuki rubbed ashes into her brother's face so that she would be sure of recognizing him. However, their tryst was discovered and so ashamed was the Moon that he made sure that, from that day forth, he has always remained far away from his sister. When he has to approach her in the western sky, he makes himself as thin and inconspicuous as possible.

Unktehi NORTH AMERICA – GREAT PLAINS (*Dakota*)

The spirit of water.

Upholders-of-the-Heavens NORTH AMERICA – GREAT PLAINS (*Skidi Pawnee*)

Name given to the spirits who maintained the space between heaven and Earth. They were instrumental in the creation of the Earth after BRIGHT STAR commanded them to strike the surface of the primordial waters with their clubs. As they did so, the waters divided and land appeared. Again

under the orders of Bright Star, they began to sing about the shaping of the Earth. As the song progressed, the wind, lightning and thunder spirits shaped the Earth into hills and valleys. As these spirits left, the song changed and the Earth was clothed with trees and grass, its waters purified and seeds germinated.

Urpi-huachac SOUTH AMERICA (*Quechua*)

The goddess of fish whose daughter spurned the god CONIRAYA who, in retaliation for the snub, emptied Urpi-huachac's fishpond into the sea which is the origin of sea fish.

Ursa Major

A famous constellation of the northern celestial hemisphere that is seen by a number of AMERINDIAN peoples as the heavenly incarnation of a god or hero.

1 CENTRAL AMERICA – MEXICO (*Aztec*)
The personification of the god TEZCATLIPOCA who every night may be seen falling towards the sea into which QUETZALCÓATL threw him.

2 CENTRAL AMERICA (*Maya*)
Said to possibly represent the god C in spirit form.

3 NORTH AMERICA – ARCTIC (*Inuit*)
The heavenly incarnation of a polar bear that was chased into the sky by a group of hunters who may also be seen in the night sky as the beautiful star cluster the PLEIADES[1], still chasing the animal with their dogs.

Urus SOUTH AMERICA – BOLIVIA (*Aymará*)

Name given to a group of despised Indians who spoke a different language from the AYMARÁ and say that they were born from the slime of Lake TITICACA when the Sun first warmed it. The Aymará, however, say that the Urus were brought from the coast by TACUILLA to be their slaves.

Usukun CENTRAL AMERICA – YUCATÁN,
MEXICO (*Lacandone*)
A troglodyte, the brother of NOHOCHA-
KYUM, he governs earthquakes and is thus
greatly feared.

Usumacinta, River CENTRAL AMERICA
(*Maya*)
River that for a part of its course forms the
border between Mexico and Guatemala. It
was down this river that the mysterious
character VOTAN was said to have sailed to
found PALENQUE, which lies a short distance to the east of the river.

Uti Hiata NORTH AMERICA – GREAT
PLAINS (*Pawnee*)
The goddess of corn and patroness of the
harvest.

Utiu CENTRAL AMERICA (*Maya*)
The name of the COYOTE who, together
with the forest cat YAC, the parrot QUEL
and the crow HOH, sought out and brought
the maize seed needed by the gods to
create mankind.

Utsanati NORTH AMERICA –
WOODLANDS (*Cherokee*)
'Rattlesnake', an animal spirit who is, perhaps perversely considering the dangerous
nature of the animal itself, considered as a
helper of mankind.

Utset NORTH AMERICA – PUEBLO,
SOUTHWEST (*Sia*)
The creatrix of the SIA who, together with
her sister NOWUTSET, was created by SUS-
SISTINNAKO, the primordial spider. When
the UNDERWORLD was flooded, she led the
people up to the Earth through a hollow
reed while she carried a sack containing all
the stars on her back. She entrusted this
sack to BEETLE but he could not resist
having a look and almost all the stars
escaped, which explains why there is no
order to their distribution in the night sky.
Utset managed to catch a few of the escaping stars, from which she made the planets,
and then created corn for her people to eat
by planting pieces of her own heart.

uwan(n)ami NORTH AMERICA – NEW
MEXICO (*Zuñi*)
'Rainmakers', a group of shadowy deities,
spirits of departed ZUÑI ruled over by the
Sun, who live at the very edge of the world
where they collect water from the six great
springs of the six sacred mountains of the
Zuñi. Vapour from the springs carries the
uwannami skywards. Hidden from those
on the Earth by the clouds, the uwannami
move between heaven and Earth and pour
or sprinkle the water they have collected
through the sieve-like clouds.

Uxmal CENTRAL AMERICA – MEXICO
Important archaeological site on the Yucatán peninsula a short distance to the west
of the city of Ticul. The centre was of
importance to both the MAYA and
the AZTEC nations. Within the ruins is a
small temple known locally as the
Dwarf's House. This clearly demonstrated
that dwarfs were held in high esteem, a
fact supported by the journey of QUETZAL-
CÓATL from TOLLAN to TLILLAN-
TLAPALLAN when he was accompanied by a
retinue of dwarfs who died of the cold,
their death causing Quetzalcóatl much
sorrow. Uxmal was also the centre from
which the XIU clan ruled the Maya
people.

Uyuuyewe NORTH AMERICA – PUEBLO,
SOUTHWEST (*Sia*)
The twin brother of MAASEWE.

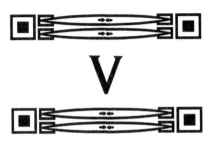

V

Vab SOUTH AMERICA – BRAZIL (*Tupari*)
The younger brother of VALEDJÁD who was born in a similar manner to his older brother, from a block of stone that split in half, from which Vab was born amid a great stream of blood.

Vagoniona CARIBBEAN (*Taïno*)
A variant name given to GUAGUGIANA.

Valedjád SOUTH AMERICA – BRAZIL (*Tupari*)
The older brother of VAB, both brothers being born in a similar manner from blocks of stones that split in half, amid streams of blood. Valedjád was inherently evil and, in a fit of pique, flooded the world, an act that led the Sun to consider how he might be disposed of. Eventually a sorcerer named ARKAONYÓ used liquid beeswax to seal Valedjád's eyes and nostrils, and to stick his fingers together so that he could not use his magical powers. Now having him captive, the people went in search of a bird that was large enough and strong enough, to carry him away to the north, and after many attempts watched as he was carried away. He lives in the north in a stone hut, and whenever he gets angry, it rains.

Valum Chivim CENTRAL AMERICA (*Maya*)
The as yet unidentified home village of the mysterious VOTAN.

Valum Votan CENTRAL AMERICA (*Maya*)
Town or village through which the mysterious VOTAN is said to have travelled *en route* from his home village of VALUM CHIVIM to travel up the River USUMACINTA to found PALENQUE.

vamoa-pod SOUTH AMERICA – BRAZIL (*Tupari*)
Primitive beings who lived in a tent and inhabited the Earth before mankind came up from the UNDERWORLD. Just two vamoa-pod are named: AROTEH and TOVAPOD. After the vamoa-pod had had their food stolen by some of mankind who had sneaked up from underground, the two dug in the hole to which they tracked the thieves. By so doing, they let streams of the people out, until Aroteh and Tovapod blocked up the hole again. These first people had tusks which Tovapod removed, and webbing between their fingers and toes, which he also removed, thus giving the people their present beautiful teeth, hands and feet.

Vaugh'eh SOUTH AMERICA – BRAZIL (*Tupari*)
The female of the giant SHAMAN rulers of the village of the dead, with whom male PABID must have ritual intercourse before being admitted to their eternal home and introduced to their new companions. Vaugh'eh had her male counterpart in MPOKÁLERO.

Venus

The second planet of the solar system that was commonly perceived among many peoples, and not just the AMERINDIANS, as the personification of one, or more usually, two deities. This is due to the fact that the planet appears early in the morning before sunrise, a time when it is referred to as the MORNING STAR, and shortly after dusk, before any of the stars are visible, a time when it is referred to as the EVENING STAR. The following is not a complete list of all the native American personifications of the planet, but rather a representative list.

1 NORTH AMERICA (*Skidi Pawnee*)

The characterization of BRIGHT STAR when seen as the Evening Star, and of GREAT STAR when seen as the MORNING STAR[4].

2 CENTRAL AMERICA (*Maya*)

Seen by some as the characterization of the god C, the MAYA called the planet NOH EK, the GREAT STAR. They had great respect for the planet Venus, as clearly demonstrated in the calculation of their CALENDAR which was, to a great part, based on the rotational period of the planet, as well as governing their rituals and warfare by careful observation of the planet. The planet was given its own day, LAMAT, the eighth day of the AGES OF MAN, the Maya spiritual pilgrimage on which mans spirit plunges into the lowest, infernal regions of the UNDERWORLD, whose depravations he must then overcome if he is to progress.

3 NORTH AMERICA – ARCTIC (*Inuit*)

Seen low in the western sky as spring approaches, the planet Venus is said to be the spirit of an old man, who was chased into the air by the parents of some children he had imprisoned after they had disturbed him when he was hunting seals.

4 CENTRAL AMERICA (*Aztec*)

The personification and symbol of QUETZALCÓATL as the Morning Star.

Village of Souls NORTH AMERICA – WOODLANDS (*Algonquian*)

The home to which HARE retired after his work on Earth had come to an end. Situated in the far west, Hare still lives there with his grandmother NOKOMIS and his brother MOQWAOI, who had gone there before him. Sometimes braves have journeyed there to visit him. One story tells of how four, though some sources say seven, braves made the perilous journey and entertained Hare who promised each brave a wish. One man asked to be a successful hunter. Another wanted to be a great warrior. However, the last wished for immortality, so Hare turned him into a stone (some say a tree).

Ville au Camp HAITI (*Voodoo*)

The name of the underwater capital of the LOA.

Viracocha SOUTH AMERICA (*Inca*)

Also known as CON TICCI VIRACOCHA (perhaps his most correct form) or TICCI VIRACOCHA, this creator figure was the most widely accepted deity among the many peoples of the INCA empire. His cult did not attract a wide following until PACHACUTI developed it, and combined the true aspects of the creator with those of long-worshipped culture heroes. The multifaceted origins of Viracocha have, regrettably, left a startling confusion in the surviving stories in which he plays a role.

viracocha SOUTH AMERICA (*Collao*)

The name given to the followers of the earliest cult of CON TICCI VIRACOCHA.

Von Humboldt, Friedrich Heinrich Alexander, Baron

German naturalist and traveller (1769–1859) who for five years, accompanied by Aimé Bonpland, explored South

America (1799–1804) which led to his monumental twenty-three volume *Voyage de Humboldt et Bonpland aux Regions Equinoxales* (1805–34) in which he dealt with the legends of EL DORADO, disproving that the mythical lake PARIMA lay beyond the ORINOCO in a fabled land called MANOA or OMOA.

voodoo HAITI

The name given to a religious cult that is made up, in the main, of magical beliefs and practices. Today it is followed principally on the Caribbean island of Haiti, but also has followers in some parts of Africa, South America and the West Indies. The cult arose on slave plantations in the seventeenth century as a combination of the Roman Catholic teachings of the plantation owners and West African religious traditions. Initiates into the voodoo religion also retain their membership of the Roman Catholic church, though this does not necessarily indicate an acceptance of the cult on the part of the Church of Rome.

The most common belief of voodoo is that of the LOA, a spirit who involves itself in human affairs, some of which are clearly based on the lives of Roman Catholic saints. The loa is invoked by the HOUNGAN (priest) or MAMBO (priestess) at ceremonies during which the loa takes possession of the celebrants.

The HOUMFORT (temple) has a central post from which the loa is believed to descend to 'mount' the initiate, the particular loa being identifiable from the characteristic behaviour exhibited by the possessed worshipper. Notable loa are ERZULIE, the Earth-goddess; LEGBA, the lord of the road who acts as an interpreter between humans and spirits – he corresponds to Saint Anthony the Hermit; OGU, a warrior who corresponds to the Roman

Catholic Saint James the Great; and Baron SAMEDI, the lord of the land of the dead.

The voodoo religion is highly secretive, and even today initiates live in fear of their lives if they reveal too much about the cult and its pantheon. For this reason, whilst the names of a great many loa are known, the exact purposes and attributes of only a handful are known to outsiders.

Votan CENTRAL AMERICA (*Maya*)

A mysterious traveller who declared himself to be a serpent, and thus is likely to have been an incarnation of the great QUETZALCÓATL. Arriving from an unknown origin, the traveller said that he had been ordered by the gods to go to America and found a new culture. Having received implicit instructions on what he was being expected to do, Votan left his village of VALUM CHIVIM, to date unidentified, and passed through VALUM VOTAN before travelling up the River USUMACINTA to found PALENQUE. From there Votan made several visits to his homeland, on one of which he came across the ruins of a tower that had been started in an attempt to reach the heavens, but which had collapsed due to confusion between the builders caused by their many languages.

Votan was supposed to be the guardian of the TEPANAGUASTE, a sacred hollow wooden instrument that is similar to the TEPONAZTLI, the AZTEC ceremonial drum. Greatly venerated, he was sometimes referred to as the 'heart of the cities'. His consort was IX CHEL, the goddess of the rainbow, though she was sometimes referred to as IX-KANLEOM. Votan's priests were of the same caste as those of Quetzalcóatl, and it is clear that he was a sufficiently outstanding leader to have extended his religious doctrines over a wide area so that they endured for a great many centuries, over which they only gradually degenerated away from their original message of redemption.

Vucub Caquix CENTRAL AMERICA (Maya)

Simple variant of VUCUB CAKIX that may just be due to a transcriptive error.

Vukub Ahpu CENTRAL AMERICA (Maya)

The brother of HUNHUN AHPU, and thus the son of XPIYACOC and XMUCANÉ. He and his brother were keen players of the game TLACHTLI and gladly accepted the challenge to play the game against the lords of XIBALBA. They set off for the UNDERWORLD and, after many days' travel, came to a cross-roads where they were tricked into taking the black road by the guardian of the junction. All they found at the end of that road were enthroned statues. Returning to the junction, they were again tricked, this time into sitting on red-hot stone thrones. Finally, they were furnished with torches and taken to the House of GLOOM, into which they were shut with implicit instructions that their torches should be kept burning all night long and still be alight when they were let out the following morning. The torches quickly burned down and the two brothers were condemned to death. HUNHUN AHPU was beheaded, but there is no record of what became of Vukub Ahpu.

Vukub Ca ~ kix, ~ quix CENTRAL AMERICA (Maya)

'Seven Macaws', a giant who, together with his sons ZIPACNÁ ('Mountain-Maker') and CABRACA ('Earthquake'), appears to have ruled over the second era of the creation. Extremely arrogant, Vukub Cakix professed to be the Sun, the light and the Moon. His sons were no less boastful. Zipacná claimed that he could move the Earth, while Cabraca said he could overturn it and shake the sky. It soon became clear to the gods that, while these giant characters inhabited the Earth, true men could not be created. They sent the twins HUNAHPU and XBALANQUÉ to deal with the monstrous problem.

Vukub Cakix lived off the fruit from a tree he owned, a fact that led Hunahpu and Xbalanqué to hide among its branches. When the giant began to pick some fruit, the twins shot him in the cheek with a poisoned arrow which caused him intense pain, but not so much that he could not tear off one of Hunahpu's arms as the twins escaped.

The twins then went to the home of Vukub Cakix disguised as doctors and offered their services to cure the pain which they diagnosed as toothache, adding that they could easily do so by pulling out the bad teeth. Vukub Cakix refused, for his teeth were made of emerald, and he said that it was by virtue of those teeth that he was king. However, the twins promised that they would substitute new teeth for the old ones, and so Vukub Cakix gave them permission to go ahead. The twins quickly extracted all the emerald teeth and replaced them with ones made from maize. They then gouged out Vukub Cakix's silver eyes, and, having lost all his splendour, the giant quickly died. Hunahpu then recovered his arm from CHIMALAMAT, Vukub Cakix's wife, who had been roasting it, and the twins departed.

A variant story says that it was not the twins who went to tend to Vukub Cakix, but rather an old couple who offered him their services. Whoever it was who pulled his teeth and plucked out his eyes, the result was the same; Vukub Cakix died and true men could finally be created.

Vukub Came CENTRAL AMERICA (*Maya*) One of the rulers of the UNDERWORLD, together with HUN CAME. He is also named as one of the lords of XIBALBA in the myths of HUNAHPU and XBALANQUÉ, in which he was burned to death after the twins had promised to rejuvenate him, something they, of course, did not do.

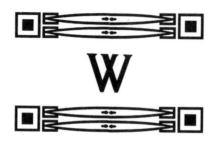

W

W'Atira North America – Great Plains (*Pawnee*)
Mother Corn who was symbolized during the HAKO fertility rite by an ear of maize.

wabanunaqsiwok North America – Woodlands (*Algonquian*)
The red-dressed people of the dawn of whom it is said that, if anyone dreams of them, they compel the dreamer to prepare a ball-game as soon as they awake. The ball in this game is an image of the Sun and is coloured red denoting the east, and yellow denoting the west. The underlying symbolism of this ritual ball-game is the perpetual alternation between night and day.

Wabasso North America – Woodlands (*Potawatomi*)
The brother of NANABOOJOO who fled to the north as soon as he witnessed the rising of the Sun for the first time. There he was transformed into a white rabbit and is honoured as a powerful MANITOU.

Wabus North America – Woodlands (*Menominee*)
The MENOMINEE say that Wabus, the Great HARE, originally grew from a bowl of blood that FLINT, the son of NOKOMIS, took from his mother. Later Wabus became a man when he took the name MĀNĀBUSCH, the famous hero-TRICKSTER.

Wakdjunkaga North America – Woodlands (*Winnebago*)
The TRICKSTER.

Wakinyan North America – Great Plains (*Dakota*)
The spirit of thunder.

wakonda North America – Great Plains/Woodlands border (*Sioux*)
The indwelling spirit or soul which all things, animate and inanimate, possess.

Wakonda North America – Great Plains/Woodlands border (*Omaha*)
The GREAT SPIRIT, though he is only vaguely personified. The OMAHA say that in the beginning all things existed in the mind of Wakonda. Men and animals then came into existence as disembodied spirits, who wandered through space searching for a home where they could take on bodily forms.

They visited both the Sun and the Moon, but found that neither was suited to their needs, and so descended to the Earth. Here, though it appeared that the Earth would be suitable for them, they could not find any land for the entire surface of the Earth was covered with water.

As the spirits flew over the surface of the water, a huge rock suddenly rose from the depths and burst into flames. The waters rose in clouds into the air and dry land appeared on which trees and grass immediately grew to maturity. The spirits

landed, took on their bodily shapes, and
fed themselves from the fruit of the trees
and the seeds of the grasses. The new
Earth reverberated with the happiness of
the people and the animals who, in unison,
raised their voices in gratitude to Wakonda.

Wala NORTH AMERICA – GREAT PLAINS
(*Fox*)
The spirit of the dawn.

Walala NORTH AMERICA – NORTHWEST
COAST (*Haida*)
A variant of ULALA (cf. TSONOQUA).

Wan NORTH AMERICA – NORTHWEST
COAST (*Klamath*)
The red fox who was set in the forests,
together with KETCHKATCH, the grey fox,
and MUSHMUSH, the white-tailed deer, by
KEMUSH during the final stages of the
Creation.

Wangol loa HAITI (*Voodoo*)
Generic name given to spirits derived from
the gods of Angolan peoples.

Wasco NORTH AMERICA – NORTHWEST
COAST (*Haida*)
Renowned mythical hero who is the HAIDA
equivalent of the TLINGIT hero KONAKAD-
SET.

Watauineiwa SOUTH AMERICA – TIERRA
DEL FUEGO (*Yahgan*)
The benevolent supreme spirit who lives
in the skies. Though worshipped as the
supreme spirit, Watauineiwa was not the
creator, but instead acts as the sustainer of
life and life's morality. He is a vague spirit
who plays an important part in initiation
rites, but not in the myths of the YAHGAN
people.

Water NORTH AMERICA – SOUTHWEST
(*Navajo*)
According to some accounts, Water was
the father of THOBADZISTSHINI by YOLKAI
ESTSAN. Thobadzistshini and his brother
NAYANEZGANI are, however, usually said to
be the twin sons of ESTANATLEHI and
TSHOHANOAI who, in the accounts that
name Water and Yolkai Estsan as the
parents of Thobadzistshini, are simply said
to have been the parents of Nayanezgani.

Watsusii NORTH AMERICA – PUEBLO,
SOUTHWEST (*Zuñi*)
The twin brother of KOWWITUMA who,
together with his brother, was involved
with the HOZONI chant and the CORN
MAIDENS.

Wekwek NORTH AMERICA –
SOUTHWEST COAST (*Miwok*)
'Falcon'. He took part in a stone-slinging
contest against the giant KELOK, a contest
which he lost and was killed, but was then
restored to life by COYOTE.

Well Beloved CENTRAL AMERICA –
MEXICO (*Aztec*)
The divine child born to the goddess PRE-
CIOUS FLOWER. Well Beloved immediately
died and was buried. Many of the plants
that were to satisfy man's needs grew from
the body of the dead infant. Cotton grew
from his hair; seed-bearing plants (corn
and so on) grew from his ears; a herb used
to cool a fever grew from his nostrils; the
sweet potato grew from his fingers; maize
from his finger-nails; and so on until his
body had produced around 1,000 different
varieties of fruit and grain.

Wemawe NORTH AMERICA – PUEBLO,
SOUTHWEST (*Zuñi*)
Generic name given to animal deities who
are governed by the Sun.

Wheememeowah NORTH AMERICA –
GREAT PLAINS (*Yakima*)
'The Great-Chief-Above', the creator.

White Body NORTH AMERICA –
SOUTHWEST (*Navajo*)
One of the four gods of the people of the
fourth world through which the NAVAJO
people passed during their ascent to the
Earth (see ASCENT OF THE NAVAJO). The
other three gods of this world were BLACK
BODY, BLUE BODY and YELLOW BODY.

White-Corn Boy NORTH AMERICA –
SOUTHWEST (*Navajo*)
One of the tutelary deities of the NAVAJO
who was set on the sacred mountain
Mount SAN FRANCISCO, together with
YELLOW-CORN GIRL, by ATSE HASTIN and
ATSE ESTSAN after those deities had cre-
ated the Navajo land.

Wigit NORTH AMERICA – NORTHWEST
COAST (*Haida*)
'Raven', the TRICKSTER.

Wilolane NORTH AMERICA – PUEBLO,
SOUTHWEST (*Zuñi*)
The spirit of lightning.

Wind-Ruler NORTH AMERICA –
WOODLANDS (*Onondaga*)
The husband of GUSTS-OF-WIND and thus
the father of TASWISCANA and YOSKEHA.
He presented his son Yoskeha with a bow
and arrows and some maize, symbols of his
lordship over all the animals and plants,
after Yoskeha had been banished from
Earth following Taswiscana's false accusa-
tion that Yoskeha had caused the death of
his mother.

Windlgo NORTH AMERICA –
WOODLANDS (*Ojibway*)
The giant ice-monster who prowls the
woods in winter looking for people to eat.

Winnebago NORTH AMERICA – GREAT
PLAINS
Indigenous North American AMERINDIAN
people from a part of the GREAT PLAINS
culture region, and one of the many SIOUX
peoples who first entered the region from
the north c.AD 800. Their linguistic neighbours included the ASSINABOIN, CROW,
DAKOTA, MANDAN, OMAHA and OSAGE
tribes.

Wisgatcak NORTH AMERICA –
WOODLANDS (*Cree*)
The TRICKSTER.

wishinu SOUTH AMERICA – ECUADOR
(*Jivaro*)
The name given to the tribal SHAMAN who
has, among his duties, the task of inter-
preting the hallucinogenically induced
visions of warriors planning a raid.

Wixalagillis NORTH AMERICA –
NORTHWEST COAST (*Kwakiutl*)
One of the two main tutelary deities of the
KWAKIUTL, the other being BAXBAKUALA-
NUCHSIWAE, the CANNIBAL MOTHER[3].

Wodziwob NORTH AMERICA –
CALIFORNIA/NEVADA BORDER (*Paiute*)
An historical prophet who led the first
wave of GHOST DANCES in 1870. Wodziwob
claimed that he had been told, in a vision,
that the spirits of their ancestors would
return on a large train (the railroad had
just been completed) and would announce
their arrival with a great explosion, during
which all the white men would be swallowed up leaving their goods for the Indians. The GREAT SPIRIT would then come
down from his home to live among them.
The Ghost Dances he had been taught in
the vision would, so he announced, bring
on the cataclysm. A second series of dances followed in 1890 that were started by

WOVOKA, the son of Wodziwob's assistant.

Wokuk NORTH AMERICA – SOUTHWEST
COAST (*Wintun*)
A huge and resplendent mythical bird with bright red eyes from whose feather sprang a large number of the animals that now inhabit the Earth.

Woodlands, North American Indians of the NORTH AMERICA
The Woodlands region of North America covered a huge geographical region. From Alaska across northern Canada to Labrador, from the Great Lakes south to the swamps that are the Everglades in Florida. The forestation ranged from the coniferous forests of the north, through birchwood, to the hardwoods to be found in the Everglades. The AMERINDIAN peoples who lived in this vast area depended on a mix of hunting and agriculture, and expressed their vivid sense of the powers of nature in elaborate ceremonies of thanksgiving that were commonly called 'dances'.

Occupying such a vast tract of North America, there were, not surprisingly, a great number of different tribes to be found. Linguistically, however, they were only divided into three main groups: the ALGONQUIAN of the far north; the IRO-QUOIAN of the Great Lakes region; and the Muskhogean of the south. Naturally, among these broad groupings there were many tribal variations. The Algonquians included the CHIPPEWA, CREE, DELAWARE, MENOMINEE, MONTAGNAIS and POTAWA-TOMI. The Iroquoian included the CHERO-KEE, HURON, MOHAWK, ONEIDA and SELISH,

while the main Muskhogean tribes were the CREEK (MUSKHOGEE) and CHICKSAW.

The Algonquian and Muskhogean Indian peoples were, in the main, peaceable, but sandwiched between them were the ferocious and internecine Iroquois. It was their internecine warring that led to the establishment of the Iroquoian confederacy in the sixteenth century, though it was not formed without considerable opposition as related in the legends of HAIOWA-THA (see HIAWATHA).

Wovoka NORTH AMERICA –
CALIFORNIA/NEVADA BORDER (*Paiute*)
The son of the assistant of the prophet WODZIWOB. Wovoka led the second series of GHOST DANCES that started in 1890 and promised initiates the complete destruction of all the white men and the return of the GREAT SPIRIT who would descend to live amongst his people.

Wurekaddo SOUTH AMERICA – GUYANA
(*Arawak*)
'She-Who-Walks-in-the-Dark', one of the two wives of the creator KURURUMANY, the other being EMISIWADDO. Her name was thought by some to consider that Wurekaddo was an ant-spirit.

Wyandot NORTH AMERICA –
WOODLANDS
The true name of the AMERINDIAN people better known as the HURON. A nomadic people who lived near Lakes Erie, Huron and Ontario, and were all but wiped out by the IROQUOIS.

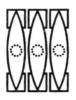

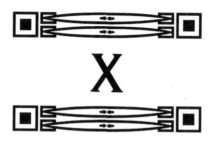

X

Xa ~ m, ~ n SOUTH AMERICA – PERU
(*Mochica*)
The make-up man to NAYMLAP who accompanied his king when he and his retinue came to CHIMOR on a fleet of BALSAS.

Xan CENTRAL AMERICA (*Maya*)
The animal that was sent ahead by the twins HUNAHPU and XBALANQUÉ into the UNDERWORLD realm of XIBALBA with orders to prick the leg of everyone he came across. Whenever Xan did this, the other lords of Xibalba called out asking what the matter was, and thus the twins learned all the names of the lords of the realm so they were later able to address each lord correctly, much to their astonishment.

Xanan Ek CENTRAL AMERICA (*Maya*)
The spirit of the pole star.

Xbalanqué CENTRAL AMERICA (*Maya*)
One of the twin sons of XQUIQ and HUN-HUN AHPU, his brother being HUNAHPU, the two being born after Xquiq had been impregnated by the head of their father, Hunhun Ahpu which had been hung, in a tree in the UNDERWORLD kingdom of XI-BALBA. Almost from birth the two brothers were brilliant magicians which aroused the jealousy of their older brothers HUNBATZ and HUNCHOUEN who plotted to kill them. Hunahpu and Xbalanqué got wind of the plot and transformed their brothers into ridiculous monkeys.

The two brothers then determined to clear a part of the forest for a field, but every night the animals restored the forest to its former state. Lying in wait the next night, the brothers saw the animals summon the felled trees to rise and return to their allotted places. They tried to trap the creatures, but at first only managed to catch the tails of the rabbit and the deer, which is why these animals have such short tails. Then they managed to trap a rat who, in exchange for its life, showed the twins where their grandmother had hidden Hunhun Ahpu's TLACHTLI equipment.

The brothers soon became enthusiastic players of the game, the vibrations of their vigorous game-play arousing the interest of the Lords of Xibalba who wondered who the new champions might be. They sent their owl messenger to challenge the twins to a series of games, a challenge the twins readily accepted. However, before leaving they planted two reeds in their grandmother's house, telling her that if any harm befell either of them, their reed would then wither and die.

Hunahpu and Xbalanqué then set out on their journey to the Underworld. *En route* they crossed a deep ravine, a boiling river, a river of blood, and then a fourth river before reaching a cross-roads where red, yellow, black and white roads met. Like their father and their uncle before them, Hunhun Ahpu and VUKUB AHPU, they took the black road, but were more cautious than their ancestors and sent an animal named XAN ahead of them with orders to prick anyone he met. The two enthroned statues at the end of the road made no noise, but each of the lords that Xan came across and pricked called out in pain, to which the others enquired what the problem was. By this ruse the twins learned the names of all the lords of Xibalba, and much to their annoyance and astonishment were able to address each in turn by his correct title: AHALCANA; AHALPUH; CHAMIABAK; CHAMIAHOLOM; CUCHUMAQIQ; HUN CAME; PATAN; QUIQRE; QUIQRIXGAG; QUIQXIL; VUKUB CAME; and XIQIRIPAT.

The lords offered the twins two stone thrones to sit on, but they politely refused to sit on the chairs that had previously badly burned their father and uncle. They were then sent to the House of GLOOM with instructions to keep their torches alight until the following morning when the first game would be played. While their father had failed at this first test, the twins preserved their torches by substituting the fire with red painted flames.

Hunahpu and Xbalanqué won the first game the following day which only served to madden the Xibalbans further who now despatched them to the demonic House of LANCES for the night with orders that they should emerge the following morning with four vases of flowers. When inside, the twins tamed the fiends by promising to send them the flesh of all the animals on the Earth, and then persuaded the ants that crawled all over the floor to bring them flowers from the gardens of Vukub Came and Hun Came.

The twins won each successive game, and were subjected to further trial houses every time. They survived the House of COLD by lighting pine cones and the House of TIGERS by throwing bones to the rapacious jaguars; and passed unscathed through the House of FIRE. However, in the House of BATS they were not so lucky

for Hunahpu injudiciously raised his head from the ground and was immediately decapitated by the dreadful CAMAZOTZ[2].

Xbalanqué called all the animals to his aid, the turtle touching Hunahpu's bleeding trunk to which he immediately stuck. With the help of the other animals, Xbalanqué managed to transform the turtle into the likeness of his brother so that the twins could return to play the final game the following day. They won the game with the help of a rabbit which distracted the lords of Xibalba just long enough for Xbalanqué to be able to take down his brother's head from the place where it had been hung in scorn and fully restore his brother.

The twins fully realized that they would be condemned to death for having won every game. Thus they conferred with the two magicians XULU and BACAM who arranged that they should be resurrected. Thus, when the time came, they willingly mounted the funeral pyre from which their ashes were spread across the sea of the Underworld. Five days later the twins reappeared in the guise of poor fishermen in which disguise they astonished the Xibalbans with their amazing powers – they burned houses and immediately restored them. They even burned each other and brought each other back to life.

This prowess came to the attention of Vukub Came and Hun Came, who summoned the twins who reverently went through their amazing repertoire. They then immolated and restored one of the lord's dogs after which they said they would even burn and restore the two lords themselves. Vukub Came and Hun Came agreed, but the twins simply scattered their ashes. The other lords of the Underworld fled in terror but all but one of them suffered the same fate, after which the twins condemned their subjects to become potters living on the flesh of wild animals and sharing only the bees with the civilized people of the Earth.

The twins then took the heads of their father and uncle and returned to the Earth where they honoured their dead ancestors by placing them in the sky, one to become the Sun, the other to become the Moon.

Hunahpu and Xbalanqué also appear in a myth concerning the giant VUKUB CAKIX and his monstrous sons ZIPACNÁ and CAB-RACA, though chronologically this story would appear to fall prior to that of the story of their defeat of the lords of Xibalba, for Vukub Cakix was said to have been the ruler of the second era of the creation, a time before true men had been created. This would seem to suggest that the twins were in fact spirits who were sent down to Earth as divine trouble-shooters whenever the gods saw a need.

Vukub Cakix fed himself with the fruit from a particular tree. Knowing this, the twins hid in its branches and, when the giant came to pick some fruit, fired pois-oned arrows at him, though they did not kill him and simply caused him great pain. In the ensuing struggle during which the twins made good their escape, the giant managed to tear off one of Hunahpu's arms. The twins disguised themselves as doctors and came to the home of the giant. They offered to cure him of the pain which they diagnosed as being caused by tooth-ache, and prescribed the extraction of the bad teeth. Vukub Cakix at first refused, protesting that it was due to his beautiful emerald teeth that he was king, but agreed to the treatment after the twins promised to replace each tooth with a new one. They then pulled out all of Vukub Cakix's teeth, but instead of using emerald, they replaced the teeth with ones made from maize. They then gouged out the giant's silver eyes. Having lost all his glory, Vukub Cakix quickly faded away and died. Before leaving the house, Hunahpu recovered his arm which CHIMALAMAT, Vukub Cakix's

wife, had been roasting, and thus restored the twins set out to deal with Vukub Ca-kix's giant sons.

With the help of 400 youths they caught Zipacná in a pit-trap and hurled great trees down on to him before building a house over the pit to celebrate his death. Their celebrations, however, were premature as Zipacná had only been stunned. In the middle of the night he rose up and tossed the house and all its occupants high into the air from which the 400 youths fell to their deaths and were buried, until the twins rescued them and transformed them into the stars.

Hunahpu and Xbalanqué next tried to trap and kill Zipacná by modelling a huge false crab, Zipacná's favourite food, which they placed at the bottom of a deep ravine. They had no trouble in luring Zipacná into the ravine and then threw mountains down on top of him. In the end, as Zipacná was struggling with such ferocity that he was threatening the very Earth, the twins turned him into stone.

Cabraca, the other giant, was a much easier problem to be rid of, for the twins simply induced him into eating poisoned roast fowl, his favourite food, from which he fell dead. With Vukub Cakix and his sons disposed of, Hunahpu and Xbalanqué returned to their home, and the gods were able to complete the Creation.

Xecotcovach CENTRAL AMERICA (Maya)
One of the four great birds that were sent by TEPEU and GUCUMATZ to attack the wooden people they had created and who had turned out so unsatisfactorily. The other birds sent on the attack were CAMA-ZOTZ[1], COTZBALAM AND TECUMBALAM.

Xibalba CENTRAL AMERICA (Maya)
The name given to the UNDERWORLD, the realm of the dead, that was ruled over by HUN CAME and VUKUB CAME, and which was also inhabited by a number of other

lords whose names were learned, much to their chagrin, by the twins HUNAHPU and XBALANQUÉ. These other lords are named as AHALCANA, AHALPUH, CHAMIABAK, CHAMIAHOLOM, CUCHUMAQIQ, PATAN, QUIQRE, QUIQRIXGAG, QUIQXIL and XIQIR-IPAT.

Xibalbay CENTRAL AMERICA – GUATEMALA (*Cakchiquel*)

The UNDERWORLD whose name is most likely a corruption of XIBALBA, the MAYA Underworld. The name, like the classical Greek Hades, is not simply the name of the realm, but is also applied to the ruler of the Underworld who created the obsidian stone, the solid edifice of material life upon which man himself is based.

Xilonen CENTRAL AMERICA – MEXICO (*Aztec*)

Goddess of the young corn who is the female counterpart of CINTÉOTL and one of the wives of TEZCATLIPOCA. She is also sometimes called CHICOMECÓATL – 'Seven Snakes'.

Xingú SOUTH AMERICA – BRAZIL

Indigenous Brazilian AMERINDIAN people whose name comes from the River Xingú along whose 1,200 mile banks they live, as it flows from the Mato Grosso to the AMAZON[1] delta.

Xipe Totec CENTRAL AMERICA – MEXICO (*Aztec*)

The flayed god and god of the seedtime (spring when seeds germinate in the ground), Xipe Totec was one of the four sons of the dual god-above-all, his brothers being CAMAXTLI, QUETZALCÓATL and TEZCATLIPOCA. Xipe Totec is sometimes thought of as an aspect of NANAUTZIN, the shabby, diseased and despised deity who willingly sacrificed himself in the fire so that the Sun might continue to light the world.

The spring festival in honour of Xipe Totec is one of the most horrible of all the AZTEC rituals, excepting perhaps that connected with TLÁLOC. At this festival captives were flayed alive and then eaten at a ritual meal at which their skins clothed images of the gods as well as his priests. After the feast the skins could, upon request, be worn for up to twenty days by those who had certain skin complaints which they wished to cure. It is perhaps due to the wearing of the yellowing skins by his initiates that Xipe Totec was also considered as the patron of goldsmiths. His spring festival is one of the most important festivals, for without his blessing the crops will not germinate in the ground. Apart from this ritual importance, Xipe Totec plays little part in the narratives.

An indication to the early origin of his rites is given in the myth of the travellers from the Aztec homeland of AZTLAN. One version of this myth states that the Aztecs captured, sacrificed and flayed the daughter of the COLHUACAN ruler who was then invited to a banquet, at which the dead girl was the main dish and the attendant priest was dressed in her skin. This ritual can be none other than that connected with Xipe Totec although the deity is not specifically mentioned in the myth.

Xiqiripat CENTRAL AMERICA (*Maya*)

One of the lords of XIBALBA who was subordinate to HUN CAME and VUKUB CAME, but of equal standing to the other lords who are named as AHALCANA, AHALPUH, CHAMIAHOLOM, CUCHUMAQIQ, PATAN, QUIQRE, QUIQRIXGAG and QUIQXIL.

Xiu CENTRAL AMERICA (*Maya*)

Important ruling clan of the MAYA who were centred at UXMAL on the Yucatán peninsula. Their sacred language, ZUYUA, was the key to being elevated to the rank of ALMENHENOB in the Maya caste system. One member of the clan, AH KUKUM XIU, helped Francisco MONTEJO the younger in his conquest of the Yucatán. However, it seems that the Xiu language may have been far older and more venerable than the family that subsequently took their name from it.

Xiuhocóatl CENTRAL AMERICA – MEXICO (*Aztec*)

The serpent torch of HUITZILOPOCHTLI which he was born holding and with a single blow of which he killed his sister COYOLXAUHQUI, who had incited the CENTZONUITZNAUA to kill their mother COATLICUE.

Xiuhtecuhtli CENTRAL AMERICA – MEXICO (*Aztec*)

An ancient god of fire who is also known as HUEHUETÉOTL or OTONTEUCTLI and is of extreme importance as he governs the fifth cardinal point – the centre. He also governs the first hours of both day and night. He is described, in one myth, as the father and mother of the gods, living in the navel of the Earth from which four streams of blood flow to the cardinal points. This is evidently a very early myth, for later he is simply regarded as the god of fire to whom the pine tree, from which torches are made, was sacred, his role as creator of the gods having been supplanted by more eminently suited deities. Xiuhtecuhtli was depicted as an old, bearded man who carried a brazier on his head in which incense was burned. He had the supreme power to act upon opposites. He was light in the dark, heat in the cold, life in death. He was also greatly honoured during a festival that occurred once every fifty-six years, the end of the AZTEC 'century'.

On the cusp between one century and the next, the gods would break their contract with the people, who extinguished all their fires. This would fill them with fear at the prospect of the end of the world. However, the priests would then produce the newly created fire from their temple and proceed to take it to every home. Thus the world would be secure for the next fifty-six-year period. Xiuhtecuhtli was also the god of volcanoes and, to a lesser extent, a solar deity.

Xmucané CENTRAL AMERICA (*Maya*)

'Twice Grandfather', the husband of XPIYACOC and father of HUNHUN AHPU and VUKUB AHPU. During the creation he brewed nine broths that were used by TEPEU and GUCUMATZ to strengthen the ground maize from which the four brothers BALAM AGAB, BALAM QUITZÉ, IQI BALAM and MAHUCUTAH were formed.

Xoc Bilum CENTRAL AMERICA (*Maya*)

The god of song.

Xochicahuaca CENTRAL AMERICA – MEXICO (*Aztec*)

One of the four guardians of HUITZILOPOCHTLI together with CHIPACTONAL, OXOMOCO and TLALTECUIN. An AMOXAOQUE, he was one of those deities who remained with the travellers from AZTLAN, the ancestral homeland of the AZTECS, and was co-responsible for the invention of the CALENDAR.

Xochimalca CENTRAL AMERICA – MEXICO (*Aztec*)

'Flower-weavers', the priestly caste of a sect who was noted for passing down the secrets of how to manipulate the hallucinogens and other 'natural' drugs down from generation to generation. Their names come from the happy state the mind was said to flower into when under the influence of the hallucinogens they manipulated.

Xochimilo CENTRAL AMERICA – MEXICO (*Aztec*)

The enemy of the COLHUACAN city of TIZAPAN, against whom the AZTEC travellers on their way from their ancestral homeland of AZTLAN fought as the allies of the Colhuaca whom they helped to victory.

Xochipilli CENTRAL AMERICA – MEXICO (*Aztec*)
'Flower-Lord', the young god of flowers, beauty, love and happiness who is included among the thirteen presiding deities of the hours of the day. Xochipilli is sometimes said to be the son of CINTÉOTL, in which case he is the god of the young, immature maize, and is also called MACUILXÓCHITL.

Xochipilli-Cintéotl CENTRAL AMERICA – MEXICO (*Aztec*)
An amalgamation of the two deities XOCHIPILLI and CINTÉOTL, in which guise they were the joint guardians of the seventh hour of the twenty-two-hour AZTEC day – midday.

Xochiquetzal CENTRAL AMERICA – MEXICO (*Aztec*)
'Flower-Feather', originally the wife of the rain-god TLÁLOC, Xochiquetzal was abducted by TEZCATLIPOCA who made her the goddess of love. Xochiquetzal lives beyond the highest heaven in XOCHITICACAN, the 'Palace of Flowers', in ITZEECAYAN, the 'Palace of Cool Breezes', and in TAMOANCHAN, the 'Palace of the West'. Her lover was PILTZINTECUHTLI who is possibly an aspect of XOCHIPILLI, and the wife of her lover was said to have been born from one of her hairs. Numerous of her followers immolated themselves on her festal altar.

Xochiticacan CENTRAL AMERICA – MEXICO (*Aztec*)
The 'Palace of Flowers', one of the three homes of XOCHIQUETZAL that are said to lie beyond the highest heaven.

Xochitl CENTRAL AMERICA – MEXICO (*Aztec*)
The twentieth day of the twenty-day AZTEC, MONTH[1], the day symbolizing the flower, representing the south, and being presided over by XOCHIQUETZAL.

Xocut(z)in CENTRAL AMERICA (*Aztec*)
The second oldest of the four sisters, aspects of TLACOLTÉUTL, who appear to make that deity the corollary of TEZCATLIPOCA. Xocutzin's sisters were TEICU, TICAPAN and TLACO. The four were not usually perceived of as separate entities, but rather the four faces of a witch who, in true pan-European style, rides through the air on a broomstick wearing a peaked hat, though, unlike her European counterparts, Tlacoltéutl rides naked.

Xolas SOUTH AMERICA – TIERRA DEL FUEGO (*Alucaluf*)
The supreme being who places every soul into every body at birth, and who receives them back into his caring after death to await rebirth.

Xólotl CENTRAL AMERICA – MEXICO (*Aztec*)
The dog of the UNDERWORLD who is the equivalent of the MAYAN PEK. A solar-deity, Xólotl sacrificed all the other gods, and then himself in honour of the superiority of the Sun after it had stopped moving across the sky, an act that induced it to resume its daily travels. As a solar-deity Xólotl also presided over the Aztec ball-game of TLACHTLI which he himself played on a magical court in the sky. Xólotl was also the god of twins and all other deformed people (the birth of twins being an aberration to the AZTEC people) who were sacrificed to the Sun at the time of solar eclipses when he is said to be the Sun's companion.

The concept behind this lay in the practice of sacrificing a dog at an Aztec burial.

The animal, whose soul was then referred to as Xólotl, might then accompany the soul of his master through MICTLÁN, just as Xólotl accompanies the Sun, carrying that soul across Mictlán's nine rivers, the CHICUNAUHAPAN, to its final eternal resting place in CHICUNAUHMICTLÁN.

Xólotl appears to be a very ancient deity who possibly originated as a TOTEMIC ancestor of the CHICHIMEC people. According to at least one story, they were descended from a man and a bitch, the sole survivors of the FLOOD[2]. Later Xólotl was named as the Chichimec war leader, though this simply indicates the adoption of the name, rather than indicating that he was ever incarnate.

Though Xólotl is usually said to have sacrificed all the gods and then willingly sacrificed himself to honour the Sun, a variant of this says that in the beginning, with everything being dark, two gods, who remain unnamed, decided to immolate themselves to bring light to the world and were thus transformed into the Sun and the Moon. However, as these remained motionless in the sky, all the other gods decided that they should sacrifice themselves. Xólotl refused and transformed himself into the twin-stalked (thus deformed) maize XÓLOTL; then into the maguey plant MEXÓLOTL; and finally into the larvae AXÓLOTL before he was caught and sacrificed. The Sun and the Moon then started to move.

In another ancient myth, Xólotl is referred to as the creator. The first demigods to live on Earth had been born from a stone knife that had itself been born to CITALICUE, whom they asked to allow them to create mankind to serve them. She agreed and told them to send Xólotl to Mictlán to secure a bone or some ashes of the dead.

Xólotl was duly given a bone when he travelled to the Underworld, but *en route* back to the Earth he stumbled and it broke into two unequal parts. Xólotl picked up the fragments and completed his journey. He then put the two pieces of bone into a bowl and sprinkled them with blood from the gods. On the fourth day a man emerged and four days later a woman, the first people.

xólotl CENTRAL AMERICA – MEXICO (*Aztec*)
The deformed, twin-stalked maize into which XÓLOTL transformed himself as his first disguise in an attempt to avoid being sacrificed to vivify the Sun and the Moon.

Xomimitl CENTRAL AMERICA – MEXICO (*Aztec*)
One of the original AZTEC leaders to leave their ancestral homeland of AZTLAN, to which he did not return. The other leaders of the expedition are named as ACACITLI, AHATL, AUEXOTL, HUICTON, OCELOPAN, TEÇACATETL and TENOCH, together with the four guardians of HUITZILOPOCHTLI who were CHIPACTONAL, OXOMOCO, TLALTECUIN and XOCHICAHUACA.

Xpiyacoc CENTRAL AMERICA (*Maya*)
'Twice Grandmother', the wife of XMUCANÉ and mother of HUNHUN AHPU and VUKUB AHPU. At first she refused to accept XQUIQ as her daughter-in-law, but later relented after Xquiq had been impregnated by the head of her husband Hunhun Ahpu in XIBALBA, and had passed a test of maize-picking. Xquiq gave birth to the twins HUNAHPU and XBALANQUÉ.

Xquiq CENTRAL AMERICA (*Maya*)
Named by some as a maiden of XIBALBA, Xquiq was the wife of HUNHUN AHPU but was not readily accepted by XPIYACOC, Hunhun Ahpu's mother. After Hunhun Ahpu had been killed in the UNDERWORLD and his head stuck on a tree of gourds, Xquiq went to Xibalba to see the sight for

herself, wondering aloud as she approached the tree if picking one of the gourds would really prove fatal. When she persisted that she wanted to pick one of the fruits, even after Hunhun Ahpu's head had spoken to her from the tree, her husband told her to stretch out her hand to him, which she did. Hunhun Ahpu gathered up all his strength and spat into it, thus impregnating her. He then told her to flee from Xibalba. When the Xibalbans tried to kill her, she took his advice.

Xpiyacoc at first refused to accept Xquiq as her daughter-in-law, but when she sought sanctuary with her, and having passed a maize-picking test, Xpiyacoc relented and gave her the shelter she was seeking. Soon afterwards Xquiq gave birth to the twins HUNAHPU and XBALANQUÉ.

Xuhé SOUTH AMERICA – COLOMBIA
(*Chibcha*)
A variant of ZUHÉ.

Xulu CENTRAL AMERICA – MEXICO
(*Maya*)
One of two magicians, the other being BACAM, with whom the twins HUNAHPU and XBALANQUÉ conferred when they became aware that they would be condemned to death, and by this consultation arranged for their resurrection.

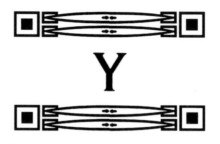

Y

Ya Tibois Quinto HAITI (*Voodoo*)
An important LOA whose origins remain unknown.

Yac CENTRAL AMERICA (*Maya*)
The name of the forest cat, possibly an ocelot, who, along with the coyote UTIU, the parrot QUEL and the crow HOH, sought out and brought the maize seed needed by the gods to create mankind.

Yagis NORTH AMERICA – NORTHWEST COAST (*Kwakiutl*)
A sea-monster that overturns canoes and eats those who find themselves in the sea as a result.

Yaguarogui SOUTH AMERICA – BOLIVIA (*Chiriguani*)
A green tiger that is said to cause eclipses when it tries to eat the Sun, but always fails as the Sun is too hot and has to be spat out again.

Yahgan SOUTH AMERICA – TIERRA DEL FUEGO
Indigenous South American AMERINDIAN people who live at the very foot of the American continent, on the islands named Tierra del Fuego that are today shared between Argentina and Chile.

Yananamca Intanamca SOUTH AMERICA – PERU (*Quechua*)
Generic name given to deities or culture heroes who were worshipped by the QUECHUA in the seventeenth century, and who were said to have been vanquished by HUALLALLO. Their story was recorded by the priest Francisco de Avila and seems to owe its origins to the legend of the expulsion of the Quechua from the fertile valleys of the cordillera to the barren highland plateau.

Yanauluha NORTH AMERICA – PUEBLO, SOUTHWEST (*Zuñi*)
The name of the first priest and medicineman who helped the people released from within the womb of AWITELIN TSITA to adjust to life on Earth.

Yáotl CENTRAL AMERICA – MEXICO (*Aztec*)
'Enemy', a title of TEZCATLIPOCA.

Yaxche CENTRAL AMERICA (*Maya*)
The tree of heaven under whose branches the souls of the righteous are thought to rejoice for all eternity.

yei NORTH AMERICA – SOUTHWEST (*Navajo*)
Generic name given to benevolent deities, the two great yei being named as HASTSHEYALTI and HASTSHEHOGAN. Led by Hastsheyalti, the yei created the goddesses ESTANATLEHI and YOLKAI ESTSAN, forming the first from turquoise and the latter from white shell. Hastsheyalti and Estanatlehi then created people, the first of the NAVAJO race.

Yeitso NORTH AMERICA – SOUTHWEST (*Navajo*)
A fearsome man-eating giant who numbered among the monstrous ANAYE.

yek NORTH AMERICA – NORTHWEST COAST (*Tlingit*)
Generic name given to all pervasive spirits which all things, animate and inanimate, possess.

Yellow Body NORTH AMERICA – SOUTHWEST (*Navajo*)
One of the four deities of the fourth world that were encountered during the ASCENT OF THE NAVAJO, the other three deities of this world being BLUE BODY, BLACK BODY and WHITE BODY.

Yellow-Corn Girl NORTH AMERICA – SOUTHWEST (*Navajo*)
One of the two tutelary deities who was set on the sacred mountain of Mount SAN FRANCISCO by ATSE HASTIN and ATSE EST-SAN following their creation of the NAVAJO land. Her companion was WHITE-CORN BOY.

Yellow-Corn Maiden NORTH AMERICA – PUEBLO, SOUTHWEST (*Zuñi*)
The leader of the CORN MAIDENS with whom PAYATAMI became enamoured. However, as the Corn Maidens could read Payatami's thoughts, they disappeared as soon as their dancing had sent him to sleep. They later returned having been promised safety by BITSITSI, and Yellow-Corn Maiden, together with BLUE-CORN MAIDEN, led a fertility dance which restored the ZUÑI lands before once again disappearing never to return.

Yellow World NORTH AMERICA – SOUTHWEST (*Navajo*)
One of the coloured worlds encountered during the ASCENT OF THE NAVAJO. Having been expelled from the BLUE WORLD, the people flew upwards under the guidance of NILTSHI who led them to an opening in the sky, through which they emerged into the Yellow World of the GRASSHOPPER people. The people were soon expelled from this world as well for making free with the wives of their hosts, and once more fled upwards, this time into a multicoloured world.

Yetl NORTH AMERICA – NORTHWEST COAST (*Tlingit*)
The demi-urge RAVEN, a wise man who was created, together with HERON, another very tall and wise man, by NASCAKIYETL who lived in a lodge in which he kept the stars, planets and light, at the source of the River NASS, together with his daughter and his two servants ADAWULCANAK and TLIE-WATUWADJIGICAN. Some say that Yetl was the child of Nascakiyetl's sister who had previously borne many other children, but they had all been killed by her jealous brother. Seeking the advice of Heron, Nascakiyetl's sister swallowed a red-hot pebble and subsequently gave birth to Yetl. He was named after the impregnable stone ITC AK, and thus called TAQLIKIC ('Hammer-Father') as he was so tough and resilient. Nascakiyetl recognized the prowess of Yetl and made him the head man of the world.

Other sources say that Yetl was really the son of the mortal man KITKAOSITIYIQA who gave him the strength he would need to create the world. Yetl then transformed himself into a splinter of hemlock which Nascakiyetl's daughter swallowed, and was thus reborn as her son. He then stole the stars, the planets and light from Nascakiyetl which had been the sole purpose of his transformation and rebirth.

Yetl next set about creating the winds. He put the west wind in a house on the top of a mountain and ordered it to hurt no one. He then created all the various Indian peoples, along with the dog who had originally been a man, but on seeing how fast he ran, Yetl had second thoughts and gave him four rather than two legs. He then turned another man, who annoyed him for some unknown reason, into the wild celery plant.

Yetl then stole fresh water from PETREL and scattered it over the surface of the arid Earth, thereby creating the streams, rivers and lakes. Yetl did not get away with this for Petrel lit a great fire underneath the escaping Yetl, the smoke from which turned his feathers from brilliant white into their present colour – black. He then forced the old woman who governs the flow of the sea to make the sea rise and fall in the sequence of tides which it still follows, and then once again came across his old adversary Petrel. They argued as to who was the older of them until Petrel put on his 'fog hat' so that Yetl became lost and had to admit defeat. He did, however, persuade Petrel to let his 'fog hat' float freely around the world.

Yetl then enticed a chicken-hawk to steal fire for him which he hid in red cedar and in some white stones (flint). He then towed ashore a huge house in which all the fish yet lived and used some of them to feast his mother, releasing the others into the rivers and the seas for the first time. Later, when some people who were fishing refused to carry him across a river, he released the Sun into the sky. The people, who had never seen the Sun before that time, fled into the woods and were transformed by Yetl as they ran into the animals whose skins they wore.

Through some deception Yetl lured all but one of the killer whales to their death and then boiled them down for their oil. He had enlisted the help of a man, but Yetl stole the man's share of the oil. The man shut Yetl in a box and threw him over a cliff, but Yetl managed to escape with ease as he had previously taught the man to secure the box with straw rather than with rope. He then invited all the 'little people' to a feast at which they sat on mats inside a circle of men. As the feast got under way Yetl shook the mats so that they all flew up into the faces of the people and became the pupils of their eyes which had, until that time, been the same colour as the rest of their eyes.

On one occasion Yetl had gone fishing with BEAR and CORMORANT but, for some reason that is unrecorded, killed Bear, after which he tore out Cormorant's tongue so that he could not reveal who the murderer was. Thus he brought death to the world. He also killed Bear's wife by tricking her into eating halibut bladders that he had stuffed with red-hot stones, and then trapped DEER in a pitfall and ate him, this last act introducing hunting and the eating of meat to mankind.

Yetl's biggest task, and one that completed the acts required for the Creation, was to solve the problem of how to prop up the Earth. Eventually, at low tide, he drained a pond of sea-water and killed a beaver who had lived in its depths. From this beaver he took a foreleg which he used to prop up the Earth and then placed HAYICANKE ('Old-Woman-Under-the-Earth') in charge of it. With his work completed, Yetl returned to the source of the River Nass where he lives to this day.

Yiacatecuhtli CENTRAL AMERICA (*Aztec*) The patron deity of the merchants, and in particular of the POCHTECA.

Yimantuwinyai NORTH AMERICA – SOUTHWEST COAST (*Hupa*) 'Old-One-Across-the-Ocean', the creator who appears to have been a volcanic deity for at his birth there was a ringing noise followed by clouds of smoke rising from the mountainside. Pieces of rotten wood then rained down and caught alight, thus bringing fire to the world.

Yiyanitsinni NORTH AMERICA –
SOUTHWEST (*Navajo*)
Generic name given to a group of unnamed deities known as the UPHOLDERS-OF-THE-HEAVENS.

Yoalli Ehécatl CENTRAL AMERICA –
MEXICO (*Aztec*)
'Night Wind', an aspect of TEZCATLIPOCA that came about through his absorption of lesser deities.

Yoaltl Ehécatl CENTRAL AMERICA –
MEXICO (*Aztec*)
Variant of YOALLI EHÉCATL.

Yolkai Estsan NORTH AMERICA –
SOUTHWEST (*Navajo*)
'White-Shell Woman', the goddess formed by the YEI led by HASTSHEYALTI. According to some accounts she was the mother of THOBADZISTSHINI by WATER. Together with Hastsheyalti, Yolkai Estsan created a new race of people by firstly making a man from an ear of white corn, and then a woman from an ear of yellow corn. She gave them the gifts of fire and maize, and then married the man to GROUND-HEAT GIRL, and the woman to MIRAGE BOY, their children becoming the first of the NAVAJO people. Yolkai Estsan then left the Earth and became the wife of KLEHONOAI.

Yolkaiaisn NORTH AMERICA –
SOUTHWEST (*Navajo*)
A variant of YOLKAI ESTSAN.

Yoltéotl CENTRAL AMERICA – MEXICO (*Aztec*)
The deification of the human heart. The ordinary AZTEC word for the heart was *yollotl*, a word that is derived from *ollín* which means 'movement'. Thus the heart is the moving organ that sustains life, but this ordinary heart may become Yoltéotl through the efforts made by the individual in life, in which case that person is said to have been motivated and sustained by the gods.

Yoskeha NORTH AMERICA –
WOODLANDS (*Onondaga*)
'Sapling', one of the twin sons of GUSTS-OF-WIND and the WIND-RULER, his sibling being TASWISCANA. Right from the start, long before the twins were born, they became bitter enemies, their ante-natal fighting actually causing the death of their mother. Taswiscana, whose name means 'Flint', was the malevolent one of the pair and soon convinced their grandmother ATAENTSIC that it had been his brother who had been responsible for the death of Gusts-of-Wind. Ataentsic immediately banished Yoskeha who went to find his father, the Wind-Ruler, who accepted him as the innocent party and gave him a bow and arrows and some maize, symbols of his lordship over all living things.

Yoskeha returned to the Earth and prepared the maize for mankind who were about to be created, but his grandmother Ataentsic spoiled it by scattering ashes over it. The maize therefore did not grow as it should have done, for which Yoskeha censured his grandmother. Yoskeha then created all the animals of the Earth, but again his good work was frustrated, this time by Taswiscana who herded all the animals into a cave whose entrance he sealed. Yoskeha managed to free most of them, but those that remained in the cave were transformed into the evil, disfigured creatures of the UNDERWORLD.

Now Yoskeha went to war against HAIDU, the source of all decay and disease, and an ally of his brother. They fought long and hard, but Yoskeha finally overcame his adversary and extracted from him the secret lore of medicine and of the tobacco ceremony that he was to later teach mankind. With the Creation coming together nicely, Yoskeha went in search of the Sun and Moon which had been created from the body of Gusts-of-Wind, but which had been hidden beneath the ground by Ataentsic and Taswiscana. With the help of all the animals he had created, Yoskeha unearthed the Sun and then evaded his grandmother and brother by passing it to the animals which ran in relay to save the Sun and bring light back to the Earth. Although it is unrecorded whether or not Yoskeha found the Moon, it seems likely that he did, the Moon having lost some of its brilliance from its extended period beneath the Earth.

With the Earth illuminated and well stocked with both plants and animals, Yoskeha now turned his attention to the creation of man. Again Taswiscana attempted to thwart his brother, but all he could create were evil monsters. Finally, having had enough of his brother, he condemned both him and the monsters he had created to the Underworld where they remain.

Yoskeha remains with the ONONDAGA to this day, for every time he reaches old age, he transforms his body back into that of a youth. Thus his ORENDA remains undiminished and nothing evil or destructive – not even Taswiscana who is the personification of the negative OTKON – can harm him in any way at all, no matter how slight or insignificant.

Yoruba loa HAITI (Voodoo)

Group of LOA who derive from the gods and spirits of the Yoruba people of Nigeria.

yoyolche CENTRAL AMERICA – YUCATÁN, MEXICO (Modern Maya)

Generic name given to giant monsters that roam the nights and who cause even the bravest heroes to tremble with fear as they pass.

Yum Cimil CENTRAL AMERICA – YUCATÁN, MEXICO (Modern Maya)

The name given by the present-day MAYA to the ancient deity depicted in the various CODEX as the god A who is usually identified with AH PUCH or HUNHAU of the classical Maya.

Yum ~ Caax, ~ Kaax CENTRAL AMERICA (Maya)

The god E who is always associated with life and never with death, the god of maize or corn and of the harvest fields, to whom offerings of blood were made, to celebrate the firing of the fields ready for the new planting. Yum Caax is the equivalent of the AZTEC deity CINTÉOTL, is sometimes also called GHANAN, and is thus also an aspect of the great KUKULCÁN.

Artistically, Yum Caax is depicted with the long profile and elongated, flattened forehead cultivated by the Maya aristocracy and found in stone portraits from PALENQUE and in the paintings of BONAMPAK. The shape is said to have represented an ear of maize. By tying boards to their heads while the bones were still soft, the skulls of Maya children were flattened by their parents who wanted them to have this sacred profile

yumbalamob CENTRAL AMERICA – YUCATÁN, MEXICO (Modern Maya)

Generic name given to beings that inhabit the first of the seven heavens, and who are given special responsibility for the care of Christians. Invisible by day, they keep watch each night by the crosses which are located at the cardinal points of each village, guarding them against evil spirits that dwell in the surrounding forests. Stylistically, the yumbalamob resemble the AZTEC deity TEZCATLIPOCA, and are said to slice the wind with their obsidian knives.

yumchabob CENTRAL AMERICA –
YUCATÁN, MEXICO (*Modern Maya*)
Generic name given to the bearded old
men said to live in the sixth of the seven
heavens. They are particularly partial to
tobacco and are revered as the lords of
rain. They receive their orders from EL
GRAND DIOS, the Great God of the Christians, who lives in the seventh heaven, and
appear to have their origins in the classical
MAYA deities CHAAC and KUKULCÁN.

Yumchakob CENTRAL AMERICA –
YUCATÁN, MEXICO (*Modern Maya*)
God of rain who seems to have derived
from the ancient MAYA deity CHAAC.

Yupik NORTH AMERICA – ALASKA
Indigenous ESKIMO people from the central
regions of Alaska. Speaking Yuk, rather
than Inuktitut, the Inupiat are referred to
throughout this book as INUIT, a term that
has come to encompass all of the indigenous peoples from the North American
Arctic regions.

Yzamná CENTRAL AMERICA (*Maya*)
The tutelary deity of a city during the
malign IX year that were ruled over by the
northern BACAB. During this time, when a
statue of Yzamná was erected in the centre
of the city, the northern gates to that city
were guarded by ZAC-U-UAYEYAB.

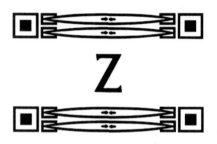

Z

Zac CENTRAL AMERICA (*Maya*)
One of the Four BACAB, or Four BALAM, the guardians of the divisions of the sacred 260-day CALENDAR. The four are named as CHAC, who was associated with the colour red and east, ED – black and west, KAN – yellow and south and ZAC – white and north.

Zac-Mitun-Ahau CENTRAL AMERICA
   (*Maya*)
The guardian of a city centre during the malign CAUAC years that were governed by ED, the western of the Four BACAB, during which time the western gates of the city were guarded by EK-U-UAYEYAB.

Zac-u-Uayeyab CENTRAL AMERICA
   (*Maya*)
The guardian deity of the northern gates of cities during the pernicious IX years that were ruled over by the northern BACAB – ZAC, and when the tutelary deity of the city itself was YZAMNÁ.

Zacatec CENTRAL AMERICA – MEXICO
Ancient civilization that once occupied what is today known as central Mexico, together with the HUASTEC people.

Zactecauh CENTRAL AMERICA –
   GUATEMALA (*Cakchiquel*)
One of the two oldest warriors under the leadership of TIUH TIUH, the other warrior of comparable age being GAGAVITZ. The warriors would have liked to have disposed of ZAKIQOXOL, the spirit of fire, but they bowed to his supernatural nature, giving him clothing and a blood-red dagger and shoes so that man could recognize him. Later, as Tiuh Tiuh led his people across the land, they came to a sea they could not cross. There the two fell asleep on the sea shore and were drowned.

Za(dieu) HAITI (*Voodoo*)
Possibly deriving from a West African deity, this LOA may be a variant of ZAHI, or vice versa.

Zahi HAITI (*Voodoo*)
One of the numerous LOA of the VOODOO religion whose name is possibly a variant of ZADIEU, though the opposite might also be true.

Zakiqoxol CENTRAL AMERICA –
   GUATEMALA (*Cakchiquel*)
The spirit of fire who was perceived as an evil killer of men. GAGAVITZ and ZACTE-CAUH would have liked to dispose of him, but even they had to bow to his supernatural quality. Instead they gave him clothing and a blood-red dagger and shoes. With these he descended to live in the forest. He became revered as the spirit of the forest who had the ability to let the forest survive unharmed, or who could destroy it at will if he so desired.

Zakitzunun CENTRAL AMERICA –
GUATEMALA (*Cakchiquel*)
The only human who was brave enough to
accompany GAGAVITZ up a mountain that
was, in all probability, a volcano.

zanges HAITI (*Voodoo*)
An alternative generic name for the LOA
which derives from the Christian French
les anges (angels).

Zapana SOUTH AMERICA – BOLIVIA
(*Collao*)
One of the two legendary chieftains of the
COLLAO, the other being CARI. It is said
that they were easily conquered by the
INCA as, at that time, they were involved in
an internecine war.

Zapotec CENTRAL AMERICA – MEXICO
Indigenous Central-American AMERIN-
DIAN people of southern Mexico who
today number about 250,000 and live
mainly in Oaxaca. Their ancestors built
the ceremonial city of Monte Albán
1000–500 BC. They speak a language that
is a branch of the Oto-Mangean family,
and has nine dialects. The Zapotec developed one of the classical Central-
American civilizations some time before
AD 300, but which declined under pressure
from the MIXTECS from AD 900 until the
Spanish conquest in the sixteenth century.

zemis (pl. zemes) CARIBBEAN (*Taíno*)
Generic term for a deity.

Zipacná CENTRAL AMERICA – MEXICO
(*Aztec*)
'Mountain Maker', the elder son of VUKUB
CAKIX and brother of CABRACA. He was
caught in a pitfall by the heavenly twins
HUNAHPU and XBALANQUÉ who had the
help of 400 young men. They hurled great
trees down on top of him and, believing
him to be dead, built a house over the pit

in which they began to celebrate their
victory. Zipacná, however, had only been
stunned and, in the middle of the night,
rose up from the pit and threw the house
and all its occupants high into the air. The
400 youths fell to their deaths, but were
repaid for their efforts to trap and kill
Zipacná by being transferred to the heavens as stars.

Hunahpu and Xbalanqué had to try a
different approach if they were to destroy
Zipacná. This time they modelled a great
crab, Zipacná's favourite food, which they
placed at the bottom of a deep ravine. It
did not prove difficult to lure Zipacná to
the ravine and then to push him over the
edge. The twins then poured great boulders and mountains down on top of him.
His struggles were so violent that the twins
had to resort to magic and turned Zipacná
into stone.

zobop HAITI (*Voodoo*)
The name given to the formal order to
which male sorcerers belong. This has led
to the term also being used to refer to the
sorcerer himself.

zombie HAITI (*Voodoo*)
A familiar concept, the term zombie actually has two meanings. It is used as a
generic term for the spirits of the dead, but
is more commonly used to refer to a corpse
that is believed to have been re-animated
by a spirit and thus enslaved. More specifically, a zombie is the spirit of a dead person
who was killed by a sorcerer or, having
died from natural causes, is then resurrected by evil HOUNGANs. Totally dominated by its evil masters, the zombie can be
made to perform any evil act as it has lost
its soul to those who control them and
become an automaton, whose sole purpose
is to do the bidding of the person control-
ling it, thus allowing that person to com-
mit any crime and escape punishment.
The idea is thought to have first arisen

from VOODOO priests who used the nerve poison tetrodotoxin, which comes from the puffer fish, to produce a semblance of death, from which the victim later recovers.

zombie errant HAITI (*Voodoo*)
The spirit of a person who has been killed accidentally. Though dead, they spend their days in the woods and walk on the roads by night, living out this ghostly existence until the term of their earthly life that had originally been assigned to them has expired.

Zotz CENTRAL AMERICA (*Maya*)
The bat god and patron of the Zotzil Indians who today live in Chiapas, as well as of some Guatemalan peoples. Zotz was important to the ancient MAYA as the patron of the twenty-day period which was known by his name. On one relief in Copán there is a depiction of Zotz struggling with KUKULCÁN, a depiction that has led some to assimilate Zotz with TEZCATLIPOCA in his eternal struggle for supremacy with QUETZALCÓATL.

Zotzilha Chimalman CENTRAL AMERICA (*Maya*)
The god of darkness, depicted as a bat, who fights KINICH AHAU, the Sun.

Zuhé SOUTH AMERICA – COLOMBIA (*Chibcha*)
Also called XUHÉ. The Sun, the visible incarnation of the invisible BOCHICA. He was created together with CHIÁ, the Moon, by CHIMINIGAGUÉ.

Zuñi NORTH AMERICA – PUEBLO, SOUTHWEST
Indigenous PUEBLO-dwelling North American AMERINDIAN people who are closely related to the HOPI and the SIA peoples.

Zuyua CENTRAL AMERICA (*Maya*)
The sacred language of the XIU clan, knowledge and understanding of which seems to have been the key to achieving the rank of ALMENHENOB in the MAYA caste system.

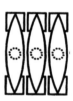

APPENDIX

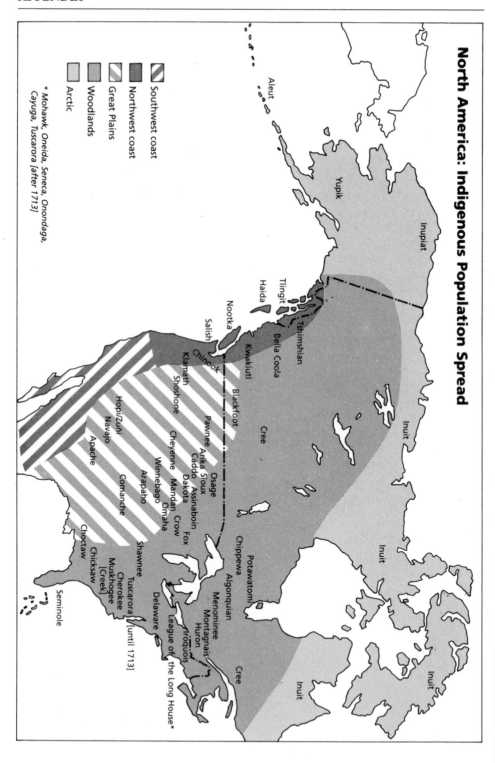

North America: Indigenous Population Spread

Legend:
- Southwest coast
- Northwest coast
- Great Plains
- Woodlands
- Arctic

*Mohawk, Oneida, Seneca, Onondaga, Cayuga, Tuscarora [after 1713]

Labels on map:

Aleut, Yupik, Inupiat, Inuit, Tlingit, Haida, Tshimshian, Bella Coola, Nootka, Kwakiutl, Salish, Chinook, Klamath, Blackfoot, Cree, Shoshone, Hopi/Zuni, Navajo, Apache, Cheyenne, Pawnee, Arika Sioux, Caddo, Dakota, Crow, Mandan, Winnebago, Omaha, Fox, Assinaboin, Osage, Comanche, Arapaho, Potawatomi, Chippewa, Algonquian, Menominee, Montagnais, Huron, Iroquois, Cree, Shawnee, Choctaw, Chicksaw, Cherokee, Muskhogee [Creek], Tuscarora [until 1713], Delaware, League of the Long House*, Seminole

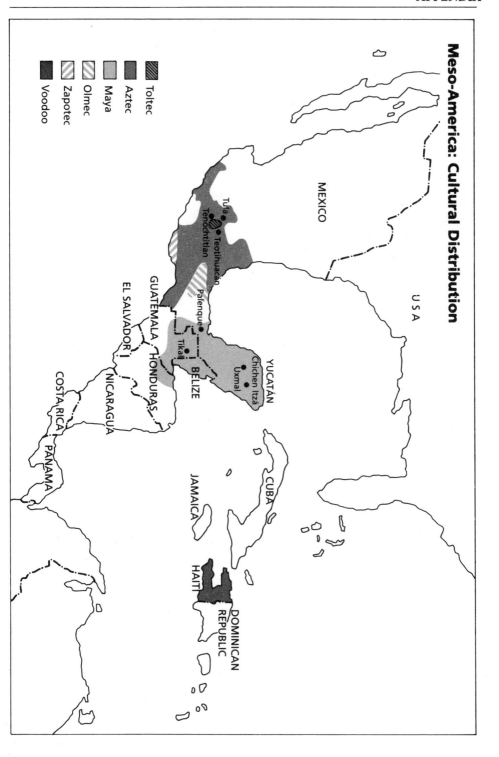

Meso-America: Cultural Distribution

Toltec
Aztec
Maya
Olmec
Zapotec
Voodoo

MEXICO

USA

Tula
Teotihuacán
Tenochtitlan
Palenque
Tikal
Chichen Itzá
Uxmal
YUCATÁN

GUATEMALA
EL SALVADOR
HONDURAS
BELIZE
NICARAGUA
COSTA RICA
PANAMA

JAMAICA
CUBA

HAITI
DOMINICAN REPUBLIC

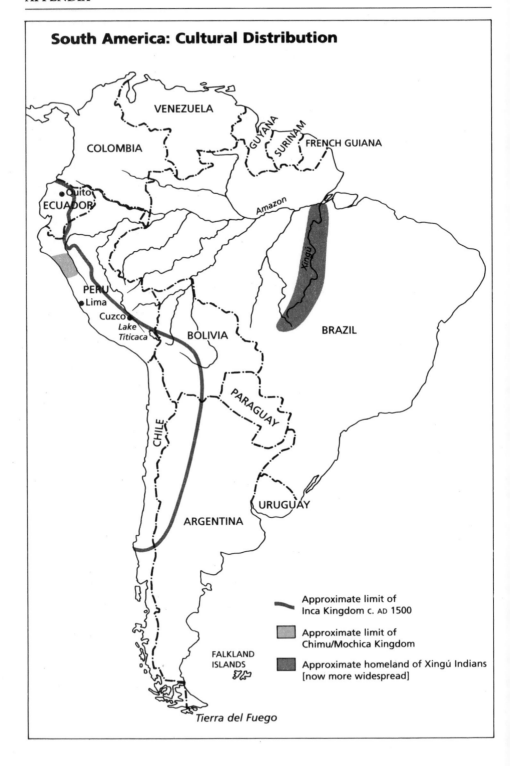

South America: Cultural Distribution

VENEZUELA

COLOMBIA

GUYANA

SURINAM

FRENCH GUIANA

Quito
ECUADOR

Amazon

Xingú

PERU
Lima
Cuzco
Lake
Titicaca

BOLIVIA

BRAZIL

PARAGUAY

CHILE

URUGUAY

ARGENTINA

FALKLAND
ISLANDS

Tierra del Fuego

Approximate limit of
Inca Kingdom c. AD 1500

Approximate limit of
Chimu/Mochica Kingdom

Approximate homeland of Xingú Indians
[now more widespread]

BIBLIOGRAPHY

The following is, by no means, a complete list of all the books that have ever been published on the subject of Native American Myth and Legend. It is, however, representative of the works that have been consulted during the preparation of this book.

Asturias, Miguel Angel *Hombres de Maíz* (Losada, Buenos Aires, 1957)

Balikci, Asen *The Netsilik Eskimo* (Natural History Press, New York, 1970)

Brogan, Hugh *Longman History of the United States of America* (Longman, London, 1985)

Brown, John Eppes *The Sacred Pipe: Black Elk's Account of the Seen Sacred Rites of the Sioux* (Penguin Books, London, 1971)

Brown, Vinson *Voices of Earth and Sky* (Naturegraph Publishers' Inc., Happycamp, California, 1974)

Brueton, Diana *Many Moons: the myth and magic, fact and fantasy of our nearest heavenly body* (Prentice-Hall, New York, 1991)

Bryant, Page *Native American Mythology* (Aquarian Press, London, 1991)

Burland, Cottie Arthur *Art and Life in Ancient Mexico* (Bruno Cassirer Ltd., Oxford, 1947) *The Gods of Mexico* (Eyre & Spottiswoode, London, 1967) *Magic Books of Mexico* (Penguin Books, Harmondsworth, 1953)

Bushnell, G.H.S. *Ancient Arts of the Americas* (Thames & Hudson, London, 1965)

Carpenter, E. *Eskimo* (Oxford University Press, Oxford, 1959)

Caso, Alfonso *The Aztecs, People of the Sun* (Oklahoma University Press, 1958)

Chamberlain, Von Del *When Stars Came Down to Earth: The Cosmology of the Skidi Pawnee Indians of North America* (Ballena Press, Los Altos, California, 1982)

Clendinnen, Inga *Aztecs* (Cambridge University Press, Cambridge, 1991)

Coe, Michael D. *Mexico* (Thames & Hudson, London, 1962) *The Maya* (Thames & Hudson, London, 1966)

Collier, John *Indians of the Americas* (New American Library, New York, 1947)

Collis, Maurice *Cortés and Montezuma* (Faber & Faber, London, 1954)

Curtis, Edward S. *In a Sacred Manner We Live* (Weathervane Books, New York, 1972)

Debo, Angie *A History of the Indians of the United States* (Oklahoma University Press, 1970)

Diaz, Bernal (trans. J.M. Cohen) *The Conquest of New Spain* (Penguin Classics, Harmondsworth, 1963)

Erdoes, Richard and Ortiz, Alfonso *American Indian Myths and Legends* (Pantheon Books, New York, 1984)

Fergusson, Erna *Dancing Gods: Indian Ceremonials of New Mexico and Arizona* (University of New Mexico Press, Albuquerque, New Mexico, 1931)

Fernández, Justino *Coatlicue, estética del arte indígena antiguo* (Centro de Estudios Filosóficos, Mexico, 1954)

Fey, Harold and McNickle, D'Arcy *Indians and Other Americans* (Harper and Brothers, New York, 1959)

Goetz, D. and Morley, S.G. *Popul Vuh: translated from the Spanish of Adrián Recinos* (William Hodge, London, 1951)

Haddington, Evan *Early Man and the Cosmos* (University of Oklahoma Press, Norman, Oklahoma, 1989)

Hook, Jason *American Indian Warrior Chiefs: Tecumseh, Crazy Horse, Chief Joseph, Geronimo* (Firebird Books, Poole, 1989)

Howard, Helen Addison *Saga of Chief Joseph* (University of Nebraska Press, Lincoln, Nebraska and London, 1965)

Josephy, Alvin M. and Brandon, William (ed.) *The American Heritage Book of Indians* (Simon & Schuster, New York, 1961)

Locke, Raymond Friday *The Book of the Navajo* (Mankind House Publishing Company, Los Angeles, California, 1976)

Lothrop, S.K., Foshag, W. F. and Mahler, Joy *Pre-Colombian Art* (Phaidon Press, London, 1958)

Lowie, R.H. *The Crow Indians* (Holt, Rinehart and Winston, New York, 1956)

MacCulloch, John A., and Gray, Louis H. *The Mythology of all Races* (13 volumes) (Cooper Square Publications Inc., New York, 1922)

Marquis, Arnold *A Guide to America's Indians* (University of Oklahoma Press, Norman, Oklahoma, 1960)

Milner, Clyde A., O'Connor, Carol A. and Sandweiss, Martha A.(eds.) *The Oxford History of The American West* (Oxford University Press, New York, 1994)

Morley, S.G. *The Ancient Maya* (Oxford University Press, Oxford, 1946)

Neumann, Erich *The Great Mother* (Princeton University Press, New York, 1963)

Nicholson, Irene *The X in Mexico* (Faber & Faber, London, 1965) *Mexican and Central American Mythology* (Hamlyn, London, 1967)

Parkes, H. Bamford *The History of Mexico* (Eyre & Spottiswoode, London, 1962)

Peterson, Frederick *Ancient Mexico* (Allen & Unwin, London, 1959)

Right, Barton V *Kachinas: A Hopi Artist's Documentary* (Northland Press, Flagstaff, Arizona, 1973)

Séjourné, Laurette *El Universo de Quetzalcóatl* (Fondo de Cultura Económica, Mexico, 1962)

Soustelle, Jacques (trans. Patrick O'Brian) *Daily Life of the Aztecs* (Weidenfeld & Nicholson, London, 1961)

Tanner, Clara Lee *Hopi Kachinas* (Ray Manley Publishing, Tuscon, Arizona, undated)

Thernstrom, Stephan (ed.) *Harvard Encyclopedia of American Ethnic Groups* (Harvard University Press, Cambridge, Mass. and London, 1980)

Thompson, J.E. *The Rise and Fall of Maya Civilization* (Oklahoma University Press, 1956)

Vaillant, G.C. *The Aztecs of Mexico* (Penguin Books, Harmondsworth, 1952)

Waters, Frank *Book of the Hopi* (Penguin Books, Harmondsworth, 1972)

Weltfish, Gene *The Lost Universe: Pawnee Life and Culture* (University of Nebraska Press, Lincoln, Nebraska, 1977)

Willis, Roy (ed.) *World Mythology: The Illustrated Guide* (Duncan Baird Publishers, 1993)

Wood, Marion *Spirits, Heroes and Hunters from North American Indian Mythology* (Schocken Books, New York, 1981)